The
Weather-Resilient
Garden

A defensive approach
to planning & landscaping

Charles W.G. Smith

Illustrations by Elayne Sears
and Bobbi Angell

Storey Publishing

The mission of Storey Publishing is to serve our customers
by publishing practical information that encourages personal
independence in harmony with the environment.

Edited by Gwen Steege and Teri Dunn
Art direction by Wendy Palitz
Cover and text design by Wendy Palitz
Front cover photographs: © Joseph DeSciose (top and middle right);
© Mark Turner (middle left); © Paul Rocheleau (bottom right)
Back cover photographs: © Joseph DeSciose (top and bottom);
© Rosemary Kautzky (middle)
Illustrations in Parts 1 and 2 © Elayne Sears and in Part 3 © Bobbi Angell
Text production by Jennifer Jepson Smith
Indexed by Susan Olason, Indexes & Knowledge Maps

The information in this book is true and complete to the best of our knowledge. All recommendations are made without guarantee on the part of the author or Storey Publishing. The author and publisher disclaim any liability in connection with the use of this information. For additional information please contact Storey Publishing, 210 MASS MoCA Way, North Adams, MA 01247.

Storey books are available for special premium and promotional uses and for customized editions. For further information, please call 1-800-793-9396.

Printed in the United States by Versa Press
10 9 8 7 6 5 4 3 2 1

Library of Congress Cataloging-in-Publication Data

Smith, Charles W. G.
 The weather-resilient garden : a defensive approach to planning and landscaping / Charles W.G. Smith.
  p. cm.
 ISBN 1-58017-516-3 (pbk. : alk. paper)
 1. Landscape gardening. 2. Landscape plants. 3. Crops and climate.
I. Title.
SB473 .S552 2004
635.9—dc22
                        2003014934

Contents

Part One: Creating a Weather-Resilient Garden 1

Part Two: Really Bad Weather:

    Healing Methods and Fresh Starts 35

        Cold 38

        Ice and Snow 63

        Salt 90

        Flood 112

        Drought 145

        Fire 174

        Hail 200

        Heat 219

        Humidity 247

        Lightning 265

        Wind 287

Part Three: Top 100 Weather-Resilient Plants 323

        Perennials 324

        Shrubs 342

        Trees 350

        Vines and Ground Covers 365

        Ornamental Grasses 371

        Annuals .376

        Lawn Grasses 382

Appendix 385

Supplies and Resources 386

Further Reading 388

USDA Hardiness Zone Map 389

Botanic to Common Name Index 390

General Index 396

In loving memory of my dear sister,

Pat Ball, whose strength, faithfulness,

and humor always encouraged

her many friends and family...

In the spirit of Hebrews 10:24

Part One

Creating a

Weather-Resilient Garden

"Things fall apart; the center cannot hold;
Mere anarchy is loosed upon the world."

— William Butler Yeats

A Closer Look

At first glance, the weather-resilient garden looks like any other beautiful garden — including yours. The plantings and design are inviting and attractive, with flower beds, shrub borders, and trees that gracefully accent the tasteful paths and walls. A stroll past a bed of perennials reveals no clue that these lovely plants can endure months of dusty drought or scalding heat. A walk through a grove of trees holds no hint that they can all survive hurricane-force winds or weeks of flooding. The qualities that allow the weather-resilient garden to survive — not only the best of times, but the worst of times as well — are not easily discerned, but they are certainly there.

The typical traits of the weather-resilient garden are well described by the classical Greek word *praus* (pronounced PRAH-os), a term usually used to describe people. This word has a compound meaning. Its first meaning — gentleness, as in a gentle breeze — is closely coupled with its second one, which is to have unbending power or the strength of steel. So *praus* means to be gentle, but also resilient and strong. In the weather-resilient garden, the gracious ambience of flowers and form is apparent every day. But behind the gentle, inviting appearance — in plants, soil, hardscape, design, everywhere you look — is a strength that resists and endures the severe, damaging weather that someday visits every garden.

In the pages that follow, you'll find a variety of ideas and methods to enable your garden to develop *praus*. You identify and use *praus* in the elements and plants of your landscape. *Praus* can be found in soils, in the form of buffers that reduce changes in pH, water, and nutrition. It can also be found in microclimates that reduce changes in pH, water, and nutrition. It is also very much a part of the constitution of the plants that gracefully endure all manner of weather. As you read, you'll learn the skills to employ and magnify your own garden's will to survive, and thus create your own weather-resilient garden.

MADE TO ENDURE. A weather-resilient landscape and the gardens within it can withstand any number of pressures, from suffocating heat and humidity to bitter cold winds.

Defensive Landscaping

No, you're not going to build a moat instead of a water garden. Defensive landscaping is simply becoming more aware of your garden as well as the factors, such as weather, that affect it. With that knowledge, you can create a garden and yard that is attractive as well as responsive to a vast array of weather events.

Get to Know Your Garden

People can work a piece of ground for decades and not really know it. It is human nature to have tunnel vision, to focus intently on something but miss how that thing fits into everything else. So regardless of whether you think you know your landscape, take a pad and pencil and take a walk around. As you walk, readjust your mind and eye. Which way does the wind normally blow? When it comes through, what does it hit, what is sheltered? Ask these questions for all the types of weather that can cause trouble for you. Then note on the paper where certain types of weather could cause the most problems. The hilltop may be windy, for example, or the soil type may change from the bottom of the hill to the top.

Triage: Evaluate, Stabilize, Fix

Triage is a term used in medicine, particularly by emergency care workers. We can take a triage approach to our gardens, too, by first ascertaining the elements in a landscape that need attention, then by prioritizing those elements. The way to think about the garden, whether it looks great or not, is that something is amiss and you've got to find out what it is. The windy hilltop might need a windbreak, but if nothing is planted on the hilltop, there is no pressing need. If there are garden plants on the hilltop, then the windbreak jumps to the head of the line.

Some problems have multiple variables. For example, the soil at the bottom of a hill will hold moisture longer than the top of the hill, which makes it a good place for growing plants in a drought. You discover that the bottom of the hill is also a cold pocket that gets frost before other places in the garden. Therefore, the plants that you set out here should be resilient to both of those conditions.

In addition to discovering aspects of your landscape that have been hidden from your view until now, you'll also find out how to install devices, such as raised beds, windbreaks, and walls, that immediately improve the resilience of your garden. Even the use of temporary devices, such as row covers, and watering can make such a profound difference in the ability of plants to withstand weather that you'll be amazed.

Making the garden more weather resilient isn't always about adding things to landscapes. Sometimes it's about taking things away: Soil can be made more amenable to plant growth by diverting water; you can remove weak tree branches to reduce the potential for wind damage.

Principally Speaking

Weather-resilient landscaping is a different approach to designing and tending the garden and yard. When selecting plants, your first consider-ations will be how plants grow under different types of stress and which ones will thrive in whatever conditions come to your garden, rather than their color, shape, or form. Once your garden can survive weather extremes, designing beds and borders is just that much more rewarding and fun. Weather-resilient landscaping changes the garden significantly, but the principles used to make the garden more resilient are simple:

• Discover each plant's cultural needs and preferences regarding weather-related conditions.
• Use the plant's natural strengths to strengthen the garden from weather.
• Magnify a plant's natural strengths by using hardscape devices, such as windbreaks.
• Use the different strengths of different plants to enhance resiliency of the group.
• Allow plants to grow in the place that best fits their strengths.
• Do all the above so that each plant will face any weather challenge at its peak of resilience.

The Partnership Begins

It is easy to think of a weather-resilient garden as being a collection of tough plants that can tolerate a wide range of nasty conditions. But that would be looking at the garden simplistically and out of context. While a garden must have plants, it is also much more than just plants. The vitality and weather resilience of the garden also depend on such elements as soil, overall climate, microclimates, topography, and amount of rainfall. All of these influence the health and strength of garden plants as well as the vigor and strength of the severe weather that may roll in. Mark Twain once wrote, "A great, great deal has been said about the weather, but very little has ever been done." It's time to put on the boots and the garden gloves, because that's about to change.

Buffers Aren't Just in Aspirin

The weather-resilient garden can resist and tolerate more severe weather than comparable gardens because it contains buffers against the harsh weather. The dictionary defines a buffer as something that lessens or absorbs the shock of an impact. In garden terms, a storm with hurricane-force winds is something that has a severe impact on the garden. The buffer that absorbs such an impact could be a windbreak that dampens the wind speed before it reaches the plantings, or it could be the proper species of tree that can naturally endure high winds.

Dozens of types of buffers that reduce the shock of a number of different types of weather exist in your garden and landscape already. They are disguised as microclimates, plant varieties, compost piles, raised beds, and even the water that comes out of the garden hose. Learning to find and use buffers can provide your garden with resilience you never thought possible. For instance, a walk around the yard can turn up hot spots or cold pockets that might differ in temperature by up to 10 degrees F (–12 degrees C) from neighboring places. Those degrees can make the difference between wilted plants and healthy ones or hard-frost damage and no frost damage.

Learning to identify buffers in your garden and yard is the first step to increasing weather resilience. The second step is to strengthen those buffers. This can be done in various ways, such as improving the soil to encourage more resistant plants and erecting a hurricane fence to block strong winds.

In many gardens, plants and structures are often not only in harm's way but also lack the resilience to endure hard times when they come. This acceptance of inevitable disaster doesn't have to be. Vulnerability is not something the garden has to live with; instead, weaknesses can be strengthened and the forces that seek to ruin can be redirected or dissipated. The tools we can use are qualities in the soil, water, microclimates, and the flexible nature of plants themselves.

Buffer #1: Soil and Resilience

Healthy soil is the single most important buffer your garden has going for it. Unfortunately, in the world of horticulture, soil has always had an image problem. It doesn't photograph well. It isn't stunningly beautiful, like a blooming peony, or majestic, like a grand old live oak. In short, its reputation is dirt. Yet soil deserves more attention and appreciation. It keeps the garden alive and its health and quality directly relate to the health and weather resilience of the landscape.

Gardening magazines and books, as well as agronomy texts, always state that the "best" soil is a type called sandy or coarse loam. Coarse loam has many qualities that provide plants with weather resilience. If you're lucky enough to have coarse loam in your garden, it's a little like being born into a royal family: When you are born a prince or princess, your future is secure, and even a series of bumbling mistakes throughout your life probably won't stop your ascension to the throne. Similarly, if you have coarse loam in your garden, you can make some horticultural mistakes and your garden will usually still grow beautifully. But if you are not so fortunate, it's possible to make the soil in your garden more like coarse loam by creating your own.

Creating Coarse Loam Soil

There is no replacement for real garden soil. In nature, it can take up to 500 years for 1 inch (2.5 cm) of soil to form, a time frame that outlasts a person's patience, not to mention life span. Simply adding sand to clay or silt soils isn't practical because of the sheer volume and weight of sand necessary to produce a significant change. The good news is that you can make a soil that offers the benefits of coarse loam in your garden, and which is actually superior to coarse loam in such qualities as drainage and nutrient retention. To do this, you'll need the following:

• A well-defined area of garden soil you wish to improve, such as a raised bed or a marked-off section of garden
• Rototiller, broadfork, garden fork, or similar tool to turn the soil
• Partially decomposed organic matter, such as compost
• Perlite
• Greensand

The Mayonnaise Jar Test

To determine the amounts of the ingredients you need to add, begin by doing a simple soil test on the present soil to determine just what it is made of. Those who get paid to do this call it *fractional analysis.* Many gardeners affectionately refer to it as the mayonnaise jar test.

Collect representative soil samples from the area of garden to be improved and from different depths, ranging from 1 or 2 inches (2.5–5 cm) to 6 to 8 inches (15–20 cm). Gather enough soil to fill the jar about halfway. Put the soil in a clean mayonnaise jar and break up any clumps as best as you can. Add a few drops of Murphy's Oil Soap and then fill the jar three-quarters full with water. Screw on the lid and shake. Set down the jar and let everything settle.

CLAY 1"
SILT 1"
SAND 2"

PUT IT TO THE TEST. Sand, silt, and clay will settle in layers in a jar of water.

When the water clears, which will take anywhere from 2 to 24 hours, look for three bands in the soil. The band at the bottom of the jar is sand. Measure the depth of this band and write it down. The layer on top of the sand is silt. This often has a darker color than the sand and has a different appearance, being made of smaller particles. Measure the depth of the silt and write that down as well. The topmost layer, composed of clay, is made of a very fine material and often blends into the silt layer. Measure this layer and write it down, too. Now add all the measurements together to get the total profile depth. The finished calculation might look like this: sand 2 inches (5 cm), silt 1 inch (2.5 cm), clay 1 inch (2.5 cm); total 4 inches (10 cm).

To determine the percentages of sand, silt, and clay in the above sample, multiply the measurement of each layer by 100 and divide by the total profile depth. For example, the percentage of sand in the soil described above is $2 \times 100 \div 4 = 50$ percent. Silt equals 25 percent and the clay is 25 percent. A coarse loam soil has about 65 percent sand and the remaining 35 percent is divided between silt and clay. To determine the type of soil your garden currently has, compare the results from your mayonnaise jar test to the approximate percentages in the soil triangle at the right.

SOIL TRIANGLE. A soil triangle illustrates the three mineral components of soil as well as how these elements combine to form other soil types

Making Amends

The three soil amendments that turn ordinary soil into weather-resilient soil are compost, perlite, and greensand.

Compost contributes organic matter to the soil and confers many beneficial qualities, including improved drainage, increased fertility and cation exchange capacity (see CEC Simplified), greater quantity and efficiency of soil organisms, better moisture holding and aeration, fewer diseases, and stable pH. Compost can be made in the backyard or purchased in bags or bulk from local nurseries or landscaping services.

Perlite is made by heating volcanic rock to 1,700°F (927°C), which results in a round, lightweight material that is inert, is disease- and pest-

CEC Simplified

Cation exchange capacity is the measure of how many positively charged molecules a soil can hold. Here's why this is important. For plants to grow and be healthy, they need to absorb nutrients from the soil. Once nutrients are dissolved in the soil water, they can be quickly leached from the soil unless something holds them there, giving the roots of plants a chance to absorb them.

Many dissolved nutrients, including calcium, magnesium, potassium, and nitrogen in the form of ammonium, have a positive charge. These are called cations (pronounced CAT-eye-ons). These positively charged nutrients are attracted to negatively charged spaces found in the organic matter of compost.

So, by adding compost to the soil, you not only increase its fertility by virtue of the nutrients the compost contains, but you also help the soil hang on to the fertility that is already there (or later added).

free, and does not alter soil pH. It helps create a low-maintenance soil with a sturdy structure that doesn't break down, even after extended cultivation or foot traffic. For this reason, perlite is often used in the base for putting greens in golf courses. Perlite comes in a range of grades. For amending the soil, use the coarse grade available at most garden centers.

Greensand, which is made of potassium silicate, is one of the more interesting soil amendments. Geologists call this greenish blue grainy material glauconite. It forms at the sea floor at a depth of about 650 feet (1950 m), at the incredibly slow rate of about 1 inch (2.5 cm) every 1,000 years. Greensand contains iron, calcium, potassium, magnesium, phosphorus, and more than 30 trace elements. It loosens thick, hard soils as well as sandy ones. Greensand is 10 times more moisture absorbent than regular sand and markedly increases a soil's moisture retention. It also stimulates soil organisms, making the soil ecology healthier and providing your plants with great resilience.

Compost

Soils are made up of mineral particles, such as sand, silt, and clay, and organic material. Most soils have plenty of sand, silt, or clay but can be woefully short in organic matter. That's where compost comes in. Compost is the partially decomposed organic material that, when added to soil, energizes the soil ecology, creates natural resilience against diseases, and invigorates plant growth by providing a balance of nutrients that are slowly released into the soil.

Many commercial facilities manufacture compost and distribute it to garden centers and nurseries. This makes soil improvement simply a matter of buying compost and incorporating it by using a garden fork or power tiller — pretty easy. If you like the old-fashioned way of creating compost, however, here's how to do it.

Making a compost pile is like baking, in that it helps to have all the ingredients you need ready to go before you start. With compost, this means gathering the material in enough quantity to produce a pile large enough to heat up fast and make compost quickly. Construct a base layer

Homemade Loam

To make good loam, first record the percentage of sand from the mayonnaise jar test (see page 8). Now calculate the volume of soil in the area you are going to amend, assuming you are amending to a depth of 6 inches (15 cm). To do this:

1. Multiply the width in feet by the length in feet to get the area (in square feet).

2. Multiply the area by 0.5 to get the cubic feet measurement (for soil 6 inches deep).

3. Divide the cubic feet by 27 to obtain the cubic yards measurement. Example: For a raised bed that is 4 feet (122 cm) wide by 10 feet (305 cm) long, the calculations look like this:

4 feet x 10 feet = 40 square feet
(3.6 sq m)

40 x 0.5 = 20 cubic feet
(0.6 cu m)

20 ÷ 27 = 0.75 cubic yards

total volume = .6 cu m

Next, evenly apply the following amendments in the proper proportions to the top of the soil. Be sure to wear a dust mask and gloves, as some soil amendments, such as perlite, can be dusty.

Compost. For soils with less than 50 percent sand, add 200 pounds (91 kg) per 100 square feet (9 sq m). For soils with more than 50 percent sand, add 400 pounds (182 kg) per 100 square feet (9 sq m) (in our example, 80 to 160 pounds [36–72 kg], evenly spread).

Perlite. For soils that contain 50 to 75 percent sand, add 20 percent by volume (in our example, 4 cubic feet). For soils with less than 50 percent sand, add 30 percent by volume.

Greensand. 5 to10 pounds (2–5 kg) for 100 square feet (9 sq m) (2 to 4 pounds, in our example) if applied as a topdressing during the growing season, and 40 to 80 pounds (18–36 kg) when turned into the soil.

Shortcut: The No-Measure Method

Less exact, but great for people who don't have a lot of time, combine the following and rototill all into the soil to a depth of 6 inches (15 cm), until the soil is uniform.

• **Compost:** 4 to 6 inches (10–15 cm) deep

• **Perlite:** 1 to 2 inches (2.5–5 cm) deep

• **Greensand:** A thin layer, little more than a dusting

of brown material from 3 to 6 inches (8–15 cm) deep and top that with an equivalent depth of green material. Now add a layer of animal bedding with manure, garden soil, or finished compost from a previous batch. This introduces the proper bacteria to the pile. Finally, lightly sprinkle everything with water. Repeat the sequence, adding layer upon layer, until the pile is about 5 feet (1.5 m) tall. To allow air to penetrate the pile so that the bacteria do their thing, some people lay across each layer of the pile a length of perforated pipe slightly longer than the pile is wide. A pile 5 feet (1.5 m) high may have four pipes crisscrossed through the mound. Cover the finished pile with a waterproof tarpaulin, such as a sheet of black plastic. This warms the pile while keeping it at the proper moisture level — moist, not wet.

Compost on Autopilot

Once the pile is built and covered, the organisms make the compost. All you do is supervise. The pile should warm up quickly so that in a few days, the internal temperature is just about 160°F (71°C). You can check the

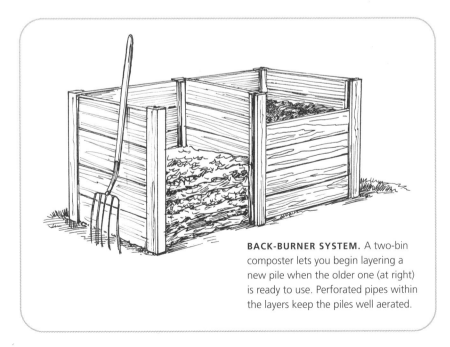

BACK-BURNER SYSTEM. A two-bin composter lets you begin layering a new pile when the older one (at right) is ready to use. Perforated pipes within the layers keep the piles well aerated.

Old-Time Compost Recipe

Compost is the result of organisms, from worms to a host of bacteria, breaking down organic matter, such as leaves and banana peels, into a nutrient-rich material that resembles soil. As in all recipes, the relative proportions of the ingredients can be juggled a bit as long as the basic directions are followed. In compost, the baseline rule is to use about 90 percent brown material and 10 percent green material.

Brown Material	Green Material
Herbivore animal manure	Grass clippings
Autumn leaves	Weeds from the garden
Straw or animal bedding	Vegetable kitchen scraps
Wood shavings	Seaweed

temperature by using a soil thermometer, which can be purchased at most garden centers, nurseries, or farm stores. If the temperature drops below about 140°F (60°C) before the compost looks brown and rich, turn the pile with a garden fork to mix up the ingredients a bit. As the layered material becomes a pile of compost, the temperature will naturally decrease, becoming close to the ambient soil temperature of the garden.

How long all this takes depends a great deal on what went into the pile. On average, a hot compost pile, such as that described above, can produce compost in as little as a week, but more often the process takes 2 to 6 weeks. Many busy gardeners pay even less attention to their compost piles and are satisfied with what is known as *cold composting*. This can be as simple as piling a mound of leaves and other garden and kitchen waste in the backyard and turning it whenever you remember to turn it. The process takes longer — about a year — but the result is still compost!

Soil Tests Demystified

When you are uncertain about the quality of your soil or its composition, it's a good idea to get it tested before making any changes. Many aspects of gardening become ingrained as you gain experience, and the longer you garden, the more you come to rely on your own good instincts. Knowing the fertility of the soil, however, isn't something you recognize by experience alone. To know just what the soil needs, you must do a soil test. Soil tests are surprisingly simple to do, and they are a very worthwhile investment.

For a small fee, a soil test provides you with an exact profile of nutrient levels in the soil. It also can determine what the pH of your soil is. Nutrients tested include phosphorus (P), potassium (K), calcium (Ca), and magnesium (Mg). Several optional tests are also available, including ones that provide levels of iron (Fe), manganese (Mn), zinc (Zn), and soluble salts. Nitrogen levels can also be tested, but available nitrogen is so water soluble that its level in the soil changes very quickly.

Most soil testing laboratories can do quite a bit more than just test soil. They can also analyze samples of plant tissue or growing mixes that don't contain soil but may be made from such ingredients as bark, sphagnum moss, perlite, and vermiculite. If the lab is aware of the plants you're growing, the recommendations that are returned can be so specific as to specify the quantity and type of fertilizer you should apply and when you should apply it, as well as how best to modify the pH to meet optimum levels.

Soil tests can be done anytime, but there are a few preferred times of year based on what the tests are likely to prescribe. If you suspect that the soil pH in the tested areas will not need modification, then spring testing is fine, although there may be a processing delay at the lab because of all the other people who waited until spring.

If you suspect that the soil pH has changed, or if you don't know one way or the other, it's a good idea to take the sample in the fall. You can then add lime (to raise) or sulfur (to lower) the pH to the proper value, and the soil has time to respond before planting time comes around again. Whenever you decide to test the soil, remember to contact the lab of your choice beforehand (often affiliated with land grant universities and county Extension offices) for the mailing labels and sample bags you will need.

How to Take a Soil Sample

For those with gardening tools of every shape and sort, the best tool to use is a soil probe. If you don't have one, use a clean, dry, long-bladed trowel.

SOIL SAMPLING. Use a trowel to get a 6–8" (15–18 cm) deep sample.

1. Remove plants and debris from a small area.
2. Using the trowel, cut a circle about 4 or 5 inches (10–13 cm) in diameter and 6 to 8 inches (15–18 cm) deep.

3. Remove one half of the circle and set aside.
4. Slice off a layer 1 to 2 inches (2.5–5 cm) thick and put it in the plastic sample bag.
5. Break up any clumps and leave the bag open in a warm, dry room.
6. When the sample is dry, remove about 1 pint (½ liter) of soil and place it in a soil sample bag provided by the lab that will do the test.

Sometimes, especially when you wish to find out the profile of a larger area (such as a lawn), composite samples are the way to go. To gather a composite soil sample, repeat the above steps in 5 to 10 places around the lawn or planting. Place the samples in a clean plastic bucket, then mix all the samples together. Take out one sample, bag it in a plastic sample bag, and label it.

Buffer #2: Water for Weather Resilience

For many of us, water is something we take for granted. In some areas, it is plentiful enough that daily supplies are not a concern, and it is so commonplace that we rarely think of it more than in passing. But water is a unique substance. Water can be used to the gardener's advantage to make the garden more weather resilient by using three specific qualities unique to water and no other substance on the planet: phase change, surface tension, and specific heat.

Time for a Change

An amazing quality of water is its ability to be three things at once. In nature, substances can exist in three states, or phases: solid, liquid, and gas. Water is the only substance that can exist in all three phases at normal temperatures present on the earth. Even more remarkable is that these three separate phases can even exist in the same place at the same time. For example, on a sunny winter day, you can see the solid phase (snow) melting into the liquid phase (water). Less noticeable is water's gaseous phase, as water vapor is formed through the evaporation of water and the ablation (changing from ice to water vapor, without becoming water) of snow.

How Change Is Good for the Garden

Aside from being a novel curiosity, this 3-in-1 property of water has some practical benefits for your garden. As water passes through its different phases, it either releases heat and raises the temperature of the nearby air or it absorbs heat, lowering the temperature of the air. For example, as water condenses from water vapor to dew, heat is released into the air in such quantity that the temperature often stops dropping for the remainder of the night. As water changes phase again, from a liquid to a solid, more heat is released to the air. As water changes phase, the liberated heat can be just enough to provide resilience to the garden and turn a hard frost into a light one or a light frost into no frost at all.

Professional-Strength Cold-Weather Help

The phase changes of water can be used in various ways to help the garden become more weather resilient. Many of these techniques stem from methods used by professional horticulturists. For example, a challenge facing many horticultural operations is how to overwinter plants so that they remain healthy through the cold months and are ready for shipping come spring. Trying to do this outdoors places the plants at the mercy of the weather, and they are often snow-covered and inaccessible when the shipping season starts. The alternative is to overwinter plants in an unheated greenhouse, called a holding house.

Because greenhouses can get warm during the day even in the depths of winter, nurserymen cover the frame of the greenhouse with white plastic (the standard thickness is 8 mil). This imitates the intensity of light under a snow cover and limits penetration of warming sunlight to keep the plants dormant. This arrangement can work alone, but the interior of the holding house may still be subject to greater swings of temperature than are desirable.

Use of water helps with this problem. A trough lined with plastic is constructed down the center aisle of the holding house. After the plants are placed in the greenhouse and watered one last time, the trough is filled with water and the ends of the holding house are sealed with white plastic. Over the winter months, the phase changes of the water in the trough effectively moderate the temperature. Early in the dormant period, the freezing water releases heat, keeping the air slightly warmer. Late in the dormant period, the melting ice keeps the air cooler, letting the plants break dormancy slowly.

Modifying the Overwintering Technique

You can adapt the same concept professionals use by making a protective or overwintering tool in an ordinary raised bed. When plants are set to be overwintered, usually after a few hard frosts, run a plastic trough, at least 8 mil in thickness, down the center of the bed, about 3 to 5 inches deep. Install small hoops along the sides of the bed and cover everything with white (opaque) nursery plastic, leaving enough surplus to seal both ends securely. Fill the trough with water and seal off the ends. This simple

Water on the Brain

There is a curious coincidence between the garden and the gardener: the human brain and a living tree both contain 75 percent water.

A SNUG WINTER HOME.
Protect plants in raised bed by creating a mini-hoop house, with a water trough running down its length.

procedure removes much of the effect of capricious winter weather, such as plants coming out of dormancy too soon and being damaged when bitter weather returns. The plants are now also resilient to wind damage, such as dieback and tip burn, sunscald, damage from deicing compounds such as salt, and freezing and thawing caused by lack of snow cover.

Warm-Climate Crisis: Smoke or Water?

Warm climates have their own troubles that the phase changes of water can help with. There were once some commercial greenhouses in central Florida filled with green tropical houseplants that needed temperatures above 45 to 50°F (7 – 10°C) in order to avoid chill damage. One cold winter afternoon, the power went out and the emergency generators served only a portion of the area, the older houses being off-line. The managers hauled out dozens of sooty things called smudge pots, stout metal containers attached to 4-foot-tall (1.2 m) metal chimneys. The smudge pots were lined up in the aisles, filled with fuel, and lit. Clouds of black smoke rolled out and hung thick in the air. The idea was that the sooty smoke would act like a layer of insulation and slow the loss of heat through the glass roof.

Water could have solved the threatened crisis more easily and much more cleanly. Rather than pour out toxic smoke, the greenhouse managers could have kept the greenhouses just as warm, if not warmer, by increasing the humidity. Water vapor, because it holds a great deal of thermal energy, provides a buffer to quick changes in air temperature. By wetting down the aisles, the temperatures would modulate because of the humidity. Even though evaporation of water requires heat, thus initially cooling the air, the resultant high humidity level would have provided a thermal buffer.

Orchids or ferns grown in a bathroom benefit from humidity in that environment. Companion planting in which taller plants grow above shorter ones works well. This is partly because of the moderating temperature effects due to the higher humidity of the air amid the plants than what is just outside them. Air inside cold frames and even moist garden soil increase humidity levels and thus increase a garden's resilience.

Ice as a Buffer: Orange Ice
Even in warm regions, the change of water to ice can prove helpful. In areas in which tropical and subtropical plants grow, a rush of cold from up north can destroy a citrus grove or other plantings. To protect trees from extensive cold damage, growers often spray the canopies with water and allow it to freeze on the branches, leaves, and stems like a misplaced ice storm. It works. The ice keeps the trees at 32°F (0°C) while the surrounding air in the grove may be in the mid- to low 20s (around –5°C).

A Good Kind of Tension
Water molecules have an attraction to one another that causes them to naturally clump together. This attractive force, called surface tension, is what holds a raindrop together, giving the drop shape. Surface tension is what allows water to move through the soil and into plant roots by way of capillary action. When the soil is properly amended, it works with the surface tension of water to make garden plants healthier, and more resilient to changes in their environment.

Holding in the Heat

Water also has the ability to absorb and hold energy like no other natural substance in the world. This ability is expressed in a measurement called specific heat which reflects the amount of heat energy needed to warm a small amount of a substance (1 g) by 1 degree C. The greater the specific heat of a substance, the better an insulator that substance is, as seen in the following comparison of water and gold.

To warm 3½ ounces (99.2 g) of gold from 10°C to 11°C requires 3.1 calories of energy. To warm 3½ ounces of water from 10°C to 11°C requires 100 calories of energy. After the temperature of both the gold and the water has increased by 1 degree C, the gold holds only 3 percent of the heat energy of that absorbed by the water. It is this absorbed energy that is useful to gardeners in making plantings more weather resilient.

A popular tool to take advantage of the specific heat of water is an insulator designed to protect warm-weather crops like tomatoes from the chill of spring nights. The device consists of a series of clear plastic sleeves joined together and rolled into a cylinder. The tube is set over a plant and the sleeves are filled with warm water. This simple little invention works amazingly well because compared with other hot caps, the water provides

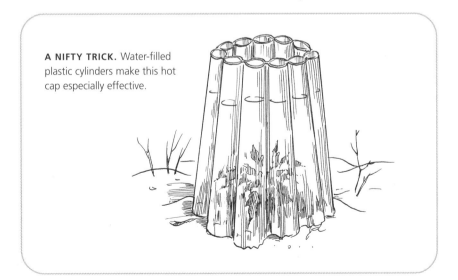

A NIFTY TRICK. Water-filled plastic cylinders make this hot cap especially effective.

not only superior insulation but also modulation of the temperature change. The air temperature inside the water-filled cylinder stays warmer longer and also warms up more slowly in the morning. In contrast, some types of hot caps can cook your plants if they aren't removed soon after the sun strikes them.

Buffer #3: Microclimates

The USDA Hardiness Map (see page 389) is one of the most detailed and accurate maps of its kind for you to determine the general hardiness zone of your garden and yard. However, whatever the map indicates to be your hardiness zone, your yard and garden are more likely a composite of two or more zones.

The USDA map provides information on the hardiness data for entire regions and thus indicates the overall climate zone of your region. Features of your yard, both natural and man-made, frequently modify the overall climate, creating small areas with distinctly different environmental conditions (including hardiness zones) from the areas surrounding them. These small distinct areas are called microclimates. Learning how to find and use the microclimates in your yard and garden will help make your entire landscape healthier and more weather resilient.

Hardiness Zone Maps Demystified: An Imperfect Science

Creating a map that accurately depicts the hardiness of plants across North America has been a goal of everyone from gardeners to scientists for decades. The difficulty in reaching this goal focuses on how to convey very complex climatic information simply and easily.

The climate of any area is an intricate blending and interfacing of every aspect of an area's environment, including precipitation, heat, wind, latitude, altitude, and cold. When the first hardiness maps were being created in the first half of the 20th century, such comprehensive data just didn't exist for much of the continent. What did exist in some quantity was weather data, including temperature records.

In 1927, Alfred Rehder (of Boston's Arnold Arboretum) wrote the classic textbook *Manual of Cultivated Trees and Shrubs,* which included a hardiness zone map. The eight zones were based on that location's annual minimum low temperatures. Rehder noted that the map was meant to render "approximately" the hardiness zones across the continent. To underscore this, question marks frequently followed the hardiness zones. Rehder's maps firmly established the precedent of using the annual minimum low temperature as the sole criterion to define hardiness and create hardiness zones.

Donald Wyman, also with the Arnold Arboretum, refined and updated Rehder's hardiness zone map many times between 1938 to 1971. Wyman's map, which adorns the endpapers of *Wyman's Gardening Encyclopedia,* is much more detailed and thorough but is still based only on annual minimum temperatures.

The United States Department of Agriculture (USDA) began producing a hardiness zone map in 1960, and by its 1990 revision, this map had become the standard. The USDA map divides North America into 10 very detailed climate zones; however, these are still based on annual minimum (low) temperature. Currently, the USDA map seems to be the one most widely used in reference books and plant catalogs.

Hardiness Is Not Just Low Temperature

Minimum annual temperatures are sometimes the dominant factor in a location's climate, but not always. A low-growing Zone 6 plant can grow in USDA Zone 4 if the area has a deep insulating snow cover each year. Meanwhile, a Zone 4 plant may not grow in Zone 6 because of more active freezing and thawing. A plant that grows in Zone 8 in California may perish in Zone 8 in the humid Southeast. In more southern regions, the minimum temperature is not nearly as important as the maximum temperature and the humidity.

The hunt for better ideas has led to the creation of intricate hardiness zone maps that are based on multiple climate factors. The *Sunset National Garden Book* has taken its complex western maps nationwide, painting the continent in 45 different hardiness zones. The Plant Heat-Zone Map from the American Horticultural Society uses annual maximum temperatures to define its zones. This map is an aid to southern gardeners but is of marginal use in cooler locations.

For years, gardeners have taken hardiness zone maps as law when they should have been taking them with a grain of salt. But knowing the limitations of your tools doesn't mean you shouldn't use those tools. Use whatever hardiness zone map makes the most sense for your area, but use this hardiness information just as a starting point. Then, visit local nurseries and talk with other gardeners regarding the hardiness of specific plants. Check to see what zones those plants are assigned.

Trust your plant supplier. Nurseries don't stay in business shipping plants to areas where they won't grow. If the catalog says that a plant will grow in your zone, believe it, but take healthy precautions too — be sure the catalog company has a good guarantee (replacement or refund) policy.

Reference books, such as plant encyclopedias, provide the hardiness range of plants. The range almost always includes multiple zones, but the hardiness of the plant may differ in different parts of the range. The zones at either end of the range may be locations in which the plant is only marginally hardy. To play it safe, select plants with hardiness ranges well within your garden's zone.

Use native plants and know what other gardeners successfully grow in your area. None of the experts who made all the maps and wrote all the books ever came to your garden. Stick with what has proved itself in your patch of earth and, when expanding, check out your neighbors' gardens.

How to Find Microclimates

Knowing that microclimates exist in your garden and knowing how to recognize them are two different things. The climate of your region is composed of many elements including heat, cold, wind, wet, dry, sun, and shade. A microclimate has the same elements, but in quantities different from the climate of the region overall. Changing the relative amounts or intensities of those elements can have a pronounced effect on the climate of that spot (and thus which plants will thrive there). These microclimates can be as small as a few square feet or as large as an acre or more.

In this example, an open sunny field has a uniform climate. When a house is built in the field, a collection of microclimates are created that didn't exist there before. The house is aligned with the four sides facing the four cardinal points and a garden bed constructed along each side. Compared with the climate in the original field, the microclimate in the north-side garden now has reduced light and increased shade, increased overall soil moisture, reduced temperatures, frequently increased winds, and slower melting of snow and ice in spring. The south garden, meanwhile, has increased light intensity, increased heat, higher rates of evaporation from plants and soil, greater incidence of drought, and less wind. These two areas are physically separated from each other by only a few dozen feet, but they have very different growing conditions — so different that some plants that thrive in one bed would not survive in the other.

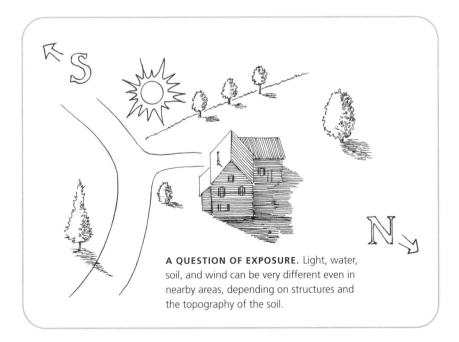

A QUESTION OF EXPOSURE. Light, water, soil, and wind can be very different even in nearby areas, depending on structures and the topography of the soil.

To find the microclimates in your yard and garden, look for distinct differences (compared to the background climate) in these elements:
• Light — intensities of sun and shade
• Water — soil moisture and nearby bodies of water, such as lakes, ponds, streams, and the ocean
• Soil — soil types
• Wind — how strong, how often
• Temperature — heat and cold, and how fast it changes

Working with Microclimates

Once you find the microclimates in your yard and garden, the task becomes how to use them to make your landscape more weather resilient. First, note how the microclimate differs from the surrounding area. Does it have more moisture, shade, and so on? Once you know how the area is different, you can determine what plants will thrive in those conditions. For example, the south side of a house can often support plants one USDA zone less hardy than the surrounding area, but those plants must also be heat and drought resilient and thrive in full sun.

Common Microclimates

Different features within and around your landscape are important in creating the climate of the yard and garden. For example, water acts as a heat sink, holding the solar energy it accumulates over the course of the day and releasing it slowly over many hours throughout the night. Large bodies of water release warmth into the air, moderating the air temperature of places near them. Thus, gardens near lakes or oceans are subject to higher night temperatures and less chance of late-spring or early-fall frosts than are gardens located away from water. Ponds and small lakes also moderate climate but on a much smaller scale, with the effect often restricted to areas immediately bordering the water.

Cities. Developed urban areas are often called heat islands because of the effect the buildings and paved surfaces have on climate. Parking lots, streets, and buildings absorb large quantities of heat during the day and release it back into the air at night. This is why cities have higher minimum night temperatures than do adjacent suburbs. Gardens in the city may be one hardiness zone warmer than nearby less developed areas but become oppressively hot in the summer months. Air quality, an important factor in determining plant health, can be poorer in urban areas. Tall buildings can also funnel winds, increasing wind velocity, or block them, making calm havens in which plants may grow.

Valleys. Valleys can produce microclimates milder or more severe than the surrounding climate, depending on the lay of the land. In some large valleys with lakes, such as New York's and Vermont's Champlain Valley, the lake serves to buffer both cold and warm air, producing a microclimate one full zone warmer than nearby areas. The valley serves to hold the warmer air produced by the lake.

Valleys without large bodies of open water respond differently. Cold air is denser than warm air and wants to find the lowest point in the landscape. The cold air sinks and flows downslope, like water running downhill. So cold air pools in valleys, creating cold pockets 5 to 10 degrees F (3–6 degrees C) colder than areas sometimes only a few yards away. Not surprisingly, valleys are prone to late-spring and early-fall frosts. They also often have more soil moisture than adjacent slopes.

Hilltops. Crests of hills can also create a microclimate, either milder or colder depending on circumstances. In winter, it's common for storms to be termed *elevation dependent*. These storms are often a messy mix of rain, snow, and ice, with the type of precipitation dependent on the atmospheric temperature of an area and the temperature a reflection of the elevation. The higher the hill, the colder the air and thus the greater the chance precipitation will be freezing rain, sleet, or snow.

The reverse also happens when hilltops are warmer than the valleys, as when a storm moves north of a region and drags warmer air over the landscape. The hilltops warm up first, while the valleys hold on to cold air until the storm winds eventually scour it out. In general, hilltop climates have less frost on clear nights but often have stronger wind, which can damage many plants.

Slopes. Between the hilltops and the valleys are the slopes. Sloped land can have a wide variety of microclimates, depending on the direction of exposure. A south slope faces the sun more directly than does flat ground and so collects more solar radiation. Slopes warm up faster in spring but

Keeping Watch: The Garden Weather Station

When you really start to become interested in the elements of weather that are constantly interacting in your garden and yard, it's almost irresistible to want to know even more about what's going on out there. The best way to do this is to create your own garden weather station. The type of station that is best for your needs depends on personal comfort, the amount of time and money you can invest, and how accurate you want the readings to be.

Personal comfort. Innovative tools or systems that make tasks easier can intensify the joy of gardening. Many home weather stations can be designed so that the readings from the instruments are electronically displayed at a convenient location inside the home.

Time and money. A functional garden weather station need not be prohibitively expensive, depending on the quality and quantity of instruments desired. Some people like more than one of certain instruments to place in different spots. A nice mix of indoor displays and an out-door, enclosed station can provide most of what you need to begin tracking your garden's microclimates. You can find these in garden-supply catalogs and in garden centers.

Accuracy. "Accuracy" in this case refers more to the accuracy of what you really want to measure than to the device measuring it. For disease control, it is far better to measure humidity in the leaf canopy than on the lawn. The convenient displays that record outdoor temperatures using a probe attached near the house won't give an accurate reading of what the temperature is in the garden. So be sure to record information from locations where you want the data, not from other spots that may be irrelevant to your garden.

What Instruments Should You Have?

The values you want to keep track of in the garden weather station reflect the requirements of the garden. The following list suggests what a garden weather staget hotter in summer. Plants on south slopes are also prone to winter-related problems, such as sunscald.

North slopes are cool and shady, meaning that they warm up slowly in spring and also tend to hold more soil moisture. Because they warm up

tion should have.
• High and low thermometer (to measure temperature)
• Barometer (atmospheric pressure)
• Hygrometer (humidity)
• Rain gauge
• Wind speed and direction indicator
• Soil moisture meter

All-in-one units. Today the easiest and most accurate way to keep up with the weather in your garden is by using a wireless weather station. These units come with remote wireless sensors that you set in various places in your garden. The sensors transmit data to a display in the house, much like a wireless telephone does. The amazing thing about these units is their comprehensiveness. They will tell you everything you want to know about your garden, including:
• Temperature — high and low, plus current indoor and outdoor
• Humidity — indoor and outdoor, plus dew point
• Wind — speed and direction, plus current wind chill
• Pressure — current plus daily trend
• Precipitation — daily rainfall total, plus rainfall rate

These devices also display the forecast. The sensors can be placed up to 400 feet (122 m) from the base station. There are many different products and models, with prices between $400 and $600.

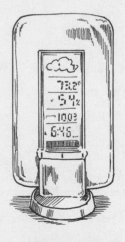

KEEPING A WEATHER EYE.
An electronic weather unit can provide at-a-glance information on conditions in your yard.

slowly, the trees come out of dormancy slightly later and more slowly. This timing allows tender buds to emerge after the hardest frosts, as well as making the buds more cold resilient longer into the season. East and west slopes are more moderate in climate but have problems all their own. Trees on west slopes are especially prone to sunscald because they receive the last sun of the day before it sets, warming the trunk before rapid cooling occurs as the sun disappears over the horizon.

Houses. Houses and other structures can steer and block the wind. Many areas have prevailing winds that come from a north to northwest

Getting to Know Your Best Friend

It has been said that gardening with microclimates is like getting to know your landscape as well as you know your best friend. For many of us, it is easy to go out and buy our best friend a gift that is personal and special because we know her so well. We know what she likes, and what she doesn't like. We know her better than just about anyone else. When we purchase the gift, it brings her joy for a long time. Just think of how your best friend would react if you bought her whatever happened to be on sale! That is often what gardeners who don't know their land like their best friend inadvertently do.

The plot of land you tend should be like a best friend, but how many of us actually know the land of which we are stewards? Do we purchase plants for our garden based on what we want or on what would make our "best friend" happy? Observing, modifying, and using microclimates is getting to know your garden in a personal way. When that knowledge is in our minds, then decorating the garden with exactly what the garden needs is so much easier — and brings joy for a very long time.

direction. The house thus produces a sheltered microclimate on the south and east sides. Other elements, from porches to stones walls, also moderate climate by blocking winds, collecting heat, and conserving moisture.

A balcony can have its own microclimate. The height above the ground makes it less susceptible to mild frosts. The placement of a balcony is important, however, as it can be windy or sheltered, depending on its exposure.

Paved or hard surfaces. Parking lots, driveways, patios, and roofs can be heat sinks. These hard surfaces absorb heat during the day, often becoming intensely hot, then radiate that heat back into the air at night. The resulting temperatures can be extreme for many plants, producing excessive heat and evaporation. In container plants, which are popular for decorating such spots, soil in pots can become quickly overheated, injuring roots and weakening the plant.

Trees. Large trees can produce a microclimate beneath their canopy by shading the area, blocking sunlight, and hogging soil moisture and nutrients. Some trees, such as black walnut, even exude chemicals into the soil that makes it difficult to impossible for other plants to grow at their feet.

Raised beds. Raised beds are gardens designed to create a favorable, very forgiving microclimate for many garden plants. Raised beds warm up faster in spring and have better drainage, and soil quality is more easily managed. Similarly, terraced beds with a southern exposure warm up even faster and absorb even greater amounts of solar radiation than do raised beds.

Rocks and rock gardens. Rocks and rock gardens can produce one or more small microclimates within them. Rocks act like pavement and other hard surfaces: They collect heat from the sun and disperse it over time. They can also serve as wind barriers, creating calm islands in the garden. The combination of warmth and calm creates a forgiving microclimate.

Fences, windbreaks, and stone walls. Fences and the like break or modify wind, creating a calm area that is much easier on plants than windy conditions. Fences and similar features not only block winds, but they also redirect winds away from one place and to another. They also help when severe weather comes, by insulating the yard from the worst of the storm.

Soils. Soil can be instrumental in creating a microclimate that may be difficult to detect. Different soils hold varying amounts of water and air, and the exact quantities of each affect the temperature of the ground. Clay soils hold more moisture than sandy ones and can keep air temperatures near the ground warm enough to prevent light early- and late-season frosts. Sandy soils, with their abundant air spaces and less water, cool off faster, allowing frost to form.

Humidity. The humidity as related on weather forecasts is a general value of the air mass presently over a region. The humidity that makes up a microclimate is different because it depends more on stable environmental factors than on the changes of air masses that come with fair weather or storms. An example can be found on the banks of some northern streams. A bank may have hemlock trees shading ferns, mosses, and liverworts, along with perennials such as Solomon's seal and miterwort. Above the bank on the floodplain, an entirely different plant community thrives, with aspen, partridgeberry, and hayscented fern. The ravine is cooler and shadier, but that alone isn't enough to account for the difference in plants. It is also more humid. The water vapor in the air not only modulates temperatures, shaving off the highs and lows of nearby areas, but it also reduces evaporation, keeping these plants thriving. An additional benefit is less ultraviolet radiation, which has been shown to reduce the growth rate of plants.

Turning Over a New Leaf

Unlike soil and water microclimates, plants have a genetic makeup that decides the type and strength of their buffering ability. Each plant's unique collection of DNA directs if it is frost tolerant, strong-stemmed, prone to disease, or capable of producing strong branches. Matching a plant's natural resilience with the needs of your landscape and garden is one of the basic goals in creating a weather-resilient garden — a garden that reflects a partnership of plant and place.

The plants we select to grow in our gardens and yards are the result of personal choice. More often than not, we choose to grow a plant because we like it; something about it appeals to us. When gardeners turn their attention to making their plantings more weather resilient, something to examine is why we choose the varieties we choose.

Buyer Beware

The daylily is one of the most adaptable, weather-resilient plants around. It has been the subject of intensive plant breeding for generations, which has resulted in tens of thousands of varieties. Some of these are exquisite and improve on the daylily's wonderful qualities. Others have pretty flowers on pitiful, weak plants that need constant care just to make it through a pleasant, uneventful growing season.

Every season, myriad varieties of plants are introduced and displayed on catalog covers and in gardening magazines. But the true qualities of these new introductions are often not known, or not described. It is fun to try out new plant selections, but when I need something for a spot that must face tougher conditions, I want a tested variety that has proved itself. Thus, in my garden new varieties get the cushy spots until I know more about them. The more challenging places, the cold pocket and the windy hill, get the tried-and-true varieties.

The Catalog Story

Many plant catalogs sorely lack information about the real qualities of plants. I don't just want to know what the plant can do under optimal conditions; tell me the rest of the story. African daisy may be described as being able to weather cold winters; hollyhock may be described as thriving in any moist, well-drained soil. But many plants thrive or fail to thrive in these conditions. Weather resilience is seldom addressed in catalogs, but when you discover those that offer specific advice, you'll find them the most useful when you are selecting plants.

Be an Educated Consumer

Even species and varieties that are not very weather resilient can be made more durable by purchasing plants at the right stage of growth. When you wander around a garden center and pass the rows of flats filled with annuals, notice how many of them are in bloom and how many are not. Now watch as people come to buy the plants. Time after time, you'll see people purchase plants that are in flower and leave the smaller, green plants behind. The plants in bloom will make a fine garden, but the plants that are slightly smaller and not in bloom will transplant better, usually be more vigorous and healthy, and as a result will tolerate bad weather better, all at no extra cost.

Whenever you purchase plants, don't fall for the allure of the bigger plant in a small pot, the tomato that is already in flower, or the annuals that are in bloom even though growing in tiny starter pots. Too often you'll bring home broccoli that will bear a head the size of your thumbnail, a pepper whose blossoms drop off the plant, or celosia that goes to flower when it is 6 inches high when it should be three times that tall. Buy potential, not instant gratification.

Part Two

Really Bad Weather:

Healing Methods and Fresh Starts

"On this day all the springs of the vast watery deep
were broken open and the floodgates of the heavens
were opened."

Genesis 7:11

THE WEATHER IS A LOT LIKE A MOODY FRIEND: amiable much of the time, but also temperamental and prone to unpredictable outbursts. Indeed, the moods of nature are more powerful than our defenses against them. After experiencing a hurricane, flood, ice storm, or other powerful natural event, the words of Yeats (see page 1) become intensely personal. It is more than "*things* fall apart" — it is *your* things! The center of your gardening world, those years of creative caring for your patch of earth, does not hold. When the worst weather takes aim at your garden, everything can seem to disintegrate in just a moment or two. The assault of an overwhelming meteorological force is devastating to both the garden and the spirit of the gardener.

There are many types of foul weather. Some come as quick as lightning and others are as measured and patient as drought. The bad weather that may affect your yard and garden can be divided into 11 distinct events: cold, ice and snow, salt, flood, heat, drought, fire, humidity, lightning, hail, and wind. While some of these events share common features, each event has a unique impact on your garden. Flood-damaged soil has different qualities and challenges from drought-damaged soil.

Just as important, once we understand the unique aspects of certain weather events, we can prepare and protect the garden and its plants far more effectively. The gardener's wonderful ally in facing bad weather's challenges is the garden itself. Healing and rejuvenation always follow injury — that is how nature works. Garden and gardener are both imbued with the qualities of the phoenix.

Because plants are made to survive, when they are injured an array of internal mechanisms designed to restore them begin to function. The chemistry and metabolism in the plant change when it suffers mechanical injury, such as broken limbs or loss of leaves. Buds that have remained dormant for weeks, months, or even years suddenly sprout. New roots and buds begin to grow where there were none before. Hormone levels change, and plant processes like photosynthesis and transpiration speed up or slow down. The plant makes dozens of internal alterations and corrections calculated specifically to heal itself. Trees with foliage being preyed upon by insects, for example, protect themselves by changing the chemical makeup of their leaves to repel the pests. More remarkable, trees at a distance but not infested also change the chemistry of their leaves simultaneously, to prepare for attack. This intricate survival scheme is standard equipment in every plant in your yard. Some plants are better adapted or tolerate more kinds of adversity than others, but they are all survivors.

As we gardeners nurture our plants, we learn more about them and what each one needs to thrive. When vandalistic weather storms through, many plants recover with only gentle care, but others need more intensive help right away or they won't make it. At the worst, some plants, including large trees, die, making your job more complicated.

Repairing weather's ravages, whether mending one damaged tree limb or rebuilding an entire landscape, can be daunting, but try to view the rebuilding and healing of the garden as a partnership between you and your plants. Derive strength from that alliance between your plants' natural survival instincts and your joy in growing beautiful, healthy plants.

At the beginning, with so much clean up to do, repairing and healing the garden may look overwhelming and can be emotionally draining. As the process unfolds, however, a new garden begins to evolve where your familiar old garden was once. Its newness is disquieting at first, its features are different and any replacement plants haven't been in place long enough to look at home. But after a while, everything once again does look like home. The garden may be different, but it is still yours, and the reassuring structure and the peace of the place gradually return.

Caring and mending is healing to both garden and gardener. This section guides you through the process of rebuilding your garden in the wake of damaging weather. Along with techniques to help heal the garden, you'll learn the best plant partners to help you create a strong, weather-resilient garden for the future, a garden as beautiful as it is undaunted.

Cold

SPRING COMES EARLY ONE YEAR, and by mid-May the memory of winter weather is far behind. Even though it hadn't been a very hard winter, the unseasonable warmth is welcome, a gleam of the long, comfortable days to come. For weeks, the temperatures climb well above freezing, coaxing the buds on the trees to open. Everywhere orchards are in bloom, the trees dressed in rose-pink buds that fade to snow white blossoms. The foliage of irises and daylilies is lush, and blooming tulips and daffodils hold high their dazzling blossoms. Impatient gardeners start to plant tender crops in the warm soil. Though it is early to plant such crops as tomatoes and melons, the weather is perfect and it seems silly to worry.

Meanwhile, far above the earth and thousands of miles away, an enormous river of air called the *jet stream* flows across the atmosphere. For many weeks, it has run in a nearly straight line from west to east. This pattern, called a *zonal flow*, brings temperate weather to much of the United States by keeping the cold air locked in Canada. Spring is early, not because there was no frigid wintry air, but because the cold air is blocked from coming south by the jet stream. In a matter of hours, the temperate zonal flow that was in place for weeks falls apart. The jet stream swings north, reaching deep into Canada, then loops south, pushing a dome of arctic air south like an ice floe drifting down a river.

At dawn, the jet stream guides the large arctic high-pressure system from Canada into the northern tier of states. The temperature is in the low 40s as the dome of cold air arrives. The sky clears and the breeze dies away. The air is completely calm, the stars sparkle, and the temperature begins to fall. *Radiational cooling* occurs when the heat absorbed by the earth during the day is released into the air at night. Humidity, wind, and a layer of clouds over the area all slow radiational cooling. Dry, still air and clear skies speed it up. Conditions are perfect for maximum radiational cooling — and the temperature drops like a rock. A few hours after dawn, the mercury is in the 20s over all the area, with some deep valleys bottoming out around 23°F.

The unexpected freeze has killed some leaves, flowers, and buds outright, but the worst damage occurs as the sun comes up and washes over the plants and trees. The strong spring sunlight quickly thaws the leaves and flowers, and even more die (see page 46). The leaves of hardy perennials, such as daylilies, are burned with cold, the upper half of the leaf blades brown and withered. The cells within the leaves, stems, and buds of unprotected vegetable plants and annuals have ruptured and collapsed. And the orchards are decimated. Though the trees seem fine superficially, they are very sensitive to temperatures before, during, and after blossoming. This one cold night has killed one quarter of the grape crop, nearly 90 percent of the cherries and apples, and large numbers of vegetables and flowers. The damage isn't confined to one valley, or even one state, but is widespread. The cold has quietly, and destructively, flowed over more than a dozen states and provinces in two countries.

The Way the Wind Blows

The jet stream is the forceful current of air that steers storms and fair-weather systems across the land. What sort of weather comes to your garden depends largely on the direction of the jet stream. A west-to-east flow brings temperate weather and weak storms. A flow that swings south to north brings warm weather and possibly strong storms, and a flow from the north drags in cold air. The jet stream changes its direction of flow frequently, and often quickly.

What Does "Cold" Really Mean?

One of the obvious differences between the gardener and the garden is the temperature of each. We stay at about 98.6°F (37°C) all the time, whether we're outside in the cold or inside a cozy house. While some plants manage a little thermal manipulation, most assume the temperature of their environment. When it is hot outside, the plant is just as hot. And when it is cold, the plant is just as cold as its surroundings. Over the course of a single average climate year, garden plants growing in many areas of North America can experience *internal* temperatures that range from far below 0°F (−18°C) to about 100°F (38°C). We humans cannot endure that.

As resilient as many plants can be over a long period, such as a calendar year, there are times during that year when they are especially vulnerable to climate change — particularly cold. But cold rarely works alone. The most widespread cold damage affecting plants, from annuals to apples, from perennials to peaches, usually occurs in concert with warm weather. However, there are ways to predict cold events; prepare your garden, yard, and orchard for them; and fix what goes wrong.

Identifying Your Yard's Cold Spots

When you plan your approach to protecting your yard and garden against damage caused by extremes like those just described, you must first identify the USDA hardiness zone you live in (see the map on page 389). But hardiness zones are just broad indicators of what you can expect. Because every backyard and garden is different, every location has its own array of cold and warm spots. To find the cold spots in your yard, think of cold air as a flood of water coming into your yard. Where is the "water" going to go? It runs to the lowest places. In other words, the low spots you find are probably also the cold spots. These areas get cold earlier in the year, stay colder later in the year, and reach colder temperatures faster than other areas of the yard. These are the places that need to be reserved for the cold-hardiest plants.

Now look around for hills and slopes, and again picture water running down these. Cold air flows much like water, and often the coldest air flows most quickly down the steepest slopes. Slopes can often be the best places to plant because they tend not to get too hot or too cold. (Orchards are often planted on slopes for this reason.) South slopes are an exception, as they can be prone to quick temperature changes.

High points that stick noticeably above the surrounding area may be windy places. Wind and cold can combine to produce a frigid environment for plants.

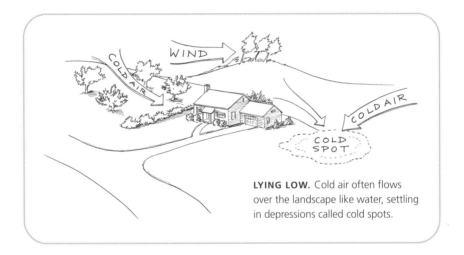

LYING LOW. Cold air often flows over the landscape like water, settling in depressions called cold spots.

How Hardiness Changes through the Seasons

Not only do you need to consider the temperatures you may experience in the coldest months, but you should also take into account the fact that the hardiness of permanent garden plantings (trees, shrubs, and perennials) changes throughout the year. While the information gardeners receive about hardiness seems graved in stone, it is most often based on one event (minimum annual temperature) during one season of the year (winter). If an apple tree is rated as hardy to $-40°F$ ($-40°C$), it seems logical that it would always be hardy to $-40°F$ ($-40°C$). But it isn't — and neither is any other plant growing in the garden.

An apple (buds, stems, and branches) is hardy to –40°F (–40°C) when it is dormant and protected from the cold. As the days lengthen and warm, the hardiness of the plant begins to change. In late winter, as the sap first begins to return to the tree, the hardiness temperatures start to climb toward the freezing point. As the buds swell in spring, the hardiness lessens until it is near 32°F (0°C) by the time the buds open. In addition, different parts of the tree have different degrees of hardiness. The flower buds are much more tender than the vegetative parts. The young developing fruit is very temperature sensitive after pollination and petal fall, and becomes progressively hardier as the season advances.

As fall approaches, the progression of hardiness changes, and the buds become hardy first. Hardiness progresses down the branches from the twigs to the trunk. The last part of a tree to become ready for winter is the union between the branch and the trunk. (The trunk itself is not as vulnerable as other parts, but isn't always ready for winter either.) This model can be used to describe many hardy plants. Just remember: Hardiness is greatest in winter and least during flowering, fruit or seed set, and fruit or seed development.

The Difference between a Frost and a Freeze

When the weather forecast calls for a cold night, you'll hear such terms as *light frost, hard frost, widespread freeze,* and *hard freeze.* All of these terms refer to conditions in which the temperature drops below freezing. Is there a difference between a plant with frost damage and a plant damaged by a freeze? Yes.

The biggest difference between frost and freeze damage is that frost injury happens to plants that are growing or acclimating, whereas freeze damage occurs to plants while they are dormant. Frosty nights can occur on evenings during which the *dew point* (the temperature at which the atmosphere is saturated and water begins to condense) is below freezing. Frost begins to form once such a dew point is reached. The water vapor solidifies on exposed surfaces, growing into the snowy, glittering ice crystals called frost.

How Freezing Kills Plants

Plants protect themselves from freezing injury in many ways, from super-cooling to desiccation (see page 46). What happens, however, when these schemes fail? Water is found inside plant cells and outside the cell in the extracellular spaces. Because there is less dissolved material in the water within the extracellular spaces, it begins to freeze while the water inside the cell remains liquid. This condition begins to draw moisture from the cell into the extracellular spaces. This process places great stress on the cell membranes and they rupture, severely damaging the cell. If temperatures continue to drop, the remaining fluid within the cell freezes, killing the cell outright.

Whereas *frost* is ice crystals that form on an exposed *exterior* surface of a plant, *freezing* is ice that forms *inside* a plant and *within* plant cells. Tender plants and hardy but actively growing plants are composed of soft, pliant cells that are easily damaged by frost crystals. Acclimated hardy plants are resilient to frost, but not always to a freeze.

The Big Chill: Injury When Temperatures Are Above Freezing

Temperatures that are cold but still well above freezing can also damage certain plants. Plants sensitive to this type of injury include those of tropical and subtropical origin, such as some annuals, tender perennials, container-grown foliage plants, and vegetables. Chill injury can also affect hardy species grown in warm environments, such as greenhouses, but that have not been hardened off (*acclimated;* see page 55) properly. After a long winter of looking at enticing vegetables in seed catalogs, many gardeners have an uncontrollable desire to get their transplants and seeds into the ground as soon as possible. The logic is that the earlier a plant is in the ground, the longer it has to grow and the more it will produce. However, this thinking is incorrect. Such crops as corn, tomato, pepper, eggplant, squash, and pumpkin can suffer damage that will affect them throughout the growing season if they are exposed to "cold" temperatures as much as 20 degrees F (11 degrees C) above freezing. If temperatures soon rise above 50°F (10°C) or so and the chill is limited to 2 or 3 hours, damage may be reversible. The tissues heal from within before any outside symptoms become evident. Longer chill periods, however, result in permanent injury that becomes progressively serious. Chill injury can affect plants at any stage of growth, from germinating seed to fruiting plant.

Chill damage occurs when the temperatures range between 33°F and about 50°F (1°C–10°C). The injuries are often invisible and most often appear when the temperature rises above the 50°F threshold. Symptoms of chill injury may not appear immediately, but become evident days or sometimes weeks later. Signs of damage include slowed growth; delayed flowering and fruit set; reduced yield; blackening and death of the leaves; water-soaked lesions on leaves, stems, or fruit; wilting and drooping of foliage; and water-soaked and spongy spots on leaves, stems, or fruits. Less obvious injury includes reduction or stopping of photosynthesis, poor seed germination, slower growth, and reduced water and nutrient absorption from the soil.

How Chill Does Its Damage

Freezing injures plants through formation of ice crystals in plant cells. In contrast, chilling injury happens when temperatures are too warm for ice to form. When temperatures drop into the chill zone, some physiological changes occur at a molecular level that alters the biochemistry inside plant cells. Plant cells contain many smaller parts, among them the all-important chloroplasts, which contain the chlorophyll a plant needs for photosynthesis. These small parts are vital to the function and survival of the cell and, ultimately, the plant. The parts are contained within thin membranes that are the gatekeepers of the cell. Everything that enters or exits these cell parts has to pass through the membranes. If the membranes don't function properly, the plant doesn't function either. The result is injury to tissues and perhaps death to the plant.

In some plants, it takes only 4 to 6 hours of chilling, or less, for noticeable and irreversible damage to occur in some cell membranes. In both freezing and chill injury, there is a thermal Rubicon that once crossed inevitably produces damage. While the precise temperature and time of exposure required for chill injury varies with the species and variety, the type of damage is consistent and affects a wide range of plant parts.

As cold seeps into a plant, the cell membranes begin a physical transformation from a flexible, watery consistency to a translucent solid that resembles gelatin. Once they turn to jelly, the membranes don't function normally anymore. Water that should be confined by the membranes slowly leaks through them and fills the spaces among the cells, from which it evaporates. The loss of moisture produces wilting due to irreversible damage to the plant itself. The plant affected by chill injury is falling apart inside. Toxins, such as aldehydes, and injury-induced hormones, such as ethylene, accumulate. Oxygen, sugars, organic acids, and proteins all show abnormalities in structure or quantity. The longer a plant must endure the cool temperatures, the more injury results.

The Origin of the Species

Chilling injury affects a wide variety of plants from tropic and subtropical climates. The average minimum annual temperature runs from 45 to 50°F (7–10°C) for the tropics to 33 to 40°F (0.5–4°C) for the subtropics. This temperature range also reflects the boundaries of chill-temperature damage in many sensitive plants. This could suggest that sensitivity is a function of the environment in which the plants grow and the adaptations to cold they have never had to make to succeed in their natural environment.

In the midst of chaos, an interesting paradox develops. The same cool temperatures that destroyed cell membranes and altered the internal workings of the cell now hold everything together, only tenuously, like a horticultural house of cards. While surrounded by cool temperatures, many chill-sensitive plants look fine. It is only when they are warmed to normal temperatures that cells collapse, plants wilt, and other injuries, such as water-soaked lesions and soft mushy areas, appear.

How Plants Survive Cold Temperatures

For not having any brains, plants have some very ingenious ways of protecting themselves from cold. Unlike animals, which can transport themselves from a cold place to a warmer one, plants have to survive where they are, where they happen to grow.

Supercooled. Pure water freezes at 32°F (0°C). If the water contains some dissolved materials, such as sugars, the water will remain unfrozen even after the temperature drops below 32°F (0°C). This effect is called *supercooling*. It is an effective way of avoiding deadly ice formation in a plant — to a point. Plants that use supercooling as part of their overwintering strategy include many shrubs and trees. In these plants, the wood goes through winter in a supercooled condition. Because of the materials in solution within many of these shrubs and trees, the water in the wood can remain liquid down to about –40°F (–40°C). Below this temperature threshold, however, the water often freezes, causing massive cell injury and death.

Dry as a bone. Whereas the wood in trees and shrubs survives by supercooling, the tissues in some other plants avoid injury in a different but no less ingenious way. Throughout the colder months, many plants slowly move liquid from the interior of plant cells to empty areas outside the cells called *extracellular spaces*. This process is akin to cleaning out the house and putting all the stuff you don't need in storage. In cold weather, the liquid in the extracellular spaces freezes, while the cells, now nearly devoid of moisture, remain dormant and uninjured. As the temperatures fluctuate, the amount of moisture within the cells changes, too.

Hardiness Mysteries

Long ago, the Swedish scientist Carolus Linnaeus devised a way of naming plants that was designed to define and catalog all life on earth. Under this system, which still serves as the basis of modern scientific nomenclature, every living thing is assigned two names: the first for the genus and the second for the species. This system was expected to consolidate like kinds of living things while separating dissimilar ones. Many times it works well, but sometimes it displays its imperfection.

Surprising toughness. The majestic yellowwood tree *(Cladrastis lutea)* is found in the wild in the southeast United States in Zones 6 and 7. Within its range, it seems to be declining in numbers, but outside its range it is a popular ornamental and thrives in climates as cold as Zone 4. The reason for the large disparity between native range and adaptive range is an unanswered question.

Hardiness within a genus. Flowering dogwood *(Cornus florida)* grows naturally from the Deep South all the way to New England. Throughout its native range, it is considered one species. But a flowering dogwood that is hardy in the South isn't as hardy in the North. In addition, the intensity and duration of the fall color display differs in trees from different places. The same is true for the blossoming of the trees in spring. Even named varieties (cultivars) have significant variations in hardiness. Despite the lack of predictability in hardiness, however, gardeners can take steps to make flowering dogwoods more hardy: Researchers at Michigan State University have found that trees grown in sunny locations are hardier than those grown more traditionally as understory trees.

Unexplained reluctance. Fringe tree *(Chionanthus virginicus)* is a small tree with nondescript, simple leaves that grows to about 15 to 20 feet (4.5–6 m). In late spring, the branches are covered with airy puffs of lacy, fragrant white flowers. The gray branches appear lifeless long into spring, but just when you're sure the tree died over winter, leaves pop from buds. Fringe tree is native from east Texas to the Atlantic Coast and north to near the Ohio River. When fringe trees are planted north of this boundary, they thrive just as well as they do in their native range. In fact, while the northern limit of their native range corresponds to Zone 6 on the USDA Hardiness Zone map, fringe tree is fully hardy throughout Zone 5. Why fringe tree grows naturally only to Zone 6 when it can grow in harsher climates remains a mystery.

For example, in some broadleaf evergreens, such as rhododendrons and a few viburnums, the appearance of the leaves provides an indicator of the degree of moisture in the leaf cells. As the temperature drops, the leaves roll into increasingly tight cylinders. The more tightly the leaf is rolled, the less moisture the cells contain. In cold weather, the foliage is so desiccated that it is technically wilted, but in the frigid temperatures the lack of moisture is a benefit rather than a problem.

Pollen illustrates well how controlled desiccation protects cells from freezing injury. Pollen grains contain very little moisture and can survive temperatures far lower than those found naturally on earth, down to an incredible −320°F (−196°C). Add a little moisture, however, and the same grains die within a few degrees of freezing.

As long as the temperatures move up and down in a normal rhythm, allowing the water to flow in and out of the cells in advance of large temperature shifts, this overwintering strategy works very well. If the temperature goes from warm to cold very fast, however, the system fails.

When the plant cells cannot move the liquids from inside the cells to the extracellular spaces fast enough, the water freezes inside the cells rather than outside. The resulting apparent damage includes bark splitting, in which vertical cracks split the bark.

Creating Protection against Cold

Much cold damage to the garden and yard can be avoided by using a little careful forethought when planning, planting, and preparing for winter.

Planning. Site needled and broadleaf evergreens on north and northeast exposures to reduce the chance of such problems as winter sunscald (see page 60). These plants should also be away from windy areas where the combination of wind and cold can result in dieback (see page 62). Choose plants that are unquestionably hardy to your yard, and for the coldest spots in the yard, select the hardiest plants.

Planting. There's strength in numbers. Group shrubs and trees to create small, more plant-friendly microclimates. And whenever you plant,

LET'S GET TOGETHER. An assemblage of shrubs and trees can be the foundation for a more temperate microclimate.

add generous amounts of compost to the soil. Compost improves drainage, soil fertility and structure, and moisture balance. These improvements reduce the chances of winter damage through such events as fluctuations in temperature, while providing an environment that keeps the plants as healthy and resilient as possible. And don't forget to mulch around plants during the growing season to keep temperatures moderate and the soil moist.

Preparing. Avoid pruning the lower branches of shrubs and trees with south or southwest exposures. Wrap exposed trunks and stems of plants with white plastic to deter sunscald and frost cracking. Add a deep layer of mulch in fall around plants after a few hard freezes to inhibit heaving. Keep soil moist entering into the winter season. Fertilize during spring and early summer to provide plants with proper nutrients. Thick layers of fallen leaves that stay around the base through winter encourage disease, so use bark mulch instead (this pertains particularly to rhododendrons and other ericaceous plants). Set screens of burlap or snow fence in front of evergreens.

Devices That Protect against Frost

Anyone who heats a home throughout the winter knows how much energy it takes to keep the house warm, and how much money that energy costs. So the idea of moderating the temperature outdoors, even a little, can be intimidating. Protection from frost, however, is very important if the potential of gardens, orchards, and yards is to be realized. The farmers in the example at the beginning of this chapter lost their primary source of income for the better part of the year in just one night. Gardeners in the region lost scores of different plants and had others severely damaged. Frost protection is important to everyone who grows plants in cool climates, and it can be achieved in surprisingly clever ways.

Frost protection is meant to provide a temporary thermal buffer for plants when temperatures sink to near the freezing point. The devices are most often used to protect vegetables, herbs, and flowers so that the growing season can be extended a few days or weeks. Most types of frost protection for the garden are called *passive protection* and are placed in the garden before the cold weather arrives. The most popular ways to protect the garden from frost include the following.

Row covers. A long sheet of specialty fabric that admits light and insulates from cold, row cover "fabric" is actually made of pressed polyester fibers, smooth and light to the touch. Row covers are readily available through garden-supply companies and local garden centers. Be sure to also acquire row cover pins, so you can secure the row covers to the soil. Row cover pins are about 6 inches (15 cm) long and look like large hairpins. For taller-growing plants, you can set down a series of metal hoops over the row or flower bed and lay the fabric over the hoops. The heaviest models, called *frost blankets,* can keep the area beneath a cover about

COVER-UPS. Row covers are simple tools that produce "portable microclimates."

Beware Bacteria: They Can Make Frost Worse

Many kinds of bacteria live on the surfaces of plants, including leaves and flower petals. Most of these bacteria are not harmful — except when frost arrives. Frost crystals need something to grow on before they can form, and the bacteria on the plants provide a place for an ice crystal to begin growing. Experiments with an antibacterial spray applied before a frost showed that the absence of bacteria caused an absence of frost.

6 degrees warmer than the outside temperature. (For the best protection, be sure that no parts of the plants beneath the cover actually touch the top of the cover.)

Hot caps. Made of everything from a plastic gallon milk container to a water-filled plastic tepee (see page 21), hot caps are often used by vegetable gardeners to keep their early transplants warm and growing. These devices work well, but their true measure of protection is difficult to gauge because of the many types available. One problem with them: Hot caps are labor intensive because they have to be placed and removed by hand each day.

Cold frames. Models made from insulated, translucent materials such as polycarbonate are especially wonderful tools for protecting small numbers of plants. Traditional cold frames help harden off plants. Newer types not only harden off plants but also help plants grow. More like miniature greenhouses than like traditional cold frames, they can be calibrated to open and close all by themselves. They also provide even better thermal protection than do frost-blankets.

Water and Sensible Warmth

Water is often used as a means of frost protection all by itself. Water stores and releases energy as it changes from a gas to a liquid to a solid and back again. When water warms up, evaporates, or changes from ice to water, heat is removed from the air and stored in the water molecules. These events cool the air. When the process is reversed and water condenses from a gas to a liquid, or water cools in temperature or freezes into ice, heat is surrendered by the water molecules and released into the air. These events warm the air.

The relative amount of heat released as water goes through its various phase changes helps show how it helps buffer temperatures and protect from frost. A gallon of water that cools from room temperature to 32°F (0°C) releases more than 72,000 calories of heat. As it freezes, 1 gallon of water releases nearly 290,000 calories.

Traditional covers, such as row covers, are good frost protectors. The addition of water can provide an even greater thermal buffer. To install a water component in a garden, hollow out a trough down the aisle or along the side of the aisle. The trough should be at least 1 foot (30 cm) wide and 2 or 3 inches (5–7.5 cm) deep. (If the garden has raised beds, there is probably no need for the trough.) Lay some plastic sheeting (6 mil or greater works best) down the bottom of the trough. Pin down the sides with landscape fabric pins or anchor with mounded soil so that water won't leak out. Fill the trough with water. In theory, warmer water works better, but it costs money to heat the water.

Mulch versus Lawn

Help avoid frost in your garden by having a little less lawn around it. Large areas of lawn are more prone to frost than nearby areas with a surface of mulch. This is because the lawn doesn't absorb as much heat during the day compared with such surfaces as mulch. Thus, at night, less heat is available for the ground to release into the air.

Does an Ice Cube Melt Faster in Arizona or North Carolina?

Humid air holds a lot of heat energy in the particles of water vapor, especially compared with dry air. This stored energy can affect the environment, acting like a blanket to deter frost. In other words, when it's humid, the garden is less likely to be hit with frost. On the other hand, given the same air temperature, an ice cube will melt faster in the humid climate of North Carolina and more slowly in the dry desert of Arizona.

Reducing Chill Damage

Water is also an effective way of protecting your plants against damage from chill. The amount of time the plant is exposed to chill, nutrition, and ripeness are others.

Water. In chill-sensitive plants, high humidity levels can slow or prevent injury caused by chilling. The humidity reduces evaporation of moisture through the leaves. To raise humidity levels around plants, grow them under lightweight row covers (described on page 50). The covers do a good job of trapping both warmth and humidity. In addition, keep the soil moist, because moist soil raises humidity levels as water evaporates from the ground.

Time. If temperatures dip into the chill zone, it takes a certain amount of time for irreversible damage to occur. Keeping chill exposure to less than 2 hours often prevents lasting injury.

Nutrition. Fertilizing is needed for plants to grow optimally. The proper type of fertilizers can increase the hardiness of chill-sensitive plants by a few degrees. As the fruits of sensitive vegetables are ripening in spring and summer, apply fertilizers containing calcium and magnesium. Calcium and magnesium help stabilize cell membranes in plants, making the plants less susceptible to cold damage.

Chill Injury in the Refrigerator

The refrigerator is where much of a gardener's hard work ends up — and where it is ruined. Warm-season crops, and those from tropical climates, are damaged when placed in the cool temperatures of refrigerators. Tomatoes, peppers, melons, and eggplant are some crops that should not see the inside of a fridge. Peppers often develop soft, watery lesions on the skin. Tomatoes gracefully self-destruct as the tissues grow soft and watery. Be kind to all your gardening efforts and keep your produce out of the refrigerator.

Ripeness. When cool weather comes, some people go to the garden and pick the ripe tomatoes and leave the greener ones. Here's one of the ironies of gardening: The ripe tomatoes are more chill tolerant than the greener ones. When temperatures drop below about 50°F (10°C), the greener, still-ripening tomatoes suffer more damage from cold than the red ones would have suffered. In cool weather, then, take steps to protect all the fruits that have set, not just the ripest ones.

A Note on Container Plants

For plants, growing in a container is not a natural thing. Some adapt very well to it, but container plants are always more sensitive to changes in the environment than are plants with roots firmly in the garden. Here are some ways to protect container plants when winter comes calling.

Bring plants indoors. Many container plants spend their lives moving from the deck to the living room or enclosed porch as the seasons change. Tropical and subtropical plants are sensitive to chill and should usually be brought indoors when cool-weather temperatures drop below 50 to 55°F (10–13°C).

Overwinter in a cold frame. Hardy plants can be overwintered in a cold frame by packing the containers pot to pot as cold weather approaches. Be sure the soil is adequately watered, so it enters the winter moist, not wet or dry. A coarse-grade mulch, such as bark nuggets, can be used to fill the spaces among the pots to provide increased moderation of winter temperatures. The top of the frame can be covered with greenhouse-grade white plastic (usually 8 mil).

Sink plants in mulch. Hardy plants can be sunk into a thick bed of organic mulch somewhere outdoors. You might want to put them in a pile spread out in an unused area, preferably a northern exposure, where they will experience fewer heat-and-freeze cycles from the late winter sun. Use a coarse- or medium-grade mulch, such as pine bark. Make a hole for each pot and sink it in up to its lip.

Hard Times: Preventing Cold Injury

Hardening is an old-time garden technique that protects warm-weather vegetables, annuals, and other crops and ornamentals from cold injury. The idea behind hardening is that plants will adapt to a more challenging growth environment if they are introduced to that new environment gradually. Hardening has a proven record of protecting many plants from cold injury. But to be effective, it must be done correctly.

Many people harden plants each spring by bringing them outdoors during the day, then hauling them back indoors at night. Others keep the plants to be hardened outdoors all the time in a cold frame. Is there a difference in the effectiveness of the techniques? Yes. By moving plants in and out of two distinct temperature regimens, the plants often do not harden completely or suffer damage from quick changes in temperatures. Two weeks on a protected porch or within a cold frame is always better for the plants in the end.

Plants can be hardened when outdoor temperatures are above the minimum night temperatures demanded by the plant. This range can be wide, spanning more than 30 degrees F (16.5 degrees C). So just as you know to sow peas in early spring, well before pumpkins, harden off your hardier plants before you work with your chill-sensitive ones.

You will get the most uniform hardening of your plants if you use a cold frame with thermally activated venting. If you prefer a more low-tech and traditional approach, locate them under a shady tree, on the back porch, or in some other convenient spot away from wind and sun. Wherever you place them, don't allow any other type of stress to affect the plants. For instance, be sure that they are not in direct sun, that they remain well watered, and that they are not exposed to the wind. The hardening-off process takes about 2 weeks, so allow that much time before transplanting them to the garden.

Paracelsus once said, "It is the dose that makes the poison." Too much stress is bad for plants, but a little stress applied in a controlled way improves and strengthens them. It is important to remember that hardening is intentionally bringing controlled stress to a plant. It is tempting to think that keeping plants in a perennially stress-free condition produces the biggest, strongest, and most floriferous or fruitful specimens. Just as the pampered child raised without caring discipline does not become self-reliant and fruitful, the plant not properly acclimated will be weaker and more prone to weather damage.

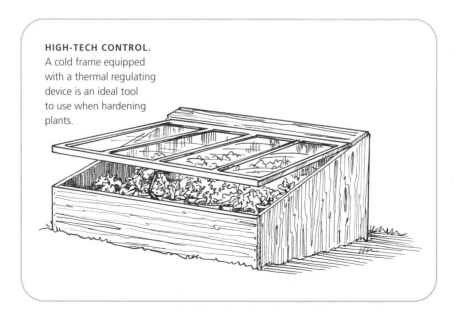

HIGH-TECH CONTROL.
A cold frame equipped with a thermal regulating device is an ideal tool to use when hardening plants.

How Hardening Works

Hardening allows a plant to adapt to different growing environments that are within the limits of its genetic makeup. It lessens transplant shock and helps the plant stay healthier and grow better. What hardening can't do is change the genetics of a plant and make it do something it can't. Hardened plants still need to stay away from temperatures below the chill threshold for that plant (minimum night temperature).

The process of hardening significantly changes a plant to help it survive both the new growing environment and the transplanting process. Here's how: Growth of leaves and stems slows down, while growth of the roots increases. Carbohydrate levels, or food reserves, increase in the plant as the water content slightly decreases. New leaves are darker green in color, smaller, and thicker, with a thicker waxy layer to reduce water loss. Some plants also generate a pinkish tinge on the stems, leaf veins, and leaf petioles (it is not known whether this helps protect plants).

Which Temperature for What Plant?

Chill-sensitive plants do not have a uniform temperature at which damage occurs. Some plants, such as eggplant and watermelon, are very chill sensitive and are injured when exposed to temperatures in the 60s (16°C–21°C). If hardened at the lower temperatures required for tomatoes, the eggplant and watermelon would be injured. To obtain the proper hardening temperature for a plant, look at the seed packet or consult a comprehensive plant encyclopedia, such as *The Gardener's A–Z Guide to Growing Flowers from Seed to Bloom* or the *American Horticultural Society's A–Z Encyclopedia of Garden Plants*. These resources provide the minimum night temperature for individual species and cultivars.

The minimum night temperature is also the threshold temperature for chill injury in sensitive plants. Harden the plants in temperatures *above* the minimum night temperature. After transplanting, be sure to grow the plants in an environment that remains above this crucial temperature.

Chill-sensitive plants growing in warm, bright surroundings often exhibit luxurious growth that is very susceptible to damage in cool temperatures. Seedlings and transplants of hardier species are also sensitive to cold temperatures when first placed outdoors. In the hardening process, all aspects of the plant are conditioned to survive and thrive in cool weather. The essentials of this process are the same for both chill-sensitive and hardy plants. Only the temperatures at which the plants are hardened differ. This means that plants should be hardened according to their own relative hardiness and, by extension, when the outdoor conditions are within the proper range.

When Cold Strikes

In spite of your best efforts to protect your garden, winter woes may strike. Here is some advice to help you recognize the damage, apply some "first aid," and create more protection for another year.

Frost Heaving

Description: Freezing and thawing — most gardeners would gladly endure a consistently cold winter rather than one that bounces back and forth between freeze and thaw. As refreshing as warm stretches in winter can be for humans, they aren't good for plants growing in certain soils. Heavy clay soils, those with a high organic content, and wet soils are prone to heaving through freezing and thawing cycles. As the wet ground freezes, the expanding ice lifts sections of the ground above other parts, exposing roots to cold air. When the thaw comes, the ground unevenly settles, further exposing the roots.

Symptoms: Patches of soil are raised above the surrounding ground. Edges of raised areas may look dry, with roots exposed to the air.

Remedies: Reset raised plants at the proper level. Avoid disturbing soil when possible.

Strategies: Amend heavy, wet soils with compost. Add a 2- to 3-inch (5–8 cm) layer of mulch, such as cocoa hulls, over plants as soon as the ground begins to freeze. This is especially important for plants that have been planted within the last growing season, as they are most susceptible to damage from heaving.

Cold-Damaged Roots

Description: The roots of plants are not nearly as hardy as the portion of the plant that is above the ground. For example, many varieties of apple trees can weather temperatures as low as –30 to –40°F (–34 to –40°C). But the roots of the same trees can incur massive cold damage if soil temperatures dip 10 or 20 degrees below freezing. Soil is a wonderful insulator compared with air, so the ground is not subject to rapid fluctuations in temperature. Most root damage in winter comes from long, uninterrupted cold spells during which little or no snow cover protects the ground. Root damage also occurs in areas with chronically wet, gravelly, stony, or sandy soils. In these circumstances, the cold can settle progressively deeper into the soil.

Symptoms: Root injury from cold symptoms resembles that of roots damaged by flooding (page 122). Leaves, branches, and stems may all suffer because of root damage. Minor damage probably goes unnoticed. More extensive damage often remains hidden for weeks or months after the spring thaw, only to reveal itself late in the growing season. Symptoms include slow growth, thin foliage, and yellow leaves.

Remedies: Reduce stress around the plant, especially the root zone, by maintaining proper soil moisture, avoiding soil compaction or mechanical injury, and improving air circulation.

Strategies: To prevent root damage from cold, apply mulch to the root area of shrubs and smaller trees. Large trees can be protected by growing a thick ground cover over the root zone, such as a densely planted grass, pachysandra, or lilyturf.

Winter Trunk Sunscald

Description: The weather conditions that are most favorable to winter sunscald are also those that make a beautiful late-winter day — a cloudless sky, bright sunshine, and a deep snow cover. The sun strikes the trunk of the tree, warming it to many degrees higher than the air temperature. As the sun edges toward the horizon, the last rays strike the southwest side of the trunk (in northern areas) or the northwest side (in southern regions), warming it to well above freezing. When the sun sets, the combination of snow cover and clear windless sky produces fast radiational cooling. The temperature plummets, and the thawed bark freezes so rapidly that large areas of the cambium (beneath the bark) are killed.

Symptoms: Patches or strips of cracked or peeling dead bark appear on the trunks of shrubs and trees, most commonly smooth-barked types, such as beech, birch, apple, pear, and cherry.

Remedies: With a sharp horticultural knife, trim loose bark by making a clean cut just inside live bark. Use a complete fertilizer in spring.

Strategies: For trees that are strictly utilitarian, such as orchard trees, a whitewash using exterior white latex paint on the susceptible side is helpful. Be sure to reapply it every 3 to 4 years. Wrapping the trunk with a white plastic trunk protector is effective and more aesthetically appealing, as this can be removed seasonally. Avoid unneeded pruning of lower branches, because these branches can partially shade the trunk and thus offer some protection.

Winter Leaf Sunscald

Description: As winter sun warms foliage, tissues in leaves begin to transpire, losing moisture to air. When the ground is frozen, replacing lost moisture through roots is difficult. Leaves can desiccate, and tissues progressively die back. The result is winter sunscald.

Symptoms: A brown scorching of foliage on trees, shrubs, and woody perennials, leaf sunscald most often affects needled and broadleaf evergreens, such as pines, spruce, and rhododendrons. It often occurs on the southeast, south, and southwest sides of a plant. In needled evergreens, damage first appears as a light brown discoloration on the tips of needles. On broadleaf plants, the leaf blade tips turn brown, or patches of brown appear on the leaf faces of those most directly exposed to sun. If unchecked, damage can injure entire branches or even kill a plant.

Remedies: Light cases in which just the tips of leaves are scorched often recover after a normal growing season. Trim back foliage with more severe sunscald that does not recover. Remove dead branches as needed. Fertilize injured plants with a complete fertilizer per label directions, so plants get adequate nutrients to replace lost foliage.

Strategies: Block direct rays of sun from striking plants. Site susceptible species with a northern exposure, or grow them as understory plants beneath large conifers. Erect burlap screens or wood-plank tepees. It is necessary to screen only the southeast to southwest exposures.

Bark Splits Down a Trunk

Description: Bark splits are most noticeable on smooth-barked trees, such as sweet cherry, but can form on many other species. Two weather conditions cause bark split: protracted very cold weather and sudden changes in temperature. During very cold weather (well below 0°F [−18°C]), the tree's tissues freeze to the point where they are very brittle. The split occurs — with a loud crack — as pressures produced by ice deep

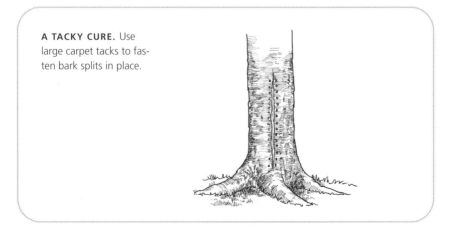

A TACKY CURE. Use large carpet tacks to fasten bark splits in place.

within the trunk snap brittle tissues. The second type forms when unseasonably warm, late winter or spring weather is followed by sudden cold.

Symptoms: Long, narrow fissures appear in the bark of trees and shrubs, most commonly near or at the base of plants. This damage is often seen on azaleas and other thin-barked shrubs and trees.

Remedies: Some cracks are narrow and knit themselves together with no help at all. Tack wider cracks in place as soon as you see the injury. If bark near the crack dies, trim back dead bark to green tissue.

Strategies: Moderate temperature fluctuations by wrapping the lower trunks of shrubs and small-caliper trees with white tree wrap.

Dieback

Description: Dieback can occur anywhere on trees, shrubs, and perennials. On evergreens, the first sign is browning foliage similar to sunscald; on deciduous trees, dead branches fail to leaf out in spring. Young, quick-growing trees are more prone to dieback than are more mature trees. Dieback is a bit of a catch-all term used to describe damage from diseases, pests, and environmental conditions that produce similar-looking damage. It most often affects twigs and branches that were not sufficiently hardened off while entering winter, perhaps because of late growth, or because the plant is only marginally hardy in the area, or because the winter was especially cold.

Symptoms: Plant tissues die back from the twigs' tips toward the trunk.

Remedies: To treat minor damage, wait until buds break in spring, then prune back to first strong bud. Prune more extensive damage as needed.

Strategies: Choose plants that are hardy to the coldest weather you might experience, rather than just the average winter. Fertilize in spring; avoid fertilizing late in the season. (If you fertilize too late — within 8 to 10 weeks of frost — it may spark a flush of new growth, which doesn't have time to harden off before cold weather arrives and is either severely damaged or killed outright.) Mulch around plants in late fall to moderate soil moisture and temperature. In areas with cold winters, soil should be evenly moist, not dry or overly wet, before it freezes for the season.

Ice and Snow

THE DULL GRAY LIGHT that seeps through the February clouds is weak and flat. It doesn't allow details to crystallize but brings images to your eyes that seem softly blurred and two-dimensional. Living in the heart of winter is like spending the days within the faint grays of clouds that never fully go away. But the pewter light so peculiar to winter days isn't an accident of the moment — it is a product of the weather processes that are right now evolving thousands of feet above you.

The boundary between a mass of cold air to the north and slightly warmer air to the south lies nearly east to west. It moved south as a cold front a few days ago, stalled, then slowly returned north as a warm front heavy with clouds. Although this border between air masses is invisible, in the atmosphere it has form, serving as a pathway for weak troughs of low pressure and spawning areas of precipitation to roll along it.

This morning, a layer of air about 3,500 feet thick blankets the surface of the earth. The air is very moist, with the relative humidity close to 100 percent. The temperature of this air layer is about 28°F at 1,500 feet and near 30°F for several hundred feet above and below that altitude. From 3,500 feet to 10,000 feet, the air is warmer, with temperatures from 40°F to near 45°F. Air temperatures are well below freezing above 10,000 feet and drop to below zero thousands of feet higher.

In the higher, colder clouds, the moist air is lifted by the winds, carrying billions of specks of dust. Occasionally, a speck of dust contacts a supercooled droplet of water and instantly grows into a snowflake. At other times, water vapor crystallizes on a speck of dust. Some supercool droplets simply freeze in the frigid air. No matter how they form, the myriad tiny ice crystals soon begin their descent through the clouds toward the earth.

As they drop through the clouds, the ice crystals bump into each other and grow in size. When they pass from the cold upper layer of air into the warmer band, they melt into raindrops. The drops fall quickly through the sky, and at about 3,500 feet they pierce the top of much colder air and convert to very cold rain. When the raindrops finally land on the leaves and branches of plants, driveways, walkways, steps, and roads, they will freeze on contact.

All morning, the temperature is steady at 29°F, and the rain falls and freezes. Within several hours, the limbs of the trees are glistening with a patina of glassy ice. These limbs begin to creak when nudged by even the weakest breeze. Meanwhile, shrubs are encased in frozen crystal, bent over and burdened by a load they cannot shake off. Just before noon, a loud report cracks through the air as a huge branch snaps and drops from the large silver maple, crushing a cluster of rhododendrons below as it plummets. More and more cracks echo from the trees. Minutes later, the electric power goes out.

By midafternoon, the rain has changed to freezing drizzle. Nearly 1½ inches of ice have glazed the garden and yard, the weight snapping dozens of branches and breaking off the tops of the maples and ash. Smaller woody perennials, such as lavender, are encased in ice but for the most part unharmed. Many shrubs have had branches torn from the stem, or the trunks have been simply split in half.

The trees are the most pathetic sight this day. Many look like they fell prey to a monster string trimmer that clipped their upper branches and left them toppled or hung upside down. Dozens more branches litter the ground. Before the weak winter sun sets, it peers out from the clouds and ignites the landscape with diamonds of sunlight that reflect from the catastrophe, creating a sparkling beauty that graces the torn landscape in spite of the damage. Yet as the rays of light retreat, the carnage again comes into focus — all of it caused by three layers of air with a slight difference in temperature.

Ice and Snow: A Fearsome Twosome

Winter is when the earth closes down. The ground freezes shut and instead of moisture soaking into the soil, piles of snow and ice build up on the impermeable surface. In these inhospitable months, the gardener can retreat to the warmth of hearth and home. But the garden cannot. The shrubs and trees are locked in the ground, slapped by icy winds, and gently buried in snowfall. There are ways we can help make the garden and landscape better resist the stresses of winter, long before winter ever comes. Ice and snow come to the garden at the same season of the year, and sometimes in the same storm, but they affect your garden and landscape in very different ways.

The Uniqueness of Snow

We learn as children that no two snowflakes are alike. At first glance, this is an interesting fact, but meditate on it a moment and see what that simple statement entails. If you were to scoop up a handful of snow and try to count the snowflakes, it would soon become clear that the task is as exhausting as it is impossible. There are just too many of them! Now, can you ponder how many snowflakes are in a typical snowstorm, or the number of flakes in all the snowfalls over the duration of an entire winter? Is there a number large enough to relate the quantity of snowflakes that have ever fallen upon the earth over all of history? Now, let's go back to that fact learned in childhood — no two snowflakes were, are, or ever will be alike. Amazing!

Shape. However, all is not random. Snowflakes come in six shapes, and all snowflakes have six sides. This is because the cornerstone of every snowflake is a molecule of water. Water contains two atoms of hydrogen and one of oxygen. When ice crystals form, the hydrogen atoms come together and the oxygen fits between them, forming a hexagon. As the snowflake grows, the hexagon pattern is followed. The different types of hexagonal shapes are due to differences in humidity, temperature, and other factors that influence how the crystal grows.

Color. What is the color of a snowflake? Most people say that snowflakes are white, but what something *seems* to be is not always what it really *is*. Snowflakes are ice crystals and are therefore by definition clear; thus, snow really has no color at all. Snow *looks* white because each snowflake crystal has an abundance of reflective surfaces that bounce the light off the crystal and to our eyes. Because the entire light spectrum is reflected, a snowflake appears to be white — the color of light when all the colors of the spectrum are combined.

Winter Wildlife

Once a snowstorm is over and the landscape is immersed in a fresh blanket of white, it is tempting to think that the threat to the yard and garden is over, at least temporarily. But a deep snow cover can be a precursor to damage to trees and shrubs in some unexpected ways.

Rodent damage. If you could float into the air, how high do you think you could go and still see a mouse scurrying over the lawn? The answer is usually about 150 to 200 feet (46–61 m). If you were a hawk, you could see that mouse even from thousands of feet up in the sky. Now, put that mouse against a clear white background of snow, and it doesn't stand a chance. To remedy this, mice and voles use the snow to protect themselves from predators by making runways under the snow, thereby staying out of sight as they move around.

Although the little rodents are preyed on by shrews, ermine, martens, coyotes, and foxes, as well as by owls, which have hearing so precise that they can locate and grab a rodent as it scurries through a tunnel inches below the surface, all this doesn't seem to put a dent in the number of rodents ready to eat your landscape in winter. A single acre of lawn, garden, and landscape can provide habitat for hundreds of voles. And their winter food supply may be the woody plants you love, as they like to gnaw the bark at or just beneath the soil line. Small amounts of bark may be gnawed away without seriously harming a plant, but if they actually girdle a tree or shrub (remove bark all the way around), the effects are serious (see page 78).

Ice and Snow: The Past 20 Years

Over recent decades, there have been five memorable North American storms that resulted in damages totaling $19.7 billion and costing 541 lives.

December 1992: A violent nor'easter rolled up the East Coast, pounding New England. It caused $2.4 billion in damages and 19 people were killed.

March 1993: What was then called the "storm of the century" dumped up to 4 feet of snow over a wide area of the East Coast. The great blizzard of '93 cost $6.6 billion and claimed 270 lives.

February 1994: A massive ice storm covered Texas, Oklahoma, Louisiana, and Arkansas with thick layers of ice that tore down trees and power lines and killed nine people. Total damages were $3.3 billion.

January 1996: A coastal blizzard dropped up to 3 feet of snow from the Mid-Atlantic states through New England. Damages totaled $3 billion, and 187 lives were lost.

January 1998: An ice storm that left ice up to 3 and 4 inches thick destroyed much of the power grid in southeastern Canada, northern New York, Vermont, New Hampshire, and Maine. At one point, 80 percent of the state of Maine had no electrical power, and over the entire affected area, 3.5 million households were without power. Total damages were $4.4 billion and 56 deaths.

Deer to my heart. Deer have the knack of causing many kinds of trouble in the garden and landscape. Some problems caused by deer are made worse by weather with lots of snow, especially deep snow crusted with ice. When deep, crusted snow covers the landscape, it becomes increasingly difficult for deer to forage for food. Hunger and a tasty menu lead many animals to browse the ornamental plants in our gardens and yards. Although a starving deer will eat almost any plant out of desperation, the following plants are low on the list of desirable foods and so can be considered resilient. These plants are also resilient against voles and rabbits.

Deer-Resilient Plants

Autumn sage (*Salvia greggii*)

Barberry (*Berberis* spp.)

Bearberry (*Arctostaphylos uva-ursi*)

Bottlebrush buckeye (*Aesculus parviflora*)

Boxwood (*Buxus sempervirens*)

Caryopteris (*Caryopteris* spp.)

Colorado blue spruce (*Picea pungens glauca*)

Cotoneaster (*Cotoneaster* spp.)

False cypress (*Chamaecyparis* spp.)

Ginkgo (*Ginkgo biloba*)

Heritage birch (*Betula nigra* 'Heritage')

Japanese cedar (*Cryptomeria japonica*)

Leucothoe (*Leucothoe* spp.)

Lilac (*Syringa* spp.)

Mountain laurel (*Kalmia latifolia*)

Oleander (*Nerium oleander*)

Paw-paw (*Asimina triloba*)

Pieris (*Pieris japonica*)

Privet (*Ligustrum* spp.)

Red-osier dogwood (*Cornus stolonifera*)

Rhododendron (*Rhododendron* spp.)

Rosemary (*Rosmarinus officinalis*)

Rose-of-Sharon (*Hibiscus syriacus*)

Russian olive (*Elaeagnus angustifolia*)

Scotch pine (*Pinus sylvestris*)

Serviceberry (*Amelanchier* spp.)

Texas mountain laurel (*Sophora secundi flora*)

Wintergreen (*Gaultheria procumbens*)

Yaupon (*Ilex vomitoria*)

Yucca (*Yucca* spp.)

Changing Personalities: Snow to Ice

As snow falls, each delicate ice crystal lands gently on those that fell before. The resulting accumulation is a snowy layer that is a matrix of air and angled icy snowflakes arranged randomly in incalculable complexity. Sometime after a snowfall, become a kid again, grab a magnifying glass, and get on your hands and knees in the snow. Under magnification the snow is a universe unto itself, weightless snowflakes stacked on weightless snowflakes, creating microscopic passageways that go on forever.

Now, while you are still looking at the snow with the magnifying glass, gently exhale onto the snow. The snowflakes turn into small clear droplets of water that soon freeze into little balls of ice. In the garden, this same change happens, although the melting takes place from both above and below.

As the snow begins to naturally compact in the days after a storm, the heat in the ground radiates up into the snowpack. The snow that melts turns into a layer of ice that rests directly on the soil surface. The snow that melts from solar or thermal radiation at the top of the snow layer either forms a crust or produces granular icy particles.

Coping with Ice

Ice is heavy. One pint (0.5 liter) of water, when frozen, becomes a block of ice weighing about 1 pound (0.5 kg). Here's a way to gain an appreciation for what plants must endure in an ice storm. Fill a quart container with water. Then grasp the container, now weighing about 2 pounds (1 kg), and extend it at arm's length — horizontal to the floor. Now hold it there while I tell you what a plant goes through.

Freezing rain is liquid precipitation that freezes as it contacts a surface that is at or below freezing. As each drop hits the surface, it produces a very thin glaze of ice. That icy film then serves as the surface for the next drop to strike and freeze. As the coating of ice accumulates, the weight of the ice increases.

If you held the quart container of water close to your body, you could carry it for a long time comfortably. Likewise, ice that forms on a branch close to the trunk poses no real problem, because the strongest part of a branch is where it joins the trunk. However, if weight is added to the end of the branch, as happens with ice in an ice storm, the force on the branch and its union with trunk is markedly increased.

Now put down the quart container. Can you feel how and where the added weight strained your arm? When the branches of trees and shrubs become covered in ice, they can't remove their burden, and sometimes a branch or tree cracks and breaks under the weight.

Once ice has formed on a plant, there is no reliably safe way to remove it without subjecting the plant to unnecessary harm. The best way to help plants through an ice storm is to strengthen them before the ice forms.

Unexpected Benefits: Snow and Soil

It seems only right that anything as beautiful as snow would have some practical qualities as well. And it does. Snow is beneficial to the garden for the following reasons.
• Prevents soil heaving
• Maintains microorganism activity in the soil
• Conserves nutrients
• Moderates soil temperature
• Conserves and recharges soil moisture

When the soil freezes in fall and winter, the biotic activity in the upper layers of soil just about stops. The bacteria and fungi so vital to the health of plant roots — and, by extension, the plants — stop functioning. In addition to microorganisms, larger soil dwellers, such as worms, head deep into the subsoil, where winter never penetrates. The frozen soil also puts a halt to root growth and absorption of moisture and nutrients. The life contained in the soil enters a quiescent period.

These months of chill stillness are like storing food in the freezer for months before preparing it. It will still make a good meal, but the difference between frozen-thawed and fresh is obvious. Soil is healthier if the microorganisms within it are actively maintaining it. A snow cover insulates the soil so effectively that in many cold regions, the soil microorganisms can maintain activity through the entire snow season.

Conserves nutrients. The biological activity of soil microorganisms throughout the winter keeps active the processing of organic matter into nutrients, such as nitrogen. In addition, warmer soil temperatures under the snow layer protect the tiny root hairs from freezing to death. In exposed frozen soils, the death of peripheral roots causes a loss of nutrients, especially nitrogen, through volatilization and leaching.

Moderates soil temperatures. The effect of snow on the temperature of the soil throughout the winter is dramatic. Forest soils that have both a layer of leaf duff and a snow cover are well insulated, and so the soil under the trees may never freeze during the entire winter. The snow and leaf duff combined are so effective that temperature gradients of as high as 50°F (27°C) can exist between the soil and air (the soil temperature may be above freezing while the air temperature is near –20°F [–29°C]). You can duplicate this effectiveness in your own garden and landscape by mulching garden plants when the ground is freezing in late fall or early winter. Combined with the snow that accumulates, plants would then have a natural barrier against damaging cold.

Recharges soil moisture. Snow is a reservoir of soil moisture that recharges the field capacity of the soil in spring, just when the plants need it most. Because the snow has insulated the ground all winter, the soil is in a condition to accept it when it melts, and allows the water to slowly percolate down. Snow cover is a very important part of soil–water management in drought-prone areas, as it can make up a substantial portion of the moisture needed by plants through the spring and early summer.

Fire and Ice

In the middle of an ice storm, it is sometimes difficult to foresee an even greater hazard posed by the icy catastrophe. Major ice storms leave immense quantities of dead wood throughout the forest. As this wood dries, it becomes potential fuel for wildfires. Homeowners whose property abuts large tracts of forestland should ask the landowner to be sure the land is cleaned up promptly. Municipal, state, and federal governments all have different policies regarding cleanup and salvage of storm-damaged timber.

Going on the Defensive

For those gardeners and homeowners living in regions that regularly experience snow and ice storms during winter, there are a number of ways to prepare against damage to your plants and property. The first is to select plants that are known for weathering storms.

(Too Much) Snow Falling on Cedars

Sometimes, as the snow floats down through a cold calm sky, the sound of each snowflake as it lands on the evergreens comes faintly but clearly to your ears, like the sound of pins dropping one by one. In other storms, the flakes are big and soft and settle on the foliage as gently as goose down. Snow in all of its manifestations is beautiful to behold. However, too much snow falling on cedars and many other trees can be more beauty than some trees and shrubs were meant to handle.

The degree of resilience of a tree to ice and snow damage is nearly as reliant on the age, health, and placement of the tree as it is on the species and variety. For example, the many species and varieties of false cypress range from short, sturdy slow-growing trees, such as Hinoki false cypress, which are quite resistant, to the upright and open form of Lawson false cypress, which is prone to damage. In between these extremes are many species that tolerate snow and ice but can be left a little bent by the experience, too.

Be aware, however, that an accumulation of ice to even ½ inch (1 cm) can damage plants. In the worst ice storms, 3 to 4 inches (8–10 cm) of ice will form on branches and trees, which is much more ice than any tree should be expected to bear.

Shielding Your Plants from Harm

If you've ever experienced an ice storm, you know that whatever freezing rain lands on, there the ice will form. If the rain never reaches the plants, the ice doesn't either. A shield is a device that is most often used to protect foundation plants from the ravages of ice dropping from the eaves.

Spruce Up the Garden

In the great ice storm that devastated northern New York, New England, and southeastern Canada in January 1998, nearly every species of tree was beaten and broken by ice that accumulated up to 4 inches (10 cm) thick. Birches, maples, ash, and aspens were all severely damaged. In such a destructive storm, the fact that so many species succumbed to the force of the ice is not unexpected. What may be surprising is that a few tree species came through this test with barely a scratch.

If a tree were to be designed to be nearly ice-proof, snow-proof, wind-proof, hail-proof, and storm-proof, it would look just like a spruce. Spruce trees have a steeply conical shape; dense evergreen branches that reach all the way to the ground; limbs that are fan-shaped, flat, and arranged in hor-izontal layers; and small needles. When ice forms on the upper surface of a branch, the weight of the ice holds down the branch until it contacts the next branch, which in turn supports the limb above it, and so on. When the ice storm is over, the tree looks like an upside-down ice-cream cone covered in ice — but only the outside of the tree is icy. The interior of the tree is free of ice, so there is very little strain on the trunk and little or no breakage of branches.

Spruces of the northern forest and other cool areas include red spruce *(Picea rubens)*, black spruce *(P. mariana)*, white spruce *(P. glauca)*, and Engelmann spruce *(P. engelmannii)*. Other spruces more commonly grown in the home landscape are Colorado blue spruce *(P. pungens glauca)*, Serbian spruce *(P. omorika)*, and Norway spruce *(P. abies)*, the most commonly cultivat-ed spruce species in the world.

Many designs are available, but the common feature is they are constructed of hard, durable material that will withstand the assault of large icicles as they drop from above.

Sandwich board. The most efficient design is a sandwich board composed of two pieces of plywood joined at the top with a pair of hinges. This roof-shaped shield is then set over a plant. Falling ice just glances off the sandwich board; freezing rain accumulates on the board rather than on the plant.

Plastic-covered hoops. Some of the same devices that are used to extend the growing season can also be used to protect plants from ice. If you used a series of metal hoops covered by Reemay cloth to warm the plants beneath it, you can protect against ice by replacing the cloth with white plastic (8 mil works well); the ice then collects on the plastic, not the plants. Plastic obviously isn't as strong as wood, but as the ice accumulates, it can be quickly removed: Just tap the plastic to crack the ice and send it sliding down to the ground.

Where Ice Storms Typically Happen

Ice storms occur across many regions of North America, with some areas more prone than others. The location with the most frequent storms is a bull's-eye-shaped area centered on the Finger Lakes region of New York. Central New York is the hub of a much larger area of frequent ice storms that extends from southern Michigan and northern Indiana and encompasses all the territory south of the St. Lawrence Valley to Long Island.

Three smaller areas are prone to frequent ice storms too. One is centered over the Columbia River Valley in southern Washington, the second is on the prairies and Midwest near the Iowa and Missouri border, and the third covers the Carolinas and southern Appalachians.

Brace Grafting

For plants that tend to bend under the strain of ice, such as arborvitae, brace grafting can offer a permanent strengthening. This simple graft is done in spring just as active growth begins. It joins two stems with a scion taken from the same tree. The easiest method uses an existing branch that is grafted elsewhere onto the plant without severing it from the tree. At the site of the graft, find a branch of about a pencil's thickness, growing from a main stem and angled slightly upward. This branch, called the scion, should be long enough to easily reach the stem to which it is going to be grafted.

1. Line up the scion against the stem to be grafted. Make two parallel cuts in the stem exactly the scion's width and mirror the angle at which the scion lies against the stem.

2. Where the scion contacts the stem, cut away the bark so that the bare portions of the scion and stem fit together snugly. The scion should have some bulge to it so it has some flexibility.

3. Nail the scion in place with flat-head wire nails at least twice as long as the diameter of the scion.

4. Cover the union with grafting wax to prevent drying.

5. Tie the grafted stems together to reduce wind movement until the graft grows together.

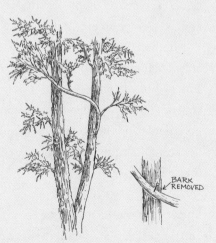

BRACE YOURSELF. Brace grafting is a method to strengthen a tree naturally, without using cables or other devices.

Braces. Braces are any devices that strengthen the existing structure of a tree or shrub. The plants most sensitive to ice storms are upright evergreens with multiple stems. To reinforce these plants, use a roll of about 4-inch-wide (10 cm) fabric tape. Begin at the bottom of the plant and tie the tape around the plant as close to the ground as possible. Wrap the plant in an upward spiral, drawing in the branches toward the center of the plant. Tie off the tape near the top of the plant.

Snow Traps

There seems to be an abundance of stories about places that receive too much snow, like the inn on Mount Rainier that once had a snowpack well over 20 feet (6 m) deep. What people don't talk about as much is how to get more snow to places that need it. This is accomplished by constructing devices that trap the snow that falls or blow it into areas that need it for insulation or soil moisture. There are many types of snow traps, including windbreaks. These can be temporary, such as those made of snow fencing, or permanent, such as hedges and hurricane fences. These structures collect snow on the upwind side of a fence and should be aligned perpendicular to the prevailing winter winds.

Another type of snow trap is used in farm fields. The farmer cuts the crop, such as alfalfa or wheat, to leave stubble about 4 inches (10 cm) tall. The stubble catches the snow as it blows over the field, creating a reservoir of snow. A gardener can adapt this technique. When you cut back perennials and the lawn in fall, leave 4- to 6-inch-tall (10–15 cm) stubs on the perennials and cut the lawn at about 3 inches (8 cm) tall. These measures will help trap the snow.

Snow-Removal Strategies

During a heavy snowfall, it is common for a foot or two (0.3–0.6 m) of snow to top every one of your prized landscape plants. Few plants in the world can carry such loads gracefully, and it is natural for the gardener to want to relieve the burden as soon as possible. Here's how to do it while minimizing the chance of damaging the plants.

THE BRUSH-OFF. Loads of snow left on an evergreen can cause distortion in the shape of the tree. Proper removal of the snow can prevent this damage.

Needled evergreens. Look over the snow-covered plant and see how many and which branches are buried. In big storms, the lower branches are often completely buried in snow and those above them just have their tips buried; the upper portions of the tree are capped in snow. Use a broom and begin at the top. Tap the leader to release the snow. As this snow falls, it often knocks some snow off the lower branches. Work your way down, gently sweeping off the snow with a side-to-side motion. When you reach the branches that are buried, carefully move the topmost of these to see if they will pop out of the snow. If there is any resistance, stop and let the buried branches stay buried.

Breaking the Ice

It is tempting, when faced with a thick glaze of ice covering your plants, to give each icy branch just a tap with a broom handle. As with all risky things, sometimes it works — but sometimes it doesn't. Even if branches don't break, the bark is likely to get bruised, which can lead to disease or pest infestation later during the growing season.

Broadleaf evergreens. Different types of broadleaf evergreens react differently to snow loads. Small-leafed rhododendrons, like the PJM varieties, have an open, upright branching pattern that makes the branches collect snow and then droop toward the ground. It is tempting to lift a branch from the middle, but this often results in snapping the limb. Instead, support the branch directly under the cap of snow and gently shake the snow free. If the tip of the branch is buried, let it stay buried. This same method should be used for deciduous shrubs with an open, loose branch habit (such as spirea and beautybush).

Rodent Damage

Description: Rodent damage is most often gnawing of the bark very close to ground level, sometimes even a bit beneath the soil line. In mild cases, the gnawing removes a small amount of bark, and healing proceeds without supplementary care. In worse instances, the branch or stem has bark removed from more than 50 percent of the perimeter. And in the most severe cases, the branch or stem is completely girdled. When this much bark has been chewed off or otherwise removed, the flow of food produced during photosynthesis down the stem to the roots stops.

Symptoms: Bark has been removed in thin strips or so completely that bare wood extends around the circumference of the stem and often many inches up the stem as well. Thin-barked species of shrubs and young trees with juvenile bark (which is much smoother and thinner than the rough-textured bark of older trees) are the most frequently injured.

Remedies: Some trees, such as pecan and many species of elms and cherries, can heal themselves of even extensive damage. But most plants, particularly those that have been girdled, cannot heal themselves and the only repair, not always successful, is a technique called *bridge grafting*. The goal is to reestablish the flow of food so that the plant won't starve to death. This type of graft takes bits of the damaged plant and grafts them over the injured portion, spanning the damage and reconnecting the downward flow of food from the leaves. For people who do grafting all the time, such as orchardists, successful bridge grafting is pretty easy. For

Bridge Grafting

1. Collect the scions from branches elsewhere on the plant from wood that is 1 year old and at least ½ inch (1 cm) in diameter. Be sure the scions are a few inches longer than the wound to be bridged. Store in a plastic bag in the refrigerator until needed.

2. Trim the wound with a horticultural knife, leaving straight clean horizontal edges on both the top and bottom border of the wound.

3. Make two 1- to 1½-inch-long (1–1.5 cm) vertical and parallel cuts in the bark at the base of the wound. The cuts should be the width of the scions and penetrate to the wood. Make a matching pair of cuts in the bark above the wound and directly above the first pair of cuts.

4. Make a shallow horizontal cut at the base of each pair of parallel cuts. Remove the exterior part of the flap of bark, leaving a thin tab.

5. Cut the scions to fit between the base of the bottom cut and the top of the top cut.

6. Prepare a scion by making a sloping cut about 1 to 1½ inches (1–1.5 cm) long; cut completely through the wood.

7. On the opposite side, make a short (about ½ inch [1 cm] long) cut at a steeper angle. Repeat at the other end of the scion.

8. Insert the wedge of the base of the scion under the flap of bark at the base of the wound and the top of the scion under the flap at the top of the wound. Be sure the scion is aligned in the direction of growth (right side up).

9. Using thin nails, tap the scion into place. Cover the unions with a thick coating of grafting wax.

You'll know whether a graft is successful in a few weeks because the buds on the scion will open.

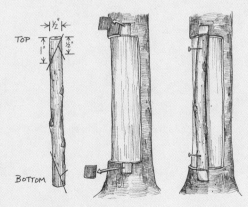

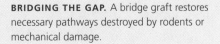

BRIDGING THE GAP. A bridge graft restores necessary pathways destroyed by rodents or mechanical damage.

Resiliency versus Sensitivity

What makes some trees resilient to ice is often a combination of traits, as well as the degree to which those traits are manifest in the plants.

Resiliency Traits

Here are some traits to look for in plants resilient to ice buildup:
• Branches are pliant and yield under load (such as hemlock)
• Shape is steeply conical (such as spruce)
• Tree has a single strong trunk (such as ginkgo)
• Tree is slow growing (such as white oak)
• Mature height is short (such as serviceberry)
• Branch unions are strong (such as mountain laurel)

Snow- and Ice-Resilient Evergreens

American holly *(Ilex opaca)*
False cypress (*Chamaecyparis* spp.)
Fir (*Abies* spp.)
Hemlock *(Tsuga canadensis)*
Jack pine *(Pinus banksiana)*
Japanese umbrella pine *(Sciadopitys verticillata)*
Lodgepole pine *(Pinus contorta)*
Mountain laurel *(Kalmia latifolia)*
Rhododendron (*Rhododendron* spp.)
Spruce (*Picea* spp.)

Snow- and Ice-Resilient Deciduous Trees

Amur maple *(Acer tataricum ginnala)*
Bald cypress *(Taxodium distichum)*
Beech (*Fagus* spp.)
Black gum *(Nyssa sylvatica)*
Black walnut *(Juglans nigra)*
Catalpa (*Catalpa* spp.)
Dawn redwood (*Metasequoia glyptostroboides*)
Dogwood (*Cornus* spp.)
Ginkgo *(Ginkgo biloba)*
Kentucky coffee tree *(Gymnocladus dioica)*
Littleleaf linden *(Tilia cordata)*
Northern red oak *(Quercus rubra)*
Norway maple *(Acer platanoides)*
Redbud *(Cercis canadensis)*
Serviceberry (*Amelanchier* spp.)
Sweetgum *(Liquidambar styraciflua)*
White oak *(Quercus alba)*

gardeners not used to grafting, however, the technique can be frustratingly precise.

Bridge grafting should be done in the early spring when buds are breaking and bark "slips" from wood (due to plentiful sap between bark

Sensitivity Traits

Vulnerability to ice damage can be seen long before the ice actually damages the plants. Examining your plants for the qualities listed below will help you separate the weak from the strong:

• Branch unions are at a shallow angle to the trunk (such as Bradford pear)

• Trees are the clump-forming type (such as birches)

• Tree is fast growing (such as Siberian elm)

• Tree has brittle wood (such as willows and locusts)

• Tree has multiple trunks (such as arborvitae)

• Branch unions are incurved rather than ridged (such as box elder)

Snow- and Ice-Sensitive Evergreens

Arborvitae *(Thuja occidentalis)*
Atlantic white cedar *(Chamaecyparis thyoides)*
Azalea *(Rhododendron* spp.)
Japanese cedar *(Cryptomeria japonica)*
Juniper *(Juniperus* spp.)
Lawson false cypress *(Chamaecyparis lawsoniana)*
Live oak *(Quercus* spp.)
Red pine *(Pinus resinosa)*
Shortleaf pine *(Pinus echinata)*

Snow- and Ice-Sensitive Deciduous Trees

American linden *(Tilia americana)*
Aspen *(Populus* spp.)
Birch *(Betula* spp.)
Black cherry *(Prunus serotina)*
Black locust *(Robinia* spp.)
Box elder *(Acer negundo)*
Bradford pear *(Pyrus calleryana* 'Bradford')
Chinese elm *(Ulmus parvifolia)*
Crab apple *(Malus* spp.)
Hackberry *(Celtis* spp.)
Honey locust *(Gleditsia triacanthos)*
Pin oak *(Quercus palustris)*
Siberian elm *(Ulmus pumila)*
Silver maple *(Acer saccharinum)*
Willow *(Salix* spp.)

and wood). However, scions used for the graft must be dormant and should be gathered some weeks beforehand.

Strategies: Bridge grafting puts stress on the tree, much like an operation stresses the body of the patient. So if the graft doesn't take, the plant is sometimes in a worse state than before. A second attempt can be made immediately if the bark is still in the slipping stage, or a year later when the bark begins to slip again. Some people elect to let things be and see if the plant recovers on its own. As noted above, some species, such as cherries, elms, and some hickories and oaks, can, to a great degree, recover.

Tree Limbs Pulled Down by Compacted Snow

Description: In years when snowfall accumulates to form a snowpack 3 or more feet (0.9 m) deep, young trees especially can be damaged by slow changes in the snow. As the snowpack builds up over repeated storms, it slowly compresses and sinks. Branches frozen into layers of snow are pulled down as the snowpack increases in density. Pressure breaks limbs from the trunk at the top of branch unions with stems, often leaving the bottom portion of unions attached.

This injury is frequently seen in orchards. In fruit-bearing trees, the limbs of mature trees must carry substantial weight; the partially attached branches are often viewed as irreparable and are removed. On the other hand, when the same damage appears on young ornamental trees, such as false cypress, many times the injured limbs can be repaired.

Symptoms: Broken or damaged limbs.

Remedies: The most important thing in repairing snow-compaction damage is to repair the break as soon as it is discovered. If the open wound is exposed to the air for too long (many hours or days), the injury worsens to the point that it is essentially irreparable.

Strategies: The best way to avoid snow-compaction damage is to periodically rescue trapped branches from the grip of the snow. Ideally, do this within a day or two of the snowfall, before the snow has a chance to compress upon itself. Avoid pulling on the branches, as this often breaks the limb. Use a child's lawn rake or a small adult version of the same tool. Carefully remove snow from the branches by dragging it away from the trunk. Once the limb is exposed, gently shake and lift it out of the snow. Also, remove as much snow as possible from beneath the limb. See also Shielding Your Plants from Harm, page 72.

Repairing Breaks

1. Clean the break, removing any foreign material, such as shreds of bark. If ragged edges exist along the torn bark edge, cut them cleanly with a horticultural knife. Remove broken splinters from the exposed branch union.

2. Set the branch back in place so the bark edges are flush and the union looks natural.

3. Drill a hole slightly smaller than the screw you will use to secure the limb through the base of the branch union into the trunk.

4. Drive the wood screw into the branch so the head of the fastener is flush with the wood (the wood screw should be about 1½ times as long as the depth of the broken portion of the branch).

5. Wrap the limb and trunk with grafting tape to secure and strengthen the union during healing. In a pinch, you can use duct tape; wrap the tree with the shiny side against the tree and the sticky side exposed.

A TIMELY ATTACHMENT. A partially torn limb can sometimes benefit from being reinforced with a wood screw inserted to penetrate the branch and trunk.

Soil Heaving

Description: Heaving of soil occurs when the upper layers of the soil are subjected to a succession of freeze–thaw cycles. The air temperature during these cycles fluctuates between being just above freezing to dipping just below. Heaving is most common in spring, when day and night temperatures frequently hover near freezing and soil moisture is often high.

As the moisture in the ground freezes and thaws, it expands and contracts, producing a physical force that lifts blocks or portions of soil out of the ground. The fracturing and lifting of the soil exposes plant roots to the air and to much colder temperatures than those found in undisturbed soil nearby. Adverse effects range all the way from some root damage to death of a plant.

Symptoms: Heaving is common in heavy soils, such as clays and silts; soils with abundant moisture; and soils where the temperature is near freezing. Exposed soils (soils that have little or no snow cover) are especially vulnerable.

Remedies: In this case, the remedy is the same as the strategy, except for the timing. If heaving occurs, it is important to protect the exposed roots as soon as possible. Cover the heaved area, and beyond for a foot or so, with straw or other airy organic mulch to a depth of 1 foot. Allow the plant to remain "as is" until the spring thaw, when the straw can be removed and the plant settled back to a proper growing posture.

Strategies: If good snow cover is not present, try compensating. Although not as effective as snow, an organic mulch can help reduce the possibilities of heaving.

Bending under Pressure

Description: Robert Frost wrote a poem about the flexibility of birches and how a child could climb up the trunk, kick out, and while hanging on to the trunk allow it to gently bend and deliver him softly to earth. Birches can do that, but if boys and girls choose to just hang on the tree rather than letting go, then even birches may not rebound. In ice storms, it is not only how much ice forms on a tree but also how quickly the ice melts or cracks and falls away that determines whether the bending tree will be able to bounce back.

Most ice storms last for a few hours and deposit less than ½ inch (1 cm) of ice. It takes about ½ to ¾ inch (1–2 cm) of ice to produce damage on trees and shrubs. Depending on the species and the amount of ice and wind, a number of different types of damage can result, each with its own characteristics. If trees bend during a storm, they usually quickly recover, depending on the species and the amount of ice, as well as whether winds have added to the damage. If the ice accumulation is heavier and the ice stays on the trees, the bend will stay in the trees too.

Symptoms: Tree trunks and branches are temporarily or permanently bent out of shape by the weight of ice. Clump birch trees and arborvitae are known for bending under pressure and remaining in that nearly prone posture thereafter.

Remedies: A tree with a bend in the shape of a gradual curve can sometimes be straightened by pulling the tree back into position and staking it in place. Trees with angular bends have probably suffered structural damage and may not be salvageable. The errant stems of arborvitae should be pulled together as soon after the storm as possible to minimize damage and tied in place to restore their attractive form and strengthen them against further storms. You can remove the ties in midspring to see whether the tree maintains its shape. If it is still floppy, retie the stems, keep them in place for a year, and then reassess. Birches, on the other hand, may seem to prefer the lazy look, and don't easily respond to the gardener's wish for them to stand up straight.

Strategies: See Shielding Your Plants from Harm, page 72.

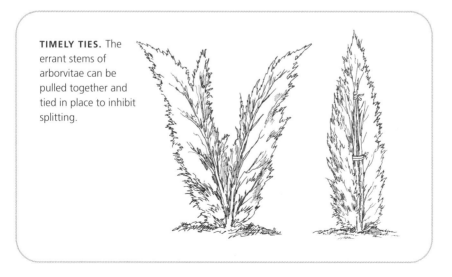

TIMELY TIES. The errant stems of arborvitae can be pulled together and tied in place to inhibit splitting.

Broken Branches

Description: By far the most common type of injury to trees is broken branches. This can range from the loss of a few skinny twigs to splitting or fracturing of major limbs. The magnitude of branch damage is often very closely tied to how an individual ice storm interacts with the unique aspects, such as branching patterns, of a tree. Loss of a substantial number of branches (more than 50 percent) puts the survival of the tree into question. Ice storms that break branches also create wounds of different sizes all over the tree, allowing pests and diseases easy access.

Symptoms: Some trees lose an abundance of smaller branches, all of similar caliper, and from all over the trees. And whereas one species may lose large limbs, another tree may be unscathed.

Remedies: Larger branches should be pruned back either to the trunk or to a major branch fork.

Strategies: In the years *before* a storm, prune the trees in the landscape to reduce weak, damaged, or diseased limbs. In the years *after* the storm, keep an eye on the damaged trees for signs of infestation of insects or infection from disease. See also Shielding Your Plants from Harm, page 72.

Broken Treetops

Description: Breakage of the main leader of a tree high in the canopy is most often caused by an ice storm. Many trees with this damage survive, with a new leader rising from below the break.

Symptoms: A broken treetop, ranging from a few feet to dozens of feet in length, falls to the ground or hangs top end down and is snagged in the upper branches.

Remedies: Rid your yard of danger by having a professional arborist cut out the damage from the tree in spring. The main worry is pests or diseases that use the break as a way to enter the tree. Keep on the lookout for those problems; clearing up the damage promptly and neatly may reduce the possibility.

Strategies: See Shielding Your Plants from Harm, page 72.

Broken Trunks

Description: The trunk may break when the main stem, or dominant growing stem, fractures just above or below the first set of branches. If the break is above and includes only about 25 percent of the branches on the tree, the tree may survive. If the break occurs below the lowest branches, the tree is not salvageable.

Symptoms: A tree is broken off anywhere along the trunk.

Remedies: A tree with a storm-damaged trunk may still be alive and even survive for years, but it won't look very attractive anymore. Unless it has special sentimental value, you should take it out and replace it.

Strategies: See Shielding Your Plants from Harm, page 72.

Uprooted Trees

Description: Thunderstorms, hurricanes, floods, and ice storms can uproot trees. Some trees that are uprooted in the first three events can be set upright again and staked. Over the years, they can produce new anchor roots and thrive. But when an ice storm uproots trees, trying to set the trees right again is very difficult. The cold frozen ground, snow, and ice make restoration tricky or impossible. The cold also inhibits recovery because the chill air easily damages exposed roots.

Symptoms: A tree is torn out of the ground with its roots exposed.

Remedies: Sadly, though an uprooted tree might be savable at another time of year, winter-uprooted trees are usually goners.

Strategies: See Shielding Your Plants from Harm, page 72.

Split Stems

Description: This injury is not reparable in larger trees, but smaller species, such as 'Little Girl' hybrid magnolias, can be saved.

Symptoms: Some trees split right down the center.

Remedies: Undertake your repair of a split stem as soon as possible after the damage occurs. Clean the wound to remove shattered wood or frayed bark. Gently set the split back together, making sure the pieces match as exactly as possible. Use flat-head nails to hold the two sections together. The nails should be long enough to join the pieces but short enough not to poke through the other side of the stem. Finally, wrap the entire wound from bottom to top with duct tape, with its shiny side against the bark.

Strategies: See Shielding Your Plants from Harm, page 72.

When Spring Comes

Description: Some years, the ice- and snowmelt come in spring, the moisture seeps into the ground, and everything is fine. In other years, however, a deep snowpack long outstays its welcome. The ice that lies against the soil has been there for months, creating an environment nearly identical to a flood. The mask of ice over the ground effectively blocks out air. The surface of the ground then turns into an anaerobic environment rather than one that uses oxygen for its chemical processes. While there isn't as much biological activity going on in the soil during winter as there is at other times of the year, a good amount still happens if the ground isn't frozen.

Symptoms: A long spell of ice can leave behind two things when it melts in the spring: (1) black-colored grass, leaves, and other vegetation lying on the ground or on living vegetation, the result of the anaerobic processes that began to function after the oxygen supply was cut off; (2) snow molds that appear at the edge of the melting snowpack. Gray- or pink-colored snow molds often look something like cotton candy. Pink snow mold can appear on many grass types, but is more prevalent on bent grass varieties.

Remedies: Fortunately, minor snow molds disappear, or "melt away," in the sunshine and warmth of spring. Dead material turns black because it has begun to decay in the absence of oxygen, so its natural color does not return. Rake up the blackened material and put it in the compost pile. Live things that blacken often just "shake it off" and green up.

Strategies: It is very difficult to control the depth of snow on the lawn or the time it persists into spring, two important factors in proliferation of snow mold. What can be done is to toughen up the lawn to make it less vulnerable to snow mold infestation. Avoid applying more than the recommended quantity of fertilizer and apply nutrients only at the suggested times. If your lawn is prone to pink snow mold, avoid fertilizing in late fall, especially with high-nitrogen formulations. Avoid adding compost to soils with high organic content in fall. If gray snow mold is more likely in your area, be sure to fertilize with a high-phosphorus, low-nitrogen fertilizer to strengthen plants. In any case, always look for fertilizers formulated for use in fall; often these have reduced nitrogen levels and increased phosphorus and trace minerals. Keep the lawn clean of debris, especially fallen leaves. Reduce thatch in grass types prone to heavy thatch production, and top-dress with screened compost to promote better surface drainage.

A Moldy Tale

Pink snow mold. Caused by an organism closely related to *Fusarium* (a fungus responsible for many rot and wilt diseases of flowers and vegetables), pink snow mold is not usually as virulent as its relatives. The disease is seen at the edge of a retreating snowpack and appears as patches of grayish white mycelia, often with a pinkish tinge, growing on grasses that have been bleached to tan-white.

Gray snow mold. Common in cooler parts of eastern North America, gray snow mold shows as fluffy mats of light gray mycelia rising from the grass and turning pale tan at the edge of the snowpack. Identify this fungus by blades of grass peppered with dark fawn-colored dots. Like pink snow mold, gray snow mold usually disappears as the weather improves in spring. The disease lingers in areas of shade longer than spots with full sun, but all traces of the infection are usually gone in a month or two.

Salt

MARY AND MARTHA ARE FRIENDS WHO GARDEN and chat about perennials and vegetables and how global warming seems to be making winters milder than ever before. They live across the street from each other in a quiet New England town, Martha in a small-shingled Cape Cod cottage and Mary in a little gambrel-roof cabin. Over coffee one late November day, they speak of what still needs to be done to winterize their gardens. Mary tells Martha about the plastic snow fence she bought to protect her roadside evergreens from salt spray, but Martha decides to protect her plantings with the old burlap fence she always uses. No matter, they conclude, each will work fine.

There isn't gardening to be done during the winter, but there is shoveling. Winter comes in late November and decides to stay late. For months on end, there seems to be an endless succession of storms. Some are all snow; others add some freezing rain or sleet. Keeping the paths open from the house to the driveway is a constant ordeal. When spring finally comes, it feels good to stop shoveling and know all the troubles of winter are in the past.

The spring-flowering bulbs are blooming and the grass and perennials are greening up and growing. But the lawn beside Martha's flagstone walkway looks terrible — unhealthy and brown. The blades of grass are failing to green up, and the plants look weak and frail. The damage is a wide irregular swath that follows along the edges of the walkway.

A mistake many of us make is that we think of gardening as a seasonal activity. In northern climates especially, when plants die back and go dormant, the gardener in us goes dormant too. When snow covers the lawn and garden, they disappear from our consciousness, and we might think that what we do outdoors in winter doesn't affect the garden and yard now that they are covered in winter white. But it often does.

Mary is a frugal New Englander who reads product labels in the supermarket and recycles everything. She used a deicing product all winter long, and she read the directions first and followed them. Martha, on the other hand, is not a perfectionist and not as careful as most. She also used a deicing product all winter long, by the handful, and replied to a query from Mary with a startled "Directions? Nonsense, everyone knows how to use rock salt." Unfortunately, Mary's carelessness resulted in damage she didn't anticipate, and she felt worse than if her yard had been struck by a storm over which she had no control. But it also raised her awareness. The resilient garden must be tended by the resilient, humble gardener who can learn from mistakes.

Getting Some Soil Savvy

When gardeners talk about garden soil, the names and relative importance of various chemical elements in it are tossed about like popcorn popping over a hot stove. You'll hear talk of nitrogen, phosphorus, potassium, calcium, iron, magnesium, and more. An element that is rarely mentioned is sodium. If you look on a bag of fertilizer, sodium isn't listed. Check a botany text, and sodium isn't among the elements essential for plant growth and health. Even though it isn't an essential nutrient, however, sodium is very important for plant growth because of how it can change the soil in which plants grow.

As sodium accumulates in soil, it progressively makes that soil a less fit place for plants to grow. Sodium slowly damages soils in three ways: through accumulation of salts, which leads to saline soils; through excessive amounts of free sodium, which produce sodic soils (see page 94); and by creating soils with extraordinarily high pH values. Soils compromised in any of these ways are unhealthy homes for many plants if the damage is mild and home to nothing at all if extreme.

How Salt Gets in Soils

Soils have been around far longer than the plants that grow in them. Soils form through the slow weathering of what scientists call geologic material (what we call rocks). Some of the eroded material is the sand and clay that you feel as you rub soil in your hands. But rocks are also chemically weathered, dissolving in solution and changing into other compounds, such as salts.

A salt is formed when the positively charged hydrogen atoms of an acid are replaced by the negatively charged atoms of a base. This happens in nature all the time and is how oceans became salty. As salts are formed from the bedrock, they get washed into streams by runoff and eventually find their way to the sea. Sometimes this transportation system isn't quite so efficient, and the salts get stuck in soils. This happens in low-altitude areas where drainage is poor and little water movement exists. The salts flow in as runoff but have nowhere to go, and they begin to accumulate in the soil.

Routine gardening practices can also contribute to salt accumulation in soil. Fertilizers are salts. They include the nitrates and phosphates that provide the necessary nitrogen and phosphorus to plants. When you add fertilizer to the soil, you are adding salts. In many soils this is not a problem, but in soils where the drainage is poor or in dry soils where the amount of water applied to the soil is less than the amount evaporated from it, salts can accumulate to harmful levels. Salt is also delivered to soils through the addition of organic fertilizers, such as manure and compost, and even through irrigation water.

A Low-Sodium Diet for Your Yard and Garden

No one adds salt to his or her garden on purpose. But the use of salt to de-ice walkways and provide a safe walking surface opens the way for accidental introduction of salt to the garden and lawn. Fortunately, we can control how we use these products to manage ice and snow in our yards. The most efficient way to use melting agents is also the most conservative and environmentally conscious, providing people safe footing while ensuring that the garden and surrounding area receive the minimum exposure to salt possible. Of course, the right way to use deicing products is not the way most people do use them. By being salt conscious through the winter, you can put your garden and yard on an environmentally healthful, low-sodium diet. In other words, you don't have to eliminate walkway salting; you just have to do it discriminately.

Identifying Saline Soils

Saline soils naturally exist in regions where the amount of rainfall is less than the amount of moisture lost to evaporation. The hallmark of saline soils is the accumulation of excess salts at the top of the soil. The salt layer can be very thin and look like an opaque white paint stain or it may be as thick as a snowfall. The salts accumulate at the soil surface as a result of evaporation and capillary flow. Three factors combine for salt to come to the surface of soil and then stay on the surface: water, salt, and heat.

Here's how to picture the dynamics of saline soils. Imagine that the water is a truck, the salt is the cargo the truck carries, and the soil capillaries are the roads the truck uses. The road system (soil capillaries or

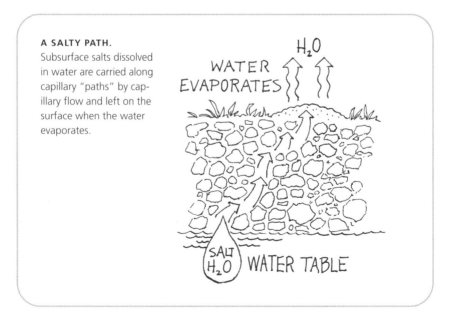

A SALTY PATH. Subsurface salts dissolved in water are carried along capillary "paths" by capillary flow and left on the surface when the water evaporates.

passages) runs from the water table, where the soil is saturated, to the soil surface. The water contains dissolved salts (loading the truck with cargo). The water is drawn through the capillaries to the surface by capillary flow (like a dry sponge soaking up water). At the soil surface, the water evaporates in the heat. The salts can't evaporate and are left behind (the truck unloads the cargo). Once this process starts, it tends to keep going, and more and more salt is transported to the surface and left behind as the water evaporates.

Capillary flow is different from water movement produced by the force of gravity, and in fact often moves contrary to the force of gravity. Its ability to move water upward depends on the size of the capillaries, which in turn depends on the type of soil. Clay soils have very small capillary diameters and can move water through about 5 feet (1.5 m) of soil. Sandy soils, with larger passages, can move water through a little over 2 feet (0.6 m) of soil. The cycle of capillary action is dependent on a high water table or equivalent water source to continually transport salts into the root zone. Find a way to remove the water, and you break the capillary flow cycle and stop adding more salts to the soil. This is the first step in repairing saline soils.

High-Sodium (Sodic) Soils

Soils with high levels of sodium are called *sodic soils*. The difference between a saline and a sodic soil can be puzzling. Even though both saline soils and sodic soils contain an abundance of sodium, the sodium affects each of these soils very differently. Saline soils are high in soluble salts but low in a form of sodium called exchangeable sodium. Sodic soils are low in soluble salts but very high in exchangeable sodium.

Effect of sodium on saline soils. The soil structure is not damaged and the ability of water to percolate through is still satisfactory. In clayey soils there is sometimes surface crusting, but in most instances the soil structure is normal.

Effect of sodium on sodic soils. Sodic soils contain so much sodium in the form of exchangeable sodium that it damages the soil structure. The exchangeable sodium disperses clay and silt particles and then prevents them from re-forming into the vital soil particles that produce soil capillaries and other soil spaces. The result is a breakdown of the soil that causes the characteristic, easy-to-identify look of sodic soils.

When dry, sodic soils have a hard, crusty appearance and most often are black in color. The high sodium content and subsequent scattering of clay particles destroys the soil capillaries and makes the ground nearly impermeable to water. A healthy sandy soil can allow 6 to 8 inches of water to percolate through it in 1 hour. A sodic soil allows only ¼ to ½ inch (0.6–1 cm) of water to seep in every hour.

Sodic soils can be found throughout western North America in the Great Plains, from Texas and Kansas to North Dakota; in the Rockies, at locations such as Utah and Colorado; and in the arid Southwest, from Nevada to Arizona. They are most common in low areas with high water tables. Very little grows in sodic soil, in part because the soil structure is so poor but also because the pH can be very high, sometimes reaching values above 10.

The Lesson of the Clay Pot

In many parts of North America, the most common place to encounter saline soils isn't the great outdoors, but in the pots that hold houseplants and other container-grown plants. Plants that are stingy with water, such as jade plants, produce conditions very similar to natural environments that create salty soils — that is, the amount of water added to the soil is less than the amount evaporated from it. The salt appears as a white powdery deposit on the outside of clay pots. Plastic pots don't solve the problem; they just hide it a little. Because plastic pots aren't permeable, the salt residue most often collects on the inside lip of a pot and on the soil-mix surface itself.

Salt accretion on a clay pot is attractive to some gardeners. The blotches and stains give the pot an antique look, as if it were thousands of years old, the relic of some ancient civilization. Less romantic people see these salted pots as items in need of a good scrubbing. Certainly, many houseplants can tolerate a saline soil, but how many of us cheerfully smile when asked to endure a "tolerable" situation with no end in sight? To manage the saline soils of many houseplants, follow these simple rules:

• Flush the pots of container-grown plants once a month with enough water to thoroughly soak the root-ball. Then allow the soil to drain completely before watering again.

• Avoid watering plants and then letting them stand in a saucer full of water. This acts as a shallow water table and encourages salt deposition on the soil surface.

• For slow-growing plants that don't need potting up to a larger pot very often, change the soil once a year. Clean or replace the pot at the same time.

• With plants for which changing the soil is impractical, scrape away the top inch or two of soil and replace with fresh growing mix.

• Fertilize lightly. Too much fertilizer introduces too much salt. (Overfeeding can also encourage a plant to outgrow its quarters too quickly.)

How Plants Cope with Salty Conditions

In gardening as in life, one of the conditions to strive for is equilibrium — a state of stability and balance. In scientific terms, *equilibrium* is "the state of a reaction where the concentration of the reactants doesn't change with time." To understand how some garden plants are resilient to saline conditions, we must look at how salt interferes with a plant's normal physiological equilibrium.

Great quantities of salt in the soil inhibit roots from absorbing water. Plants that are growing in saline soils may look like they are suffering from drought damage when it is really salt injury. If the soil water is concentrated with salt, then to reestablish an absorption flow into the plant, the plant must concentrate something in the fluid in its cells to match the soil water. Some plants produce amino acids and other materials, called *compatible solutes,* within their cells that restore the compatibility between the soil environment and the physiological state of the plant, and thus achieve equilibrium.

The roots of plants contain tiny and very fragile hairs that absorb from the soil most of the water a plant uses . Excess sodium in the soil damages the root hairs by removing calcium from the membranes, resulting in leakage of cellular fluids. Salt-resilient plants handle this sodium toxicity in a variety of ingenious ways. Some grab the toxic sodium ions before they can do damage and transport them to a cell feature called a *vacuole*. The vacuole is a place within a plant where toxic materials can be stored but remain isolated from the rest of the cell and thus do no damage. The vacuole may look like a bubble in the middle of the cell.

Other plants have found different places to hold the sodium ions so that they do no harm. Some plants have tiny cells called *bladder cells* on the leaf surfaces. The excess sodium is transported up a shoot to the leaf, where it is deposited in the vacuole of the bladder cell. When the vacuole becomes filled to capacity with sodium, the cell falls off the plant. An example of this is found in the ice plant *(Dorotheanthus bellidiformis)* — a seemingly strange name, as the plant is native to Zone 10. Ice plants grow in saline environments. The extra sodium that is absorbed along with the soil moisture is transported to the vacuoles of bladder cells in the leaves. As the bladder cells fill with sodium, they bulge through the leaf surfaces like balloons. These bladder cells cover the leaves and reflect the sunlight like frost crystals — hence, the name ice plant. The bladder cells then drop off the plant and the process starts over again. In fact, ice plants may actually be used as an indicator of saline conditions. If the ground is too saline, it will stop the growth of young ice plants; they will resume fast growth as soon as the salt concentrations are reduced.

Finally, some plants get rid of salt by returning the excess to the environment, by either depositing the salts on their leaves or excreting it through their roots. Prairie cordgrass *(Spartina pectinata* 'Aureomarginata'), an attractive ornamental grass reaching 5 feet (1.5 m) tall, with green leaves edged in gold, uses this process to rid itself of salt.

The fact that so many species of plants have developed so many ways of coping with salty environments has encouraged plant breeders, who are experimenting with salt-tolerant ornamental and food crops.

Plants for Salty Soils and Salt Spray

Salty soils challenge the resiliency of roots, and salt spray attacks the foliage. Being tolerant of either is a wonderful quality for a plant to have. Being able to survive and thrive in both shows valuable resilience!

Trees. Some trees seem to have chosen saline environments as their own. These trees show remarkable resiliency to saline conditions, even far from the sea:
Eastern red cedar *(Juniperus virginiana)*
Gingko *(Gingko biloba)*
Horse chestnut *(Aesculus hippocastanum)*
Live oak *(Quercus virginiana)*
Ohio buckeye *(Aesculus glabra)*
Russian olive *(Elaeagnus angustifolia)*
White ash *(Fraxinus americana)*

Palms. The image of a palm swaying by a tropical lagoon can convince people that all palms are tolerant of salty conditions. However, many are not, and some are more tolerant than others.
Cabbage palmetto *(Sabal palmetto)*
Coconut *(Cocos nucifera)*
Palmetto *(Sabal palmetto)*
Texas palmetto *(Sabal mexicana)*
Thread palm *(Washingtonia robusta)*
Washington palms *(Washingtonia* spp.)

Shrubs. A multitude of shrubs are superb garden plants, but the number de-creases considerably when only saline-tolerant plants are sought. Here are some of the best of this group, plants that are at home from the coast to the mountains, in a variety of climates.
Bayberry *(Myrica pensylvanica)*
Juniper *(Juniperus* spp.)
Lantana *(Lantana* spp.)
Oleander *(Nerium oleander)*
Pittosporum *(Pittosporum* spp.)
Rugosa rose *(Rosa rugosa)*
Southern wax myrtle *(Myrica cerifera)*
Sweet fern *(Comptonia peregrina)*
Yaupon holly *(Ilex vomitoria)*

Vines. Because vines grow up supports and along the ground, plants are vulnerable to salt from both saline soils and salt spray, and garden vines that can tolerate salt are few, but here are some of the most reliable.
Algerian ivy *(Hedera canariensis)*
Bougainvillea *(Bougainvillea* spp.)
English ivy *(Hedera helix)*
Star jasmine *(Trachelospermum jasminoides)*
Virginia creeper *(Parthenocissus quinquefolia)*

Perennials and annuals. There seems to be a clearer line between salt-tolerant and -intolerant herbaceous plants. Here are some very popular perennials and annuals that are counted as salt-resilient plants.

Ageratum *(Ageratum houstonianum)*
Allwood pink *(Dianthus x allwoodii)*
Artemisia *(Artemisia spp.)*
Blanket flower *(Gaillardia spp.)*
Century plant *(Agave americana)*
Daylily *(Hemerocallis spp.)*
Dusty miller *(Senecio cineraria)*
Ice plant *(Dorotheanthus spp.)*
Lily-of-the-Nile *(Agapanthus africanus)*
Lilyturf *(Liriope muscari)*
Moss rose *(Portulaca oleracea)*
Pot marigold *(Calendula officinalis)*
Red-hot poker *(Kniphofia spp.)*
Rose mallow *(Hibiscus moscheutos)*
Rosemary *(Rosmarinus officinalis)*
Sea lavender *(Limonium latifolium)*
Sea thrift *(Armeria maritima)*
Sedum *(Sedum 'Autumn Joy')*
Sweet alyssum *(Lobularia maritima)*
Verbena *(Verbena spp.)*
Yarrow *(Achillea filipendulina)*
Yucca *(Yucca spp.)*

Lawns. Most turfgrasses lack tolerance to saline environments, but some reliable, and even truly remarkable, grasses exist. Seashore paspalum is a tropical turfgrass, so it's not for everyone, but it can even be irrigated with ocean water and survive tidal flooding. The following have varying degrees of salt resilience.

Alkali Grasses

Bermuda grass *(Cynodon dactylon)*
Fine fescue *(Festuca spp.)*
Seashore paspalum *(Paspalum vaginatum)*
St. Augustine grass *(Stenotaphrum secundatum)*
Tall fescue *(Festuca elatior)*
Wheatgrass *(Agropyron spp.)*

Ornamental Grasses

Many of these graceful plants are as tough as nails when it comes to resistance to salt. Take your pick.

Blue fescue 'Elijah Blue' *(Festuca glauca 'Elijah Blue')*
Feather reed grass *(Calamagrostis x acutiflora 'Karl Foerster')*
Fountain grass *(Pennisetum spp.)* (perennial species)
Giant beach grass *(Leymus racemosus 'Glaucus')*
Mondo grass *(Ophiopogon japonicus)*
Northern sea oats *(Chasmanthium latifolium)*
Prairie cordgrass *(Spartina pectinata 'Aureomarginata')*

Avoiding Salt Damage

Your approach to keeping your garden and yard as salt-free as possible should be two-pronged: (1) Prepare the soils and plants to handle any salt exposure that comes their way, and (2) limit that exposure to the barest minimum possible.

Assessing Vulnerable Areas

Building up your garden and yard's ability to handle some salt spillover from winter begins as soon as the growing season starts in spring. Before doing the raking and cleanup from winter, take a stroll around the edges of the driveway and walks. As the snow piles melt, they usually leave behind a veneer of gritty sand. Lawn grass may look pressed and matted from the ever-present weight of snow and ice. Mark the boundaries of the gritty deposition and note evidence of any rivulets of runoff that emanate from the salty area. These are the areas that will require work in the coming months to prepare them for next winter.

Lawn areas. The area of your yard and garden subject to the greatest salt exposure is directly adjacent to sidewalks and driveways where melting agents are used. The goal is to increase the ability of the soil to accept small amounts of salt while affecting the plants that grow in it as little as possible.

Begin in spring with a thorough raking. Irrigate the grass with clean water to leach out any salt. If you know what types of turf grow in your lawn, check to see how salt tolerant these varieties are. If they are salt sensitive or if the grass seems to have some salt damage, consider oversowing with a salt-tolerant turfgrass such as fine or turf-grade tall fescue.

Also beginning in spring and then continuing once a month until the end of the growing season, spread a thin layer of screened compost over the sections of lawn nearest the snow-removal areas. Fertilize with a water-soluble complete fertilizer per label directions.

Garden beds. In beds that are replanted each year, such as those growing annuals, allow soil to dry out until it holds normal moisture levels.

Add clean water to leach out any salt. Let it dry out again, then turn it and loosen as deeply as practical. Next, incorporate compost into it. The compost improves drainage, which facilitates the leaching of any salts that do end up in the soil and inhibits changes in the pH of the soil. Compost also increases soil fertility, keeping plants more vigorous and bolstering moisture-holding capacity, thus helping reduce water stress on plants.

In beds with established plantings, rake them out each spring and leach the soil where possible with clean water. Incorporate compost where practical. Prune back any obvious damage to woody perennials and shrubs. Cover the soil with a thin [1- to 2-inch (2.5- to 5-cm)] layer of organic mulch, such as cocoa mulch or buckwheat hulls. In late fall to early winter, apply a new layer of mulch. And finally, when replacing plants, choose salt-resilient species and varieties when possible.

Salty Soil and the End of Empires

Remember Carthage? Not many people other than history buffs do. But one reason this once mighty center of a world empire is all but forgotten is salt. Back when Rome wanted to control the world, Carthage was a similarly ambitious and powerful city-state across the Mediterranean Sea on the north coast of Africa. Rather than work things out peacefully, Rome and Carthage ultimately fought a series of wars that ended with Carthage losing. The Romans destroyed the city of Carthage, but took their vengeance a step further: They covered the fields with salt so that the crops needed to sustain a city could not be grown there again.

Throughout history, many other empires and some civilizations have disappeared because of poor agricultural practices that allowed their once fertile fields to become fallow, salty wastelands.

Salty versus Slippery Sidewalks

When we purchase a new product, something we're unfamiliar with, most of us read the directions before we use it. But some things have been a part of our lives since we were kids. We think that there is no need to read the directions for those kinds of products because everyone already knows how to use them. A little investigation, however, often reveals that we have been using them incorrectly, and have been doing so for years. Understanding how melting agents like salt actually work helps show the best way to use them.

Melting away. Deicing products work by lowering the freezing point of water, thus turning ice back into liquid water. The lower the temperature, the less effective the melting agent becomes. This means that salt melts ice and snow most effectively when the temperature is closest to freezing — and is progressively less efficient as the temperature drops.

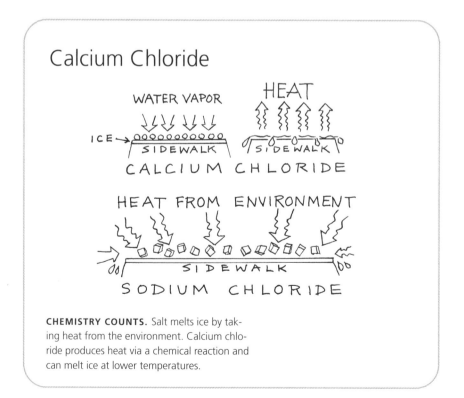

CHEMISTRY COUNTS. Salt melts ice by taking heat from the environment. Calcium chloride produces heat via a chemical reaction and can melt ice at lower temperatures.

Turning on the heat. Turning ice into water requires heat, and different melting agents acquire that heat in different ways. Salt takes heat from the environment, such as the sidewalk, the driveway, or the air. The colder the environment is, the less able salt is to melt the ice. Other melting agents, such as calcium chloride, produce heat through a chemical reaction and are effective at melting ice at much lower temperatures than is common salt.

More isn't better. The amount of salt spread on a sidewalk or driveway is important, in the same way the amount of flour that goes into a cake recipe is important. Salt melts ice when a specific concentration of salt exists in the meltwater. If too much salt is spread on the surface, the extra salt does *not* speed up melting, but instead slows it down and can even stop it completely, so not only does excess salt harm your yard and garden and pollute the environment as it runs off into the water table, street, or storm drains, but it is also less effective.

Here are some guidelines for the most environmentally friendly program to remove snow and ice.

• Remove as much snow and ice as possible with scrapers, shovels, snow blowers, plows, or power shovels.

• Apply deicing agents according to the manufacturer's recommendations and rates. The amount you need is probably less than you think!

• Thin layers of ice require very little melting agent, sometimes just a couple of ounces per square yard. For thick layers, apply only enough melting agent to weaken and loosen the ice, then remove by hand.

• Apply melting agent a few hours before ice and snow hit. This inhibits the bonding of ice to the surface.

• Shaded surfaces need slightly more deicing products than sunny areas because of reduced heating of surfaces.

• If traction is a concern, mix in an abrasive, such as sand, with the deicing agent. (This is especially important when using calcium chloride, as unlike rock salt, this product leaves the surface wet rather than dry.)

• Never use any salt product solely as a traction agent. Use 100 percent sand or dirt if traction is your objective.

• When you shovel after salting, do not toss the salt-laden ice and snow onto your lawn or garden. Instead, pile it up by the road, at the end of the driveway, or in any other spot where there are no significant plantings.

Repairing Saline Soil

Getting rid of excess salt in the soil seems so simple that it should be child's play. After all, the salts are water soluble. If water put the salts in the soil, then water should be able to take them out as well. In theory, this is absolutely correct. However, before the salts can be leached from the soil, the added water must have a place to drain to, or the dynamics of capillary flow will simply redeposit the salts where they were. Repairing the soil means the water dynamics that created the salinity problem must be changed.

Step 1: Fix the Drainage

Poor drainage is a prime cause of saline soils. In many areas of North America, especially from the Great Plains westward, saline soils are a fact

Sodium Chloride versus Calcium Chloride

Sodium chloride and calcium chloride are used extensively to remove ice and snow from surfaces. Here's a comparison of these two chemicals.

Sodium Chloride (Salt)	Calcium Chloride
Effective from 15°F to 32°F (–9 to 0°C)	Effective from -20°F to 32°F (–29 to 0°C)
Leaves surfaces dry	Leaves surfaces wet, can refreeze
Least expensive	Costs a little more than rock salt
Widely available at home-supply stores	Popular with municipal crews

Test First!

The amount of sulfur needed to lower the pH value of the soil in your garden is probably different from the rate required for a soil in the yard down
the street. This is because soils have different amounts of organic matter
and other materials that influence the effectiveness of amendments designed to alter soil pH. Soil tests provide solid baseline information from
which to improve your soil and grow weather-resilient plants.

of life. But repairing them is either financially or physically impractical.
Farms with very large acreage can't afford to install drainage systems over
vast areas. And in places like the prairies, the natural slope of the land is
too shallow to support a drainage system. For gardeners, however, practical options for reclamation of useful yard and garden space exist, primarily in the form of raised beds.

Raised beds. The raised bed cures many soil problems, including salinity, in one fell swoop. By installing a raised bed, you change the drainage
pattern of the soil, break the capillary flow engine, and reformulate (both
physically and chemically) the soil. Often, installing a simple wooden-
plank raised bed will provide good growing space that is free of salt. If a
more intensive solution is needed, you can combine a raised bed with a
drainage system that is designed to stop capillary flow.

Mark out the area for the raised bed and excavate the soil to a depth of
2 or 3 feet (0.6–0.9 m). Where possible, dig out a V-shaped hollow down
the center of the trench so that the V flares up to the sides of the trench
and looks like the inside of a boat, with the keel running down the center.
Backfill the trench with coarse sand, gravel, or pea stone. Rake the fill
level and set the raised bed atop the fill.

Once you've gone to the trouble of creating the raised bed, don't ruin it
by filling it with bad soil. Start fresh with a blend of the folowing: coarse

sand (10%), compost (40%), perlite (15%), pine or fir bark (15%), and loamy soil (20%) with a low salt content.

Drainage systems are valuable in areas where the slope is adequate to accommodate the system and where a ready supply of low-salt irrigation water exists to leach the soil. The most common drainage system is the tile drain (see the Floods section, page 112), which can substantially improve the drainage in yards and gardens.

Step 2: Leach the Soil

Once good drainage has been established, the saline soils must be leached to remove the excess salts. Use clean water with low soluble-salt content to flush out the salts. Allowing 6 inches (15 cm) of water to percolate through the soil can remove up to half the soluble salts. Keep in mind that many garden irrigation systems supply from ½ to 1 inch (1–2 cm) of water per hour; thus, leaching can take hours. The flow of water must be slow and steady, so that little or no runoff is produced — the water must drain *through* the soil rather than run over it.

Step 3: Adjust the pH

Saline soils often have pH values around 8.0, which is too high for vigorous growth of many garden plants. Adding elemental sulfur at the rates recommended on soil tests will decrease the pH to a range suitable for good plant growth (see Test First!, page 105).

Repairing Sodic Soils

Repairing sodic soils is generally more difficult than fixing saline soils. Unlike saline soils, where the offending salts need only to be removed, the sodium in the soil structure of sodic soils first has to be replaced with something else before it can be removed. The "something else" is calcium, which is supplied by adding gypsum to the soil. Gypsum is a rock that is ground into a powder and used as a soil amendment. It is packaged in bags and is readily available at garden centers and nurseries.

Gypsum is made of calcium sulfate. When it is applied to a sodic soil,

When Not to Add Gypsum

The addition of gypsum (sometimes called *white alkali*) can improve sodic soils but can complicate matters in saline soils. In many parts of western North America, a major part of the white crusty stuff on saline soils isn't just sodium chloride (table salt) but also calcium sulfate (gypsum). Adding gypsum to saline soils worsens rather than improves them (because adding gypsum increases the salt content of the soil.)

the calcium molecule splits away from the sulfate molecule. The sulfate combines with water to form sulfuric acid, which is then neutralized by the calcium. This is why adding gypsum supplies calcium but doesn't change the soil pH. The sulfur portion of the gypsum binds to the sodium, forming sodium sulfate, which is easily leached from the soil, leaving behind the calcium to replace the sodium in the soil structure. Add gypsum to sodic soils per the results of soil tests, usually at a rate of about 50 pounds (25 kg) per 1,000 square feet (93 sq m), in the spring and fall.

Simply adding gypsum doesn't improve soil by itself, because it doesn't remove sodium. The calcium in gypsum replaces the sodium in soil, freeing it up for leaching. Thus, drainage must also be made satisfactory so sodium can be leached out. The same drainage methods that work for saline soils also apply to sodic ones (see page 104).

Finally, the pH of the sodic soils must be modified by adding elemental sulfur at recommended rates, so that a suitable growing environment can be established.

Reversing Direct Salt Damage

If you live on along a seacoast, it comes with the territory that salt spray is going to affect your garden. Most of the effects of salt spray on plants are limited to a band about 1,000 feet (305 m) wide and inland from the shore. This isn't shocking to gardeners in coastal areas, because everyone knows the ocean is salty. You might not think the same thing would happen to gardens in Iowa or Ohio, but it does, in a sense — every time a deicing agent is applied to the roads in winter. Whenever you plant anything near a roadside, imagine you are planting it a few yards from the beach. Here are some approaches to specific situations.

Road Salt Spray

Description: Those of us who live many miles from the coast and in cool climates forget that every year we voluntarily bring the equivalent of sea spray to our yards and gardens. Each time the plow truck passes or we sprinkle deicer on the walk and steps, it is like high tide has come into our yard. The damage anti-icing agents cause to plants can be divided into two types: injury from direct contact with the salt and damage caused from excess sodium in the soil.

When salt is applied to road surfaces, the salt dissolves, lowering the freezing temperature of the solution and melting the ice. The salt is now part of the liquid on the highway. Every speeding car and truck kicks up a foggy cloud of salty mist that covers roadside plants. Winter can last a long time in some places, and that means days and days of salt baths for the plants that border an interstate highway or your yard by the road.

Symptoms: Damage from salt spray does not appear right away. Instead, in a matter of days in late winter, coinciding with a slowing down of salt application and the plants' breaking dormancy, roadside conifers suddenly turn brown. The brown color appears to be less damaging than the dried-out leaves and needles left behind by sunscald. Salt-spray damage most often appears on the side of plants directly facing the road, and the damage penetrates the foliage only a few feet.

Deciduous trees and shrubs hide their damage until bud break, when injury to buds and twigs that occurred months before finally becomes noticeable. Leaves rising from damaged buds can be malformed and smaller than normal. When buds or terminal twigs have been killed, the new growth from the injured tip can contain more shoots than usual, producing a form of witches'-broom.

Any roadside trees and shrubs can suffer salt damage in winter, but some locations are worse than others. Here are some of the places most likely to suffer damage:

• Sides of roads with the heaviest traffic (most damage occurs within 25 feet (7.5 m) of the road, with the heaviest injuries sustained within 10 feet (3 m) of the curb)

• Corner yards near intersections

• Yards located on a hill or at the bottom of a hill

Remedies: Prune carefully to remove disfigured portions of a deciduous plant while maintaining the plant's form.

Strategies: Physical barriers can prevent salt spray from reaching the plants and producing damage. For smaller shrubs and young trees, a snow fence erected between the roadside and the plants is often enough protection to stop injury. The fence can be made of plastic, wooden slats, burlap, or anything else that intercepts the salt drift. Plant salt-tolerant plants in regions where salt spray is a problem. Keep all plants in as healthy and vigorous a condition as possible, especially as they enter the winter season.

Damage from Sidewalk Salt

Description: When salt is spread on driveways and walkways, inevitably some is spilled to the sides. The salt seeps into the ground and produces a band of saline soil in which lawn grass, flowers, trees, and shrubs may be growing. As the weather warms and the growing season progresses, lawns and garden plants can be damaged by excessive sodium concentrations. Hot, dry summer weather can exacerbate the injury.

Symptoms:

• Blades of grass turn brown from the tip down, and sometimes the margins of a leaf curls slightly.

• Growth is slower than normal and all parts of the plant are stunted.

• Foliage is yellowed.

• Leaves are "burned" at the margins.

• Growing points die back.

• Leaves drop.

• Foliage changes color earlier than normal in the fall.

Remedies: Fixing salt-damaged soil along sidewalks and driveways is similar to repairing saline soils anywhere, with one big plus: The soil of your yard and garden is healthier than chronically salt-damaged soils of some semiarid areas. Your garden soil has more organic matter, a better nutrient balance, and strong structure. These benefits allow the offending salt to be leached out and amendments to be added to help repair any damage.

To remove salt from bare soil with good drainage, first till in some finished compost. Next, irrigate the ground with 6 inches (15 cm) of water (that amount translates roughly to a sprinkler running for 6 to 8 hours). Set the flow rate at low, so that the water seeps into the ground rather than running off.

If plants are already growing in the soil, apply a 1-inch (2 cm) layer of compost to the surface of the soil before watering and space out the irrigation over a few days. Leach the soil twice over 1 month. After that, apply a complete fertilizer.

Strategies: Saline soils can be managed and even avoided by paying attention to three primary factors: water, drainage, and soil type. Salts may be added to soil through irrigation water. Have it checked for soluble salts if you think your water may be the culprit. Second, remember that poor drainage locks salts in the soil by not letting them leach away. Improve drainage by using raised beds, installing tile drains, or methodically adding topdressings of compost. Heavy soils like clays also prevent adequate drainage and hold on to salts more efficiently than soils with light structure. Add compost to these soils to lessen salt buildup. Last, remember that water is the substance that carries away the salt from the growth zone of soil. Be sure to apply enough water during irrigation to carry salts down through soil layers rather than up through soil capillaries, where they are deposited on the soil surface as water evaporates.

Sea-Salt Damage

Description: Growing a garden close to the ocean offers a blend of unique beauty and special challenges. One of the most omnipresent and unpredictable is salt. Salt most often affects seaside gardens in the form of salt spray, which blows inland off the water. In most locations, sea-spray effects are limited to about 0.2 mile (0.3 km) from shore. During heavy storms, such as hurricanes and, on the East Coast, nor'easters, strong winds can send salt spray up to 50 miles (80 km) inland. Even without storms, many ocean sites are subject to persistent winds off the water that drive salt spray into the garden.

Symptoms: Damage from salt spray is very similar to, and many times indistinguishable from, salt damage along inland roadways in winter. Symptoms include a tan or light brown scorching or burning of the foliage that has come in contact with the sea-salt spray. On monocot plants like ornamental grasses, this manifests first as discolored strips and advances to complete browning followed by leaf drop. In dicots, including trees and shrubs, the leaves have a brownish mottled discoloration before they turn mostly or completely brown and then drop. If the soil is not high in salts, the damage is limited to the portions of the plant that have come in contact with the salt.

Remedies: The best approach is to remove the salt from a plant as soon after exposure as possible. Wash off the residue with water. High light seems to worsen the effect of salt on foliage, so washing it off after the storm and under cloudy skies is best.

Strategies: The most popular ways to deal with ocean spray are to grow plants indigenous to seaside locations and to choose garden plants known to be salt-spray resilient. Using these criteria still provides plenty of lovely plants that won't succumb to sea spray's ravages. Some gardeners near the sea like to construct a "safe microclimate area" in which they grow just about anything they want. With stockade, stone fences, or other windbreaks, wind and spray that come off the water are forced up and away from the garden. This tactic can considerably reduce the amount of salt exposure. (For more information about windbreaks, see pages 302–310.)

Flood

IT IS THE MIDDLE OF MAY, AND THE WEATHER HAS BEEN about average. The temperatures are comfortable and the rainfall near normal. Flowers, shrubs, and trees are growing vigorously, and many are in bloom. The grass is lush and green. The trees are nearly leafed out.

A slow-moving spring storm soaks the lower Mississippi Valley and slowly moves up the Appalachians, while a mound of high pressure is anchored off the Atlantic Coast. Working together, the two weather systems pull a dense stream of warm, moist air from the Gulf of Mexico and drive it northward. As the plume rides over cooler air, its clouds thicken and deepen, shading the land beneath them in a gray overcast. The air is still; the leaves on the trees are motionless. And then it begins to rain.

The circulation of the storm and that of the high-pressure system act like a conveyor belt for rain, continuously shuttling moisture northward. And the rain keeps falling. The slow movement of the weather systems keeps the rain shield relatively stationary, so that the rain continues to fall over the same places. The first day, more than 1 inch falls. The soil soaks up nearly all of this precipitation and then becomes overloaded. All of the smaller pores are filled with water, and it is raining faster than the larger pores can funnel the water through the soil. As the soil becomes saturated, puddles large and small form in roads, yards, and fields.

Overnight and through much of the next day, heavier bands of rain pass overhead, and the rainstorm becomes a deluge. Over 8 inches of rain pound the ground. The waterlogged soil can hold no more. Streams of runoff course down roads, driveways, and grassy slopes, flooding pavement areas and washing out gullies. Storm drains are choked with water and dump jets of muddy water into streams and rivers. The low areas of yards, containing gardens, lawns, and trees, become shallow ponds. Small creeks and rivers rise rapidly to their banks as torrents of seething brown white water push logs, uprooted trees, and trash downstream. As it floods, the sodden soil loses much of its strength, and the roots of the trees are less able to grip the ground. Some tall trees with large leafy canopies become top-heavy and begin to lean.

In the continuing rain, the swollen streams overflow onto the flood-plain. Backyards become a swirl of eddies and currents of floodwater. Trash of all kinds is carried in, mingling with downed branches and green leaves. Rafts of branches and sticks are temporary homes to displaced snakes, and colonies of fire ants bob on the water like venomous basket-balls. The roots of a tall tree snap with loud, penetrating cracks. In slow motion, the tree falls from its place in the grove and it splashes with a heavy crash into the muddy ground.

Two days after the rain begins, the sky has wrung itself out, the clouds thin to silvery gray, and the day brightens. The rain slows to a persistent, annoying drizzle that lingers for a few hours and finally disappears. The rain is gone, but the sound of water is everywhere. Storm drains echo as water gurgles into the pipes. The streams and rivers are awash with sounds like breaking surf as standing waves rhythmically build up and col-lapse onto themselves. Drops fall from the trees and splash into puddles. The backyards and gardens in the surrounding square miles are affected by one or another of the most common types of floods: "green" floods, ponding floods, and riverine floods.

In the Garden, before the Rain

Most forms of bad weather, such as wind and lightning, affect plants directly. Floods, however, affect plants primarily by damaging the soil.

According to the United States Geological Survey, floods are the most common natural disaster in the country. Floods occur in all regions, from Alaska to Florida, and in every season of the year. There are many types of floods — ice-jam floods, flash floods, storm-surge floods, landslide floods, and regional floods, for example. When flooding flows into your garden and yard, a chain of events begins that has an impact on soil and plants, sometimes extensively. It helps to understand what is happening in garden soil *before* the flood arrives, so that the changes it brings may be interpreted correctly.

At the simplest level, garden soil is a mix of solids, liquids, and gases. The solids are mineral and organic materials, such as sand, silt, clay, and humus. These are arranged into a matrix or structure that is composed of 30 to 60 percent empty spaces. In normal conditions, about half of these spaces, called *pores*, are filled with water and the remaining half with air.

Soil has mechanisms to retain an optimal balance of moisture and air. It does this by losing what it doesn't need and keeping what it does need. The pore spaces in soil are of varying sizes. When it rains, the water soaks into the soil and fills all the pores, large and small. Once the pores are filled, any extra water runs off. The water in the larger pores is pulled by gravity to deeper layers of the soil, and the water that remains near the surface is held there by surface tension and is ready for use by plant roots and soil organisms.

Microorganisms in soil. Garden soil appears inanimate but is actually a thriving ecosystem. Much of the microscopic life, primarily bacteria but also fungi, is constantly making the soil more fertile by producing nutrients that plants can easily use. Nitrogen-fixing bacteria, which most often grow in symbiotic association with legumes, use oxygen to convert nitrogen directly from the air to forms that plants can use. The nitrifying bacteria rely on oxygen to make nitrates, a readily available form of nitrogen, from ammonia, a product produced as organic matter in the soil decays. Because most of the oxygen in soil is found in the top few inches, this area also contains the highest concentration of bacteria.

As quickly as soil bacteria use up oxygen, more seeps in from the atmosphere to replace what is lost. This natural replenishment keeps the proportion of oxygen in the soil's air spaces nearly equal to that in the air above ground. The most beneficial soil bacteria are also the most dependent on oxygen. When soil has no oxygen, aerobic bacteria activity stops.

Roots and root hairs. While bacteria grow and fertilize the soil, the roots of plants, from perennials to trees, grow through the soil. The amount of roots that infiltrate the soil, even from a small plant, is staggering. In H.J. Dittmer's famous experiment with winter rye, it was discovered that the roots of one rye plant had a total length of 2 million feet (about 6 million m), or close to 380 miles (612 km). Roots not only anchor a plant in place, but also absorb water and nutrients from the soil and then move these materials to the base of the stem. Some roots also serve as a carbohydrate storage area.

Roots can be thick and massive, but the portions of roots responsible for the absorption of water and nutrients so vital to a plant's health and survival are so small that you can barely see them. Root hairs are tiny tubes, extensions of a root's epidermal cells, that appear only at the very tip of the roots. Plants need an enormous number of root hairs to survive. (Dittmer's single rye plant contained 14 billion root hairs.) Root hairs are exceedingly fragile and very sensitive to changes in the environment.

A Word on Worms

Of all the creatures that live in yard and garden soil, perhaps the most important are worms. Worms tunnel through the soil, creating channels through which air and water pass in and out. As they move through the ground, worms process the soil and turn organic matter into humus, which increases soil fertility.

Worms live in the same upper regions of the soil as soil bacteria, mycorrhizae, and plant roots, and they are sensitive to the same changes. If conditions change slowly, the worms get out of the way, tunneling deeper into the soil to wait out the trouble. But worms are pretty defenseless, and if change comes quickly, most of them will die.

Because they do not live very long, they must also be continually replaced, a process that can occur only if the plant, and the plant's root, is growing.

Roots and fungi. Many trees, shrubs, ferns, herbs, and perennials do not rely on root hairs alone to absorb water and nutrients, but instead use a symbiotic partnership with a soil fungus called a *mycorrhiza*, which fulfills the same function. The fungus invades the root, forming a pathway between the root and the fungus. The fungus then provides nutrients for the plant, and the plant provides growth-enhancing substances to the fungus. Roots with mycorrhizae are blunter, with less of a taper, than roots with large numbers of root hairs. Mycorrhizae rely on oxygen to function and are very sensitive to changes in the soil environment.

Types of Floods

To the unpracticed eye or the disheartened gardener, a flood is a flood. But it's not that simple. There are several different kinds of floods, and knowing which one — or which ones — is affecting your property can help you understand what has happened and how you can cope with the damage to your yard and garden.

Green Floods

When the ground is saturated but not inundated, the event is known as a *green flood*. This sort of flood is found on all types of terrain, from slopes to basins, but persists longest in areas of poor drainage. It is usually a temporary occurrence after heavy rains, but a green flood can also be a perennial condition caused by a high water table or magnified by shallow soil above hardpan or ledge. Persistent green floods are less damaging than temporary events, because the plants that remain in permanently flooded areas adapt to that condition. Green floods that affect normally well-drained areas temporarily impose an environment on plants to which they cannot easily adapt, and injury results. In deep, well-drained soil, gravity pulls excess water through the soil pores in a matter of hours, dispersing the flood and returning the soil to normal. In level areas and in fine clay or silt soils, the gravitational movement of water is slowed and the green flood may last for days.

Green floods can damage soil structure and fertility; injure or kill soil organisms; and injure or kill annuals, perennials, and some shrubs with thin roots. Some ways to control green floods are to install French drains, tile drains, or dry wells, and to create raised beds.

Ponding Floods

A *ponding flood* consists of standing water that covers portions or all of a garden and yard. Ponding floods can be the result of heavy rain or can be the stagnant puddles left behind as the waters of a riverine flood (see below) recede. A ponding flood can also occur in late winter, when melting ice and snow pool in low areas atop the still-frozen ground. Ponding floods have all the negative effects of green floods, plus a few of their own. For example, the standing water acts as a barrier to oxygen reaching the soil, and this increases the damage to organisms in the soil and plant tissues, especially roots. In addition, the water may cover the leaves of low-growing plants, a condition that most herbaceous plants cannot survive for more than a day or two (some succumb in mere hours). As the ponding flood recedes, it often transforms briefly into a green flood until the last of the excess water is gone.

Ponding floods damage soil structure and fertility, injure or kill soil organisms, and injure or kill herbaceous plants, including annuals and perennials. Plants that are submerged for more than a day are often severely damaged or killed. Most trees are unharmed by ponding floods that last less than 1 week. Ponding floods that occur when plants are dormant, as in meltwater floods, are less damaging. Ponding floods can be managed by installation of French drains, tile drains, dry wells, swales, and berms. Control floods of shallow depth with raised beds, as well.

Riverine Floods

In a *riverine flood*, a river or stream overflows its banks and inundates the yard and garden. This type of flood is highly variable in force and size. The water can move fast or slowly, scour a landscape, or deposit sediment over it. The flood can cover a small area or drown a dozen states at a time. Riverine floods also commonly carry debris ranging from sewage to floating trees to fire ants, which pose additional hazards. Riverine floods are often deep, ranging from 1 foot (0.3 m) to 10 feet (3 m) or more. When floodwaters reach a magnitude that they can swamp the ground floor of homes, nothing can lessen their impact. However, proper preparation hastens the departure of the floodwaters and, thus, the garden's recovery.

The *ice-jam flood* is a specific type of riverine flood that occurs when winter ice breaks up following a rain. As a channel swells with water, it breaks up the ice, which then floats downstream. When the floes reach an obstacle, such as a bridge abutment, they often pile up or jam, forming a dam of ice. The river then rises very quickly upstream of the dam and spills over the banks, inundating the adjacent floodplain. One of the greatest hazards to plants from an ice-jam flood is the blocks of ice themselves, because these impressive objects can crush plants or scar trees by tearing away bark.

A riverine flood carries all the damage potential of a ponding flood, plus other risks. The moving water can erode gullies in the landscape, even those already underwater. Trees can be undermined, making them more prone to toppling and root damage. Parts of the garden, from structures to plants, can be picked up and floated away. Hazardous material can drift into the yard, making the garden home to everything from toxic waste to insects. Moving water can break limbs and snap stems. Short-term floods (less than 1 week) do damage mostly to herbaceous plants. Longer floods can severely injure all types of plants in the garden.

Another concern in riverine floods is sedimentation. Many floods leave behind a coating of fine mud that, if not removed, will block oxygen into the soil and damage plants. Drainage techniques, such as French drains, are of benefit if the water is shallow or when deep water recedes. A berm can act as a dike and hold back floodwaters or divert water to another location. Raised beds are of benefit if the flood is shallow.

Flash Floods

A *flash flood* can occur along a running river or within the seasonally dry drainage channels of intermittent streams. Even bone-dry washes can become muddy-water torrents in a flash flood. They form when heavy rain falls on terrain that is steep and incapable of absorbing very much precipitation. The runoff drives downslope and gathers into drainage areas, such as ravines and gullies. Flash floods can be deadly because they form very quickly, in just minutes. Rather than the typical overflow of water of a riverine flood, a flash flood is often a wall of water that roars down a canyon with enough force to destroy buildings, sweep away cars, and eradicate gardens. The type of flash flood most encountered by gardeners is a rapid rise and overflow in a stream or river. The currents in this riverine type of flash flood can be very strong, with extensive erosion and debris that leave short-duration ponding floods in their wake.

Flash floods most often do mechanical damage to the garden, in the form of erosion and scouring, broken limbs and stems, and uprooted plants. Berms are the best defense against flash floods.

How a Flood Damages Your Garden

Often the first damage a flood brings to the garden is to the soil — and the damage can occur in very little time. As rain falls on the ground, it seeps into the soil, filling the channels and spaces while driving out the air. During heavy rains and floods, the upper few inches of soil become saturated, and excess water runs off to low points or pools atop the sodden ground.

The roots of most garden plants are concentrated in the top foot of soil. Even massive trees have a primary root zone that typically extends only about 4 feet (1.2 m) deep. Thus, most plants have no trouble surviving a heavy rain and a few inches of soggy soil. But in areas of the garden that flood, the soil saturation continues to expand and deepen until the ground in the entire root zone is waterlogged. Suddenly everything that lives in the soil — bacteria; fungi; garden; lawn, and landscape plants;

What Happens in a Flood?

1. Water removes oxygen from the soil.

2. Beneficial bacteria and fungi that need oxygen stop growing.

3. Growth of plant roots slows down.

4. Bacteria that do not need oxygen begin growing, removing nutrients and adding toxins to the soil.

5. Floodwater damages soil structure.

6. Primary plant processes, such as photosynthesis, transpiration, and respiration, slow or stop.

7. Growth throughout entire plant slows or stops.

8. Disease organisms flourish and invade some plant tissues.

9. Plants die.

and worms and other organisms — is suffocating beneath an oppressive blanket of floodwater. The flood starts a domino effect that can devastate plants in the garden and yard.

Domino #1: Good Bacteria Out, Bad Bacteria In

Oxygen is the fuel that powers the metabolic processes of nearly all living things that inhabit or use the soil. Without it, the process of life, and eventually life itself, stops. A flood puts an airtight cap over the soil, stopping the free exchange of oxygen between the air and the root zone. After the flood has shut off the flow of oxygen, the plants and soil organisms continue to burn whatever oxygen remains in the soil until the supply is exhausted. Lack of oxygen is catastrophic to both plants and aerobic soil bacteria, but in different ways.

Nitrogen-fixing bacteria enrich legumes and some other plants with nitrogen they take from the atmosphere; they need oxygen to grow.

Nitrifying bacteria that change ammonia into fertile nitrates also depend on oxygen to grow. In a flood environment, these bacteria so essential to life in the soil just stop working.

Another large group of versatile bacteria also uses oxygen to break down organic matter into humus and enrich the soil. When the oxygen supply is cut off, these organisms switch from working with oxygen (aerobic) to working without it (anaerobic). Anaerobic bacteria break down organic matter into other compounds just as aerobic bacteria do, but in a much less desirable way. As the aerobic bacteria shut down, the anaerobic bacteria gear up. Through the processes of fermentation and anaerobic respiration, these bacteria denitrify the soil, removing the fertile materials that the aerobic bacteria put in. As by-products of their work, they leave behind a brew of toxic compounds that taint the soil, often with such foul-smelling materials as hydrogen sulfide and methane. Through a process called reduction, the anaerobic bacteria chemically change some essential elements, such as manganese and iron, from forms that plants can easily use to forms that are toxic to plants.

Domino #2: Destruction of Soil Structure

The texture of the soil is determined by what the soil is made of, such as sand, clay, or silt. How those ingredients fit together forms the structure of the soil. The building blocks of soil structure are called *colloids*. The colloids act as glue, binding together the solid portions of the soil into such structures as pores and channels. Picture colloids as the mortar holding together the bricks of a house.

Once the soil is saturated in a flood, the colloidal structure of the soil begins to weaken and dissolve. To illustrate, imagine that the billions of capillaries and channels in the soil are like mine shafts in a mountain. Strong timbers support these mine tunnels, and the mine operates normally. Colloids provide support for the soil channels, and air moves in and out of the ground normally. If the timbers in the mine should weaken and fail, however, the tunnels will cave in and the mine stop working. Similarly, when floodwaters weaken the structure of the soil, the channels and capillaries collapse in much the same way as a mine shaft collapses when its structure is weakened. And to make matters worse, the longer the flood lingers and remains over the soil, the more it is likely to damage the soil.

A flood soaks the soil so much that its structure begins to dissolve and disintegrate. Soil aggregates — the tiny bits of mineral and organic matter that hold everything together — begin to fall apart. Clay particles that cling to other soil particles and are needed for soil fertility are scattered into the water. As the soil structure weakens and begins to break down, the chemical composition of the soil also begins to change. The aerobic chemistry of normal soil yields to the anaerobic chemistry of flooded soils. The soil is made less fertile as the bacteria remove nitrogen from the soil and make some elements unavailable to plants. Sulfates are changed to hydrogen sulfide, and the soil loses nutrients vital to plant growth. Dozens of compounds are released into the saturated soil, creating a poisonous soup of carbon dioxide, methane, alcohol, hydrocarbons, phenolic acid, and cyanide-based compounds. The pH of the soil changes too: Acid soils become more alkaline and alkaline soils become more acid. The flooded yard and garden is a soggy environment that most plants find uninhabitable.

Domino #3: Plants Begin to Be Damaged

Photosynthesis is very sensitive to changes in the environment — so sensitive that the process shuts down in most plants within a few hours of being flooded. Transpiration rates plummet, and the movement of water through the plant drops almost 50 percent after just 1 day of flooding. In many plants, the leaf pores (or *stomata*) close. (For more information about stomata, see page 297.) The roots stop taking in essential nutrients like nitrogen, phosphorus, and potassium, and growth slows.

As submersion continues, the softer, nonwoody roots of trees and shrubs die. Perennials and annuals suffer great losses of their root system. Low oxygen levels in the soil encourage infection by plant diseases, such as are caused by *Phytophthora*, and roots begin to rot.

Flood Timetable

Relative Resilience of Plants to Flooding

How long a plant can survive a flood depends on many variables, including the time of year, depth and temperature of the water, and condition of the plant. All things being equal, the following time-table gives general projections for the tolerance of plants to inundation.

1 to 3 days. Most plants can survive a flood of this duration. Exceptions are sensitive lawn grasses, such as Bahia grass *(Paspalum notatum)*, and popular garden annuals, such as sweet alyssum *(Lobularia maritima)* and geraniums *(Pelargonium* hybrids).

1 week. This is the limit of tolerance for many annuals and herbaceous perennials. Most lawn grasses die as well. Slightly more resilient turfgrasses, such as Kentucky bluegrass *(Poa pratensis)*, incur extensive but reversible damage. Some perennials, including lavender *(Lavandula* spp.), santolina *(Santolina* spp.), silver-mound artemisia *(Artemisia schmidtiana)*, and thrift *(Armeria maritima)*, die.

10 days to 2 weeks. Most turf-grasses, garden annuals, and forage crops die, including red and annual clovers and moderately resistant turfgrasses such as Bermuda grass and St. Augustine.

Perennials noticeably suffer, and such plants as delphiniums, many alliums and artemisias, and coreopsis die. Many small trees are severely damaged or begin to die; these include redbud *(Cercis canadensis)*, flowering dogwood *(Cornus florida)*, and wild plum *(Prunus americana)*. Some large trees, including most hickories and pecans *(Carya* spp.), black walnut *(Juglans nigra)*, red mulberry *(Morus rubra)*, loblolly pine *(Pinus taeda)*, black cherry *(Prunus serotina)*, and red and black oaks *(Quercus rubra, Q. velutina)*, also die.

2 weeks to 4 weeks. This is the limit of tolerance for even the most resilient herbaceous plants, whether annuals or perennials. Even flood-tolerant turf species, such as tall fescue *(Festuca elatior* var. *arundinacea)*, will be damaged or die. The remaining terrestrial woody perennials, small trees, and shrubs that have survived show significant damage or soon die. Some perennials that can survive floods of this length are some iris *(Iris* spp.), daylilies *(Hemerocallis* cultivars), turtlehead *(Chelone lyonii)*, and lobelia *(Lobelia* spp.). Trees that reach their limit at this time include most elms *(Ulmus)* and oaks *(Quercus)*, black gum *(Nyssa sylvatica)*, and sassafras *(Sassafras albidum)*.

How Bad Is It?

Every flood has subtle differences, but the damage left behind is similar. Knowing what to look for during a flood will help you determine the extent of damage after the water recedes. The most important criteria to consider when determining flood damage to plants are:

• What time of year the flood occurs
• How long the flood lasts
• Depth and temperature of the water
• Species of plants
• Amount of water movement
• Amount of sediment the water leaves behind

Time of year. Whether your garden has perennials or pine trees, the time of year a flood occurs greatly determines how damaging that flood is to plants. In general, dormant plants can endure floods much better than can plants that are actively growing. Many dormant plants can weather floods for weeks or months without damage, whereas those same plants flooded during a period of active growth may die in days. Plants are most vulnerable to flood damage during or just after the vigorous flush of growth in spring, when they have depleted most of their food reserves. Different plants enter this period of growth at different times. A flood may

How Much of the Plant Is Above Water?

Flood injury increases as more of a plant is submerged. Plants can be somewhat resistant to floods that cover their roots and stems, but when leaves are underwater, the damage increases markedly. Many flood-tolerant species die after complete submersion for 1 month; even a couple of weeks of submersion can cause extensive damage. Intolerant species suffer much more quickly.

damage one species of plant and leave another unharmed. Other suscepti-ble plants are those weakened by disease or naturally low in vigor.

How long it lasts. Plants are wonderfully adaptive. Even during a flood, plants try to conform to the conditions around them and endure. Flooded trees, for instance, take in oxygen through openings on the bark called *lenticels* and transport it to the roots. Some flooded plants produce adventitious roots along their sodden root system. These roots absorb nutrients and detoxify some of the harmful compounds produced by the anaerobic bacteria. However, if a flood lasts too long, many plants will be damaged or die. Many flowering bulbs and herbaceous perennials are very sensitive to flooding and will die within a few days to a week. Woody plants, including many shrubs and trees, show major injury if the flood lasts 1 to 4 months.

Depth and temperature of the water. The depth of a flood is a major fac-tor in the damage it causes to plants. Plants can best endure a flood that saturates the soil but doesn't result in standing water. Injury is more like-ly once standing water develops and increases substantially if the foliage becomes submerged. The temperature of the water also makes a big dif-ference in terms of when or whether damage occurs. The warmer the water, the lower the level of dissolved oxygen and the more quickly plants are injured. The cooler the water, the more dissolved oxygen it contains, and the speed of injury is thus reduced.

Species and preferred habitat. Many species are designed to grow in moist or wet conditions, and common sense will tell you that the plants in a water garden may weather a flood much better than those in a drought-tolerant flower bed. But there are many important exceptions, such as the turfgrass tall fescue, which tolerates both flood and drought conditions.

Water movement. The water of some floods, such as flash floods and storm surges, have currents or waves that scour the soil or physically damage plants. The water movement can undermine roots, exposing the fragile root hairs to the water and then to the air as the water recedes. Undermined trees can topple, and bark, stems, and branches may be fur-ther damaged by floating debris.

Perennials Sensitive to Flooding

Generally speaking, owing to their more vulnerable herbaceous nature and smaller size compared to woody plants, perennials struggle after a flood. Plants adapted to drier conditions, of course, may simply expire. However, plants adapted to wet environments, such as the marginal plants used near garden ponds, are just as susceptible to flood injury if the flood occurs during warm weather in spring. The following perennials are sensitive to flooding.

Basket-of-gold *(Aurinia saxatilis)*
Blanket flower *(Gaillardia* spp.)

Clematis *(Clematis* hybrids)
Coralbells *(Heuchera* spp.)
Coreopsis *(Coreopsis* spp.)
Delphinium *(Delphinium* spp.)
Geranium, hardy *(Geranium* spp.)
Lavender *(Lavandula* spp.)
Lavender cotton *(Santolina* spp.)
Lily leek *(Allium moly)*
Penstemon *(Penstemon* spp.)
Pink *(Dianthus* spp.)
Russian sage *(Perovskia atriplicifolia)*
Silvermound artemisia *(Artemisia schmidtiana)*
Thrift *(Armeria maritima)*

Sedimentation. Many floods leave a layer of sediment, from sand to silt to gooey mud, atop the garden. This layer often blocks air from reaching the soil and roots below. It covers low-growing plants, impeding resumption of photosynthesis. It can also contain toxic compounds that weaken plants. Remove accumulated sediment when possible.

Strategies for Preventing Flood Damage

If you prepare for a flood like you're constructing a set for a disaster movie, the process will be tedious and your yard will look like it's *waiting* for a flood rather than simply *prepared* for one. Your best bet is to use different techniques, such as berms and French drains, as gardening elements that enhance, rather than detract from, the beauty of your yard. Your attractive, uniquely landscaped garden will thus just happen to also be ready for flood. Each of the following methods is rated for its effectiveness as protection from green, ponding, riverine, and/or flash floods.

Raised Beds

Installing raised beds is like building an ark for the garden. Raised beds are perhaps the easiest, most versatile method to protect against minor floods. Even if the raised beds are submerged for a time, the soil in them will dry out faster after the waters recede than will soil in the main garden. Raised beds protect plants from minor flooding by:
• Keeping the plants and soil above the water
• Allowing soil to dry out more quickly than ground beds and lawns
• Allowing oxygen levels and aerobic bacteria activity in soil to return to normal faster
• Inhibiting nutrient loss from soil
• Protecting plants and plant roots from injury

The best type of raised bed for flood protection is one that has solid sides. It can be made of many materials. Wooden planks are the most common, but artificial wood made with recycled materials (plastic and real wood) is perhaps the best material — it never rots, always looks attractive, can be nailed or screwed like wood, and is environmentally friendly.

The frame of the bed is simply made from boards screwed in place to form a rectangular, bottomless box. For added flood protection, you can

Know and Respect Conservation Laws

Many flood-prone areas are near wetlands, streams, rivers, or other areas that are protected by local, state, and federal environmental laws. Before constructing any flood-control techniques in a protected area, always check with your town's conservation commission regarding the laws and regulations in your area. In many locations, modifying the land within the buffer zone of a protected resource in any way, even cutting down a tree, is severely restricted.

install a modified French drain under the bed first. Dig out 1 to 2 feet (30 –60 cm) of soil from the base of the bed and fill the hole to within about 4 inches (10 cm) of the top with coarse sand. Then set the raised bed atop the French drain and fill with soil and plants.

Efficacy of Raised Beds

Green flood	Excellent
Ponding flood	Excellent
Riverine flood	Fair to good
Flash flood	Fair to good

Berms

A berm is a long mound of earth that is used to keep something in or to keep something out. For example, berms are frequently used to keep out traffic noises and unsightly views, while at the same time they "keep in" peace and quiet and a sense of privacy. To control flooding, berms can be used singly to direct water away from the garden or in tandem to channel unwanted water away from the garden in a manner similar to a swale (see below). Single berms work well along small streams, washes, roads, trails, paths, and other areas where moving water can overflow.

When building a berm, the key point to remember is that it is meant to direct water away from the garden. Many people make the mistake of building a berm around a garden or yard — which collects water rather than deflects it!

Efficacy of Berms

Green flood	Poor
Ponding flood	Fair to good
Riverine flood	Good to excellent
Flash flood	Good to excellent

Swales

A swale is simple but can provide a remarkable degree of flood protection. To visualize a swale, imagine a valley running between two mountains. In the garden and yard, a swale is a small valley that runs from one part of the yard to another. When it rains, the swale performs two important tasks: It funnels away water from the rest of the yard and it directs that water to another place. A swale can also act as a catch basin if the exit slope is shallow and the swale tends to hold runoff rather than to drain it away.

Swales can be made of myriad shapes: Some are narrow; others are wide and shallow. It doesn't matter what they look like, as long as the appearance is pleasing to you. Most swales are constructed by using large equipment, so that the finished slopes can be graded and the final landscape has a soft, worn appearance. Lawn grass is the usual topping; this allows excess water to flow quickly from the yard into the drainage system.

In areas in which a swale remains consistently wet, many people plant wetland plants, such as cattails and Joe-Pye weed, to enhance the ornamental value of the site. Swales also offer nice opportunities for using hardscape elements, such as bridges and stonescapes, to beautify the yard.

Efficacy of Swales

Green flood	Fair
Ponding flood	Good to excellent
Riverine flood	Fair to good
Flash flood	Fair to good

Dry Streambeds

A close cousin to the swale, the dry streambed is a drainage system consisting of a narrow swale lined with cobbles. The slopes often have a greater vertical drop than do other systems. The drainage principle is the same as that of other active systems, and the dry streambed must carry water to a benign place.

Larger stones, such as cobbles, should be used because the water draining down a streambed is often moving faster than that through other drains, and the heavier rocks serve to stabilize the system. To avoid erosion of the bank edges, be sure the stones continue up the stream bank. Many people use water-permeable landscaping cloth as a base before setting the stones in the streambed. If you do this, however, be warned that during times of fast runoff, the cloth may increase the force of the water descending the stream and thus increase the risk of erosion.

Efficacy of Dry Streambeds

Green flood	Poor
Ponding flood	Poor to fair
Riverine flood	Good
Flash flood	Good

French Drains

A traditional French drain is a sloped trench filled with loose stone and topped with a layer of coarse sand. In a flood, the excess water percolates through the sand and stone and away from your lawn and garden. The slope of the trench then carries the water away from your garden. French drains can be made to any depth and width to suit your situation. They can be very helpful in removing persistent small puddles and diverting downpours.

The key to making a French drain work well is to be sure that the trench is sloped enough to allow the water to flow through it. On flat areas, this is done by digging the head of the trench to the desired depth. Measure this with a tape measure held against a crosspiece set

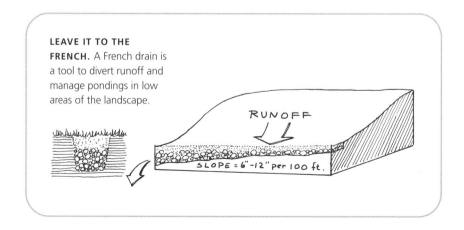

LEAVE IT TO THE FRENCH. A French drain is a tool to divert runoff and manage pondings in low areas of the landscape.

RUNOFF

SLOPE = 6"-12" per 100 ft.

perpendicular to the trench. Continue digging the trench and measuring every 10 feet (3 m) or so. At each measurement, the trench should be deeper than the previous point. A recommended slope for a drainage system (including French drains and tile drains) is 6 to 12 inches (15–30 cm) per 100 feet (30 m). This means that a 100-foot-long (30 m) trench that is 2 feet (0.6 m) deep at the start will be about 3 feet (1 m) deep at the end. Make the trench as wide as you need to accommodate the extra flow, generally between 1 foot (30 cm) and 3 feet (1 m).

Fill the trench with stone large enough to allow fast gravitational flow of the water; stone about 2 inches (5 cm) in diameter usually works well. The stone should come to within about 4 inches (10 cm) of the surface. Fill the remainder with coarse sand.

Now comes the creative part. The traditional topping for French drains is grass. This works well if a drought-tolerant turf is sown, because the sand beneath the roots drains so well that it dries out faster than nearby turf areas. Another potential topping is a walkway, such as a boardwalk, that is raised above the ground a few inches. This solution allows easy access to the yard, is universally accessible, needs little maintenance, and is attractive. In addition, the drain beneath protects the walkway from frost heaves, the bane of many garden paths.

Efficacy of French Drains

Green flood	Good
Ponding flood	Excellent
Riverine flood	Fair to good
Flash flood	Fair

Dry Wells

The dry well is a cousin to the French drain. The only difference between them is that the French drain works for a living whereas the dry well is a couch potato. By definition, a dry well is a hole in the ground that is filled with fast-draining material, such as stone. You can make it whatever size you desire, but most are no more than 5 feet (1.5 m) across. After you have dug and filled the well, cap it with sand and sow over the top with grass

Avoid Building a Drain That Fails

Water that drains through the soil is described as either gravitational or capillary. *Gravitational water* rapidly flows into the soil and then out of the soil through the largest soil pores. When you water a potted plant, the water that pours out the bottom is gravitational (or excess) water. *Capillary water* is found in very small soil pores. In these tiny spaces, the surface tension of the water is stronger than gravity. This causes the moisture to sit there and not drain away.

A French drain must be made of materials that enhance gravitational flow of water and minimize capillary flow. That is why the material used to top or cap the system is important. Never use fine-textured soils or sand — these materials have too much capillary potential and will block excess water from entering the drainage system.

seed. Dry wells are most effective in areas that have deep soil; in ground that lacks obstacles, such as rock ledges; and in regions where there is a shallow water table. Dry wells can be helpful in controlling minor flooding.

To build, first observe the lay of the land, looking for natural drainage patterns and low spots. It is helpful to do this after a rain or even during a storm, so you can survey the precise drainage pattern. Site the well in a low point, a place where runoff will gather.

Efficacy of Dry Wells

Green flood	Excellent
Ponding flood	Good to excellent
Riverine flood	Fair
Flash flood	Poor

Tile Drains

When I was a kid and much smarter than my father, I removed a small tile drain that he had installed in the backyard years before. I figured it was not needed anymore because the ground around it was dry. Within a day or two, the area was saturated and a mess. Humility can never be learned too soon!

Tile drains work well and, when properly installed, are just about invisible. In essence, a tile drain is a French drain with perforated pipe at the bottom of the trench. Be sure that the piping leads to a place where excess water will do no harm, such as a low point.

To install a tile drain, dig a trench in the same manner as for a French drain. Depending on how cold your winters are, it might be wise to set the entire run of pipe below the frost line to protect from heaving. Lay about 6 inches (15 cm) of stone in the bottom of the trench and set the perforated piping atop the stone. Wiggle the piping into place and use a mason's level to check that the slope is uniform. Fill and top as in building a French drain.

Efficacy of Tile Drains

Green flood	Excellent
Ponding flood	Excellent
Riverine flood	Fair to good
Flash flood	Poor to fair

Physical Damage after the Flood

Gardeners feel a driving need to get out and fix things that are wrong in the garden. Floods, especially floods involving streams and rivers, carry a lot more than water into your yard. Other potential risks to beware of are chemical and sewage pollution and hazardous debris, such as metal and glass. An abundant water supply often increases the number of breeding mosquitoes, which may raise the chance of contracting diseases like encephalitis and West Nile virus. In addition, floods often force animals, from snakes to insects, from their preferred homes into your yard.

(In warmer regions, look out for — and stay away from! — fire ant colonies floating on the water.) So stay aware of potential problems as you work in your yard, and always wash thoroughly when you come back inside.

At the beginning of this chapter, you learned what is happening to your plants below the ground in a flood. But you still don't know how much injury has occurred, and to which plants. During the flood and after it recedes, much information can be gleaned by carefully looking at

Some Top 10s for Flood-Prone Areas

The 10 Best Trees

Forest trees can be divided into two groups: the understory, which is composed of smaller trees and shrubs, generally under 30 feet (9 m) tall, and the taller, dominant trees that grow above and reach 100 feet (30.5 m) tall or more. Understory trees include flowering dogwood, redbud, and flowering plum. Dominant trees include live oak, red maple, and cottonwood.

In general, the dominant tree species survive flooding better than smaller understory species. The most flood-resistant are those in prime of life. Seedlings and very young trees of even flood-tolerant species can be damaged and killed by floods. Less vigorous old trees or those in decline are also vulnerable.

Bald cypress *(Taxodium distichum)*
Eastern cottonwood *(Populus deltoides)*
Green ash *(Fraxinus pensylvanica)*
Honey locust *(Gleditsia triacanthos)*
Persimmon *(Diospyros virginiana)*
Silver maple *(Acer saccharinum)*
Sweetgum *(Liquidambar styraciflua)*
Sycamore *(Platanus occidentalis)*
Water hickory *(Carya aquatica)*
Water tupelo *(Nyssa aquatica)*

The 10 Best Perennials

Cardinal flower *(Lobelia cardinalis)*
Daylily *(Hemerocallis* cultivars)
Japanese iris *(Iris ensata)*
Marsh marigold *(Caltha palustris)*
Monkey flower *(Mimulus* spp.)
Rose mallow *(Hibiscus moscheutos)*
Siberian iris *(Iris sibirica)*
Speedwell *(Veronica* spp.)
Yarrow *(Achillea* spp.)
Yellow flag *(Iris pseudacorus)*

your garden and landscape, especially foliage. The leaves of a flooded plant often provide very specific clues as to what part of the plant is damaged and how well, or not so well, the plant is repairing itself.

Epinasty

Description: Although epinasty indicates root damage, it can also be viewed as a favorable sign. Epinasty is a side effect of production of the hormone ethylene, which is most often used by plants to promote fruit ripening. In saturated soil, ethylene assists in making additional roots that increase the plant's tolerance of flooding.

Symptoms: Leaf stems (petioles) turn downward when epinasty is present. It differs from wilting in that the leaves have plenty of moisture (that is, they are turgid) and seem normal, other than pointing down. Sometimes the leaf margins of epinastic foliage are slightly curled. You'll see this condition most readily on trees and shrubs, but you may also recognize it on other ornamental and edible garden plants.

Remedies: None.

Strategies: None.

Chlorosis

Description: Chlorophyll has a fairly short life span in plants and must be continually replaced during the growing season for leaves to remain green. If the chlorophyll is not replaced, the leaves begin to turn yellow. This yellowing is also a sign that some vital plant processes are shutting down. Sometimes this shutting down is normal: As healthy trees and shrubs go dormant in autumn, the resulting beautiful foliage colors are actually caused by chlorosis. In flooded plants, however, chlorosis is an entirely different indicator.

Photosynthesis is very oxygen dependent. Within hours of the soil being deprived of oxygen, photosynthesis stops. Nutrients become more difficult for plants to absorb from the soil, and transport of water and nutrients throughout the plant slows or stops. As the chlorophyll molecules break down, the leaves take on a yellow color. In flooded plants, the change from green to yellow most commonly advances from the bottom of the plant to the top. It indicates that the roots are still providing moisture to the leaves, but that root damage has occurred and is advancing into and through the aerial portions of the plant.

Symptoms: Leaves on a plant turn yellow, caused by the reduced presence of chlorophyll.

Remedies: None.

Strategies: None.

Wilting

Description: Most commonly, wilting is viewed as a sign of dry soil. It should more accurately be seen as a sign that the roots are not absorbing adequate moisture from the soil. Leaves constantly lose moisture through evaporation and so must continually replace that moisture with water the roots absorb from the soil. In floods, the softer, nonwoody roots tend to die, sometimes within days of inundation. These roots contain the tiny hairs that absorb the water from the soil. As more of the root hairs die, the flow of moisture to the leaves slows down.

Symptoms: Leaves lose internal moisture and droop. Wilting leaves often look desiccated and wrinkled, and they develop a muted green color. In some species, the foliage tends to curl in from the sides as it wilts. Sometimes wilting indicates a marginal soil moisture condition, such as when the leaves droop during the day and recharge at night. At other times, the leaves wilt and stay that way. Regardless, wilting usually results from extensive root damage, and you can often expect such diseases as root rot to follow.

Remedies: None.

Strategies: None.

Leaf Drop

Description: In nearly all actively growing plants, a little leaf drop is normal. Sometimes a change in the growing environment, such as water availability or amount of sunlight, can trigger modest leaf loss. It becomes a concern only when large numbers of leaves fall at abnormal times. In flooded plants, there are two types of leaf drop to watch for. The first is when the leaves turn yellow before dropping; the second is when green leaves fall from the branches. Both forms of leaf drop indicate injury to the plant, especially to the roots. In flood-damaged plants, the older leaves usually drop first. Newer leaves are often more vigorous and have more chemicals, including plant hormones, that allow them to withstand changes better.

During some abnormal weather conditions, flood-type defoliation occurs when no flood exists. Called green floods (see page 116), these conditions can appear in summer when tropical moisture rides up on a stagnant weather front and dumps repeated downpours on a normally temperate location for days on end. Even though no standing water exists, the soil around the root zone is saturated for days. Under such conditions, shallow-rooted trees, such as sugar maple, are prone to leaf spot. Dark, circular lesions appear on the leaves and they drop to the ground in great numbers for weeks after the ground becomes wet. Once on the ground, fallen leaves often turn black. Because there is no standing water over the ground, the soil can return to normal moisture levels more quickly than in a standard flood, so recovery of the tree is common.

Symptoms: Leaves drop from trees during the growing season. The foliage can be either green or yellow. Leaves may drop a few at a time or the plant may undergo a large defoliation. Plants adapted to drier environments typically drop leaves within 2 weeks of flooding, whereas wetland species may take up to 2 months to show noticeable leaf drop.

Remedies: None.

Strategies: Plant flood-tolerant species when planning a landscape in flood-prone areas.

Erosion

Description: Floods can undermine roots, making trees and shrubs prone to toppling. While underwater, the roots can absorb some oxygen directly from the water, postponing root damage. However, as soon as the roots are exposed, they dry out very quickly. Repair must therefore be a top priority.

Symptoms: Soil has been washed away by flowing water.

Remedies: Fill in scoured spots around the root zone with a mix of moist soil and compost or sand and compost. Gullies can be repaired after the soil dries out. To slow the runoff and reduce erosion, set rows of cobbles (like small stone dams) in gullies a few feet apart, perpendicular to the direction of flow. Then fill in areas with soil and tamp into place.

Strategies: See pages 126–133.

Broken or Injured Limbs

Description: Shifting earth, roiling water, and the winds that often accompany flood conditions can easily damage the branches of woody plants.

Symptoms: Broken or hanging limbs along with torn and bruised bark appear on affected plants.

Remedies: Pruning is the traditional remedy for many types of injury, but in the case of flood damage, it is best not to be too hasty with the shears. Of course, you should cut back or remove plants that present a safety hazard, and prune back broken branches and other obvious damage. Flooding saps the reserves of many types of plants, however, and pruning green portions of a plant hinders rather than helps the plant recover. Refrain from pruning plants that have suffered other types of injuries, such as root damage that leads to defoliation. Although these plants may eventually die, there's still a chance they'll recover, and pruning now would decrease their chances.

Branches that have been completely broken from the tree or are hanging have a ragged wound and some torn bark at the break site. When the break is toward the tip of the branch, make a clean cut a few inches below the break. When the break is close to the trunk, prune the branch a fraction of an inch outside the branch collar.

Strategies: Do protective pruning of trees by removing limbs with weak branch–trunk unions or by thinning branches from trees with top-heavy canopies. Under most conditions, this should be done while a tree is dormant. However, if the tree is damaged, remove the broken limbs immediately.

Saturated Soil

Description: Have you ever seen an old abandoned barn that was leaning and sagging so much that you wondered how it could possibly stay upright? Waterlogged soils are a lot like that old barn. So much of the structure has been removed or weakened that just a few footsteps can damage it, collapsing and compacting the remaining pores, like knocking down the main support of the old barn.

Symptoms: Saturated soil is like a sponge that is filled with water. Press on it with your finger and water oozes out. Step on it and water squeezes out from under the soles of your feet. Saturated soil that has been disturbed is called mud. Mud has all the ingredients of soil but nothing to hold it together, the structure having been lost. A plant with its roots in saturated soil has a better chance of survival than does one with its roots in mud.

A LIGHT TOUCH. Before walking or driving equipment over wet soil, lay down planks, which will distribute the weight.

Remedies: Walking or driving equipment over saturated soil will compress and compact it, damaging it further. To reach plants that need pruning or to fill eroded areas, lay a boardwalk of planks to serve as a walkway. Bring materials over the boardwalk in smaller amounts — fill a wheelbarrow only partway, for instance. If there is no immediate need to cross a sodden area after a flood, give the land a chance to dry out completely first.

Loose, sodden soil provides poor support for established plants and even less for newly planted trees and shrubs. As a general rule, during good weather, staking of plants is strongly discouraged because it fosters weak stems and top-heavy canopies. After flooding, however, landscape plants may benefit from added anchorage while the soil dries out and the roots heal. When staking a tree after a flood, use two wires, set in line with the prevailing wind direction and an equal distance apart, to evenly distribute the strain. Secure the cables to sturdy stakes about 4 to 5 feet (1.2–1.5 m) tall and set parallel with the trunk. Drive them into the ground deep enough that they won't pull out (in most cases, 18 to 24 inches [45–60 cm] long will be sufficient). Keep the plant staked for one growing season if it seems to be growing normally, or until it has done well through one growing season.

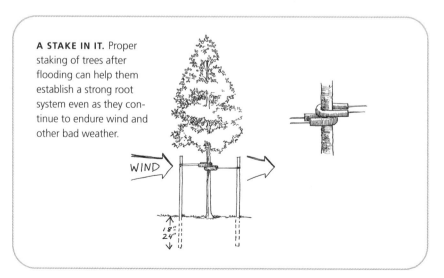

A STAKE IN IT. Proper staking of trees after flooding can help them establish a strong root system even as they continue to endure wind and other bad weather.

Lawns Damaged by Saturated Soil

Description: Lawns deserve special mention because sodden turf is exceedingly fragile.

Remedies: Stay off saturated lawns, as foot traffic will tear pieces of sod from the lawn. As the grass dries, rake out the dead turf to make room for new seed and to remove plant material that could attract disease and pests. Avoid raking until the grass and soil are dry. Raking too soon will pull healthy grass plants out of the ground.

Strategies: Depending on your region, you may ultimately over-sow with a sturdy turf blend that contains native species, such as buffalo grass. Plants that send roots deep into the soil are more firmly locked into earth than shallow-rooted species and can thus better endure times when the topsoil layers are saturated. Plants with a taproot (a root system with a dominant central root, as, for example, bur oak) are damaged less, and often recover faster than their shallow-rooted counterparts. When dealing with a class of plants without taproots, such as lawn grasses, select the most vigorous, deeply rooted types, such as buffalo grass, that can resist uprooting in fragile saturated soils.

Nutrient Imbalance

Description: Both floodwater and the actions of anaerobic bacteria make a mess of the nutrient profile of the soil. The flood has wreaked havoc with soil levels of nitrogen, phosphorus, and potassium as well as sulfur, magnesium, and calcium. The pH level of the garden and yard has changed — flood-affected acid soils become more alkaline and alkaline soils become more acid.

Symptoms: Many complex combinations of deficiencies can arise that manifest in a wide variety of symptoms. Foliage may show abnormal color (yellowing in between veins), shape (emerging leaves malformed), or form (leaves are curled).

Remedies: The nutrient deficiencies usually last only as long as the flood. To help diagnose problems that are potentially nutrient related, however, keep a record of the progress of any abnormality you observe, in case it continues beyond the flood time. It's possible to test foliage for indications of nutrient deficiencies, but that's expensive. These tests can be performed before the soil has returned to a stable nutrient profile. Spraying the foliage with the proper nutrient can then sometimes alleviate the symptoms if the tree is growing normally. Remember that floods slow or stop growth in many trees and plants, and growth returns to normal only slowly over time.

Strategies: Your first step should be to order soil tests for your garden beds and lawn: Contact your nearest Cooperative Extension office or ask for advice and a test kit at your local garden center. Soil-test recommendations may call for adding an amendment, such as phosphorus, potassium, or dolomitic limestone. Wait until the soil has dried out before taking the sample and adding amendments. Nitrogen should be applied sparingly, with an application of between ½ and 1 pound (0.2–0.5 kg) per 1,000 square feet (93 sq m); after this, do not apply a nitrogen fertilizer again for the remainder of the current growing season. Avoid using trace elements for at least 1 year. Flooding can significantly change the availability but not necessarily the quantity of many trace elements in the soil. Consequently, deficiency symptoms may appear when the soil holds adequate quantities of a nutrient, but not in an available form. Adding more of the trace element can result in toxity symptoms as the soil returns to normal and the trace elements again become available. Retest your soil next year and add further amendments in accordance with those results.

Sedimentation

Description: Floods that have flowing water can leave behind a sloppy mess. The rapid flow allows the water to carry a large amount of clay, silt, sand, and gravel downstream. When the water spills over into the floodplain, it slows down and releases its load of sediment. The larger material, such as gravel, is dumped first, closest to the stream, whereas the fine material settles out farther from its source, after the water becomes almost stagnant.

Symptoms: Sediment depths after a flood can vary from a thin film to many feet. Some trees, such as silver maple, can tolerate or even thrive in such conditions. But most plants cannot handle them, and even if a plant can tolerate many feet of sand, few gardeners would find such a thing acceptable. Sediment that covers the ground buries smaller plants, robbing them of sunlight and normal gas exchange. Larger plants also suffer because the oxygen they need is in the top few inches of soil, which has moved away from their roots.

Remedies: Under most circumstances, sediment deposits are manageable and can be removed fairly easily. For small areas, gently loosen the sediment with a rake, watching out for and gingerly working around exposed roots. Rake a little at a time onto a flat-bladed shovel and put it in a wheelbarrow.

Strategies: None.

Lack of Growth

Description: Plants injured by flooding often show little or no measurable growth during the growing season after the flood. They just sit there — some looking healthy, some not — but not growing. Many plants bear fewer leaves than usual, and the leaves are smaller than normal.

Symptoms: Lack of growth indicates damage, especially to the root system, but of a magnitude that is often impossible to determine. Some plants recover after about one growing season; others die suddenly.

Remedies: To give a plant the greatest chance of recovery, avoid compacting the soil near its root zone by keeping foot traffic or machinery off it until the soil has dried out. For smaller areas, such as borders and gardens, work compost into the soil when you are cultivating the surface. Sometimes it is difficult to protect an area from traffic and still go about daily life. Use whatever method and reminders work best in your situation — quiet homes with adults only may need just a warning-cloth strip on a stake, whereas homes with kids may need more obvious and impenetrable fortifications, such a blockade of lawn furniture or hay bales. Once the soil has dried out, try to keep the soil moisture near optimum. Plants damaged by flood are very susceptible to drought injury in the coming months or even years.

Strategies: This is a problem that can be lessened by choosing plants with the strongest flood tolerance, as these plants will recover more rapidly than less resilient species. Keeping plants as strong and healthy as possible throughout the year will allow faster recovery from damage. Finally, reduce stress on flooded trees by avoiding soil compaction near the trees.

The Comatose Garden

Description: Many perennials, shrubs, and trees have an amazing ability to recover after trying conditions, but others just don't make it. After a flood, leaves can fall off and perennials can just disappear, making your yard look as if it were in midwinter. These features may indicate that some plants are dead, but sometimes they indicate a condition called the *comatose garden.* A comatose plant has sustained severe injury, and most of the life processes within it have slowed or shut down to conserve whatever energies remain so that the plant can attempt to heal itself.

Symptoms: Comatose plants look dormant or dead. Unlike dormancy, however, which is a period of inactivity, these injured plants are active, but in a way that is largely unobservable.

Remedies: If you can be patient, it is best to wait and see whether plants that look dead have really succumbed or are playing possum while they recover. As you wait, keep moisture levels in the soil near perfect. Any stress now will be more than they can handle. Many of these plants recover completely and regain every bit of their beauty. I once saw a Pinxter azalea *(Rhododendron nudiflorum)* regress from a sturdy 6-foot-tall (1.8 m) plant to a leafless stick 2 feet (0.6 m) tall. Five years later, it is now over 8 feet (2.4 m) tall and provides a beautiful display of pale pink flowers each spring.

Drought

THE EQUATORIAL TRADE WINDS THAT BLOW EAST TO WEST over the Pacific Ocean are weakening. In normal years, the winds interact with the water to create pools of warm water off the coast of Southeast Asia and to draw cool water to the surface off South America. As the winds weaken, the reverse occurs and the warm water edges eastward, usurping the mass of cold water. This event is called El Niño. As the waters continue to warm in the eastern Pacific, they further diminish the trade winds overhead and create a thermal shield that blocks deep cold-water currents from rising to the surface. Cold-water fish disappear from their indigenous waters, and the food chain begins to crumble.

The higher surface temperatures of the water cause the enormous storms that rise from the Pacific each winter to generate farther east than normal. This causes a domino effect on storm genesis across the tropical zones. The change in the weather of the tropics rejuvenates the jet stream and pulls it far south, where it spawns massive storms that pummel California, the Southwest, and northern Mexico with a succession of floods, landslides, and mountain blizzards. To the east, across the wide prairies of the Great Plains, a completely different, though just as extreme, type of weather settles over the grasslands. The Great Plains is a drier place than many other areas of North America. Droughts occur here more regularly and more often than elsewhere on the continent— and also more severely.

The last soaking rain tapped against farmhouse roofs late last fall, 8 long months ago. After that rain, the farmers checked their fields for moisture content, called the field capacity, and found the soils were holding almost as much moisture as they could. In winter, most of fields were fallow but the gardens, lawns, shrubs, and trees across the landscape slowly drew down the soil moisture until the ground froze for the winter.

The winter snows are light. By late spring, the lack of rain has deepened from a dry spell to a drought. The long days and warm weather hasten the loss of moisture from the ground, and field capacities drop to about 50 percent. In the area hardest hit by the drought are a botanical garden with an extensive collection of trees, a home with beds of perennials, and a large nursery with field-grown perennials. Water restrictions have limited watering, and as the days wear on, the endless procession of dry blue skies diminishes optimism.

The botanical garden's trees include many Japanese maples, red maples, and flowering dogwoods, all of them set amid lawns and paths. While the garden's drought-resilient trees, including Kentucky coffee tree and white oak, are tapping moisture deep within the ground, many drought-sensitive trees are clearly suffering. The leaves of Japanese maples are losing moisture faster than it can be replaced, and edges of their leaves are turning brown and dying. The foliage on the red maples is turning color many weeks early. The flowering dogwood leaves are curling at the margins. The shallow roots of these trees are in soil that has not been recharged by rain in months, and the existing moisture has been wicked away by the lawn. With the top foot of ground so parched, it is near the permanent wilting point, a degree of soil drought so extreme that plants growing in it are certain to suffer grave injury and perhaps death.

The perennial nursery hasn't legally been able to irrigate for many weeks, and the rows of daylilies and other plants have baked in the sun every day with no relief. The owner of the farm is from the old school of agriculture, which taught to conserve soil moisture. He has thus lightly cultivated the space between the rows of plants, which has made a dust mulch. The theory is that by breaking up the soil surface, the capillaries that carry moisture to the surface will be broken, thus trapping the moisture in the ground and reducing evaporation. As the tractors roll over the fields, clouds of topsoil float into the air and are carried away on the wind. Some of the crops — daylilies, candytuft, coneflowers, black-eyed Susans

— manage to thrive despite the horticultural intervention. Other, more drought-sensitive crops stop growing and die. The dust-mulch theory turns out to be wrong. The mulching pulverizes the top of the soil, causing erosion and reducing the ability of the rain to soak into the soil. Because the upward movement of water in the soil ceases once the top layer dries out, cultivation only damages the soil.

Meanwhile, perennial gardens at a home at the edge of town are holding up. Each bed has underground soaker hoses, and the gardener uses a moisture meter and keeps records in a notebook. The irrigation system hasn't been used for a long time, but the gardens are still full and lush. Even the more drought-sensitive plants are thriving. This garden's survival secret is its soil. Where the botanical garden and field nursery relied largely on the soil that was there (with minimal improvement), the home gardener used a rich, highly organic soil with a field capacity far superior to that of the unimproved soils. A layer of organic mulch over the ground is also helping the garden retain moisture.

Getting to Know the Water Thief

Climate is like a clock whose pendulum swings in uneven rhythms and uncertain gradations. There are stormy times, wet periods, dry and cold intervals, and seasons of extreme heat. Each of these variations, including drought, is a natural occurrence in many climates. Drought appears and disappears at irregular intervals and with unpredictable severity in areas as vast as a continent and as specific as your garden. Much remains to be learned about why these variations occur. But what is known is that many droughts, including some of the longest and most severe, seem to begin at the interface of wind and current, ocean and atmosphere, half a world away from the garden they affect.

Drought has been called many things, but perhaps the most descriptive image is that of the "water thief," for drought really does steal the source of life from the soil — and by extension, the plants in the garden. But how does drought rob the ground of water and how quickly does this happen?

How Water Moves in Soil

As rain falls from the sky and seeps into the soil, water fills the empty spaces (or pores) that are defined by the soil's structure. When all of the pores are saturated with moisture, any remaining water that falls flows away as runoff. The soil is now saturated, but over the next hours or days, the excess moisture, called gravitational water, drains away. *Gravitational water* is soil moisture that moves through the ground in response to gravity. The water that seeps out the bottom of the pot after watering a container plant is gravitational water.

Once drainage has stopped, any water that remains in the soil is called capillary water and can be categorized as free, available, or unavailable. It is capillary water that plants rely on for nearly all their water needs. As drought progressively dries out the ground more completely and more deeply, the capillary moisture in the soil becomes ever harder to obtain.

Free capillary water is moisture that is held within the soil but moves up, down, or laterally in response to differences in the concentration of water elsewhere. For instance, the water in a moist plot of ground moves

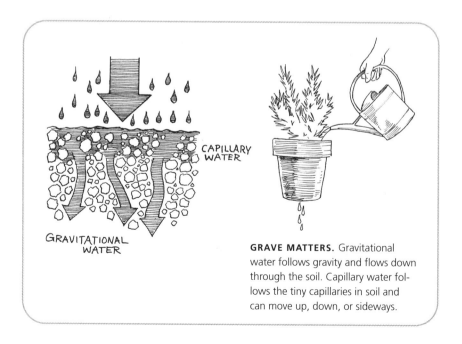

CAPILLARY WATER

GRAVITATIONAL WATER

GRAVE MATTERS. Gravitational water follows gravity and flows down through the soil. Capillary water follows the tiny capillaries in soil and can move up, down, or sideways.

toward an adjacent, drier plot of ground. Another example: When you water a container plant by pouring water in the saucer beneath it, the moisture seeps up through the soil ball through free capillary movement. The free capillary water is eventually removed by evaporation from the soil surface and through absorption of moisture into plant roots.

Once the gravitational water is gone and the movement of the free capillary water has stopped, soil is at the optimum moisture level to grow most plants. The soil surface appears dry, but just below, the soil is moist. The quantity of water held in the soil at this point is called the *field capacity*. Field capacity varies among different soils. The field capacity of a sandy loam is 10 percent; silt loam averages 20 percent; and a clayey soil, about 40 percent.

Bad to Worse: Reaching the Wilting Point

For plant roots to absorb water, either the root has to grow to the water or the water has to go to the root. As a drought progresses, the soil continues to dry out and the percentage of moisture in the soil drops. As the quantity of moisture in the ground decreases, the remaining moisture becomes harder for the plant roots to absorb. Basically, moisture in soil exists as a thin film that adheres to soil particles. As this film is thinned and reduced, the forces holding the moisture to the soil increase. This makes it more and more difficult for the roots to absorb that water.

When the percentage of moisture in the soil reaches about half the field capacity of the soil, the *permanent wilting point* is reached, a point at which a plant can no longer draw any remaining moisture from the ground. A sandy loam at the permanent wilting point still contains about 5 percent moisture, but that moisture is attached to the soil particles with a force of over 200 pounds per square inch (91 kg per 6.5 sq cm). Compare that with the little over 14 pounds per square inch (6 kg per 6.5 sq cm) of atmospheric pressure we feel every day, and it's easy to see why plants can't pry out any more moisture from droughty soil.

Plants wilt when the rate of transpiration from their leaves exceeds the amount of moisture absorbed by the roots for a period of time. When soils reach a moisture level where plants can no longer draw moisture from them, the plants cross a point of no return. The water thief has robbed the garden, but hope may remain. Wilting can be reversed if the balance between absorption and transpiration is restored. The length of time a plant can endure wilting is different for different plants. Drought-resilient plants, which have moisture-conserving traits, survive longer than do plants without such resources. Sometimes they even survive until rain.

A Matter of Measurement

Not so long ago, there was no way to reliably or accurately determine which areas of the country were suffering from drought and which ones weren't, or how bad a drought was. In the 1960s, Wayne Palmer rectified this by inventing the Palmer Drought Severity Index (PDSI). His system

Daily Water Stress

Daily water stress is different from drought. *Daily water stress* reflects a short-term, usually diurnal, water deficit that is often self-remedying. Drought and daily water stress are similar only in that they both are conditions in which water loss from the plant exceeds water absorption.

The temporary wilting associated with daily water stress is due to more moisture being lost through the leaves than can be absorbed from the soil. Even though the plant is wilted, the soil still has moisture in it. The plants that have a tendency to wilt during hot, sunny days generally have thin leaves composed of thin-walled cells. These plants tend to be drought sensitive as well. Examples are impatiens and many vegetables, such as squash and tomatoes. Drought-resilient plants can modulate evaporative moisture loss much better than can plants that suffer from daily wilting.

portrays the relative dryness of an area by numerical value ratings from - 6 to +6. Figures with minus values represent dryness and positive numbers indicate excess moisture. The index best displays conditions of long-term drought; it isn't as reliable in depicting short-term events or assessing areas in which moisture is seasonally locked in snowpacks, such as the western mountains.

Soon after creating the PDSI, Palmer went on to devise the Crop Moisture Index (CMI). This system addressed the shortcomings of the PDSI. The CMI uses the same scale as the PDSI and is based on the normal moisture values for each area. The CMI is so responsive, however, that it can reflect weekly changes in soil moisture. This makes it a valuable tool for people in all areas of the United States.

If a good thing can come from a drought, it may be a renewed appreciation for water and its inherent and continual value. We all need water to live, and when water becomes less abundant, water conservation assumes a fresh immediacy. One way to conserve water is to know how much falls on your garden, as opposed to the amount measured at the international airport where the nearest weather station is located, and to know how moisture is actually in the soil so that you know exactly how much to supply. This knowledge can be gained by using two simple devices: a rain gauge and a soil moisture meter (see page 161).

The Drought of the Century

For 7 years in the 1930s, over two thirds of the United States was in the grip of the worst drought of the 20th century. On the PDSI, a rating of −4 signifies extreme drought. In 1934, values estimated to have equaled −6 extended from California to New York and from North Dakota to Texas. In portions of the Great Plains and the Southwest, years of damaging farming practices had stripped the land of its natural plant cover and exposed the topsoil to brutal wind erosion. In one area, covering Colorado, New Mexico, Texas, Oklahoma, and Kansas, the erosion was especially dire. Enormous dust storms, unlike anything ever seen in the country before, swirled over the plains to such an extent that the region was called the Dust Bowl. Storms threw dust so high in the sky that it didn't settle back to earth until it reached the Atlantic Coast.

As the drought dragged on, the desiccated topsoil blew against homes and barns in drifts like brown snow. Indoors, the fine gritty dust was inescapable. It found its way into cupboards, food boxes, and even the refrigerator. Outside, the dust was life threatening. Emergency hospitals were opened in Colorado, Kansas, and Texas to care for thousands of patients with ailments nearly unknown before. People died of silica poisoning from inhaling the dust. Respiratory infections were rampant, and a form of pneumonia called dust pneumonia became common. Yet perhaps the most horrific injuries took place on April 14, 1935, when a violent dust storm swept through Stratford, Texas. The dirty air became so thick with soil and so forcibly driven by the winds that many residents actually suffocated to death from the dust they inhaled.

The Dust Bowl years are most often seen as one massive drought extending over the better part of a decade. Its duration and depth make it the stuff of folklore, a climate-altering catastrophe. Yet the Dust Bowl wasn't caused by a single event, but by a series of closely spaced droughts interspersed with more normal weather. The first drought began in 1930 and continued into 1931. The second one didn't arrive until 1934. That event lessened in severity the following year, but then deepened into a third drought in 1936. The last event lasted from 1939 into 1940.

Just as the Dust Bowl wasn't the result of a single drought, the recovery to a normal climate was gradual, proceeding intermittently over many seasons, even beginning before the last drought started. In the spring of 1938, rainfall began to return to normal. By 1941, the droughts that created the Dust Bowl were finally over.

There have been other, more recent droughts, some that even rival those of the legendary Dust Bowl in intensity (such as events in the 1950s and 1980s). But these later events were made less severe by implementation of practical soil- and water-conservation methods. These days, there are even more ways to modify and combat periods of drought and help the garden and the landscape through troubled times.

The Disaster of Drought

Drought is not a spectacular weather event in the manner of a hurricane, a tornado, or a flood. It is menacingly slow and patient, wearing down the vitality of the landscape. Damage may go unnoticed until it is irreparable. Occasionally, a drought clears the way for a wildfire that takes advantage of the tinder-dry landscape and scorches the earth in a firestorm. In the years between 1993 and 2003, there were 10 droughts or drought-induced wildfires, which led to damages in excess of $1 billion each and together totaled $36.3 billion. Revisiting these recent events is sobering.

1993: A drought smothered the southeastern states during the summer, leaving 16 people dead and causing $1.1 billion in damage.

1993: Autumn drought and winds fanned flames into wildfires across southern California, killing four and causing $1.1 billion in damage.

1994: Drought across much of the western United States created ideal wildfire weather. Blazes ignited and burned over many states from summer through fall, resulting in $1.1 billion in damage.

1995: Severe drought devastated a large area of the southern Great Plains from fall 1995 through the summer of 1996. In Texas and Oklahoma, total damages across the affected area were estimated at $5 billion.

1998: A catastrophic drought during the summer crippled the South from Texas to the Atlantic Coast, claiming 200 lives and costing $9 billion in damage.

1999: Summer drought covered the eastern states with very dry, hot conditions. Over 500 people died, and there was $1 billion in damage.

2000: Drought and wind in spring and summer produced extensive wildfires, resulting in $2 billion in damage.

2000: The South was again subject to devastating drought and heat, with more than 100 deaths and damage totaling $4 billion.

2002: Drought and winds through spring and fall combined to spur wildfires over 11 western states. Over 7 million acres were burned, 21 people died, and damage totaled more than $2 billion.

2002: Extensive drought stretching from coast to coast and crossing 30 states lasted from spring through fall. Costs were estimated to be at least $10 billion.

The Uniqueness of Droughts

A thunderstorm in Oklahoma is like a thunderstorm in Indiana. A hurricane in Texas is like one in North Carolina. Most weather disasters have their individual fingerprints, but they all tend to be variations on a common theme — except droughts. Droughts are unique to the place they affect.

For example, California normally receives much less rainfall than does Florida, so if Florida received California's normal annual rainfall, Florida would be in a severe drought, whereas California is not.

To illustrate, imagine that both California and Florida are suffering through a drought rated at -2 on the Palmer Drought Severity Index. How much rainfall over 3 months is required to end both droughts? California would need about 3 inches of rain to end its drought, whereas Florida would require more than 18 inches — about six times as much. It takes less rain to end droughts in the western states than it does to end them east of the Mississippi River, and the Great Plains are between the two in terms of rainfall needed.

Designing the Garden for Drought

The flower and herb garden often has more plant diversity collected into one space than any other part of the home landscape. This variety provides some valuable tools for managing soil moisture in the garden.

When designing and planting, take a moment to research the native climate of the plants you are using. Then group plants first according to their geographic similarity, such as all the plants originating from the Mediterranean region. If you want to expand the group, include all plants from a Mediterranean-type climate, such as southern California.

This technique also groups plants by their similar moisture needs. For best results, grow them together in blocks. You'll find that sorting plants out this way creates some interesting and potentially very pleasing combinations. Using the above method and species and varieties found in many gardens, you would get plant groupings such as these:

Dry climate. Lavender, rosemary, coralbells, salvia

Intermediate climate. Daylily, lupine, penstemon, oenothera

Moist climate. Astilbe, filipendula, cardinal flower, impatiens

The Jug-or-Not Tree-Watering System

It would be nice to craft a garden of nothing but resilient plants that adapt to all sorts of conditions and weather. But that isn't what our gardens look like. Many of the plants that we choose to grow are picky. Sometimes, however, we are unaware that a plant we grow is finicky until it is in the ground and adversity, in the form of drought or other bad weather, appears. On page 156 is a list of trees that are popular landscape and garden plants that don't do well during the dry periods. They need irrigation when other plants don't, and they need to be monitored for water stress.

In addition to these drought-sensitive trees, many other trees when newly transplanted need 4 or more gallons (15 liters) of water per week to establish good root systems. Traditional watering methods can produce runoff or otherwise be wasteful of water resources, which need to be conserved at all times and especially during droughts. Here is an inexpensive homemade system that uses recyclable materials to create a watering device. You will be able to deliver precise amounts of water to a tree, with no runoff and almost no surface evaporation.

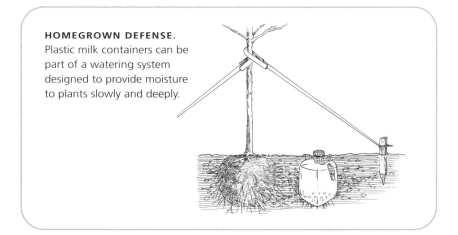

HOMEGROWN DEFENSE. Plastic milk containers can be part of a watering system designed to provide moisture to plants slowly and deeply.

Drought-Sensitive Trees

Arborvitae (*Thuja* spp.)

Fir (*Abies* spp.)

Flowering dogwood *(Cornus florida)*

Hemlock *(Tsuga canadensis)*

Japanese maple *(Acer palmatum)*

Red maple *(Acer rubrum)*

Sugar maple *(Acer saccharum)*

Sweet birch *(Betula lenta)*

Yellow birch *(Betula alleghaniensis)*

To create the system, you'll need a plastic 1-gallon milk container (opaque white plastic containers are more durable than the more common translucent types), a rubber band, and an empty onion bag.

Thoroughly wash out the milk container to remove all food residue. If the container has a slip-off plastic label, remove it and discard. Poke four pencil-sized holes in the bottom of the container.

Dig a hole between the tree stem and one of the stakes you've installed for the guy wire that supports the tree. Be sure the hole does not damage the root-ball of the tree. Level the bottom of the hole and set the container in the hole. The opening of the container should be a fraction of an inch higher than the surrounding soil. Cut out a swatch from the onion bag and fasten it over the opening with a rubber band to keep out bugs and debris.

To use, fill the container with water, refilling as often as necessary to keep a steady supply of water flowing. Smaller trees need about 4 gallons (15 liters) a week; larger ones [over 4 inches (10 cm) in diameter] require up to 8 gallons (30 liters) a week. Space the watering schedule over the week so that the plant receives moisture as evenly and steadily as possible.

Drought and the Vegetable Garden

While it's possible to list plenty of drought-resilient trees, flowers, and shrubs, there are no such lists for vegetables. This isn't to say that some vegetable plants can't survive drought. Yet when drought touches vegetables, it removes the sweetness, tenderness, and juiciness and replaces these virtues with bitterness, toughness, and a mealy texture. So with vegetables, surviving a drought isn't the goal. For best quality, the vegetables must sail through the ordeal as if nothing out of the ordinary has happened. Under all but the worst conditions, you can still supply vegetables with the moisture they need by using tools that allow more precise watering and by conserving the soil moisture for as long as possible.

Preventive Strategies: Before Sowing and Planting

Prepare your growing beds with an eye to maximum growth and water conservation before sowing and planting. The key here is to construct wide raised beds. This approach not only uses water resources most efficiently, but it also maximizes the soil volume that plant roots can use. This results in plants with deeper roots and more vigorous growth. Raised beds can be constructed from hard materials, such as planking and timbers, or they can have no sides at all, a design in which each bed is a wide mound of soil that can be sculpted with a shovel or hoe in a few minutes. (See pages 127–128 for more details.)

Compost Really Helps!

Finished compost is a powerful drought-fighting tool. When you add it to your garden beds, it:

• Increases soil porosity

• Increases the amount of moisture the soil can hold (that is, it increases field capacity)

• Improves soil drainage (and well-drained soil reduces the chances of destructive salt buildup, to which soil is especially vulnerable during periods of drought)

The wide raised bed creates the needed soil volume, but to work well it should be filled with quality soil that will hoard moisture. Do this by loosening the ground to a depth of up to 2 feet (0.6 m), if possible) with a broadfork or garden fork. Follow by incorporating finished compost into the garden soil.

Planting Strategies

Jethro Tull was an Englishman who decided that a little more order and structure would improve farming. Essentially, from the creation of agriculture until the 1600s, when Tull lived, crops were sown by broadcast seeding, which was basically tossing seed out on the ground as if feeding chickens. Tull believed that each plant should be the proper distance apart from its neighbor so that all the plants could grow their best and the entire field would yield better and more uniformly. It is from his influence that today's vegetable seed packets have information on how to grow in straight rows. Although Jethro Tull's straight rows work well, planting in straight rows wastes garden space and soil moisture, too. Another, better way to grow vegetables involves sowing staggered rows and practicing interspecies planting.

Staggered rows. Planting a raised bed in a staggered pattern can provide the proper growing distance between plants and at the same time

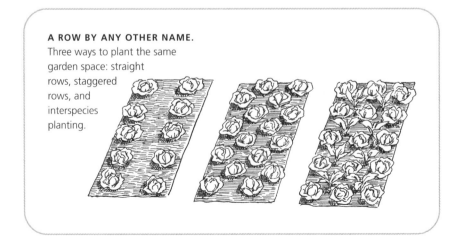

A ROW BY ANY OTHER NAME. Three ways to plant the same garden space: straight rows, staggered rows, and interspecies planting.

increases the number of plants within that space. You can have an entire bed or bed section planted in the same vegetable, or model the raised bed after a windbreak, with shorter plants on the sides and slightly taller plants in the center.

Interspecies planting. Planting different plants in the same bed helps conserve soil moisture. Many plants have roots that grow at different depths, so mixing plants allows a more even distribution of roots in the soil. This practice leads to a more even utilization of soil moisture. For example, plants with very deep roots, such as carrots and potatoes, can be planted near crops with more shallow roots, such as beans and lettuce.

Mulch Means More

Drought means less rain and more sun. If there is moisture in the soil, the additional sunshine can mean bumper crops, especially of longer-season vegetables, such as beefsteak tomatoes. A layer of mulch over the growing bed drastically reduces evaporation of moisture from the soil.

In vegetable gardens, it has become fashionable to use colored plastic mulches or reflective mulches, especially beneath tomatoes, to hasten maturity and control pests. The trouble with plastic mulch of any color is that it doesn't allow the rain (which will eventually come) to soak into the ground and recharge soil moisture. During a drought, that feature is a major drawback.

Your best bet is to use organic mulches, such as cocoa and buckwheat hulls. These provide an effective evaporation barrier, allow rainfall to easily percolate into the soil, and enrich the soil as they slowly decompose.

Watering Tools of the Trade

Drought doesn't just rob the soil of water. The water that remains underground can become tainted with salts and other impurities as the drought deepens. That makes watering the garden and all the assorted plants of the landscape a task that requires both efficiency and conservation. Years ago, watering equipment was nothing more sophisticated than a watering can or a hose with a sprinkler. Today, many tools are available to help the gardener send water directly to where it is required, in the amounts that are needed:

Soaker hoses. These hoses are made of a single layer of rubber that allows water to sweat through the casing and into the soil. They can be laid on the surface of the growing bed or set in a shallow trench and covered with an organic mulch. Use the soaker hose in conjunction with a soil moisture meter (see next page) to be sure that the moisture is of the proper amount and delivered just to the root zone.

Drip irrigation. These systems consist of thin, impermeable tubes with evenly spaced small openings that enable water to dribble out, delivering water to the root zones of individual plants rather than to the growing bed in general. The tubes are often covered with mulch to keep the water in the tubes cooler and to reduce evaporation as the water is applied.

WHAT A DRIP. Drip irrigation is an excellent way to conserve water. You irrigate only the plants you want to grow, letting the weeds fend for themselves.

Timers. Timers allow the garden to be watered when it should be, not when your schedule permits. They range from uncomplicated devices that simply turn the water on and off for a certain period of time to fancy touch-pad types that can be programmed days in advance.

Soil moisture meters. These easy-to-use tools can make a huge difference in keeping the garden well watered while conserving water. The meter consists of a probe topped with a needle gauge that swings from left (dry) to center (just right) to right (too wet).

Soil needles. These probes attach to a hose and inject water below the soil surface. They are most often used to water trees and shrubs. To use a soil needle, penetrate the ground at an angle so that the probe doesn't extend deeper than 8 inches (20 cm). (Even with large trees, most of the roots are found in the top 8 inches of soil.) Water for about 5 minutes at each location within a circle formed by the tree's drip line.

Rain gauge. Perhaps the simplest watering tool in the garden, a rain gauge is just a graduated container to measure rainfall. The gardener uses it to determine how much supplementary water is needed for plants by subtracting the amount provided by rain.

Tough Turf: Lawns and Drought

When people talk about gardening, the topic of lawns usually doesn't come up. Many people don't view their lawn as a garden. But in reality, your lawn is probably the biggest garden you have — and a very thirsty one at that.

A lawn is composed of millions of individual grass plants, each one with leaves and roots in need of nutrients and water. Water makes up about 90 percent of the weight of every grass plant (though not all turf species are equal when it comes to hanging on to the limited amount of water provided them in dry times). Ideally, a drought-resilient turfgrass looks good even when conditions are hot and dry. This ability to maintain "grace under pressure" is a sign that the grass type is physiologically prepared for drought.

Drought-Resilient Lawn Grasses

Bahia grass

Bermuda grass

Blue grama grass

Buffalo grass

Kentucky bluegrass

(moderately resilient)

Tall fescue

Western wheatgrass

Zoysia grass

Strategies for Helping Your Lawn During Droughts

Water sparingly but deeply. One of the easiest ways to waste water is to let it evaporate. Frequent, shallow watering soaks the top of the plant but doesn't allow moisture to seep into the soil, where it is needed. Remember that the water a plant needs comes from the soil; thus, water the soil and not the plant. Be sure the moisture extends deep into the ground, so that deeply rooted species, such as tall fescue, can use it.

Reduce evaporation. Water during times when the potential for evaporation is lowest. This is usually after dark and at dawn, when the wind is calm, and on cloudy days.

Mow tall and less often. Raising the mower deck to 2 to 3 inches (5–8 cm) helps cool the soil and roots of the grass and reduces evaporation. It also strengthens grass plants.

Hold off on fertilizing. It isn't a good idea to add more salts to dry soils, which is what happens when fertilizer is added to a drought-stressed lawn. In addition, a nitrogen application can produce soft growth that requires more water to stay green and scorches easily if it doesn't get it.

Reduce the size of your lawn. The typical lawn uses more water, whether natural or supplemental, than any other part of the landscape. Add low-maintenance gardens or convert a part of the lawn into a lawn alternative, such as low native grasses, wildflowers, or ground covers.

Change is good. Replace drought-sensitive grasses with drought-resilient ones. This can be done all at once by removing one grass and replacing it with another, or, in some cases, by overseeding.

Drought-Resilient Plants

Plants native to arid climates are by necessity tolerant of chronic drought. They are superbly adapted to their desiccating environment. For example, a barrel cactus can survive for months and months in soil that seems as dry as dust. Its secret: It retains a nearly normal supply of moisture in its tissues. Plants adapted to perennially dry conditions are called *xeriphytes*. Xeriphytes range from the cacti of the southwestern deserts to sedums that happily grow in dry sandy soil in moist, temperate climates.

Dressed for Drought: What Well-Prepared Plants Look Like

In spite of their variety, tough, drought-resistant plants have many traits in common, including where they originated and grow naturally, and ingenious ways of reducing moisture loss and thus the negative effects of droughts. Some of these are easily identified and can provide the gardener with a good idea of whether a plant has drought-resilient properties.

Place of origin. Many drought-resilient plants are indigenous to regions with little rainfall. For example, the total average precipitation for much of northeastern North America is about 40 inches (102 cm) per year; in drought years it may fall to 30 inches (76 cm) or less, causing water stress in many native species. Native to the Rocky Mountains, where annual precipitation is about 25 inches (63.5 cm), Colorado blue spruce *(Picea pungens)* grows well in the wetter northeastern climate, yet it also prospers in the western mountains' drier climate. So when the Northeast experiences drought, conditions actually become more like the species' native environment, to which it is naturally adapted.

Soil type. Some plants located in regions with adequate rainfall may nevertheless endure near constant drought conditions because of the soil they are in. Many northeastern native junipers, such as eastern red cedar *(Juniperus virginiana)* and common juniper *(J. communis)*, receive abundant rainfall but often grow in sandy, poor soils that are almost constantly dry. These and similar species have developed drought resilience and can thrive in dry or moist climates.

Gray foliage. The gray foliage of some plants, such as dusty miller, reflects sunlight, which keeps the leaves cooler and reduces transpiration.

Leaf hairs. Leaf hairs serve multiple purposes, including reflecting sunlight (cooling the leaf), blocking sunlight (cooling the leaf), and increasing the humidity at the leaf surface (reducing the transpiration rate).

Glossy or shiny leaves. No matter their shape, from big, serrated leaves like those of holly to tiny cotoneaster leaves, all are polished to a gloss with waxes that not only reflect sunlight but also reduce transpiration.

Plump, juicy leaves. Succulent foliage (as in sedum) serves as a storage area for moisture that can be drawn on when other sources become low.

Small leaves. Small leaves, whether round (cotoneaster) or needle-shaped (rosemary), conserve moisture by limiting the area that can be heated by solar radiation and reducing the evaporative effects of wind.

Drought Tolerance by Region

The list of garden plants with drought tolerance is lengthy and contradictory. Even the definition of the term *drought tolerance* remains a matter of debate among experts. To accommodate a wide range of possibilities, the lists that follow on pages 165–168 are divided into three major regions: the area west of the prairies, the area east of the prairies, and peninsular Florida.

Most of the region west of the prairies has normal annual precipitation levels that would constitute drought conditions farther east. Thus, plants in this region need to tolerate generally drier conditions all the time and are less likely to encounter sustained periods of wet soils. The reverse is true through most of the region east of the prairies, which host a moist environment most of the time. Drought-resilient plants here need to endure dry soil and minimal, if any, supplementary water during droughts. Yet they also thrive in soils of normal moisture. Many plants labeled "drought resilient" in the East would not be considered drought resilient in the West, and vice versa.

Finally, the uniqueness of Florida's environment merits its own list. This region manages to combine heavy rain with drought-prone soils.

Drought-Tolerant Plants for All Regions

From the Prairies East

Trees

Bur oak (Quercus macrocarpa)

Eastern red cedar (Juniperus virginiana)

Honey locust (Gleditsia triacanthos)

Jack pine (Pinus banksiana)

Kentucky coffee tree (Gymnocladus dioica)

Live oak (Quercus virginiana)

Pin oak (Quercus palustris)

Russian olive (Elaeagnus angustifolia)

Shumard oak (Quercus shumardii)

White oak (Quercus alba)

Shrubs and Small Trees

Amur maple (Acer ginnala)

Bayberry (Myrica spp.)

Cotoneaster (Cotoneaster spp.)

Dry-land blueberry (Vaccinium pallidum)

Flowering quince (Chaenomeles spp.)

Japanese barberry (Berberis thunbergii)

Juniper (Juniperus spp.)

Lead plant (Amorpha canescens)

Nine-bark (Physocarpus spp.)

Pignut hickory (Carya glabra)

Potentilla (Potentilla spp.)

Privet (Ligustrum spp.)

Rugosa rose (Rosa rugosa)

Siberian pea shrub (Caragana arborescens)

Staghorn sumac (Rhus typhina)

Sweet fern (Comptonia peregrina)

Virginia rose (Rosa virginiana)

Washington hawthorn (Crataegus phaenopyrum)

Perennials, Annuals, and Ground Covers

Anacyclus (Anacyclus depressus)

Artemisia (Artemisia spp.)

Barren strawberry (Waldsteinia ternata)

Bearberry (Arctostaphylos uva-ursi)

Black-eyed Susan (Rudbeckia spp.)

Blanket flower (Gaillardia spp.)

Blue lyme grass (Leymus racemosus 'Glauca')

Blue oat grass (Helictotrichon sempervirens)

Butterflyweed (Asclepias tuberosa)

California poppy (Eschscholtzia californica)

Carpet bugle (Ajuga reptans)

Coreopsis (Coreopsis spp.)

Cosmos (Cosmos bipinnatus)

Echinacea (Echinacea spp.)

False indigo (Baptisia australis)

Gayfeather (Liatris spp.)

Globe amaranth (Gomphrena globosa)

Hen-and-chicks (Sempervivum spp.)

Hollyhock (Alcea rosea)

Lamb's ears (Stachys spp.)

Lavender (Lavandula spp.)

Lavender cotton (Santolina spp.)

Mexican sunflower (Tithonia rotundifolia)

Morning glory (Ipomoea spp.)

Musk mallow (Malva moschata)

Oregano (Originum spp.)

Penstemon (Penstemon spp.)

Plume grass (Erianthis ravenae)

Prairie coneflower (Ratibida columnifera)

Prickly pear (Opuntia spp.)

Drought-Tolerant Plants (continued)

Pussytoes (*Antennaria* spp.)

Rock rose *(Portulaca grandiflora)*

Sage (*Salvia* spp.)

Sea holly (*Eryngium* spp.)

Snow-in-summer *(Cerastium tomentosum)*

Spurge (*Euphorbia* spp.)

Stonecress (*Aethionema* spp.)

Stonecrop (*Sedum* spp.)

Strawflower *(Helichrysum bracteatum)*

Sundrop (*Oenothera* spp.)

Sun rose *(Helianthemum nummularium)*

Thrift (*Armeria* spp.)

Thyme (*Thymus* spp.)

Verbascum *(Verbascum thapsus)*

Yarrow (*Achillea* spp.)

Yucca (*Yucca* spp.)

Zinnia (*Zinnia* spp.)

From the Prairies West

Gardens in climates with low annual rainfall and frequent water restrictions require plants that are adapted to such conditions. The plants that follow are a mix of xeriphytes and mesophytes (plants that require moderate moisture) that perform well in the complex mix of arid, semiarid, coastal, montane, and high plains environments found throughout most of western North America.

Trees

Afghanistan pine *(Pinus eldarica)*

African sumac *(Rhus lancea)*

Aleppo pine *(Pinus halepensis)*

Blue Atlas cedar (*Cedrus atlantica* 'Glauca')

Bottle tree *(Brachychiton populneus)*

Brazilian pepper *(Schinus terebinthifolius)*

Brisbane box *(Tristania conferta)*

California pepper *(Schinus molle)*

Carob *(Ceratonia siliqua)*

Catalina cherry *(Prunus lyonii)*

Chinese pistachio *(Pistacia chinensis)*

Flaxleaf paperbark *(Melaleuca linariifolia)*

Giant dracaena *(Cordyline australis)*

Ginkgo *(Ginkgo biloba)*

Golden-rain tree *(Koelreuteria paniculata)*

Hybrid locust (*Robinia* x *ambigua* 'Idahoensis')

Jacaranda *(Jacaranda mimosifolia)*

Jerusalem thorn *(Parkinsonia aculeata)*

Laurel *(Laurus nobilis)*

Mesquite *(Prosopis glandulosa)*

Olive *(Olea europaea)*

Pinyon pine *(Pinus edulis)*

Red ironbark *(Eucalyptus sideroxylon)*

Russian olive *(Elaeagnus angustifolia)*

Silk tree (*Albizia julibrissin* 'Rosea')

Shrubs

Chitalpa (*Chitalpa* x hybrids)

Chuparosa *(Justicia californica)*

Compact myrtle (*Myrtus communis* 'Compacta')

Crimson spot *(Cistus ladanifer)*

Desert olive *(Forestiera neomexicana)*

English lavender *(Lavandula angustifolia)*

Flannel bush (*Fremontodendron* x 'California Glory')

Japanese pittosporum (*Pittosporum tobira* 'Variegata')

Lantana *(Lantana camara)*

Mexican buckeye *(Ungnadia speciosa)*

Mountain mahogany *(Cercocarpus ledifolius)*

Purple hop bush (*Dodonaea viscosa* 'Purpurea')

Sandankwa viburnum *(Viburnum suspensum)*

Spanish lavender *(Lavandula stoechas)*

Staghorn sumac *(Rhus typhina)*

Texas ranger *(Leucophyllum frutescens)*

Wormwood senna *(Cassia artemisioides)*

Yeddo *(Rhaphiolepis umbellata)*

Perennials

Achillea (*Achillea* x 'Coronation Gold')

Asparagus fern (*Asparagus densiflorus* 'Sprengeri')

Autumn Joy sedum (*Sedum* x 'Autumn Joy')

Blackfoot daisy *(Melampodium leucanthum)*

Bunny ears *(Opuntia microdasys)*

California fuchsia *(Zauschneria californica)*

Candytuft *(Iberis sempervirens)*

Coralbells *(Heuchera sanguinea)*

Daylily (*Hemerocallis* spp.)

Desert spoon *(Dasylirion wheeleri)*

Dusty miller *(Senecio cineraria)*

Eaton's penstemon *(Penstemon eatonii)*

Lamb's ears *(Stachys byzantina)*

Missouri primrose *(Oenothera missouriensis)*

Octopus agave *(Agave vilmoriniana)*

Prickly pear *(Opuntia fiscusindica)*

Red yucca *(Hesperaloe parviflora)*

Red-hot poker *(Kniphofia uvaria)*

Sulfur flower *(Eriogonum umbellatum)*

Threadleaf coreopsis (*Coreopsis verticillata* 'Moonbeam')

Victoria Regina *(Agave victoriae-reginae)*

Yucca *(Yucca elata, Y. whipplei)*

Florida

Florida poses gardening challenges like no other region of the United States. Much of the peninsula has subtropical or tropical temperatures, humidity, and precipitation, but the ground and bedrock are so porous that the upper levels of the soil can be drought-dry an hour or so after an afternoon downpour. The result is that Florida is in a constant state of green drought: That is, there's usually plenty of rain, but frequently inadequate soil moisture. Drought-resilient plants down here must be able to endure soaking rains and dry soils at the same time.

Trees

Bald cypress *(Taxodium distichum)*

Beauty berry *(Callicarpa americana)*

Drought-Tolerant Plants (continued)

Blue Atlas cedar *(Cedra atlantica glauca)*

Bottlebrush *(Callistemon* spp.)

Bur oak *(Quercus macrocarpa)*

Cherry laurel *(Prunus caroliniana)*

Cotoneaster *(Cotoneaster* spp.)

Crape myrtle *(Lagerstromia indica)*

Cypress *(Cupressus* spp.)

Flowering quince *(Chaenomeles* spp.)

Holly oak *(Quercus ilex)*

Honey locust *(Gleditsia triacanthos)*

Jacaranda *(Jacaranda mimosifolia)*

Japanese black pine *(Pinus thunbergiana)*

Laurel *(Laurus nobilis)*

Laurel oak *(Quercus luarifolia)*

Live oak *(Quercus virginiana)*

Loquat *(Eriobottya japonica)*

Oleander *(Nerium oleander)*

Pignut hickory *(Carya glabra)*

Pin oak *(Quercus palustris)*

Rugosa rose *(Rosa rugosa)*

Sand pine *(Pinus elliottii)*

Shumard oak *(Quercus shumardii)*

Southern magnolia *(Magnolia grandiflora)*

Southern red cedar *(Juniperus silicifolia)*

Sweet fern *(Comptonia peregrina)*

Tamarisk *(Tamarix* spp.)

Turkey oak *(Quercus laevis)*

Wax myrtle *(Myrica cerifera)*

Zelkova *(Zelkova serrata)*

Palms

Cabbage palm *(Sabal palmetto)*

California fan palm *(Washingtonia filifera)*

Queen palm *(Arecastrum romanzoffianum)*

Sago palm *(Cycas revoluta)*

Saw palmetto *(Serenoa repens)*

Washington palm *(Washingtonia robusta)*

Perennials and Vines

Aloe *(Aloe* spp.)

Artemisia *(Artemisia* spp.)

Bougainvillea *(Bougainvillea* spp.)

Carolina yellow jasmine *(Gelsemium sempervirens)*

Century plant *(Agave americana)*

Creeping fig *(Ficus pumila)*

English lavender *(Lavandula angustifolia)*

Lantana *(Lantana* spp.)

Lead plant *(Amorpha canescens)*

Morning glory *(Ipomea* spp.)

Prickly pear *(Opuntia* spp.)

Rosemary *(Rosmarinus officinalis)*

Sea oats *(Uniola paniculata)*

Star jasmine *(Trachelospermum jasminoides)*

Trumpet creeper *(Campsis radicans)*

Virginia creeper *(Parthenocissus quinquefolia)*

Wintercreeper *(Euonymus fortunei)*

Yucca *(Yucca* spp.)

Beauty Beats the Beast

Drought-Resilient Roses. Few plants can match the beauty of a rose in fullbloom. Roses as a group aren't known for their ability to muscle their way through drought and other challenging weather conditions. Yet some species and varieties have managed to merge the splendor for which roses are famous with the ability to endure dry periods. It's not easy being tough and beautiful, but these roses manage to pull it off.

Rugosa roses. The original species of this remarkable group of plants, *Rosa rugosa,* is indigenous to eastern Asia, where it endures cold to −50°F (−46°C), salt spray and salty soils from coastal environments, and drought from the dry, sandy soils. The rugosa hybrids below are drought resilient and have retained their ancestor's resilience to salt and cold.

'Therese Bugnet': A strong-growing, upright shrub rose reaching 6 feet (1.8 m) tall. The double, ruffled blossoms are pink and satisfactorily fragrant.

'Jens Munk': A bushy shrub rose growing to about 5 feet (1.5 m) tall. The semi-double, soft pink blossoms are strongly fragrant, with a spicy rugosa perfume.

'Hansa': One of the most drought-resilient choices, it actually thrives in dry, sandy soil. Plants are thickly branched and very thorny and reach over 6 feet (1.8 m) tall. The double blossoms are magenta-red, with a strong fragrance.

Species roses. These are wild roses that are so versatile and beautiful, they need no improvement from breeders to find a prominent place in the garden. Species roses as a group hail from diverse habitats, ranging from swamp to sand dune. The species that follow have shown they can endure drought while maintaining an attractive appearance.

Prairie rose *(Rosa setigera):* Prairie rose is native to the dry grasslands that are home to other drought-resilient favorites, such as black-eyed Susan and coneflower. The plants are relaxed and sprawling, reaching 4 feet (1.2 m) tall and much wider. Flowers are single, dark rose-red, and richly fragrant.

Why Not Everywhere?

The adaptations required for a plant to thrive in the southwestern desert, an area of perpetual drought, are such that the plant can't survive in most other environments. You don't find barrel cacti, century plants, or other desert plants in a perennial border in Pennsylvania, a vegetable garden in Indiana, or a rose garden in Georgia. Why? Because plants in most regions of North America have to contend with not only transient drought but also floods, snow, cold, and other extreme weather events. The plants in these regions need to be able to endure all of the weather factors that make up that area's climate, not just drought and heat.

This reality produces plants in every climate type across the continent with resilience to drought and to many other, sometimes opposing, conditions. The most practical drought-resilient plants come from these conditions because when a drought is over — and it will eventually be over — these same plants that endured the dry times must thrive in the normal, much wetter, conditions.

Sierra Nevada rose *(Rosa woodsii* var. *fendleri):* Native to British Columbia all the way south to western Texas, this plant's alternate name is mountain rose. A rambling, shrubby rose, it grows to 5 feet (1.5 m) high and sports single red blossoms. It thrives in dry conditions.

Wingthorn rose *(Rosa sericea pteracantha):* The inch-long thorns of this plant are actually more spectacular than its small, whitish yellow flowers. The plants make an excellent barrier hedge.

Scotch rose *(Rosa spinosissima):* Hailing from the sandy coastal banks of Scotland, this stalwart grows to 3 feet tall (0.9 m), with ferny foliage and single, pale yellow blossoms.

Drought-Resilient Windbreaks

Colorado spruce *(Picea pungens)*

Potentilla *(Potentilla fruticosa)*

Rugosa rose *(Rosa rugosa)*

Russian olive *(Elaeagnus angustifolia)*

Scotch pine *(Pinus sylvestris)*

Siberian pea shrub *(Caragana arborescens)*

One Genus, Very Different Genes

Often, different species of the same genus do not have similar drought resilience. Even though two plants of different species may look alike, their ability to fend off dry conditions may differ completely.

For example, there are two species of larch in North America. A third species, Siberian larch, is also a popular landscape tree here. All three species look similar, with an attractive conical shape and soft green deciduous needles that turn golden bronze in fall. The major difference among the trees is in their respective ability to endure drought. Eastern larch *(Larix laricina)* is native to bogs and swamps; it is well adapted to wet places but not to dry ones. In contrast, western larch *(L. occidentalis)* is a tree native to much drier environments and is drought resilient. And Siberian larch *(L. siberica)* comes from a land of extreme cold and persistent drought and is even more reliably drought resilient than the western larch. When selecting a plant for drought tolerance, be sure to probe beyond the attributes of the genus into the qualities of species, and even varieties, to find the most drought-resilient one.

The Challenges of Drought

Growing in dry soils with little relief from irrigation or rainfall weakens plants and makes them susceptible to a number of opportunistic pests and diseases. Many trees produce substances called oleoresins, which, among other things, help repel harmful insects. Trees stressed by dry conditions produce less oleresin than normal and subsequently suffer a greater degree of infestation from insects (such as bronze birch borer and pine bark beetle). Drought also produces nonparasitic disorders that affect a diverse group of plants.

Black End

Description: Black end indicates extended drought injury to a tree.

Symptoms: Black end disease appears on walnuts as black areas on the blossom end of the nuts. Inside, the nutmeat has become shriveled and inedible.

Remedies: The nut harvest, unfortunately, is lost by the time this disease is evident.

Strategies: In future dry spells, try to keep the tree irrigated, especially during that critical period when nuts are developing.

Blindness

Description: Dry soil conditions in winter and spring can damage the roots of spring-flowering bulbs.

Symptoms: Plants fail to blossom.

Gardening Shouldn't Be Bore-ing

When choosing birches for an area prone to drought, consider species and varieties that are not only drought resilient but also resistant to the number one pest of birches: the dreaded bronze birch borer. The following birch (*Betula*) species are resistant:

River birch (*Betula nigra*)

Heritage birch (*B. nigra* 'Heritage')

Paper birch (*B. papyriferya* 'Varen')

Remedies: Dig up the bulbs. If they are clearly shriveled, they are not viable and should be discarded.

Strategies: Incorporate plenty of compost into the planting bed to help the ground retain its critical moisture and spread a light mulch for the same reason.

Blossom-End Rot

Description: This disease of tomatoes, peppers, squash, and melons is caused by a calcium deficiency in the fruit of the affected plant. As plants and fruit grow, the need for calcium, a mineral necessary for proper cell formation and growth, skyrockets. If the demand for calcium outpaces the supply, blossom-end rot results. This means that the disease can affect a garden in which there is not only *adequate* calcium in the soil, but adequate *available* calcium in the soil as well. However, the calcium that is in the soil can't get to the fruit because of an imbalance in soil moisture. During drought conditions limited to the calcium in the plant concentrates more in the leaves than in the fruit, resulting in a calcium deficiency that is limited to the fruit, the plant and soil both having normal calcium levels. That is one reason why normal and consistent moisture levels are so important.

Symptoms: A circular spot appears at the blossom end (bottom) of the developing fruit. This spot grows in size and the tissues within it collapse into a moist, mushy mess.

Remedies: None of value. Calcium sprays seem to have little positive effect.

Strategies: Keep soil moisture at near normal levels at all times by watering regularly and using mulches to reduce evaporation. Watch the weather during the growing season. If a period of wet weather is followed by dry, avoid letting the soil become droughty, as this is the time the disease most often appears. Before the growing season, test the soil for mineral deficiencies. Use lime or gypsum to correct calcium deficits and maintain pH of soil at 6.5–6.7.

Fire

THE WEATHER HAS BEEN CLEAR AND DRY FOR WEEKS. Bright sun glimmers on the Pacific surf as music bounces from boom boxes on the beach. Inland, the busy drone of cars and trucks is as constant as the view of the dusky brown mountains off to the east. It is a normal summer day in busy Los Angeles and its environs. But hundreds of miles away, two huge weather systems are drifting toward each other. A high-pressure dome with clockwise-turning winds is settling over the Rocky Mountains. To the south, a whirlpool of low pressure with counterclockwise winds tracks into the southwestern desert. As the systems close in on each other, the pressure gradient between them compels the atmosphere to form and flow into currents of wind that head toward California.

The Santa Anas are a form of wind called a *foehn,* a German word for a warm dry wind that blows down the slopes of mountains. (It originally referred only to a west wind, but now all warm mountain winds are included.) The winds sweep up the slopes of a mountain, then down the other side. On the trip upslope, the air cools and much of the moisture it holds condenses and falls out as precipitation. As the winds crest the ridges and descend, a remarkable transformation takes place. The rapidly descending air dries out and warms as it rolls down the mountain, reaching speeds of up to 70 to 80 miles per hour. The now dry, hot air floods the valleys and canyons.

The Santa Ana wind blows at a steady 35 miles per hour for 3 days, day and night for 72 hours. Plants already suffering from drought are dried to tinder. Bark beetles have killed many trees in the nearby forests, and the dead trees stand like torches awaiting a match. At the edge of a canyon where many homes are tucked into the hills, an illegal barbecue ignites a bit of scrub. In minutes, a trace of smoke leaves a smudge against the sky, and the sound of distant sirens hangs in the air.

It takes only minutes for the canyon to become a furnace of wildfire. The chaparral pops with sparks as the flames lick the slopes and climb up the canyon walls and along the roads. The homes near the canyon have been beautifully landscaped with trees, shrubs, and gardens. Residents hastily retreat in their cars as fire equipment arrives, trying to negotiate the narrow roads. The Santa Ana wind breathes hot life into the fire, and clouds of smoke swirl up from flames as the blaze reaches the first house. As acrid smoke sweeps across the lawn, crackling sparks loft into the air. The wind whips the flames, and temperatures inside the inferno rapidly climb, reaching well over 1,000°F.

The fire destroys four homes in the neighborhood, yet in the middle of the blackened mess, another house is essentially unscathed. The yard is charred in spots and some of the shrubs and trees look like they've had a very bad day, but the house is still there. The important difference between the homes that were lost and the one that was spared was the landscaping. A type of planting known as defensible space landscaping (see page 180) produces a garden and yard that defends a house by moderating the effects of an encroaching fire whether or not someone is there to fight the flames.

Fire has always been somewhat mysterious to humans. It can seem alive at times, and always behaves unpredictably, a characteristic that has become an increasing threat to homeowners who live in areas prone to wildfires. By landscaping with foresight and ingenuity, however, you can create gardens and landscapes that bring you joy as a gardener but which simultaneously, if need be, slow down and moderate the chemical reactions caused by fire.

The Awesomeness of Fire

Hurricanes are given people's names because sometimes they seem to act as if they can think. Fires are named after the place where they are thought to start, like "the Boulder Canyon Fire." Although many different kinds of weather can menace your landscape, it is fire that acts most like a living thing. It is not just unpredictable; it can seem at times calculating and even predatory. These are qualities of fire itself, but when it joins other forces of nature, such as wind and drought, it actually becomes a creator of weather, the firestorm. To withstand fire, the garden and landscape must be designed not just to be resilient, but also to use that resilience to protect house and family.

How Fire Works

Fire is a very fast and enduring chain reaction that releases heat and light. But how does that reaction happen? Traditionally, the elements of fire have been reduced to three items: fuel, heat, and air. To burn, or even to begin to burn, a fire needs all three in good supply. If any of these things is removed or substantially reduced, the fire goes out.

Fuel. The fuel for fire can be a solid, a liquid, or a gas. But no fuel can burn until it is transformed into a vapor. This may sound strange if you gaze into the fireplace and watch flames consume your firewood; the wood looks like a solid rather than a gas. But in reality, that bit of firewood is simultaneously a solid and a gas. The heat of the fire volatilizes flammable compounds in the wood. It is these vapors that burn, leaving behind the ash (which does not contain flammable materials). Removing fuel from a fire starves the fire and extinguishes it.

Heat. Heat is needed to change fuel into a state that can burn. If heat is reduced, fuel cannot burn. Adding water reduces the fire by cooling the fuel to the point where vaporization cannot take place. Removing heat from a fire therefore removes fuel from the fire and extinguishes it.

Air or oxygen. Approximately 20 percent of the air we breathe is oxygen. Fire uses oxygen as a constituent of the chemical chain reaction that releases heat and light. Because the fire uses up oxygen as it burns, the oxygen must be replaced. Without air, the fire stops. How much air does a fire need? When the oxygen content of the air falls below about 15 percent, the fire begins to extinguish itself. This is why fire safety guidelines recommend that when a blaze threatens your home, keep doors and windows closed — this reduces the inflow of oxygen-rich air. Restricting the air to the fire limits and may actually extinguish the fire.

Types of Fires

Different fires produce different temperatures as they burn. The cooler the fire, the more likely it is to burn only dead material and the less likely to kill living plants. The fires that plague California are different from those of such regions as the northern Rockies and Florida, yet all can be grouped into several broad categories: ground fires, surface fires, and crown fires. Spot fires may follow on the heels of any of these.

How Fire Changes Soil

In agronomy laboratories, soil samples are placed in ovens to remove the organic material. When the samples go into the ovens, they look like rich garden soil; when they come out, all that's left are powdery piles of sand or clay. Wildfires do much the same to soil. Soil is made of mineral and organic portions arranged in a structure of channels and spaces; these are held together by gluey substances produced by soil microorganisms. Some soils are more resistant to fire damage than others. The more resilient soils are loams, especially sandy loam. Muck, peat, and clay soils are most vulnerable. When a wildfire burns the soil, the ground is damaged in a variety of ways:

- Soil becomes less able to absorb and hold water.
- Compaction of soils is more likely.
- Erosion increases.
- Soil shows large temperature fluctuations.
- Essential nutrients are lost, especially nitrogen.

Ground fires. Ground fires, also called bog fires in some areas, are the coolest of fires. They have a narrow leading edge that limits the time that plants are exposed to flames. The mildest grade of wildfire, ground fires do the least overall damage to the landscape. They burn slowly through forest litter and over short grasses. The burn is characterized by a well-defined leading edge with flames about as tall as the front is wide (normally less than 1 foot [0.2 m]). The fire smolders as it burns, producing a cooler fire than more intense types.

Surface fires. In surface fires (also called brush fires), plants are under flame for a longer period than in ground fires, and the flames are higher and hotter — which results in more extensive damage. A ground fire is somewhat well behaved if it stays on the ground. When a ground fire encounters taller ignitable material, such as 8-foot-tall *Phragmites* reeds or high grasses, it explodes into a surface fire. Surface fires produce enough heat and air movement that they begin to assume a character all their own. The height of the flames grows, and the width of the leading edge of flames increases, too. As the temperature of the fire rises, it dries out fuels in its path and quickly brings those fuels to ignition temperatures. As the fire grows in intensity, it moves more quickly — and also more unpredictably.

Crown fires. These fires are very hot, frequently destroying every plant in their path. Whereas ground fires and surface fires are concentrated on the ground, in a crown fire the flames become established in the canopies or crowns of trees. The flames make the leap to the trees by climbing a vegetative ladder created by shrubs that are of an intermediate height between the grasses and the treetops. Once in the canopy, this type of fire can race through the forest like tree squirrels leaping from tree to tree at amazing speed. Without a doubt, a crown fire is the most intense type of wildfire, with temperatures so extreme that trees can explode and lightning bolts can thunder from the towering clouds of smoke.

Spot fires. These fires are started by sparks thrown up from an existing fire. They can be blown out from the leading edge of the fire or may be generated from a smoldering tree or similar source.

Designing a Fire-Safe Yard and Garden

Hundreds of homes are destroyed by wildfires each year. Many more are spared damage because the garden and yard stopped the fire from igniting them. When firefighters contain a wildfire, one of their tactics is to build a firebreak. They bulldoze or otherwise clear a strip of land, creating a band of earth devoid of combustible fuel and too wide for the flames to cross. When the fire arrives at the firebreak, there is nothing left to burn and nowhere to go. A well-planned yard can act as an exceptionally beautiful firebreak.

The Worst Wildfires

Peshtigo, Wisconsin, 1871. The worst wildfire in U.S. history occurred at the same time as the Great Chicago Fire. Because the blaze in Chicago received most of the media attention, many people never learned of this horrific fire. It began on October 8, 1871, in Peshtigo and for most of the next week it scorched the earth as an uncontrolled crown fire. About 1,500 people died and nearly 4 million acres burned in the fire.

Hinckley, Minnesota, 1894. This forest fire consumed more than 160,000 acres and killed about 600 people, over half of whom lived in the town of Hinckley.

Acadia National Park, Maine, 1947. Fire raged over the coastal areas, killing 16 people and burning over 200,000 acres and a portion of the quite popular tourist town of Bar Harbor.

Florida, 1998. A series of wildfires burned 500,000 acres in northeast and central parts of the state.

Texas, 1988. Wildfires burned through 330,000 acres.

Laguna, California, 1970. A wildfire in September burned over 175,000 acres.

Southern California, 1993. In a 10-day span in October, wildfires fed by the Santa Ana winds burned 300 square miles and destroyed 1,000 structures.

Los Alamos, New Mexico, 2000. A prescribed burn that went wild destroyed nearly 50,000 acres near the famous Los Alamos National Laboratory.

Hayman Fire, Colorado, 2002. The largest wildfire in Colorado history burned in the Pike National Forest in early summer, consuming 137,000 acres and 100 homes.

Defensible space is a term used to describe the buffer space around your home. It includes the gardens, lawns, and hardscape of the yard. The fire-safe yard uses strategic placement of areas of fire-resistant open space, interspersed with flame-resilient barriers, such as hedges and perennial borders. The open space is often fortified with fire-resilient turf or ground covers. The topography of the yard is adapted to slow a fire's advance and deprive it of any advantages the lay of the land might offer. Hardscape elements, including paths, stone walls, water gardens, and swimming pools, are all designed and placed to discourage fire. The goal is to have a beautiful landscape of shade trees, flower gardens, hedges, and lawn that is also a practical tool to prevent the ravages of wildfire from coming to your door.

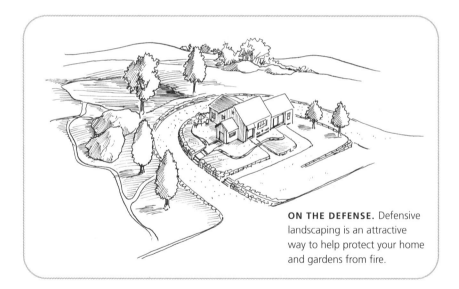

ON THE DEFENSE. Defensive landscaping is an attractive way to help protect your home and gardens from fire.

Open Space in the Landscape

Open space can be many things, from lawns to areas planted with ground covers to tennis courts. Yet all open spaces in the landscape can serve a common purpose: to provide a buffer around the home that is devoid of fuel for fires. Open-space areas work best in this capacity if they are at least 30 feet (9 m) wide.

Lawns. Turfgrass is the traditional plant grown around homes and probably fills more open space than any other landscape plant. Fires most often happen in the countryside during times of drought, when even fire-resilient plants can become desiccated. Some turfgrasses, such as Bermuda grass, that are selected from warm, humid areas but grown in warm, dry climates, become tinder-dry and ready to burn. To allow open space to perform its function, plant your lawn with grasses hardy to all aspects of your region's climate. Buffalo grass is an excellent fire-resilient grass. Keep grasses mowed short near the house and no more than 6 inches (15 cm) tall near the perimeter of the defensible space.

Ground covers. Areas near homes are sometimes waste areas where weeds grow or bare surfaces have appeared. Ground covers can make waste areas more attractive and at the same time offer protection against fire. Ground covers are also excellent lawn alternatives. When they are planted on slopes, they can slow a fire's advance. To provide the maximum protection against fire, select ground covers that are succulent throughout the season, such as ice plant, or those that can weather fire, such as Algerian and English ivy.

After the ground cover has been planted, surround the plants with an organic, moisture-retentive mulch. The mulch layer should be no more than 2 to 3 inches (5–8 cm) deep; thicker layers promote disease and pest problems. Keep the ground cover free of litter, such as leaves, that can provide fuel for advancing fires.

Hedges as Heat Shields

In landscape design, hedges have traditionally been used as barriers. They act as visual screens to promote privacy, block wind, and outline boundaries. In fire-prone areas, they serve an additional function as heat shields and fire barriers. Hedges should be strategically placed with regard to the prevailing surface winds around your home. The goal is to break a breeze — slow it, divert it, or dissipate it.

Use hedges to define the perimeter of the open-space "buffer areas." This doesn't mean your yard needs to have rings of hedges surrounding your home like battlements. Instead, allow each hedge to have a curved and natural course. The preferred plants for fire screens are those that are drought and salt tolerant and that can adapt to a wide range of growing conditions and hardiness zones. The rugosa rose, for instance, meets all these requirements and is also beautiful.

Tough Trees

Trees — tall species and short ones, densely branched and sparse, evergreen and deciduous — give a landscape a feeling of permanence as well as beauty. In fire-prone areas, they can also be either a tool to fight fire or fuel that turns a fire into a conflagration. In areas where fire is a common threat, the choice of trees to have growing in the landscape is very important, as is where in the landscape they will grow. First, inventory what is growing on the grounds now.

You often hear that native trees already growing on a site are the preferred trees to keep growing there, based on the belief that they are best adapted to the conditions and climate. If you live in an area that depends on fire as part of the natural ecology, however, the native plants may burn quite quickly but are said to be fire resistant because they resprout well after the fire is over. This definition of *fire resistant* is unacceptable from the homeowner's standpoint. In choosing trees for the yard and landscape, seek out those with some of the following qualities.

Thick bark. Thick bark insulates the living portion of the stem and branches from heat and flames. Many oaks have thick bark.

Deciduous. Trees that drop their leaves provide less fuel for fires and retain more moisture.

Neat and sparse. Choose trees with little litter, such as seedpods, and those that have an open, branching pattern (rather than a dense habit). Whatever trees grow in the yard, maintaining them in a healthy state is important to keeping them fire resilient. Prune out diseased and broken branches as well as lower limbs. Water and fertilize to keep them as vigorous as possible. Do not allow branches of different trees to touch. And keep all trees away from structures.

Defensive Shrubs

Shrubs provide important visual effects in the garden and landscape, filling the space between the low-growing plants of the lawn and garden and the tall trees. Unfortunately, this same "bridge" effect is what fire can use to climb from the low points in your landscape to the treetops, and turn a ground fire into a crown fire in minutes.

Keep shrubs away from trees, therefore, as well as from the base of structures. Instead, plant shrubs in island beds or use them in shrub borders that serve a similar purpose as hedges. These shrub areas can provide a background for perennial borders and flower gardens while providing fire protection. Place the perennial bed downslope, which will slow a fire, with the shrub border immediately upslope of the perennial bed to slow it further. Just uphill from the shrubs, leave open space that won't support the blaze either. Many shrubs are excellent fire-resilient plants that also offer stunning beauty; examples are many species of viburnum and azalea.

Integrating Hardscape

Given the proper conditions, any plant will burn. Well-designed and well-constructed garden hardscapes provide guaranteed fire resiliency because they won't burn. Integrating hardscape elements into your yard's defensible space adds attractiveness while increasing the effectiveness of plant buffers.

Decks and patios. These features are part of many homes and are often constructed of wood. Wooden decks can burn, and the space between the timbers can hold flammable debris, such as pine needles. Where possible, build decks and patios of stone, concrete, brick, slate, or other noncombustible material. If a wood deck exists, consider constructing a buffer area of crushed or washed stone around its perimeter. Keep landscape plants away from wood decks.

Retaining walls. Walls can be a major aid in keeping fire away from structures and minimizing damage to a yard. Fire often races up slopes, intensifying as it climbs. Retaining walls serve to cut the slope and block the fire. The upright face of a retaining wall steers heat and flames up and away from structures. Where possible, retaining walls should be made of noncombustible materials, such as stone. If wood is used, construct the wall from heavy timbers that can endure a fire much longer than can lighter materials.

Stone walls. Walls made of stone are attractive assets to any landscape, but in a fire-prone area, they are wonderfully functional too. Use stone walls as you would hedges, to create a physical barrier against fire. Stone walls also help direct the heat of the fire up and away from rather than along the ground. Use these in conjunction with such elements as hedges and stone walkways to increase fire-deterrent potential.

Walkways. Paths and walkways provide a small but useful physical barrier against fire. Construct a path from stone, tile, or flagstone to produce a firebreak and to improve ease of access to your home and surroundings.

Swimming pools. A swimming pool isn't just a pleasure on hot days; it's also a large safety tool for those in fire-prone areas. Pools and, to a lesser, extent, water gardens provide water to fight the fire if necessary.

Keeping Plants Fire Resilient

Fires tend to strike during the driest time of year. In spring, rains and cool weather can make nearly any landscape resilient to fire. To keep plants as resilient to fire as possible, you must keep them vigorous and healthy.

Watering. Water puts out fires by cooling the blaze and reducing the flammability of the fuel. A well-watered plant contains large amounts of moisture in its tissues, which naturally inhibits fire. Because fires most often break out during drought or dry periods, the use of water may be restricted. Here are three ways to keep your plants moist even during times of water restriction.

• Use organic mulches to reduce evaporation from the ground.

• Use drip irrigation or buried soaker hoses rather than sprinklers.

• Reduce moisture loss through transpiration by watering on cloudy days or when plants are in the shade.

Pruning. Judicious pruning of landscape plants reduces potential fuel for fires and increases the health and vigor of the plants. As a defense against fire, remove the lower limbs of trees and prune so that branches do not touch. To improve the health of a plant, it helps to prune out thin, weak, or damaged branches as well. Pruning helps direct the energies of the plant toward the strongest branches. Tactful pruning also reduces the canopy slightly, which tends to enhance the health of the tree.

KEEP THEM UP.
Evergreens with branches to the ground can be ignited by even small ground fires.

Clean up. Keeping a tidy landscape amounts to reducing the potential fuel that a fire can burn. Keep ground covers free of litter. Shrub borders and perennial gardens can be traps for windblown debris, so rake them out routinely. Remove litter from around the base of structures. When applying new mulch, avoid flammable materials, such as pine needles.

Careful inspection. Gardeners notice changes in their plants and soil around them. In areas prone to fires, this skill is essential to detect unhealthy conditions before they become liabilities or downright dangerous. Pest infestations and disease may indicate unhealthy conditions that if left unchecked could result in fuel for a fire. Watch the water status of your plants, and prune back tall perennials and wildflowers before they dry out after flowering. These steps can keep the fuel for fire to a minimum and your yard beautiful.

Selecting Plants for Fire Gardens

All plants will burn, but some plants increase a fire's intensity, whereas others can dampen it. Fire-resilient plants have traits that distinguish them from fire-intensifying plants.

Plants to Avoid

Some people call a plant that readily burns a *pyrophyte*, a word derived from the Greek meaning a plant that is disposed to burn. These plants do not just catch fire — they enhance fire or carry it to other places. Check plants in your yard for the following fire-prone qualities, and do not choose pyrophytes when purchasing new plants.

Needled and blade-leafed evergreens. Both needled and blade-leafed evergreens enhance fire, but by slightly different mechanisms. *Needled evergreens* include trees with foliage shaped like sewing needles; examples are pine, spruce, and fir. They range from small shrubs to tall trees. Needled evergreens usually have flammable resins in the wood and needles, plus a dense conical growth pattern that enhances a fire once it starts. These trees and shrubs burn hot and fast, with plentiful sparks. *Blade-leaf evergreens* are those with fan-shaped leaves and include arborvitae and false cypress. These plants also contain flammable resins and oils, and they accumulate dry material in their dense branch structure. These trees and shrubs burn hot and fast, with plentiful sparks.

Plants with high concentrations of fats and oils. All plants produce fats and oils, but the amount and type they produce varies considerably. These compounds include the volatile oils that make flowers fragrant, give balsam fir forests their refreshing smell, and provide many herbs with their aroma. These materials can also burn like a torch. The goal is not to dismiss every plant that contains some flammable chemicals, but to recognize plants that have high enough concentrations of these compounds to pose a fire hazard. Here are some traits that indicate which plants have a high content of flammable substances:

• Foliage with waxy surfaces

• Wood, bark, or foliage that is aromatic
• Plants with sap that is thick, gummy, sticky, or resinous or has a strong smell
• Plants with sticky, hairy buds

Fire-friendly foliage. Some plants bear leaves shaped to maximize surface area and oxygen availability; however, these assets are also tinder for fires. Look out for plants with foliage that has these qualities:
• Leaves are small
• Leaves that are hairy or fuzzy
• Leaves are lacy, delicate, and dissected
• Leaves are stiff or leathery
• Leaves are shiny

Finding just one of these traits on a plant may not be cause to shun it as a fire-vulnerable plant. But the more of these foliage traits that appear on the same plant, the greater the likelihood that the plant is flammable.

The wastebasket syndrome. Some plants, especially shrubs, are very good at catching all the debris that blows through a yard. Other plants, such as those growing beneath tall trees, seem to collect all the droppings sent down from above. Add the dense accumulation of leaves and twigs produced by their own growth and these plants can, over time, become a powder keg of ignitable material. Unlike the previous plants to avoid, many wastebasket plants can be cleaned up and made less dangerous. Some qualities of wastebasket plants are:
• Dense network of branches
• Evergreen foliage
• Multiple stems
• Thorns on branches

Features of Fire-Resilient Plants

Fire resiliency in plants should be viewed as a relative quality. Some plants may be very resilient to small surface fires but succumb to larger, more intense blazes. Still more are called fire resilient because they reliably sprout from the burned-over stumps left behind after a fire toasted

A Gardener's Take

Most of the time, it is fairly easy to look up the qualities of a plant and see what light requirements it has, how tall it grows, or the hardiness zones it thrives in. In addition, this information tends to be unambiguous. A rare instance in which reliable sources of horticultural information contradict one another is when the topic turns to *fire resilience*. The reason for the confusion seems to stem from the definition of fire resilience and how it applies to homeowners rather than forest managers and other professionals.

To a homeowner, the term *fire resilience* implies that plants with this quality will survive a fire. To some forestry professionals, on the other hand, a tree that survives a fire is one in which the entire top is killed but the plant sprouts from the crown or roots later. That's a big difference. Here, then, are some plants that can be considered fire resilient by a *gardener's* standards.

10 Reliable Fire-Resilient Trees
California palm *(Washingtonia filifera)*
Joshua tree *(Yucca brevifolia)*
Mojave yucca *(Yucca schidigera)*
Monterey pine *(Pinus radiata)*
Sabal palmetto *(Sabal palmetto)*
Sassafras *(Sassafras albidum)*

Southern magnolia *(Magnolia grandiflora)*
Sweetbay *(Magnolia virginiana)*
Western larch *(Larix occidentalis)*
White oak *(Quercus alba)*

10 Trees That Are Fire Resilient When Large
Black tupelo *(Nyssa sylvatica)*
Douglas fir *(Pseudotsuga menziesii)*
Hop hornbeam *(Ostrya virginiana)*
Live oak *(Quercus virginiana)*
Oregon white oak *(Quercus garryana)*
Pin oak *(Quercus palustris)*
Ponderosa pine *(Pinus ponderosa)*
Sugar pine *(Pinus lambertiana)*
Tulip tree *(Liriodendron tulipifera)*
Yellow birch *(Betula alleghaniensis)*

Trees That Are Top-Killed by Fire but Resprout
Gray dogwood *(Cornus racemosa)*
Pacific dogwood *(Cornus nuttallii)*
Persimmon *(Diospyros virginiana)*
Redbud *(Cercis canadensis)*
Rocky Mountain maple *(Acer glabrum)*
Vine maple *(Acer circinatum)*

Trees That Are Intolerant of Fire
California hazel *(Corylus cornuta californica)*
Hackberry *(Celtis occidentalis)*
Hickory *(Carya spp.)*

Pacific madrone *(Arbutus menziesii)*
Paper birch *(Betula papyrifera)*
Red maple *(Acer rubrum)*
Red oak *(Quercus rubra)*
Scarlet oak *(Quercus coccinea)*
Silver maple *(Acer saccharinum)*
Sugar maple *(Acer saccharum)*
White ash *(Fraxinus americana)*
Witch hazel *(Hamamelis virginiana)*

Fire-Resilient Plants

The following plants will slow a fire's advance and survive most fires, even though they may be top-killed.

Five Fire-Resilient Shrubs

Cotoneaster (*Cotoneaster* spp.)
Mahonia *(Mahonia aquifolium)*
Pittosporum (*Pittosporum* spp.)
Rock rose (*Cistus* spp.)
Rugosa rose *(Rosa rugosa)*

Fire-Resilient Turfgrasses

Creeping red fescue
Buffalo grass

10 Fire-Resilient Ground Covers

African daisy *(Arctotheca populifolia)*
Carpet bugle *(Ajuga reptans)*
Creeping rosemary (*Rosmarinus officinalis* 'Prostratus')

Ice plant *(Dorotheanthus bellidiformis)*
Ivy (*Hedera* spp.)
Lilyturf *(Liriope)*
Spring cinquefoil *(Potentilla neumanniana)*
Star jasmine *(Trachelospermum jasminoides)*
Stonecrop (*Sedum* spp.)
Vinca *(Vinca minor)*

10 Fire-Resilient Perennials

The perennial garden is home to a wide variety of plants that have different abilities to recover from fire. The most resilient plants are those with thick roots or roots designed for storage, such as hosta and daylily. Another tough group is clumping perennials, those that voluntarily produce shoots from the base of the plant or spread easily, such as phlox and bee balm. Here are 10 especially good plants to choose for their resilience:

Candytuft *(Iberis sempervirens)*
Daylily (*Hemerocallis* spp.)
Lavender cotton (*Santolina* spp.)
Mock strawberry *(Duchesnea indica)*
Red-hot poker (*Kniphofia* spp.)
Snow-in-summer *(Cerastium tomentosum)*
Stonecrop (*Sedum* spp.)
Thyme (*Thymus* spp.)
Wormwood (*Artemesia* spp.)
Yarrow *(Achillea millefolium)*

the rest of the plant. Taking all this into consideration, plants that are fire resilient can generally be identified by these characteristics:

• Leaves are succulent and watery
• Foliage is supple, with a high moisture content
• Sap is clear and watery, with little or no odor
• Foliage is thin, not dense
• Branching is open and airy, with few branches near the ground
• Plants tend not to accumulate dead leaves and twigs
• Plants are deciduous and slow growing
• Plants are drought tolerant
• Plants are not troubled by serious pests and diseases
• Trunks have thick bark
• Roots burrow deep into the soil (including plants with taproots)

Improving with Age

Many plants are fire resilient at one point in their lives but not resilient in another. Woody plants are often vulnerable to even relatively cool ground fires when they are young. The trunks are small and the bark is thin. As most trees grow, their bark thickens, providing a layer of insulation between the fragile cambium under the bark and the heat of the flames. As a trunk grows, it expands in diameter, making it more difficult for flames to girdle the tree. A good example of this is the canyon live oak (*Quercus chrysolepis*), which grows in California. This tree should not be

Home Test

You can check a plant's flammability with a simple test. Take a stem or twig and hold it to a flame. Plants with high fat and oil content often burn with a little flame, like that of a candle. Plants that are fire resilient will merely blacken and smolder.

considered fire resilient when young, but as it ages it becomes much tougher. Even old specimens, however, are not always reliably resilient. Hot fires can penetrate bark that is fairly thin for an oak, and the scaly bark can serve as a ladder for flames to climb the trunk into the canopy.

If Fire Breaks Out

In rural areas, homes are often far away from the nearest firefighting unit. Long distances mean longer response times in case of emergency. That's why homeowners in such areas should be prepared to take some actions and make some choices themselves until firefighters are able to arrive. Preparing for a fire event in advance makes dealing with emergencies safer. The following measures are designed to get you and your family out of dangerous areas and to safer places without injury:

• Keep emergency-response-unit contact information in readily accessible places, such as near telephones or on bulletin boards. Program those numbers into your cell phone, too, if you have reliable cell phone service in your rural area.

• Develop a variety of escape routes from your home, according to different modes of transportation, such as car, off-road vehicle, motorcycle, bicycle, and on foot. The routes should be discussed and written down, have a confirmed destination, and include strategies for all household members to meet up later.

Protecting Your Home

If the response units are still miles away and you choose to stay until help arrives, you can take some action to help hold off the fire and fire damage.

• Break out potentially helpful tools, including a long-handle round-point shovel, grub ax, leather work gloves, pruning saw, chain saw, ax, rake with metal tines, and bucket or backpack sprayer that is already filled with water.

• Set an extension ladder against the house to provide access to the roof.

• Block windows, glass doors, and openings like vents with thermal covers to help keep out the heat from the fire. Covers can be anything from sheets of plywood to metal window blinds to thermal curtains.

What Emergency Units Need from You

A well-planned, well-maintained landscape that is at the peak of fire resiliency protects your home, but it doesn't put out the fire. The firefighters who respond to your home need to concentrate on extinguishing the fire, not finding a way to get up your driveway. If your home is difficult to access, it makes a more dangerous environment for the response team and makes fighting the fire needlessly more difficult. Here's how to put out a welcome mat for firefighters while providing a measure of insurance for your home and garden.

Driveways and Access

Have your name, street, and house number clearly posted near the road so that it can be easily seen from the end of the driveway. Make it legible, make it large. In descending order of importance, be sure that the following information is clearly visible:

1. House number (be sure to use numerals, not words, for faster reading)

2. Street name

3. Homeowner's name

• Ideally, your driveway should have two methods of entrance and exit. A semicircle with a large turnaround at the center is helpful. An alternate road that can be used as a secondary route, if needed, is also helpful. If one route is threatened by fire or blocked, the other can provide access or escape. Construct generous turnarounds where driveways dead-end.

• Avoid hilly driveways or access roads. Although a car or truck can easily drive up a steep driveway, fire equipment doesn't like steep slopes. Roads and driveways should have a slope of less than 10 feet (3 m) per 100 feet (30 m). Make curves as gentle as possible.

• Clear away flammable plant material, such as brush or tall grass, from the edge of your driveway.

• Some driveways or access roads use a bridge to cross swales, creeks, and brooks. The bridge must be wide enough and strong enough for fire trucks to use to reach your home. The weight rating for the bridge should be about 20 tons.

• Construct the driveway from materials that can support the extreme weight of emergency equipment without failing. At minimum, this means a base of crushed stone topped with smaller stony material, such as pea stones. In addition, be sure that areas of the driveway that cross a streambed or wetlands have proper drainage so that the structure of the road isn't compromised.

Extra Water Supplies

Your home and garden already have a water supply, of course, whether it comes from a surface source, well, or public system. But while a garden hose can effectively hold back smaller fires, it alone certainly isn't going to end a wildfire. A large source of water near your home that is accessible to firefighting equipment can go a long way toward helping you to save your home.

Pools, ponds, and rivers. Your water sources don't necessarily have to be natural. Man-made features include reservoirs known as fire ponds as well as ordinary swimming pools. Natural sources include creeks, rivers, ponds, and lakes. For the water source to be most useful to firefighters, they will need to be able to get their large fire trucks within 15 to 20 feet (4.5–6 m) of it. Bear this in mind when siting a swimming pool, water lily pool, or water garden.

Wells. The flow rate of household wells can vary widely, but most have enough water that they can be used to fight small fires or spot fires. If you have to fight a fire yourself, your underground water supply may be all you have to douse the blaze. Keep garden hoses in good condition and rolled up, ready to use. Make sure hoses reach to all the areas where you may need them. Have hose attachments in good repair and ready to use. Finally, it is an excellent idea to get an emergency generator. If the power goes off, your well water becomes inaccessible without a generator to run its pump.

Protecting Your Home from Fire

Just as your garden should be composed of fire-resilient plants, your home should be protected with fire-resistant materials and plans.

Roofs. When a wildfire approaches, embers are often carried ahead of the flames, producing spot fires. If sparks land on an unprotected roof, the structure can be set ablaze very quickly. Homes and other structures in fire-prone areas should have roofs made of noncombustible materials, such as asphalt shingles, slate, metal, and tile. Also, keep your gutters free of leaf litter.

Trees near the house. Shade trees with branches that come close to the roof can act as a pathway for a fire to enter your house. Therefore, trees should be planted no closer than 15 feet (4.5 m) from the exterior walls. Keep branches at least 15 to 20 feet (4.5–6 m) away from structures. When a tree is too close, move it if possible; if that is not an option, you should take it down.

Foundation plantings. Avoid planting conifers and other combustible plants close to your house. Choose plants that are low growing and fire resilient, or remove foundation plants in favor of noncombustible hardscape elements, such as flagstone patios and brick walkways.

Exterior and windows. The exterior of your home and nearby structures should be made of noncombustible materials, such as brick and stone. Invest in thermal windows, which can keep the heat of a fire out of your home. To increase the effectiveness of the windows, use thermal window treatments, such as curtains and window blinds.

Flammable materials. Store firewood and other combustible items at least 30 feet (8 m) away from the house, preferably uphill.

Assessing the Fire Damage

After a fire is over, the task of cleaning up the landscape begins. Fire damage can be devastating. But the aftermath of some fires can look worse that the damage really is. The extent and degree of damage and loss largely depend on the severity of the burn, the type of plants affected, the season in which the fire occurred, and the health of the plants before the fire. The type of damage has a bearing on a plant's prognosis. In general, there are four types of damage to look for following a fire: leaf scorch, fire scars, girdling, and top (or crown) kill.

Leaf Scorch

Description: The most temperature-sensitive parts of a plant during the growing season are usually the leaves and flowers. As fire passes beneath the canopy of a tree, particularly a small tree, the updrafts bathe the foliage in temperatures hundreds of degrees hotter than the ambient air. Leaf scorch affects evergreens as well as deciduous trees. Shrubs and woody perennials, such as lavender and rosemary, can also suffer scorch.

Leaf scorch is very noticeable, and the extent of damage to the crown of a plant is easy to estimate. The amount of leaf area that is scorched is a proven and valuable aid in assessing the extent of injury of a fire-damaged plant and has been used in forestry for years. (The priorities of forest management are different from gardening and landscaping, however; we gardeners want our plants not just to survive, but also to be attractive to our eyes.)

Symptoms: In deciduous plants, the leaves or flowers dry up and die in the heat, leaving the trees covered in brown, crinkled foliage. Unless they are consumed in the fire, scorched leaves remain on the plants. On these plants, leaf scorch resembles desiccation damage seen during droughts. Determining how much of a tree is dead is a bit daunting. The situation is similar to winterkill, in that knowing what parts of a tree need to be pruned out and what can recover is not immediately obvious after winter — or, in this case, the fire — is over. The presence of leaf scorch does not indicate the degree of damage to other parts of the plant (such as leaf buds), as some species tolerate scorching better than others. In general, if the foliage is browned but not burned, a tree can often recover. Deciduous plants in good health that suffer mild leaf scorch, even of all the foliage, may make a complete recovery. The exception is if the fire occurs during or just after a flush of growth, as in spring.

In evergreens, leaf scorch is a much more imprecise indicator of damage (because there are so many types and degrees). It may resemble salt injury. Conifers in general are considered to be fire intolerant, but some, such as Douglas fir, have good resilience to fire. The large buds of Ponderosa pine help the tree sprout new needles even if much of the crown is scorched. Western larch, a deciduous conifer, often sprouts new leaves quickly after a fire. The tapered shape of many evergreens also helps dissipate the heat from a fire, decreasing the chances of damage to the buds and branches.

In any tree, foliage that is burned (rather than merely browned) indicates that the fire was hot enough not only to injure the foliage but also to damage tissues deeper in the plant, such as the bark and cambium. The extent of the injury is often not seen until the following year, when the amount of surviving foliage can be ascertained. Finally, the stress plants experience from fire injury can predispose them to death from decline in health, pests, or disease many years after the fire occurred.

Remedies: Be patient. A leaf-scorched tree can suffer leaf damage while other parts of the tree, from bark to buds, survive. Avoid thinking in crisis mode, and allow things to unfold in their own time. While waiting to see if new buds break, and watching for where they might appear, take good care of the plant by making sure that the soil moisture is at normal levels. If the ground cover vegetation has been burned off, rake the area, add a sprinkling of compost, and reseed or replant.

Strategies: Have a professional arborist inspect the tree and give an opinion as to whether it will ultimately recover or should be taken down and replaced. Even an arborist may not be able to ascertain if a tree will recover until more time has passed. If it's salvageable, ask for advice regarding pruning and potential pest and disease problems to watch for. Monitor areas on scorched branches periodically for signs of life beneath the bark. Living branches often have bark that is tight and frequently a little shiny. Dead branches develop a dull cast and the bark appears loose and "bubbly" or flaky. In living, viable tissues, the area just under the exterior bark is green-colored. Prune out any branches that do die back.

Fire Scars

Description: Fire scars are wounds that fire inflicts on a tree, typically near the base of its trunk. The fire heats, and sometimes burns through, a portion of the bark on the trunk. The damage does not extend completely around the tree.

Fire scars put a tree under stress, but under most conditions, it can recover. Some old trees, such as live oaks in the South, have fire scars from four or five separate blazes over many decades. As a fire moves through an area, it often damages one side of a tree more than the other. Generally speaking, if less than 50 percent of a tree is damaged, it can survive with normal, or nearly normal, health, and retain structural strength of the trunk. The scar, however, is no longer protected by bark. The tree gradually closes wounds like this by growing in from the edges, which takes many years. Wide wounds may never close completely.

Symptoms: Fire scars resemble the scars found on riparian trees that grow right on the riverbank. On the upstream side, these trees have had large patches of bark removed by ice floes slamming into the trunks. Fire scars also occur on the "upstream" side of the fire. The bulk of a tree's trunk protects the lee side as the flames sweep past.

Remedies: Using a sharp, clean horticultural knife, remove dead bark back to living tissue. Make clean, smooth cuts so that the tree can heal itself cleanly. Watch for infection or infestation of the injured area, and treat as needed. Keep the plant well watered and fertilized on a regular schedule, so that it will be as vigorous as possible.

Strategies: It is important to monitor the scarred area, especially wide scars, for signs of insect damage. Also be on the lookout for woodpeckers or signs of them, such as excavations in the wood. These birds don't eat wood, but rather the insects that live inside the wood. Woodpeckers may detect the presence of insect pests in the wood before you do! When scars have destroyed half or more of the bark around the base of a tree, call in a professional arborist to assess the situation. In some instances, the wound can be gapped with bridge grafting (see page 79), but other times, the tree is lost and must be removed.

Girdling

Description: If a slow fire lingers at the base of a tree, the persistent heat can kill the cambium tissue all the way around the plant. This most often happens to woody perennials, shrubs, and small trees during ground or surface fires. The foods produced in the leaves are transported down the stem through special plant cells to the roots. In turn, the roots send up moisture and nutrients to the leaves through other special plant cells. Girdling kills the cells near the base of the plant that send food down to the roots, but not the ones that send the moisture up to the leaves, as these are deeper in the tree.

Symptoms: At the base of the tree, you'll see a charred area that extends around the trunk. The bark can be completely destroyed or it can look almost normal but is loose and separated from wood beneath. This last type is sometimes difficult to diagnose. The bulge above the wounded area appears over time, usually a year or more after injury.

Remedies: Bridge grafting is the best way to help some girdled plants. This is done by grafting about four branch sections (taken from the tree) to the trunk across the killed area. Bridge grafting is best done during early spring, when the bark is "slipping" (when the bark slips away from the wood when cut, and the area between the bark and sapwood is wet and slippery).

Strategies: Observe the plant for a couple of seasons following the fire. It may leaf out and seem perfectly healthy for 1 or 2 years after the fire. But in reality, it is slowly starving to death. The foods produced by the leaves can't reach the roots and instead produce a bulge at the top of the girdled area. The roots are still supplying the leaves with moisture, but the entire plant is living off stored reserves. Over time, stress increases, pest and disease problems accumulate, and the plant dies.

Top Kill

Description: Top kill, or crown kill, is when the foliage and branches are killed outright in a fire. Some trees can survive having as much as three quarters of their canopy destroyed by flames. However, most trees

You're in Control . . . Or Are You?

Wildfire is not the only cause of scorch to landscape or garden plants. In many states, it is still legal to burn outdoor brush in the springtime. Often, the plumes of hot air from brush burning billow into the canopies of nearby trees. A "controlled" fire damages trees and shrubs in the yard just by being too close to them. And ground fires can often scorch only the lowest branches of trees and leave the rest of the plant unscathed.

with crown kill become stressed and are more likely to become infested with pests and prey to diseases, dying within 5 years of the burn.

Symptoms: If it's difficult to judge the extent of damage, call in an arborist for advice. Professional help is especially worth it if the tree you hope to save is valuable to you.

Remedies: It's best to remove top-killed trees from the yard as soon as possible. Fortunately, some trees, such as oaks, frequently send up sprouts from the base of the tree when the top has been killed.

Strategies: After a killed tree has been cut, you may want to nurture a sprout or two from its stump, if your goal is to allow vegetation to return to the area. As far as restoring the ornamental aspects of the yard, however, you would be wise to replace the dead tree you have cut with a more fire-resilient species.

Burned Lawns

Description: Fires that sweep over lawns are often ground fires that consume the little fuel the grasses offer and then move on.

Remedies: Lightly rake the burned area and water regularly to encourage new growth.

Strategies: Keep the grass trimmed so that the flames don't injure the roots, rhizomes, and stolons; regeneration will be quick.

Hail

SPRING OVER NORTH AMERICA IS A TIME when winter is slowly being forced north. Humid, summerlike air from the south and chill Canadian air attempt to occupy the same places on the continent at the same time. The air masses are so different — one warm, the other cold — that the ever-moving and changing boundary they share is a perpetual skirmish line of severe weather.

Today, the cold emanates from the clockwise flow of a large high-pressure zone entrenched high in the atmosphere over Canada. A companion low-pressure system, also very high above the earth, spins over the southern high prairies. Like gigantic gears meshing and turning in the sky, the two weather systems appear harmonious, but they serve opposing goals. The circulation of the high-pressure system pours cold air into the central United States, while the low-pressure system pumps warm air, heavy with moisture, from the Gulf of Mexico northward.

The two air masses meet along a stalled weather front that runs from west to east through the open prairies. The horizon here is so wide that on clear days, the immense sky seems to pull you into it; you feel like the tallest thing for 100 miles around. Under blue skies and fair-weather clouds, the prairie makes you feel buoyant and cheerful. When the weather turns dark, however, the prairie elicits fear, for you are in "tornado alley."

Although the day begins fair and quiet, it's late spring, and the weather can change quickly. Overhead, the weather front remains stalled and seemingly benign. A weather front is not just a trace on a weather map, but rather a path, often invisible, for storms to follow. If storms form today, they will be large and strong and probably pass directly overhead.

As the day wears on, white cumulus clouds begin to gather on the western horizon. Sometimes these clouds stay linen white and beautiful all day. But on days like this one, when the atmosphere is battling with itself, the clouds can change personality very quickly. Today, driven by winds produced as the huge air masses interact, the clouds begin to grow and blend into each other. Soon the white patina of the clouds tarnishes to pewter gray. Clouds boil into the sky, the tops growing until they are far out of sight. The clouds are now a thunderhead, a massive engorged cloud system, pregnant with rain and energy. Rising to an impressive 10 miles in the air, the top of the storm is an anvil-shaped cloud of icy fog cooled to well below 0°F. The clouds at the base of the thunderstorm are indigo to black, and the shadow they cast on the earth below is a shade even darker. Beneath the storm, the only light comes from the electric blue shocks of lightning.

Inside the storm, thermals blow the air skyward like plumes of boiling water. As the air lifts higher, tiny bits of debris (dust) attract minute particles of water, the debris and moisture forming tiny droplets so small that the slightest breeze blows them around. As the droplets bump into each other, they grow larger and are swept higher into the clouds. When the droplets reach about 13,000 feet, they enter the portion of the atmosphere with below-freezing temperatures. Water droplets passing this threshold can freeze into ice or snow, partially freeze into slush, or become supercooled and remain liquid despite freezing temperatures.

Miles away, at the local office of the National Weather Service, and at the Severe Storm Center in Norman, Oklahoma, weather radar has been tracking the developing storm. The radar screen glows with data as meteorologists analyze the images. The screen reflects the image of a severe thunderstorm with wind and precipitation patterns that could lead to tornado development. In moments, warnings and watches are issued and picked up on the weather radio in the kitchen of a nearby farm. A severe thunderstorm warning and tornado watch is in effect. The automated voice ticks off the towns in the path of the storm. It is headed straight for the O'Connor farm.

The updrafts within the thunderstorm reach 100 miles per hour, with most topping off at near 60 miles per hour. The strength and persistence of the thermals easily drive the icy particles ever higher in the clouds and produce myriad collisions among particles along the way. As the particles collide they join, producing larger and larger ice particles.

At some point, a particle of ice becomes heavier than the wind holding it up, and it falls through the clouds. On its descent, the little hailstone gets larger through a process called *wet growth*. As the hailstone contacts supercooled droplets of snow, they freeze on its surface. As water freezes, it releases just enough heat to produce a thin, watery film on the hailstone. Now that the hailstone's surface is wet, all particles that collide with it are assimilated — and the hailstone grows.

The thermals in the storm act as currents of air, and the falling hailstone is swept back into an updraft for another round of growth. Layers and layers of ice accumulate on the hailstones as they grow. Soon even the thermals can no longer support the stones, and all of them fall in a torrent from the sky.

The weather radar at the weather service shows that this storm is isolated, a single thunderstorm that has grown into a massive tempest called a *supercell*. Indeed, graphic depictions of thunderstorms often look like cells, with clearly defined borders and internal features. This supercell is racing east across the plains. The updrafts in the storm reach speeds of well over 100 miles per hour, producing a wide area of hail formation called a *hail shaft*, in which huge amounts of very large hail circulate in the clouds.

The path of the storm takes it over agricultural fields of corn as well as past the O'Connor farmhouse, with its trees, lawn, and vegetable and flower gardens. The storm clouds are low and dark, an ominous greenish black. Suddenly, something happens high in the clouds. Perhaps the hail has grown too heavy for the winds, or maybe the winds have abated slightly or shifted position. Whatever the cause, the dynamics within the storm change, and the support for the hail shaft weakens and falls apart. Millions of hailstones plummet from the sky. In some areas, the stones are the size of baseballs (or in extreme cases, grapefruits). As the ice falls, it is pulled by gravity and propelled by the wind, sometimes accelerating to over 100 miles per hour before it hits the ground. Tons of hailstones drop in a matter of minutes, burying the landscape in inches of white ice. Cornstalks snap in half and leaves are shredded until whole fields look as if they were attacked by a monster line trimmer. Car windows are smashed and skylights on roofs shatter. Stands of sunflowers become fields of leafless stalks. Lily pads and hostas are shredded, and garden perennials are crushed.

As quickly as it began, the destructive hailfall abruptly stops. Four inches of hail the size of golf balls lie piled on the ground. Rain quietly falls on this blanket of cold hailstones, causing an eerie milky vapor to form and hover above the ice. The icy fog reduces visibility and accents the chill that lingers until the hail melts away, many hours later.

In the yard outside the O'Connor farmhouse, the maple trees are barren, their foliage stripped from the branches by a meteorologic temper tantrum. Flowers and vegetables are beaten and bruised. Some look like lettuce left in the freezer; others have suffered only minor damage. The corn in the fields is still small and has been knocked flat by the barrage. The field looks terrible. The farmer will wait a week and then check the growing tips of the corn to see how much of the crop will survive and how much will die. It is not an easy week.

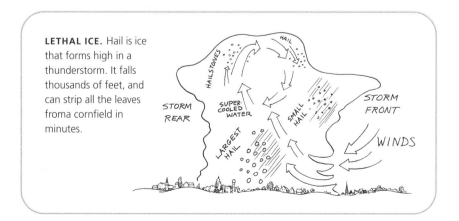

LETHAL ICE. Hail is ice that forms high in a thunderstorm. It falls thousands of feet, and can strip all the leaves froma cornfield in minutes.

Hail: A Formidable Foe

Imagine the best pitcher in major-league baseball. He's standing on the mound, waiting to throw the baseball toward home plate. At home plate, instead of a batter, is your prize tomato plant, laden with ripening fruit. The pitcher leans back and throws the baseball with all his strength. In the blink of an eye, the ball strikes the tomato plant dead center at nearly 90 miles (146 km) per hour. Instantly, the stems snap and the plant, shattered, crumples to the ground.

This illustration of how hail can damage plants isn't totally accurate, because the baseball would actually do *less* damage than a hailstone of similar size. A baseball-size hailstone is heavier than a baseball and hits the plant at a greater speed, close to 110 miles (177 km) per hour. In a storm, especially a strong one, hail forms in a large vertical column. When the hail falls out of the storm, it is like a moving dump truck jettisoning a load of stones. The hail falls thickly and intensely along a sometimes narrow area, with well-defined borders. If your yard and garden are outside the hail fall, you are fortunate.

Hail versus Sleet: What's the Difference?

Sleet is a raindrop that forms in warm air and falls through cold air on its way to the ground. The raindrop freezes in the cold air and hits the ground as a pellet of sleet. Sleet can be clear if it freezes fast on the way down, or milky if it freezes more slowly.

Unlike sleet, hail grows by adding layers of ice. A pellet of sleet cut in half has no layers. A hailstone cut in half has distinct layers, like tree rings or the rings within an onion, that mark its up-and-down passage through the clouds.

Know Your Garden's Hail Risk

In the United States, most hailstorms occur in April, May, June, and July. The most frequent time of day for hail to fall is between 1:00 P.M. and 9:00 P.M. The concerns gardeners have about hail can be simplified into two questions: Where does hail fall? How big is the hail that does fall?

Where. If you want to grow your garden without risk of hail savaging your plants, the best places to be are Alaska and Hawaii, where hail is virtually unknown. The rest of us may have to deal with hail, but to enormously different degrees.

The next safest zones, which have just a few days of hail each year, are areas on both coasts, from New England through the mid-Atlantic states in the East, and a large area of the Southwest, including Arizona, California, and Nevada.

In a large portion of the Northeast and Midwest, from central New York to Wisconsin, hail is a common event. This is also true for much of the South, the Pacific Northwest, and the northern Rocky Mountain states.

The areas that remain can be divided into those that get a lot of hail and those that get hail occasionally. A heavy hail belt (about 100 events per year per state) runs from Illinois through Iowa and Minnesota, then arcs across North Dakota to Montana and Wyoming. An even heavier band (with about 200 events per year per state) begins in Louisiana and proceeds north through Mississippi, Arkansas, Missouri, Nebraska, South Dakota, and Colorado.

The last group of states, Texas, Oklahoma, and Kansas, are known collectively as tornado alley and illustrate the close relationship that hail has with twisters. Every year, tornado alley can expect to host thousands of hail falls.

How big? Hail can be as big as a softball or as small as a lentil. It goes without saying that given a choice between being hit with a softball and being whacked with a lentil as it falls from the sky, you would pick the latter. Plants would probably also prefer the lentil. Large hail, more than 1 inch (2.5 cm) across, is much more apt to hurt plants than is smaller hail.

The largest hailstone ever recorded in the United States fell in Kansas in 1970. It measured more than 7 inches (18 cm) in diameter and weighed over 1½ pounds (0.7 kg).

Hailstorm Facts and Figures

• Each year, about 3,000 hailstorms occur in the United States. Of these, about 1,200 occur in only four states: Texas, Oklahoma, Kansas, and Nebraska.

• Hail falls of large stones most often occur in areas from the Rocky Mountains east across the Great Plains and through most of the Midwest. The location with the greatest number of storms producing large hail is Colorado.

• The South has a large number of hail events each year. Florida has the most thunderstorms of any state, yet very few hail falls of large hail. This may be due to the state's warm climate, which probably prevents the cloud tops of storms from getting as cold as elsewhere.

• Some areas, such as northern Arizona, Idaho, and Utah, do not report a lot of hail falls each year, but of those reported, a high percentage consist of large hail.

• The bull's-eye for receiving the greatest number of large hail events each year is an area on the border of Wyoming, Colorado, and Nebraska. This is where the conditions for hail, thunderstorms, and tornados come together in a way that maximizes storm potential. The combination of warm moist air off the Gulf, cold air from Canada, and the effects of weather systems coming off the Rocky Mountains conspires to create very strong storms.

Protecting Your Garden from Hail

As we've seen, hail lands a powerful punch, but there are a number of strategies you can undertake in order to protect your plants from damage.

Hail netting. Gardeners in regions where hail commonly mangles the crops desire a sure-fire way to keep hail at bay. Hail netting fills that role. This material is similar to the shade-cloth netting used by growers of everything from tobacco to interior foliage plants, such as dracaena, to dampen the light intensity reaching plants. The hail netting is laid in a horizontal sheet over and above the plants and remains in place throughout the crop cycle.

Hail nets are often made of woven synthetic fabric that is almost transparent, letting in almost normal amounts of light. The fabric is strong, ultraviolet-stabilized for endurance in the sun, and pliant so that hailstones bounce off it. It also breaks up heavy rain, which can damage flowers. Hail netting is made by agricultural supply companies, such as Conwed Plastices, producers of Hailnet (see Resources, page 387). The products are used more for large operations, such as orchards; check with your local nursery or garden center for availability.

Once the framing is in place, hail nets can be put over a garden temporarily, when you hear that a storm is impending, or for the long term if it's a particularly stormy summer. Set vertical posts around the garden and horizontal crosspieces interconnecting the posts, then lay your hail net across the top of the crosspieces.

Screens. To protect plants, such as tomatoes, that you grow in cages, drape a protective screen over the top of each one. The shield can be made of anything from old nylons to large empty onion bags. This technique works best in small gardens because when a storm is on the horizon, it may take too much time to run around your garden setting up the screens.

Cold frames. Lightweight, portable cold frames are available that can be set directly over plants in the perennial border or vegetable garden. These frames are made of almost clear polycarbonate material that stops a hailstone cold. They don't protect a large portion of the garden, but what they do shelter, they shelter very well.

Sprinklers. Another technique — though a method of last resort — is to turn on the sprinkler system around the garden when a storm is arriving. This is based on the theory that the water will slow the air speed of falling hailstones enough to make a difference to the garden's welfare. I have never tried this. It sounds akin to trying to knock down a housefly with a squirt gun, but you never know.

Designing Your Garden to Minimize Hail Damage

Hailstorms can't think, so it should be pretty easy to outsmart one, right? You would think so, but it's still not simple. Why? Because the plants we grow don't have brains either, and insist on growing in places where hail is going to fall on them. The challenge for the gardener is to design a garden environment that naturally buffers the growing space of plants while minimizing the threat of hail. Here are some devices that, when added to the garden design, can help reduce hail damage.

Windbreaks. A windbreak is anything that breaks the force of the wind: for example, tall trees or fences. Windbreaks create a *wind shadow,* an area downwind of them that is relatively calm even on a breezy day. Hail, however, does not act like the wind. Whereas wind and rain can blow across the surface of the garden at a shallow angle, hail falls at a steep angle onto the garden. This means that the shadow of protection from

Hail Can Be a Warning of Worse Things to Come

It takes strong winds to repeatedly carry a hailstone up and down through the clouds. This is why the area of a thunderstorm that is strong enough to generate hail is also the most likely place to spawn tornadoes. If hail is bouncing off the lawn, you should retreat to the safest place possible.

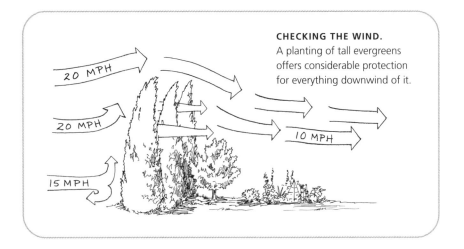

CHECKING THE WIND.
A planting of tall evergreens offers considerable protection for everything downwind of it.

20 MPH

20 MPH

15 MPH

10 MPH

hail that a windbreak offers plants is much smaller than that for wind. Also, the quality of protection varies with the materials used in the windbreak. Conifers are preferred.

Set windbreaks toward the prevailing direction that hailstorms approach your garden. If your garden has many shade-loving or partial-shade plants, a windbreak of columnar evergreens works well. These would also grow tall enough to offer a greater protective area downwind of the windbreak. For sun-loving plants, consider installing a fabric hail net that buffers wind, hail, and rain (see page 207).

Companion planting. Using a "buddy system" of resilient plants paired with more sensitive ones allows one plant or group of plants to protect others. Use dense shrubs and evergreens in the perennial border to add height, contrasting texture, and protection from hail. Try to use these resilient plants on the west and northwest to break prevailing winds and protect from hail. Plants with tall, resistant stalks, such as red-hot poker and verbascum, can be set out in groups to serve as hail buffers.

Hardscape. Hardscape is perhaps the most versatile type of hail buffer. Simple examples include using a northwest-running stone wall to protect a narrow planting on the wall's south side. Retaining walls can be used in the same fashion. Some of the largest hardscape elements you have are your home and other structures on your property. These can create great protective hail shadows or buffer space. Bear in mind, though, that large roofed structures direct hail down the roof to fall over the eaves. Hail can pile up in these spots to depths of many feet, so to avoid problems don't place plants in that path.

Protecting the Birds of Your Yard and Garden

Birds are fairly fragile creatures, and they don't fare well when struck by icy hailstones the size of musket balls. An infamous storm that occurred over Alberta, Canada, in July 1978 produced a hail fall so intense that it killed tens of thousands of waterfowl in just a few minutes. Another storm, in Colorado, killed 1,500 American white pelicans and hundreds of other birds, including American avocets, gulls, and ducks. Hail has also reportedly killed sparrows, hummingbirds, purple martins, mocking-birds, and finches.

The key to protecting your backyard birds from hail is to provide them with shelter substantial enough to ward off the hailstones and inviting enough for them to use. The most obvious shelter that many perching

Unusual, but Possible

Hail can do more than damage crops, gardens, and property. It can some-times be lethal. Only two people have died from hail falls in the United States over the past 100 years, but other areas of the world have not been as fortunate. In 1986, a hailstorm in China killed more than 100 people. On the last day of April 1888 in northern India, a region where catastrophic hail falls are fairly common, hailstones bigger than grapefruits fell so heavi-ly and so fast that they killed some people outright and buried others in piles of ice. In the end, 246 people died — the worst loss of human life from a hailstorm ever recorded.

birds, such as robins and chickadees, are instinctively drawn to is trees. The trees that offer the best protection from hail are conical in shape, densely branched, and thickly covered in needles. Some examples of these kinds of trees are spruce and fir. Other evergreens, such as pines and cedars, also offer good protection. Low-growing conifers, including common and Chinese juniper and yew, can provide shelter for ground-loving birds, such as juncos and sparrows.

Ground birds can wait out storms beneath decks or porches. Swallows and flycatchers get safety from building nests on buildings, and robins can easily take over your gazebo. You can protect cavity-nesting birds, like chickadees, titmice, and bluebirds, by setting out sturdy wooden nesting boxes. Place large-roofed feeders in the lee of buildings. If thunderstorms typically come from the northwest, site the feeder station on the southeast side.

Detecting Hail Resiliency

A hail-resilient plant isn't one that just survives the barrage from the sky. Rather, it usually comes through the ordeal with enough dignity to still look attractive. This is no mean feat, given that hail is powerful enough to kill people and animals. Hail most often damages plants in one or more of the following ways:

- Defoliation
- Breakage of stems
- Bruising and stripping of bark
- Bruising and stripping of fruit

The qualities that different plants use to resist hail damage are often contradictory but equally successful. Some plants survive through sheer size and toughness, whereas other, smaller plants manage their survival simply by presenting less of a target. Stem pliancy is an important defense, as are the short needles on such evergreens as firs and cypress. For further explanation and examples of the different ways plants survive, see the next page.

Hail-Resistant Plants

Strong and sturdy. These plants don't necessarily physically resemble each other, but they all manifest a singular ability to endure. In verbascum, the basal leaves can be damaged by large hail while the flower stalk remains in good shape. In Siberian iris, the foliage and flower stalk are smaller targets than those of other plants, and the stems can deflect potential damage from the few stones that find their mark.

Hollyhock *(Alcea rosea)*
Red-hot poker *(Kniphofia* spp.)
Siberian iris *(Iris sibirica)*
Small globe thistle *(Echinops ritro)*
Verbascum (*Verbascum* 'Southern Charm')
Yucca (*Yucca* spp.)

Small-leafed ground covers. These plants can be herbaceous perennials or woody plants, but all have small leaves that provide hail resilience. The low, spreading growth habit of the plants helps shield them from damage in most circumstances. These plants also have glossy, leathery leaves that resist hail injury much better than do the large leaves of some other ground covers (such as hosta).

Bearberry *(Arctostaphylos uva-ursi)*
Carpet bugle *(Ajuga* spp.)
Cotoneaster (*Cotoneaster* spp.)
Heather (*Calluna* spp.)
Iceplant (*Dorotheanthus* spp.)
Partridgeberry *(Mitchella repans)*
Thyme (*Thymus* spp.)
Vinca *(Vinca minor)*

Plants with pliant flower stems. These plants typically combine a modest basal rosette of weather-resilient leaves with a pliant seasonal flower stem. The cluster of leaves at the base of a plant is often not damaged by hail falls. The flower stem, rather than pick a fight with hailstones, plays a game of garden dodgeball, yielding and bending, and thus living to bloom another day. However, some of these plants produce showy blossoms that can be torn by heavy hail.

Balloon flower *(Platycodon grandiflorus)*
Peach-leafed bellflower *(Campanula persicifolia)*
Penstemon (*Penstemon* spp.)

Short-needled evergreens. This group of plants probably handles hail better than any other. They are not immune to damage, but they sustain fewer injuries, the injuries are less severe, and the damage that is sustained is less noticeable. The most frequent damage is the snapping off of the short, bristly terminal twigs that constitute the most current year's growth; these may litter the ground after a hail fall. Long-needled evergreens, including many pines, and broad-blade evergreens, such as arborvitae and false cypress, are also very resilient to hail.

Bald cypress *(Taxodium distichum)*
Fraser fir *(Abies fraseri)*
Juniper *(Juniperus* spp.)
Korean fir *(Abies koreana)*
Swiss mountain pine *(Pinus mugo)*

Plants with thin, fine leaves. A hailstorm that strips nearly every leaf from deciduous trees, such as maples, doesn't seem to touch the delicate grass plants that make up a lawn. One of the advantages of ornamental plants with thin, fine leaves is that the hail simply doesn't have much of anything to hit. A second advantage is that if the leaf is struck, the supple nature of the foliage allows it to flex and resist damage.

Blue fescue *(Festuca glauca)*
Blue oat grass *(Helictotrichon sempervirens)*
Gayfeather *(Liatris* spp.)
Lilyturf *(Liriope* spp.)
Prostrate rosemary *(Rosmarinus officinalis* 'Prostratus')

Plants with thick, heavy leaves. Although some plants with thick, heavy leaves suffer less hail damage than do some other type of plants, this trait probably doesn't deserve all the credit. Most of these plants grow in shade or partial shade; therefore, by extension, they benefit from some physical protection, such as overhead trees, as their first line of defense from the hail. Still, their leaves are more resilient than those of many other plants and can deflect hail of average size.

Bergenia *(Bergenia* spp.)
Wild ginger *(Asarum* spp.)

Growing Hail-Sensitive Plants

Some plants, such as the trees in apple and cherry orchards, are very sensitive to hail for only part of each year. Other plants are sensitive all the time, and can usually be identified by large, thin, and easily torn leaves. The plant most often mentioned as the worst to have in hail country is hosta. When hit by a hail fall, these usually attractive ground covers become shot through with holes, shredded, torn, and bruised. Lovers of hosta can still use it successfully if they site their plants in a shady place, in the lee of a large, protective windbreak, tree, or structure that acts as at least a partial shield. Indeed, any shade-loving plants that are sensitive to hail are worth the risk to grow if you can find a protected spot for them. Here are a few favorites:

Angel wings *(Caladium × hortulanum)*

Coleus *(Coleus* spp.)

Ferns

Hosta *(Hosta* spp.)

Ligularia *(Ligularia* spp.)

Maidenhair fern *(Adiantum pedatum)*

Ostrich fern *(Matteuccia struthiopteris)*

Royal fern *(Osmunda regalis)*

Trillium *(Trillium* spp.)

Lose Leaves, Lose Yield

The sensitivity of vegetable plants to hail damage can be seen in the way corn reacts to hail at different times in its growth. When young, hail can destroy 50 percent of the leaf area on a corn plant, but the total overall yield will be decreased by only about 10 percent. If the same plant suffers the same 50 percent loss of foliage when the tassels are forming, however, the yield will be cut by nearly 25 percent.

After the Storm: Post-Hail Strategies

One of the common threads that most major gardening problems seem to share, hail included, is the need for patience. In addition to obvious damage, hail causes more subtle troubles that take their toll much later. Knowing what to look for will help you repair the obvious and recognize the not-so-obvious troubles and injuries hail can bring to your garden.

Obvious Damage to Trees and Shrubs

Description: The most obvious injury to deciduous trees and shrubs is defoliation. In severe hail falls, entire canopies can be stripped. In milder events, the leaves can be torn or shredded but remain on the tree. Trees and shrubs that lose their leaves often releaf, especially if the loss of leaves occurs in spring or early summer. Broken branches are easy to see and should be removed cleanly. What are more difficult to detect are areas from which the bark has been removed or partially torn, leaving an open wound. This sort of injury occurs on thin-barked plants and on the less mature parts of other trees and shrubs.

Remedies: Where possible, tack the bark back in place. For slender branches, simply replace the bark and hold it in place with grafting tape.

Strategies: See Designing Your Garden to Minimize Hail Damage (page 208) and Hail-Resilient Plants (page 212).

Hidden Damage to Trees and Shrubs

Description: Some wounds from hailstones are too high on a tree to see. Such injuries invite disease and pests to infect or infest the plant.

Remedies: Make careful garden inspection a part of your routine, and be on the lookout for plants that seem unusually attractive to pests or that are showing symptoms, such as wilting of one branch; this could be a warning of serious troubles. Play detective and scrutinize trees and shrubs for less obvious injuries. Treat damage quickly. If the bark is torn, cut off the loose portion with a sharp horticultural knife; if you spot signs of pests or disease, use a product registered for the problem.

Strategies: See Designing Your Garden to Minimize Hail Damage (page 208) and Hail-Resilient Plants (page 212).

Damage to Vegetables

Description: As we've seen, if hail hits vegetables at a hardy time in their lives, they can be remarkably resilient. But if it smashes them at a sensitive time, the game could be over. Most vegetables are most prone to hail damage from the time they emerge, or are transplanted, until they set fruit. This is because the leaf area of the plant is smaller (less photosynthesis), the root area is smaller (less nutrient and water absorption), and the leaves are more tender (more prone to damage).

Root crops, such as carrots, that are close to harvest will produce a good crop even if much of the foliage is damaged. Root crops that have significantly damaged foliage before the roots have sized up, on the other hand, are usually lost.

Warm-weather crops, such as tomatoes, can suffer chill damage (see the section on cold, page 54), particularly if they are buried in hail for several hours. This is especially true for small plants. Watery lesions and soft spots may indicate chill injury rather than hail-impact damage. Hail fall can also break stems and strip leaves off vegetables.

Remedies: As soon as possible after a hailstorm, remove as much of the ice as you can, especially from around warm-weather plants. A small garden rake works well, as does a wide-blade trowel. Once most of the ice is pushed away, use a gentle spray from the garden hose to help melt remaining hailstones.

Next, remove broken and damaged leaves, but keep as much foliage on the plants as possible. Watch the plants for growth for about a week. If growth resumes, a plant is trying to recover. If no growth is evident, the plant is probably too damaged to produce much of a crop, and you'll have to tear it out.

Strategies: If hail damage occurs early in the growing season, there may be enough time left to replant. If you were raising corn, for example, you could remove the lost crop and sow a short-season variety that matures quickly. The yield may be reduced, but at least it is a yield. Also, see Designing Your Garden to Minimize Hail Damage (page 208) and Hail-Resilient Plants (page 212).

Damage to Seeds

Description: It is obvious how hail can damage and injure growing plants. But what happens when you've sown your seed and a hailstorm dumps a few inches of icy hail over your seedbed? The hail strikes the ground and never directly impacts the seed, yet the hail can still damage the plant. As the ice melts, the cold water seeps into the ground and lowers the soil temperature. For crops of tropical origin, such as corn and melon, this chilling can set back a germinating plant and injure it. The melting water can also produce a dense crust on the soil, especially clay soil, that can inhibit a plant's emergence.

Remedies: If you've just recently sown the crop, you can rake much of the ice out of the seed rows. However, if the seeds have begun to germinate or have started to break ground, raking can damage the seedlings and should be avoided. Instead, apply a mist of water to the ice to melt it away. This works fairly quickly. The only drawback is that cold meltwater can also damage the emerging seedlings, especially for warm-weather crops such as eggplant. Keep watch for erratic germination, slow growth, and stunted seedlings, and be prepared to resow if necessary.

Strategies: In areas prone to frequent hailstorms, such as Oklahoma and Colorado, installation of a hail net over the most vulnerable parts of the landscape, such as the vegetable garden, is helpful (see page 207).

Flowering Annuals

Description: The fate of flowering annuals in hailstorms varies. Sometimes they come through beautifully, whereas other times it looks like a mulching mower stopped by for a visit. Annuals live dangerously from a physiological point of view, racing to bloom at the expense of storing food reserves for emergencies. If hail strips or severely damages the leaves, the flowering potential of the plants is essentially lost.

Remedies: Some tender perennials that are grown as annuals, such as petunias, may recover enough to rebloom if a few leaves remain after the hail fall. Apply a water-soluble fertilizer at half the recommended rate to give them a little boost.

Strategies: Planting tough, hail-resilient annuals, such as portulaca, is helpful. For large annual displays, hail netting can stop damage.

Perennial Flowers and Herbs

Description: The outcome for perennials often depends on the condition of the plants before the hailstorm. Other plants, such as sage and English lavender, are more resilient than they may at first appear and often come through hail falls with little more than cosmetic damage. Daylily varieties with large blossoms can be tattered to pieces by hail, whereas small-flowered forms, such as 'Stella D'Oro', sustain far less damage and send up more flowering scapes in short order.

Remedies: Perennials have food reserves that can feed latent buds as they emerge and unfurl new leaves. That's why many perennials that are defoliated make a quick recovery. Remove flowers and unopened flower buds where practical, and apply a water-soluble fertilizer at half the recommended rate to give them a little boost.

Strategies: Proper plant selection based on hail resilience can reduce losses and damage considerably. Hail nets, which can be set up quickly and thus do not detract from the look of the garden, are helpful. The support posts for the netting can be camouflaged as trellises, posts, or arbors.

Heat

THE DAY BEGINS WITH A TEMPERATURE of 76°F at sunrise. The sun is like a glowing iron, red with heat. As it rises into the hazy, pale blue sky, the ember red color burns away like impurities vaporizing in a furnace, and the sun takes on the white-hot color it will hold for the remainder of the day.

At 9:00 A.M. the thermometer registers a temperature of 82°F and humidity of 60 percent. The plants in the garden seem normal. The roots are absorbing moisture from the soil and transpiring it as water vapor through the leaves. Photosynthesis is proceeding, as are the many other chemical processes that keep plants alive and healthy.

By noon, it is 93°F, with 65 percent humidity. Photosynthesis slows down, then stops. Growth of the roots and other parts of plants slows to a fraction of what it was a few hours ago. Water absorption slows down, and the plants begin to lose more moisture than they take in. Without enough moisture to cool the leaves, the internal temperature in the leaves begins to climb.

At 1:30 P.M., the leaves of the plants are noticeably wilted. A gardener, an older gentleman named David, looks out the kitchen window and sees the wilted plants struggling in the heat. He trades his slippers for shoes, forgets his hat on the peg by the door, and hurries outside. The temperature is now 96°F, with humidity of 66 percent.

The heat index is a formula that allows the calculation of what temperature it feels like when both air temperature and humidity are considered. When the temperature was 82°F at 9:00 A.M. the heat index was 84°F, a reading high enough to earn a caution advisory, meaning that fatigue is possible with physical activity. On the heat index, the noon reading of 92°F feels like 105°F, a temperature at the upper end of the extreme caution category, at which heat exhaustion, cramps, and sunstroke become possible dangers for those working outdoors. By the time David steps outside of his house, the heat index has already risen to 121°F, and work outdoors is likely to bring on sunstroke, muscle cramps, or heat exhaustion.

As David sets up the watering system, the plants he has come to rescue are in trouble. The heat has begun to attack and break down their very structure. The enzymes needed for the chemical reactions to survive are becoming deactivated. The membranes that keep all the bits of the cell separate begin to weaken and leak. The temperature of the plants continues to climb, and the structural tissues in the stems become unable to support the weight above them. It is then that the first spray of water begins to fall over the collapsed foliage.

David isn't outdoors for very long — at least, he doesn't think it has been very long — when he notices that he's soaking wet with sweat. He stops what he is doing and stands still for a moment. He is suddenly exhausted, and his muscles feel weak and rubbery. His wife, Abby, comes up behind him. "What are you doing out here without your hat?" she inquires with loving impatience. But when she sees how ill he looks, she immediately helps him indoors and into an air-conditioned room until he begins to feel better.

When the heat wave breaks days later, David has completely recovered from his bout of heat exhaustion, and most of the garden has struggled through too — but not all of it. Some plants will need to be replaced with heat-resilient ones.

Taking the Heat

The atmosphere above the planet consists of a landscape similar to that on the surface of the earth. For example, it includes mountains and valleys and rivers. Unlike the earth's landscape, however, that of the heavens is largely distant and invisible. Mountains of high atmospheric pressure are often called *fair-weather systems* because the dome of air that is their hallmark acts as a barrier to bad weather and keeps the clouds and precipitation associated with low-pressure events at bay.

As high pressure builds over a location, it often replaces dark clouds and rain with beautiful blue skies and sunny weather. Whereas storms have a dynamic presence, so much so that we sometimes personify and even name them (as for hurricanes), the seemingly benign high-pressure system responsible for a beautiful day goes unremarked. However, such systems can have destructive power if they linger too long, as when an enormous lens of air magnifies sunshine and warmth over many days into a heat wave as deadly as any hurricane.

Almost every year, in midsummer, a dome of high pressure anchors itself off the Atlantic Coast near the island of Bermuda. On the satellite images, the clouds over the Atlantic near Bermuda are pushed away by the high pressure system. The clear air looks like a hole in the clouds, but it the opposite: It is actually a mountain of air that rises above the clouds. Immense currents of air flow around the base of this mountain in a clockwise direction. As the circulation rotates around the weather system, it

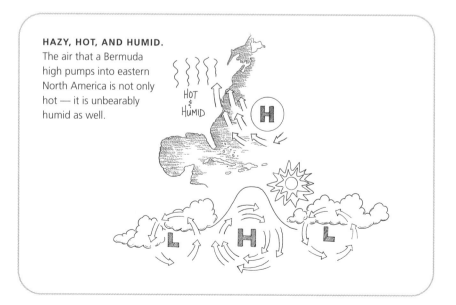

HAZY, HOT, AND HUMID. The air that a Bermuda high pumps into eastern North America is not only hot — it is unbearably humid as well.

dips into tropical latitudes, where it soaks up humidity and heat. The air currents then swing northwest over the southeastern portion of the United States, then north into the Midwest and New England. Everywhere it goes, the wind brings more and more heat and humidity, without a break night or day.

Formally defined, a heat wave is three consecutive days with a minimum shade temperature of 90°F (32°C). (This standard is still in use by the United States National Weather Service. However, in some hot dry climates, such as parts of California, the heat wave temperature can be 100°F or even as high as 105°F.) For the next 7 days, the Bermuda high phenomenon is in place, and much of the eastern United States suffocates under a blanket of hot, wet air that damages gardens and enervates gardeners. Winds that carry the heat and humidity are light, like a last exhalation, and stifling weather blankets the entire area.

Heat Isn't the Same Everywhere

A 95°F (35°C) day in Texas and a 95°F day in Minnesota look exactly the same on the thermometer. But plants that are heat resilient and thrive in

Global Warming Comes to the Garden

Through much of the final decades of the 20th century, a debate raged whether global warming was real or whether the data suggesting its existence represented normal climatic variations. Now the question has shifted from whether global warming exists to what to do about it. Over the past 50 years, the mean daytime temperature across the United States has increased, as has the average nighttime temperature. Humidity has risen, especially during the evening hours. And the occurrence of heat waves has increased markedly.

Texas often don't even survive in Minnesota, and a plant that is heat resilient in Minnesota wouldn't grow well in Texas. The overall difference in the climates of these two states more than outweighs the similarities. Climate is such a strong factor in how plants adapt to their environment that such traits as heat resilience become relative to climate and ultimately defined by it.

Natural systems hone in organisms the qualities that best allow them to use the resources around them and to endure the environmental extremes of their particular climate. Many plants cannot substantially expand these abilities to be resilient in climates vastly different from their native ones. If a plant can endure the months of heat in Florida, it probably cannot tolerate the extreme cold of Maine. Queen palms don't grow in Bangor, Maine, and lowbush blueberries don't grow in Miami, Florida.

One reason why plants cannot adapt to other climates is the extremes between the climates. A plant in northern Minnesota must survive minimum winter temperatures of –50°F (–46°C) every year, whereas it must endure heat above 85°F (29°C) for only 1 or 2 weeks each summer. A plant in southern Texas, in contrast, needs to be resistant to minimum winter temperatures of only 20 to 30°F (–7 to –1°C) but must be resilient to temperatures above 85°F (29°C) for up to 7 months annually.

Chill Requirements

It is tempting to view environmental traits out of context, as if they could exist in a climate without influencing other factors in the environment. The intricacies required for a plant to become resilient to one environmental extreme, such as cold, often interfere with its practical adaptation to the opposing environmental extreme, in this case heat. In Minnesota, the dominant annual weather extreme is cold, with heat being important but subordinate. In southern Texas, the reverse is true. For example, rugosa rose is so cold resilient that it can grow in northern Minnesota and is so heat resilient that it can grow in many warm climates. However, it can't grow in USDA climate Zones 9 and 10, such as in southern Texas, not because these areas are too hot, but because they aren't cold enough.

As fall approaches, plants from temperate climates begin to enter dormancy to survive the winter. The purpose of the chill requirement is to ensure that plants do not break from dormancy before warm spring weather is established. Chill requirements are specific to individual species or varieties and are expressed in hours of exposure to temperatures below a threshold, often 45°F (7°C).

There is a correlation between the duration of the chill requirement and the ability of a plant to grow in warm climates. For example, apples are hardy from Zones 3 to 7 and need about 1,200 hours below 45°F (7°C) to break dormancy. Figs, on the other hand, are hardy in Zones 6 to 9 and require only 200 hours of exposure to temperatures below 45°F (7°C). This points up a persistent problem in discussing heat-resilient plants: A plant that is heat resilient in New England would not survive a Florida summer. Likewise, a plant that is heat tolerant in Arizona will die in a garden in Michigan. To make heat resilience meaningful to gardeners across North America, the information must be focused on the region in which they garden.

Where Are the Heat Waves?

A heat wave is defined as three or more consecutive days with a high temperature over 90°F (32°C). About 50 years ago, locations in the eastern one third of the United States could expect perhaps one heat wave a summer, with some years having none at all. Those living in cities and towns in the western part of the country could expect the same. Localities in the central region, including the Great Plains, could reliably expect one heat wave event per year. However, that was before global warming made its impact.

At the beginning of the 21st century, the outlook has changed noticeably. No matter where you live in the continental U.S. states, an average of two heat wave events occur per year. If you live in the eastern or western third of the country, that number is closer to three events per year. And not only is the number of heat waves is increasing, but hot weather seems to last longer as well. A recent heat event in the southern plains

Ultraviolet Light and Your Garden

Just beyond the violet color of the visible light spectrum are wavelengths called *ultraviolet* (UV). Ultraviolet light gives us sunburn and is implicated in skin cancer. Much of the ultraviolet light that comes to us from the sun is blocked from reaching the earth's surface by the layer of ozone that encases the earth high in the atmosphere. Over recent decades, the ozone layer has been reduced by pollution to the point that researchers have begun to wonder about the impact of increased UV radiation on plants growing on the earth. Studies have since determined that enhanced levels of UV radiation slow growth, reduce flowering, and hamper photosynthesis in species as diverse as loblolly pine and rice.

Even though UV radiation was known to negatively affect plants, it still remained to be seen if current levels of UV radiation harmed garden plants. In a study by the USDA, a red-leaf lettuce cultivar, 'New Red Fire', was grown in the presence of natural UV radiation, just as you grow your plants in your garden. Another set of plants was grown in an environment where the UV radiation was filtered out. After 1 month, the lettuce that was protected from UV exposure contained 63 percent more fresh weight than the plants grown under garden conditions. The plants exposed to UV radiation did have something the protected plants did not, however: increased concentrations of bioflavonoids, biologically active compounds naturally produced in plants that are thought to have benefits for human nutrition. Plants are speculated to manufacture these as protection against UV rays.

was counted as one heat wave, but it baked Oklahoma and Texas with daily temperatures over at least 90°F (32°C) for over a month.

The times are changing, and the weather is getting hotter almost everywhere you go, including your garden. The good news is that the growing season in many locations has increased by about 2 weeks. But once the plants get growing, they will need increased assistance to get them through the heat.

Heat Damage, from the Ground Up

When the air is mercilessly hot, it is easy to imagine how the temperatures can have a negative effect on garden and landscape plants. But it isn't always the air temperature that damages plants; sometimes it's the temperature of the soil.

The soil insulates itself from excessive heat, as is easy to discover if you dig into the garden on a hot day. The surface layer of soil may be hot, but down just a few inches deeper, the soil is often cool and damp. The ingredients of the soil, the mineral and organic particles, moisture, and air pockets, combine to create a substance that modifies temperatures from an inch or two to several feet below the surface. When unprotected by mulch or shade, the thin layer at the surface can heat up to temperatures well over 100°F (38°C) to near 130°F (54°C). Hot soil can produce heat injuries that are easy to mistake for other problems.

Too Much of a Good Thing: How Heat Kills

All the many physical and physiological processes that go on in a plant are influenced by heat. As the air temperature increases, the plant's metabolic rate increases, chemical reactions proceed faster and more efficiently, and growth accelerates. Nutrient absorption jumps substantially: Some plants show a 10-fold increase when temperatures rise from 55 to 70°F (13–21°C). But when temperatures rise beyond the average optimum range of 55 to 90°F (13–32°C), the heat, once an ally, imposes burdens rather than conferring benefit.

Most plants grow well at temperatures within 40 to 95°F (4–35°C). As the temperature rises within this range, the rate of respiration (the process by which food is metabolized to release energy) increases faster than the rate of photosynthesis (the process of producing food from

Gardening in the Heat

Doing gardening, or doing just about anything, in the heat of a scorching summer day not only is uncomfortable but also can be dangerous to your health. Heat exhaustion, dehydration, and heat stroke are some of the potential consequences. About 175 people die from heat-related causes each year in the United States — more than the number that die from floods, hurricanes, lightning, wind, and tornadoes combined. Here are some tips for making the best of oppressive summertime heat:

• Plan activities that require physical exertion for the coolest periods of the day — early morning and twilight.

• Use a sunscreen with an SPF (sun protection factor) rating of 15 or higher. It will be more effective if you apply it at least half an hour before going outdoors. Don't forget to apply it even on overcast days.

• Although some plants are rated as "full sun," people aren't. Seek shade whenever possible. And wear a hat!

• Keep hydrated. Drink lots of water or natural (no added sugar) juices. Stay away from alcoholic and carbonated beverages, as well as coffee.

• Wear loose-fitting, light-colored clothing.

• Some prescription medications and herbal remedies can reduce your body's resilience to heat or make your skin more vulnerable to sunburn. Ask your doctor or pharmacist.

energy). If the temperature climbs more than 10 degrees F (5 degrees C) above the maximum optimum threshold of 95°F (35°C), photosynthesis sharply decreases and respiration consumes the plant's food, weakening it and placing it in a potentially deadly situation.

In addition to the reduction in energy reserves, excess heat induces chemical changes in critical enzymes (catalytic agents that speed up reactions) within a plant. Plant enzymes perform their catalytic actions only within a limited temperature range. As the temperature climbs, the enzymes become deactivated, the structure of plant proteins is altered, and the membranes in the cells begin to leak, damaging the cells. As the internal temperature of the plant rises, the rate of transpiration increases until the roots can no longer absorb moisture from the soil fast enough to keep up with the water loss, and the leaves wilt. Over the coming hours or days, injured tissues on the stem appear as dark, sunken lesions. Leaves become mottled with yellow and drop, and the plant dies.

Plants try to conserve moisture in hot environments and slow heat stress by closing the stomata in their leaves and other physical methods. But when excessive heat damages enzymes and causes proteins to misfold (a biochemical term that loosely equates to unraveling), the damage would seem to be irreversible, almost always resulting in massive injury.

Whereas some plants die, plants with certain characteristics take hot weather in stride. Such plants produce heat-shock proteins, which protect them from lethal heat by many means, including facilitating the proper folding of proteins in the cells to restore normal function, shoring up cell membranes, and repairing leaks. Heat-shock proteins also buffer a protein complex called photosystem II, which is essential to photosynthesis but sensitive to heat. It would be damaged or destroyed in high temperatures if it weren't protected by heat-shock proteins. Plants that produce heat-shock proteins not only acclimate to hot environments better than plants without them, but they also tolerate temperatures that would be lethal to other plants. Heat-shock proteins are synthesized within minutes of a plant being exposed to dangerous heat and endure in a plant for many hours after temperatures return to normal.

Helping Your Plants Beat the Heat

A plant's natural ability to survive the heat of summer can be increased by a little help from you. Here are some tips for readying your garden for high temperatures.

Choose the right site. Along the edge of the house is a natural place to create a garden. When designing a garden bed or foundation planting, the house itself needs to be taken into account, as it is will be a major factor in the microclimate of that garden. In the northern hemisphere, the sun rises in the east, passes above the southern horizon, and sets in the west. This makes the south side of the house the hot side. When planting foundation gardens with a southern exposure, be aware of how much warmer this microclimate can be than other areas of your yard.

A southern exposure is warmer because it receives more solar radiation than other exposures. That alone can make the south-facing garden 10 to 15 degrees F warmer than other plantings. Also, dark-colored buildings absorb solar radiation and then radiate it back as heat. The additional heat can keep plants warmer during cooler times of the year, keeping them growing longer. During warm months, though, the extra heat can be damaging to plants, especially if they are in a little alcove that inhibits air circulation. Light-colored buildings, in contrast, heat up less because they *reflect*, rather than absorb, the solar radiation. Although less heat is produced, the additional light intensity can damage some plants in a way similar to heat. When planting on the south side, choose plants that are resilient to heat and drought, amend the soil with compost each spring and at planting, and always cover the soil with organic mulch.

Amend the soil. Plenty of organic matter helps soil to stay cool during hot weather. Compost, whether commercially produced or homemade, adds organic matter. It improves drainage, builds fertility, enhances moisture retention, increases aeration, strengthens soil structure, and improves the health of the soil ecology. All of these benefits also act as buffers against the effects of heat. The best time to add organic matter is when you are setting out your plants.

Pick the proper plant. If a plant is to grow in a hot location, select a heat-resilient one that complements your garden design. Using the right plant in the right place means that you solve the problem before it becomes one.

Protect the vulnerable. Newly planted and young plants are especially susceptible to damage by a heat wave. Their root systems are still getting established and may not be operating at full capacity for a while. When transplanting, be sure to lightly shade (about 30 percent sunlight reduction) the newly planted tree or other plant from the sun and wind until it is established. Also, water deeply so that the roots will be encouraged to grow deeper.

Use a shallow mulch. Mulching should be second nature to gardeners everywhere, but some people think of it only as protection from cold, while, in fact, it has an important role to play in protecting plants from heat. The temperature of unprotected soil in direct sunlight can easily soar to over 100°F (38°C) early in the day and climb even higher later in the afternoon. Plant roots generally grow best at soil temperatures of 60 to 80°F (16–27°C). When the soil temperature climbs into the triple digits, injuries result, including death of the root system.

A shallow layer (2 to 3 inches [5–8 cm] deep) of an organic mulch such as pine bark is all you need to shade the soil and keep it much cooler than the surrounding, unprotected soil. Mulch as much of the root area of your plants as possible. (Deep layers of mulch were popular for a while, but they inhibit oxygen from getting to the roots and thus hurt plants more than protect them.)

Give adequate water. Water is absorbed from the soil into the roots, which conduct it to the leaves. Most of it is lost to the air in transpiration. About 10 percent of the absorbed water is used in such processes as respiration and photosynthesis. The remaining 90 percent is thought to be used to cool the plant. On a hot day, any large tree in your yard can lose about 100 gallons (379 liters) of water into the air. That moisture comes from the ground, and if the supply is not replaced, there may not be 100 gallons of water to absorb the next time.

Water thoroughly and deeply, being sure to apply water out beyond the canopy. This advice applies to more than just trees. Many plants, from perennials to shrubs, have most of their feeder roots just beyond the edge of their foliage, or the so-called drip line. You can use a moisture meter to regularly evaluate the moisture reserves of the soil. Keep a lookout for signs of heat stress in your plants, including scorching of leaf margins, leaf curl, and tip burn of leaves.

Fertilize properly. Fertilizing during hot weather, especially when it is hot and dry, is detrimental to a plant and can injure its roots. In hot weather, nitrates build up in plant roots just as those roots are shutting down because of the heat. Similarly, fertilizer applied a month or so before a heat wave can produce a flush of tender growth that is much more easily scorched or killed than hardened tissues would be. In heat-prone areas, improve soil and nurture your plants with compost, which supplies nutrients naturally and gradually. Alternatively, you can supply nutrients in a water solution.

Finding Heat-Resilient Plants

There are an estimated 250,000 species of plants in the world growing from the Arctic and Antarctic to the Amazon. Each of them has specific optimum growth requirements. In addition to individual species, there are hundreds of thousands of varieties with their own individual optimum growing requirements. One element of these requirements is heat. Botany seems to deal with a million Goldilocks, with each plant thriving in growing conditions that are "just right" for it and it alone.

To illustrate the diversity of optimum temperature environments, consider that English daisy grows best at 59°F (15°C), ageratum thrives at 64°F (18°C), and petunia prefers 80°F (27°C). Yet all of these plants can easily grow in your garden, sharing the same growing conditions, and all be healthy and blooming at the same time. So while "optimum" is unique and specific, "acceptable" is more generic and pliant. The same can be said for a plant's need for, and response to, heat.

Heat-resilient plants can be divided into groups that provide the greatest number of plants that are adaptable to the most diverse environments. For the greatest scope and practicality, let's divide heat-resilient plants into four categories: annuals, vegetables, trees and shrubs, and hometown favorites.

Too Good to Be True: Great Heat-Resilient Annuals

Purslane. When weeding, many gardeners spend much time uprooting purslane. Purslane is a weed that could lay claim to being better adapted to more extremes of weather than any garden plant known. The thing never seems to wilt; it loves the heat, can tolerate being flooded, and is drought tolerant too. All the qualities that make this plant so annoying as a weed would make it outstanding as a garden plant.

Also known as *Portulaca oleracea*, purslane is now available at your local garden center sporting cultivar names like 'Double Yubi'. Look for them in hanging baskets and pots. They're adorned with tight little double flowers in a wide selection of bright colors. The flowers start the season about the size of a nickel and get larger the hotter it gets.

Scaevola. Many of the plants in the sizzling hot continent of Australia don't have common names, so when this one came to North America, its scientific name, *Scaevola*, became its common name too. Scaevola has long stems covered with small green leaves and small, jaunty, fan-shaped blue-purple flowers. It makes an excellent hanging basket or container plant. Scaevola can take blistering heat but it is not drought tolerant, so don't neglect watering.

Annuals

Annuals are plants that complete their entire life cycle — from germinating from a seed, to producing new seed, to dying — in one growing season. Rather than storing food reserves for spring and going dormant during cold times, annuals have made life simple, if short. They thrive in the warm months, produce seed, and die with winter on the doorstep. Because they aren't perennials, they don't have to deal with the problems

25 Terrific Heat-Resilient Annuals

Ageratum *(Ageratum houstonianum)*

Angelonia *(Angelonia angustifolia* 'Blue Summer Orchid')

Begonia *(Begonia* x *semperflorens-cultorum)*

Blanket flower *(Gaillardia pulchella)*

Bracteantha *(Bracteantha* spp.)

Caladium (angel wings) *(Caladium* 'Pink Gem', 'Red Frill')

Celosia *(Celosia cristata)*

Coleus *(Coleus* x *hybridus* 'Burgundy Sun')

Creeping zinnia *(Sanvitalia procumbens)*

Dianthus *(Dianthus* 'Melody Pink')

Diascia *(Diascia barberae)*

Lantana *(Lantana* spp.)

Madagascar periwinkle (*Catharanthus roseus* 'Parasol')

Marigold (*Tagetes erecta,* Antigua series)

Melampodium (*Melampodium paludosum* 'Derby')

Mexican sunflower *(Tithonia rotundifolia)*

Moss rose *(Portulaca grandiflora)*

Nierembergia *(Nierembergia caerulea)*

Ornamental pepper *(Capsicum annuum)*

Petunia (*Petunia* x *hybridus* Carpet series, 'Happy Dream')

Portulaca *(Portulaca oleracea)*

Scaevola *(Scaevola aemula)*

Venedio (*Venedio* spp.)

Verbena *(Verbena bonariensis)*

that many different climates impose on plants. An annual that is heat resilient, then, can grow in any garden prone to heat and do well, from the desert, to the coasts, to the prairie. Many of these plants are native to hot areas of the world.

Vegetables

Vegetables are often divided into cool-season and warm-season crops because the two groups prefer very different weather conditions. That said, a variety of cool-season vegetable that is heat tolerant can effectively buffer unseasonable warm weather within the normal growing season or extend the normal growing season by a few weeks into times of warmer weather.

Heat not only changes the internal processes of plants, but it also changes them in visually apparent ways. Perhaps nowhere else in the landscape are these alterations more concentrated or diverse than in the vegetable garden. Some vegetable crops, such as peas, require cool temperatures to grow their best. It is therefore no surprise that peas would respond to hot weather with symptoms of heat stress. Peppers and tomatoes, in contrast, are native to the tropics and have always lived with heat. Yet even warm-weather crops can be very sensitive to hot weather. Here are some of the problems that hot weather can bring to the vegetable patch and varieties that help overcome them.

Carrots. Some varieties of carrots are very sensitive to heat, and the length and shape of the root reflect the effects of heat. Carrots prefer a temperature of 60 to 70°F (15.5–21°C) for best growth, shape, and taste. If temperatures exceed 80°F (27°C), a carrot root grows stubby, the texture can get tough and woody, and the taste sharp and bitter. Help control the growth of your carrots by keeping the soil moist and applying a light layer of mulch before a hot spell. Plant carrots next to taller vegetables that provide some afternoon shade. Grow carrots to harvest in the season most appropriate for your climate, such as winter for parts of Texas and California, spring for Arizona, and fall for northerly areas.

Beans. Both bush and pole beans need warm weather for productive yields, but hot weather is too much of a good thing. Heat can induce blossom drop in beans, a condition in which flowers and small pods fall from the plant. Keep the soil moist but avoid overwatering, as this can worsen the problem. Beans are sensitive to local conditions and the best way to find out which variety is most resilient to the specific microclimate of your garden is either to ask your neighbors what has done well for them or to experiment yourself. 'Gator Green' and 'Gold Crop Wax' are heat-resilient beans.

Corn. Corn originated in the tropics, and its warm-weather origins are evident in its growth requirements. As long as there is sufficient soil moisture, the hotter it gets (up to about 90 to 95°F [32–35°C]), the faster corn grows — and the heavier the yields. If insufficient moisture exists during hot weather, however, the yields and quality will dramatically drop. Keep soil moisture adequate and consistent. This may not be easy, as corn uses a great deal of water.

Some Like It Hot

A number of herbs and vegetables actually prefer hot weather. Not only do they grow better, but they are also more flavorful. Okra, for example, originated in Africa and was grown in Egypt in ancient times. It needs sustained warm temperatures to fruit well. Soil temperatures should be between 70 and 90°F. Seeds germinate best at 80 to 95°F (29.5–35°C). Eggplant grows best when soil temperatures are hot, between 80 and 90°F (27–32°C) and air temperatures are consistently above 70°F (21°C). The seeds germinate best at about 85°F (29.5°C). Here are some other vegetables that thrive in the heat:

Vegetables	Herbs
Eggplant	Oregano
Melons (all types)	Rosemary
Okra	Thyme
Sweet potatoes	

Lettuce. Heat is responsible for two major problems affecting lettuce. *Bolting* is the term for the premature development of a seed stalk, which rises from a rosette of basal leaves. In lettuce, bolting is spurred by exposure to hot weather; the seed rises rapidly from a plant that is a mass of bitter-tasting leaves. Choose slow-bolting varieties, sow early enough that you can harvest plants while the weather is still relatively cool, and keep the ground evenly moist.

The second heat-related lettuce problem is *tip burn*. Blackish spots appear on leaves near the larger veins, and the tips and margins of the leaves turn brown and die. Again, soil moisture needs to be consistent. Also, grow heat-resilient varieties and avoid fertilizing the plants during warm weather.

Peas. Peas and heat should be kept as far apart as east and west. This vegetable originated in Europe, not the tropics, and is not heat resilient. To date, no satisfactory heat-resilient variety of pea has been developed. Your best bet is to grow and harvest your peas in cool weather. If hot weather visits the pea patch, the yield and quality are reduced and the vines die back sooner. Even and adequate moisture may buffer some of the effects of warm weather for a time. When hot weather hits in the middle of the pea-growing season, keep an optimist's outlook — leave the peas on the vine to dry, and make pea soup at your convenience.

Heat-Resilient Vegetables

Lettuces
Black-seeded Simpson
Buttercrunch
Dark Green Boston
Centennial
Green Ice
Green Salad Bowl
Red Salad Bowl
Iceberg
Lollo Rosso
Mini Green
Red Grenoble
Red Riding Hood
Rouge d'Hiver
Ruby
Simpson Elite
Summertime

Potatoes
Anoka
Irish Cobbler
Kennebec
Norgold M
Red Gold
Shepody
Yukon Gold

Tomatoes
Arkansas Traveler
Celebrity
Heat Wave
Homestead 24
Mountain Pride
Porter
Solar Set
Striped German
Sungold
Sweet Chelsea
Sweet Olive
Valley Girl
Yellow Pear

Peppers. Another warm-weather crop from tropical America (including parts of South and Central America), peppers thrive in warm weather. However, they can't take hot, dry weather. Those conditions cause the young buds, blossoms, and small fruits to yellow and drop from plants, a seeming result of fluctuating soil moisture and heat. Cultivating or otherwise disturbing pepper plants during hot, dry weather damages roots and makes matters worse. During hot weather, keep soil moisture even and mulch lightly to help the soil retain it. Pepper varieties adapted to hot weather are just about any variety called NuMex, such as NuMex Joe E. Parker, or a TAM, such as TAM Mild Jalapeño II.

Potatoes. This warm-weather crop suffers from heat in a variety of unexpected ways, one of which doesn't even show up until dinnertime: After cooking, hot-weather-damaged potatoes turn black, especially if drought or low light was a problem while they were growing. When weather changes suddenly from cool and wet to hot and dry, tip burn may turn leaf tops and edges brown. Scald of potato tubers occurs when the ground is warmed so much that tubers are damaged in the soil.

Spinach. Like lettuce, spinach is a quick-maturing, cool-season crop that bolts when hot weather comes calling. The best defense against losing the crop is to sow it early enough that warm weather is avoided. The variety 'Melody' is bolt resistant.

Tomatoes. Tomatoes are perhaps the most popular vegetable. Native to tropical South America, they thrive in warm weather, but they have limits on how much heat they can tolerate without adverse consequences. When the weather turns hot and dry (with air temperatures exceeding 95°F [35°C]), the plants just about stop growing and often drop flower buds, flowers, and small fruit. If nighttime minimum temperatures stay above about 85°F (29°C) during ripening, the pigment that turns the fruit red doesn't form satisfactorily and the flesh softens excessively.

Tomatoes ripen best when average daytime temperatures are about 75°F (24°C). If hot weather is expected during ripening time, pick the fruit when the blossom end begins to turn pink and continue the ripening process indoors in a spot with excellent ventilation.

Heat-Resilient Plants for Almost Anywhere

Some excellent garden plants not only take the heat but also thrive in a wide range of climate zones. Their flexible nature takes a lot of the guesswork out of determining whether a plant survives the type or duration of heat in your garden. To make it onto this list, a plant must be heat resilient and thrive in at least five climate zones.

Trees and Shrubs

Part of the benefit of a heat-resilient garden is its low maintenance, a real plus in dangerously hot weather. These trees and shrubs do just fine in the heat, letting you stay indoors if you want to.

Common Name	Botanical Name	Hardiness Zones
Arrowwood	*Viburnum dentatum*	3–8
Blackhaw viburnum	*Viburnum prunifolium*	3–9
Burning bush	*Euonymus alatus*	4–9
Creeping juniper	*Juniperus horizontalis*	3–9
Eastern red cedar	*Juniperus virginiana*	3–9
Lowbush blueberry	*Vaccinium angustifolium*	2–8
Nannyberry	*Viburnum lentago*	2–8
Rugosa rose	*Rosa rugosa*	2–9

Perennials

Some perennials can take the heat with such grace that they keep the garden as cool as a cucumber. These are the superstars of hot-weather plantings.

Common Name	Botanical Name	Hardiness Zones
Amethyst sea holly	*Eryngium amethystinum*	3–8
Autumn Joy sedum	*Sedum* 'Autumn Joy'	3–10
Blanket flower	*Gaillardia* x *grandiflora*	3–8
Carpet bugle	*Ajuga reptans*	3–9
Coralbells	*Heuchera sanguinea*	3–8
Coreopsis	*Coreopsis verticillata*	4–9
Daylily	*Hemerocallis* spp.	3–10
Echinacea	*Echinacea* spp.	3–9
Eulalia grass	*Miscanthus sinensis*	4–9

Common Name	Botanical Name	Hardiness Zones
Gayfeather	*Liatris* spp.	4–9
Lilyturf	*Liriope spicata*	5–10
Mullein	*Verbascum thapsus*	3–9
Penstemon	*Penstemon* spp.	3–10
Red-hot poker	*Kniphofia* spp.	4–9
Rudbeckia	*Rudbeckia* spp.	3–9
Sweet Autumn clematis	*Clematis paniculata*	5–10
Thyme	*Thymus* spp.	4–9
Yarrow	*Achillea* spp.	3–9
Yellow columbine	*Aquilegia chrysantha*	3–8
Yucca	*Yucca* spp.	5–10

Hometown Favorites

This group of plants is heat resilient within a smaller range of climate areas.

Common Name	Botanical Name	Hardiness Zones
Heat-Resilient Trees and Shrubs for Zones 3–5:		
Cockspur hawthorn	*Crataegus crus-galli*	4–7
Freeman maple	*Acer* x *freemanii*	4–7
Hackberry	*Celtis occidentalis*	2–9
Hardy rubber tree	*Eucommia ulmoides*	4–7
Hedge maple	*Acer campestre*	5–8
Norway maple	*Acer platanoides*	3–7
Red maple	*Acer rubrum*	3–9
Sugar maple	*Acer saccharum* 'Green Mountain'	4–8
Trident maple	*Acer buergeranum*	5–9
Washington hawthorn	*Crataegus phaenopyrum*	4–8
White birch	*Betula platyphylla*	4–7
Trees and Shrubs for Zones 6 and 7:		
Cockspur hawthorn	*Crataegus crus-galli*	4–7
Freeman maple	*Acer* x *freemanii*	4–7

Heat-Resilient Plants (continued)

Common Name	Botanical Name	Hardiness Zones
Golden-rain tree	*Koelreuteria paniculata*	6–9
Hackberry	*Celtic occidentalis*	2–9
Hardy rubber tree	*Eucommia ulmoides*	4–7
Hedge maple	*Acer campestre*	5–8
Japanese cedar	*Cryptomeria japonica*	6–9
Leyland cypress	x *Cupressocyparis leylandii*	6–9
Mimosa silk tree	*Albizia julibrissin*	6–9
Norway maple	*Acer platanoides*	3–7
Red maple	*Acer rubrum*	3–9
Southern magnolia	*Magnolia grandiflora*	6–9
Trident maple	*Acer buergeranum*	5–9
Washington hawthorn	*Crataegus phaenopyrum*	4–8
White birch	*Betula platyphylla*	4–7

Trees and Shrubs for Zones 8 and 9:

Afghanistan pine	*Pinus eldarica*	7–10 (dry)
African sumac	*Rhus lancea*	9–10 (dry)
Aleppo pine	*Pinus halepensis*	8–10 (dry)
California pepper	*Schinus molle*	9–10 (dry)
Golden-rain tree	*Koelreuteria paniculata*	6–9
Hackberry	*Celtis occidentalis*	2–9
Hedge maple	*Acer campestre*	5–8
Japanese cedar	*Cryptomeria japonica*	6–9
Leyland cypress	x *Cupressocyparis leylandii*	6–9
Live oak	*Quercus virginiana*	8–10 (humid)
Mimosa silk tree	*Albizia julibrissin*	6–9
Purple hop bush	*Dodonaea viscosa* 'Purpurea'	8–10 (dry)
Red horse chestnut	*Aesculus* x *carnea*	7–8
Red maple	*Acer rubrum*	3–9
Southern magnolia	*Magnolia grandiflora*	6–9 (humid)
Texas ranger	*Leucophyllum frutescens*	9–10 (dry)

Common Name	Botanical Name	Hardiness Zones
Trident maple	*Acer buergeranum*	5–9
Washington hawthorn	*Crataegus phaenopyrum*	4–8
Yaupon holly	*Ilex vomitoria*	7–10 (humid)

Perennials for Zones 8 and 9:

Lavender cotton	*Santolina* spp.	6–9
Prickly pear	*Opuntia* spp.	5–10
Rosemary	*Rosmarinus officinalis*	8–10

Trees and Shrubs for Zone 10:

Afghanistan pine	*Pinus eldarica*	7–10 (dry)
African sumac	*Rhus lancea*	9–10 (dry)
Aleppo pine	*Pinus halepensis*	8–10 (dry)
California pepper	*Schinus molle*	9–10 (dry)
Camphor tree	*Cinnamomum camphora*	10 (dry)
Desert ironwood	*Olneya tesota*	9–10 (dry)
Flaxleaf paperbark	*Melaleuca linariifolia*	10 (dry)
Live oak	*Quercus virginiana*	8–10 (humid)
Purple hop bush	*Dodonaea viscosa* 'Purpurea'	8–10 (dry)
Prickly pear	*Opuntia* spp.	5–10
Texas ranger	*Leucophyllum frutescens*	9–10 (dry)
Yaupon	*Ilex vomitoria*	7–10 (humid)

Perennials for Zone 10:

Rock rose	*Cistus* spp.	9–10 (dry)
Rosemary	*Rosmarinus officinalis*	8–10
Snakeplant	*Sansevieria* spp.	10

Heat and the Lawn

It must be tough to be a lawn and have to endure a heat wave with no way to get out of the sun. Some lawns can't tolerate a heat wave, especially in such areas as the southern plains, where hot weather lingers for weeks. If you move to an area like this from a more temperate climate, you'll discover that some grasses you are familiar with, like creeping and chewing fescue, can't take such conditions. Some lawn grasses, however, can resist the heat and maintain their good looks at the same time, like blue grama, perennial rye, buffalo grass, Bermuda, zoysia, and Bahia grass. In addition, consider these interesting types.

Bermuda 'Princess'. This new variety has even greater heat resilience than older types of Bermuda grass.

Seashore paspalam. A grass for warm climates (it goes dormant at about 55°F [13°C]), seashore paspalam is especially good for lawns along the seashore. It is so salt tolerant that it can be irrigated with seawater. And yes, it is very heat resilient.

Endophytic tall fescue. Fescues and heat tolerance are not often mentioned in the same sentence, but this grass is the exception. Tall fescue is the tough member of the family and was developed into a turf-grade grass decades ago. Recently, tall fescue varieties containing natural endophytes (fungi that live inside the leaf) have been released. The endophytes make the grass even more resilient to disease — and to heat.

Coping with Heat Damage

Sudden Wilting and/or Dying

Description: Damping-off is a disease caused by soil fungi. It affects seedlings from germination to the true leaf stage. Damping-off is so common that whenever its symptoms appear, many people automatically assume that this nefarious disease is to blame. However, when the symptoms appear in hot weather, the damage in the seedbeds or seed flats may not be caused by damping-off at all, but rather by heat. In hot weather, especially heat accompanied by bright sun, the soil at the base of a stem can become so hot that the tissues are destroyed; thus, the plant dies.

Symptoms: In herbaceous plants, the base of the seedlings at the soil line turns brown, rots, and falls over. In woody species, a seedling wilts but often stays erect.

Remedies: Although sudden wilting and dying may indeed be heat related, to be safe you may want to follow the procedures for damping-off: Remove the entire infected portion of the seed flat, soil and all, plus a buffer area extending into the healthy seedlings a few inches. Transfer the remaining soil and plants to a new, clean flat. Use clean tools and disinfect them after touching anything that could be infected with the damping-off organism. Keep the healthy rescued seedlings slightly drier than normal to inhibit and kill the disease. When watering, keep the leaves dry by watering from below rather than overhead. You can do this by filling a larger container with an inch of water, then placing the flat of seedlings in it for a few minutes until it obsorbs the moisture.

Strategies: Shading, such as with shade cloth, maintaining even moisture, and providing good air circulation can reduce the occurrence of damping-off.

Stressed Container Plants

Description: The soil in containers where plants grow, especially dark-colored containers, can become very hot in summer. The container absorbs solar radiation, warming the pot and, by conduction, warming the soil. To maintain good growing conditions for (most) plants, the soil in a container should not exceed 95 to 100°F (35–38°C) and optimally should be much lower. However, actual conditions can be much more extreme. In wholesale nurseries that grow container plants, soil temperatures as high as 120°F (49°C) have been measured in summer from areas in cool northern climates. In southern regions with naturally hot climates, values as high as 136°F (58°C) have been recorded! That's equal to the hottest temperature ever recorded on earth. Such temperatures, needless to say, are lethal to plants.

Symptoms: Because the growing space of a container plant is small compared to that of plants in the ground, the plant reacts to stress faster

ABOVE IT ALL. Plants growing in containers need more protection from hot soil than those rooted in the ground.

and often to a greater degree than its counterparts in the garden. Also, a large plant in a small pot shows stress symptoms even more quickly than plants in larger containers. The first symptom of heat stress is usually wilting of the youngest leaves, followed by general wilting of all the foliage. Leaf scorch can burn the margins of the leaves. In woody plants, defoliation occurs. When stress is gradual, the leaves can turn yellowish before dropping, but when the environmental change is rapid, the leaves can fall like snowflakes even while still green. A similar leaf drop may occur on herbaceous plants, but an entire plant can also collapse as the stem loses its structural strength.

Remedies: Responding quickly to symptoms is important, as the problem can worsen very fast. If possible, move the plant to a shady spot out of direct sunlight. If the soil is dry, moisten it from below by setting it in a container filled with water. Try to keep the plant away from excessively breezy areas. Avoid fertilizing any plants that are under stress.

Strategies: To keep container plants cool, nurseries now use what is called pot-in-pot growing systems. A large pot is sunk into the ground so that the lip is flush with the soil line. The plant in the slightly smaller growing pot is inserted into the larger pot and a drip irrigation line is placed in the growing container. This effectively keeps the soil moist and cool while preventing plants from being knocked over by wind.

They Put Up a Parking Lot

Every landscape has hot spots where the temperature rises a little higher than anywhere else nearby. A good way to find trees that are resilient to these areas in your yard is to go to a place where only the really heat-resilient plants can thrive: an asphalt parking lot.

Parking lots have large expanses of paved surfaces that bake in the sunlight for hours at a time, often reaching temperatures above 120°F (49°C). At night the heat is radiated back into the air, keeping the temperature of the parking lot artificially high, sometimes more than 10 degrees F (5 degrees C) warmer than surrounding areas. Any plants growing in the small, carved-out beds in parking areas are subject to degrees of heat their garden cousins never experience.

The same is true for where buildings meet parking areas. Heat is reflected off the buildings and this condition creates a hot environment for trees planted in beds next to the buildings. Knowing how professionals protect parking-lot plantings from heat injury sets the pattern for protecting plants from the microclimate hot spots in your own landscape and garden.

In the home landscape, potted plants most often live out on the deck or patio. Here, using the pot-in-pot idea not only protects your plants from heat damage but it also provides a unique and versatile look to the outside landscape. Try it with larger plants, like lily-of-the-Nile and palms. On decks, where there is no ground, you can modify the pot-in-pot system to provide the same protection. Use a decorative container larger than the growing pot, which can be placed inside it.

Heat Canker

Description: Hot soil can cook the base of a plant stem for hours at a time. The heat can damage cells and kill entire areas of the stem.

Symptoms: Heat canker can affect many species of plants and appears as an area of dead tissue at the base of a stem. The lesion expands, girdling the stem and eventually killing the plant. Heat canker should not be confused with the dozens of other types of cankers that are caused by disease organisms.

Remedies: Remove the plant from excessive heat as soon as possible to limit additional damage.

Strategies: The key to management of heat canker is controlling the temperature of the soil with a layer of organic mulch and shade. Larger mulch, such as bark nuggets, works best for trees and shrubs because it increases aeration while insulating the soil. Herbaceous plants benefit from smaller mulches, such as cocoa and buckwheat hulls. Keeping the soil moist with soaker hoses also works well.

Heat canker is also common in gardens and fields when seedlings are small (less than 6 inches (15 cm) tall), and without enough foliage to shade the soil near the plant stem. A whitish band or lesion forms at the soil line. Heat canker is more common in gardens using black plastic mulch or with dark-colored soil. Mild cases do not reduce yield of crops.

Humidity

A WEAK STORM SOMEWHERE FAR OFF TO THE NORTH pushes a warm front over the valley. As it passes, the air over the valley changes, the rise in temperature and humidity making the air cling to your skin like a faintly sticky film. The changes are subtle, but toward nightfall a flicker of lightning to the northwest announces the coming of a cold front. It flashes irregularly, lighting up this quadrant of the sky with bolts so far away that they are voiceless. The warmth and humidity brought in by the warm front have turned the atmosphere into a massive energy collector, like an enormous bell jar of power, just waiting for something to release it into the night. It will take a cold front to free the energy trapped in the still, humid air.

Even as the storm approaches, the stars still glimmer in the night sky, except for the brief moments when they are eclipsed by the bright, silent bolts. Around midnight, a shower of rain pounds the roofs of houses and soaks gardens for miles around. Flashes of blue light followed by rolls of thunder that rattle the window frames announce another change in the weather. In the hours before dawn, a chill descends. As the cool, humid air reaches the valley floor, it condenses into microscopic droplets and veils of fog materialize as if from nowhere. In the morning, the sun strikes the tops of the hills but leaves the hollows in cool shadow. The brightening sky reveals valleys filled with veils of mist just above ground. Like a lacy curtain against a window, the translucent vapor simultaneously blurs and defines, outlining the fields, pastures, and windrows while hiding their details. As the sun rises, its golden warmth disperses the mist. For the moment that it exists, however, it reminds us of the images poets, painters, and musicians over the ages have tried to capture in their work.

Humidity: A Real Wet Blanket

Many types of bad weather are like the 500-pound gorilla — they are impossible not to notice. Humidity, however, is a different kind of bad weather. It is ethereal, pervasive, and invisible, and *can* go unnoticed. Even after its damage is widespread, mildew covering roses and phlox and rot destroying vegetables, it is not recognized as the cause of the troubles. But humidity is the culprit, of these and many other problems facing the garden. The key is to "see" and understand this invisible problem so you can make your garden as resilient as possible when it comes.

Phytophthera: Attacker of Plants

The humid, wet, and cool weather that produces picturesque scenes like that just described isn't always benign. Similar weather, foggy and cool, cloaked the hills and fields of Ireland in the summer of 1845. The conditions were perfect for the unbridled growth and spread of one of the most virulent of all plant diseases, *Phytophthora infestans,* whose scientific name means "attacker and destroyer of plants." Until that summer, potatoes had been grown in Ireland and continental Europe for more than 200 years with no significant loss from disease. By the middle of the 19th century, the Irish relied on the potato as their nearly exclusive source of nutrition for a good part of the year. The Irish countryside was carpeted with fields of potato plants when the weather caused one of the worst famines in history.

Phytophthora, also known as *late blight,* can spread like wildfire, destroying entire fields in a few days. As the blight wiped out the potato crop, the people struggled through the winter, awaiting the next growing season. In 1846, the few seed potatoes remaining were planted and grew until the weather again turned humid, wet, and cool. The crop was destroyed again. The famine lasted 15 years, killed 1 million people, and forced another 1.5 million to leave their homeland.

Late blight epidemics are completely weather dependent. Whenever conditions are right (temperatures in the 60s, with near 100 percent

The Most Humid Place in the World

Few people would want to live in the most humid place on earth for any length of time, because it is also one of the hottest places. It is an area of the Red Sea coastal region of Ethiopia, in Africa. Needless to say, this region is lightly populated, and it is covered over with jungle plants and inhabited by creatures that can tolerate such steamy conditions.

humidity for 2 weeks), an epidemic results. In 1946, these conditions occurred periodically in the eastern United States, and late blight swept the region, wiping out up to 75 percent of tomato crops in many areas.

In the second half of the 20th century, this devastating disease was managed effectively with chemicals, and fortunately, late blight doesn't develop resistance in the way that other diseases do. Until the 1990s, only one type of late blight existed, and the disease could not reproduce sexually. (Sexual reproduction mixes genes and encourages genetic assemblages that are resistant to present controls.) However, a second, even more virulent strain has recently been found in North America. The outlook now is that cool, humid weather could soon produce serious epidemics of late blight that cannot be effectively managed.

Transpiration: Shifting into Reverse

Transpiration is the absorption of moisture from the soil, movement of the water through the plant, and loss of most of the moisture through the leaves. This supplies many plant processes with moisture and serves to cool the plant through evaporative loss. Many weather events, from heat to drought to wind, accelerate transpiration, which threatens the plant with problems like wilting. High humidity levels, close to 100 percent, have a completely different effect. Rather than outrunning transpiration's cooling mechanism, humidity stalls it and renders it ineffective.

The shear volume of water that plants use seems unbelievable. Every single corn plant growing in your garden will transpire about a half gallon (2.3 l) of water into the air every day. Therefore, if you have a small garden with 100 corn plants, they will need 50 gallons (225 l) of water a day. An acre of corn, from sowing to harvest, transpires about 400,000 gallons (1,800,000 l) of water. As the humidity increases, transpiration slows down and a little-heard-of phenomenon called *reverse transpiration* accelerates. In reverse transpiration, moisture in the air enters the plant, as opposed to moisture in the plant escaping into the air. As transpiration stalls, the high humidity in the air and within the plant creates ideal conditions for certain disease spores to infect the plant.

Another way that plants respond to high humidity is through *guttation*. Guttation occurs when the roots absorb water from the soil faster than it is evaporating from the leaves. You'll see little beads of clear water on the tips and sometimes the margins of the leaves. Some plants produce guttation more easily than others and can be used as early-warning indicators of conditions conducive to fungal diseases. Indicator plants include nasturtium, potato, tomato, cabbage, turfgrasses, and strawberry.

The Fungus among Us

Part of the enjoyment of having a garden is to let the eye scan and appreciate the variety of plants growing there, from beds and borders to majestic trees. What even the most appreciative observer cannot see is another group of plants that share the same garden but are very different from, say, peonies and viburnums. These plants don't become noticeable until weather conditions, especially the humidity, are just right.

These small, strange-looking plants are various types of fungi — plants that contain no chlorophyll and so cannot manufacture their own food supplies, as higher plants do. Because they cannot provide for themselves, fungi must obtain their food from sources other than internal processes. Some, such as many mushrooms, are called *saprophytes;* these glean nourishment from nonliving material, such as fallen logs or compost. Others are parasites and survive by taking nourishment from another organism without benefit to the host. These fungi can attack animals and people in ailments such as ringworm, or they can cause plant diseases.

Fungi cause many devastating plant diseases involving thousands of different kinds of infections in plants across the globe and in your garden. These diseases not only need your garden plants as hosts; they also need the right humidity, or they remain invisible and innocuous.

It is easy to see the shared features of oak trees and peonies, asclepias and apples. They all have leaves, stems, flowers, and seeds, and all conduct photosynthesis. Disease-causing fungi are very different. Fungi have no chlorophyll, and instead of stems and branches they have threadlike filaments, called *hyphae*. When the hyphae become abundant and often easy to see, they are called *mycelia*. The cell walls of flowering plants are strengthened by cellulose, whereas those of fungi contain chitin, the same material that toughens the shells of insects. Flowering plants produce fruits and seeds; fungi produce spores.

Fungi are prolific producers of these microscopic spores. Everywhere you go in the garden, they are there too — on the ground, leaves, and flowers and floating in the air. Many times, when a spore lands on a leaf or petal, it just sits there because the weather conditions aren't right for germination. But when the spore settles on a surface with favorable conditions, its parasitic nature quickly becomes evident. It germinates, grows, infects its host, and produces spores to spread the epidemic. For more on fungal diseases and how to respond to them, see pages 258–264.

It's a Guy Thing: Humidity and Pollen

In addition to the disease problems that high humidity brings to your garden, it has an effect on pollination. Without pollination, creation of fruits and seeds (with some rare exceptions) is impossible. Yet the process of pollination is so fragile that sometimes it seems amazing that it works as well as it does.

In most higher plants, the pollen grain is as minute as dust but nonetheless contains the male generative cells necessary for sexual reproduction.

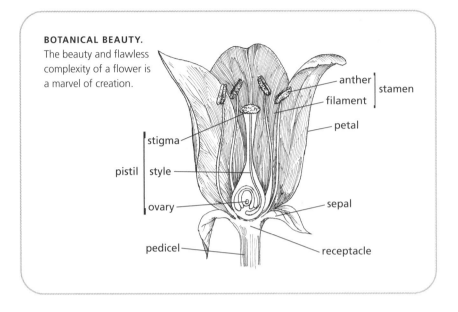

BOTANICAL BEAUTY. The beauty and flawless complexity of a flower is a marvel of creation.

anther

filament

stamen

petal

stigma

pistil | style

ovary

sepal

pedicel

receptacle

The word *pollen* comes from a Latin word meaning "fine flour," which indicates how very tiny each pollen grain is. Each grain contains two or three cells packed into a thin-walled shell. Pollen grains are produced within a floral structure called the *pollen sac*, which in turn forms part of the *anther*. When weather conditions are right, the pollen sacs open and expose the pollen to the various insects and natural forces that aid in pollination, including bees, wind, and moths. For pollination to occur, the pollen must reach a part of the female portion of the flower called the *stigma*. Once in contact with the stigma, the pollen grain germinates like a seed and pollination is completed.

How Humidity Affects Pollination

The most important weather component for the success or failure of pollination is the humidity of the air. The cells within a pollen grain are protected from the elements only by a very thin, membranelike shell. In times of low humidity, the pollen dries out. When it gets to the flower, the pollen doesn't stick to the stigma and pollination fails. It is common for the stigma to have a sticky substance on the surface, such as can easily be seen in lilies, to help the pollen adhere to it; in low humidity, this sticky film can sometimes dry out, causing pollination to fail.

Conversely, if humidity levels rise too high (generally between 60 and 90 percent, depending on the species), the pollen may never get to the flower for different reasons. For the pollen sacs to open and release the pollen grains, the air must be dry enough to encourage the splitting of the sacs. If the air is too moist, the pollen sacs do not open. In some plants, such as raspberries, the pollen sacs may open but high humidity makes the pollen grains sticky. They end up clumping together, resulting in reduced pollination.

Between the highs and the lows are humidity levels that are just right for pollen shedding and pollination. Because pollen varies in shape and size with the plant species, it isn't surprising that the optimum humidity levels for plants are often quite species-specific. For example, oak trees release pollen most effectively when the humidity is below about 45 percent; if the humidity rises higher than 60 percent, effective pollination almost stops. In contrast, raspberries require about 60 percent humidity for good pollen release, and optimal values are around 70 percent.

Many parts of the garden and landscape, from the vegetable patch to the orchard, rely on insects, such as bees, to pollinate the crops. Without the insect helpers, there would be very few foods to harvest at the end of the season. For many fruit and vegetable crops, the best weather for pollination to occur coincides with the preferred conditions for pollinators, such as honeybees, to be active. Honeybees don't like windy days, fog, cold, or rain, and pollen release is poor on such days, too. Honeybees prefer to fly on sunny, dry days with temperatures around 70°F (21°C). Once pollen is on the flower, the pollen grain germinates, grows down the *style* of the flower (see illustration), and completes pollination, which begins the growth of the squash or apple. In apples, for instance, the pollen grain germinates best within a few degrees of 70°F.

Weather has a constant effect on the quality of pollination. For many crops, the most effective release of pollen comes when the temperatures are around 70°F and the humidity is below 65 percent. These conditions allow the anthers to open, releasing the pollen, and provide ideal conditions for insect pollinators to do their job. Conditions that lead to poor pollination include cool temperatures paired with high humidity. The cool temperatures inhibit bees (only bumblebees will fly through snow flurries), and the high humidity inhibits the release of pollen.

As beneficial as bees are to producing fruits and vegetables for us to enjoy, these busy little insects aren't doing all this work because they're altruistic. What the bees get out of pollination is the nectar produced by the flowers. The bees use the sweet liquid to make honey. Logically, bees are attracted to the flowers with the sweetest nectar, but all flowers of a certain species don't produce nectar of equal quality. Sometimes the sweetest nectar is made on a tree or plant that is genetically disposed to do so, but most of the time it has to do with the weather. Sweet nectar depends on a combination of moisture, humidity, wind, and temperature. The sweetest nectar is made when the plant has adequate moisture in the soil, the temperature is about 70°F (21°C), the humidity is low, and the wind is light.

Global Warming, Humidity, and Your Garden

In the last half of the 20th century, many changes occurred in the climate of North America. For instance, precipitation increased 8 percent over much of the continent. The increased precipitation led to higher humidity levels as well. The higher levels of precipitation created higher levels of soil moisture, greater stream flow, more cloud cover, and increased humidity — all of which combined to boost plant growth across the region by 14 percent.

How these changes in climate are expressed is important to your garden. As the precipitation patterns changed, the average minimum night temperature, especially in the spring, rose. Night temperatures are often more limiting to gardening in spring than are daytime highs, so a rise in daily low temperatures has meant an earlier start to the growing season, by almost a week in many regions. At the other end of the growing season, autumn grew wetter, with slightly elevated nighttime minimum temperatures. The rise in moisture, humidity, and temperature extended the season by a few days in many areas. When these factors are combined, the growing season became an average of 10 to 14 days longer than it was half a century ago. This didn't happen everywhere, however. In some places, the changes brought about drier conditions.

The changes in the water cycle over the continent have benefits beyond a longer growing season. Soils tend to be healthier when they contain moisture levels near optimum. Soil structure is improved, fertility increases as soil organisms degrade organic material faster, and nutrient absorption through plant roots increases. Plants require less moisture to perform the same processes when they grow in humid air compared with drier air. The increased concentration of greenhouse gases that have produced global warming have also provided a buffer to help slow the increase. Plants absorb carbon dioxide, one of the global warming gases, in greater quantities in more humid environments.

When What You Need Is "More" Humidity

Anyone from the South or Northeast would think it crazy to want to increase the humidity of summer. In these regions, summer days can turn sweltering. In much of western America, however, low humidity is a problem, and raising it even a little bit can have a substantial and positive effect on crops and gardens.

The device used to increase humidity is the same one used to decrease wind: the shelter belt, or windbreak. Windbreaks of tall columnar trees have long been used on the prairies and other open landscapes to deflect wind from houses and barns. When the windbreak is set to intercept the prevailing storm winds, the barrier acts like a dam, creating turbulence that slows the wind before it even reaches the trees. The decelerated flow of air deposits windblown snow amid and in front of the barrier. This is called a *snow trap*. The most effective windbreaks are planted in zones to modify wind efficiently but with as little strain on plants as possible.

SNOW "FARMING." Snow traps harvest snow, keeping less snow near buildings and accumulating it where soil moisture will be needed in the growing season.

Over the winter, the shelter belt accumulates snow. It doesn't have to snow very much for a windbreak to gather several inches of snow: Just an inch or two (2.5–5 cm) can produce drifts 1 to 2 feet (0.3–0.6 m) deep. In spring, the snow in the snow trap melts and recharges the soil with moisture. Over the growing season, this moisture is released into the air by plants and the capillary action of the soil, resulting in an increase in humidity within that area. In arid and semiarid climates, the results can be dramatic. In the soil around windbreaks that also serve as snow traps, there is often increased growth, better fruit set, and higher yields compared with neighboring areas.

Houseplants and Humidity

Tending plants indoors brightens up the rooms of the house as well as the spirits of those who care for them. Yet the inside atmosphere of most homes is a hodgepodge of different environments and temperatures that change drastically from season to season. For example, the air in the bathroom can be warm and very humid when the shower is on but cool and dry later in the day. The kitchen can be warm when the oven is being used and cool when it is not. Central heating systems dry the air considerably, although the type of system and where the heat is delivered make a big difference in the humidity inside the house. For instance, a house heated by a woodstove in Colorado might have humidity levels as low as 10 to 15 percent, whereas a home in New England with baseboard electric heat might stay at 25 percent.

With a few exceptions, houseplants don't like low humidity, and some require higher levels of humidity to survive. Most houseplants require about 60 percent relative humidity to thrive. Many tropical plants need humidity levels close to 90 percent. On the other hand, succulents (such as cacti and jade plants) can be happy at 35 percent relative humidity. When you recognize the large gap between the relative humidity that most homes have in winter (10 to 25 percent) and what plants need (35 to 90 percent), the problem is obvious.

It is much more difficult to raise the humidity level in the entire house than in the small space around each plant. Here are 10 tips for making the environment near your plants more humid.

• Plants that are very sensitive to humidity can be grown in sheltered environments, such as terrariums.

• Some rooms, such as the bathroom, are perfect just as they are for certain plants, such as orchids and ferns.

• Some plants dry out faster than others, so check your plants frequently (if not daily) and water each plant when it needs it.

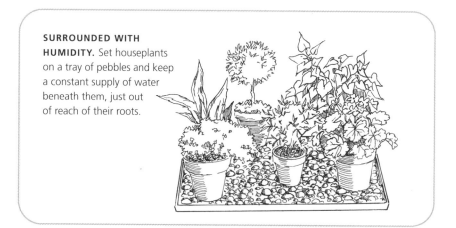

SURROUNDED WITH HUMIDITY. Set houseplants on a tray of pebbles and keep a constant supply of water beneath them, just out of reach of their roots.

• Use saucers under the plants.

• Grow plants on pebble trays (trays filled with small stones). The pot is placed on the stones so that when it is watered, the excess flows into the reservoir beneath the pebbles. The stones keep the plant out of the water so the roots won't rot. At the same time, as the water evaporates, however, it raises the humidity of the air near the plant.

• Grow plants closer together, so that the moisture each plant transpires adds to the humidity of the air around all of them.

• If a room in the house has a humidifier, by all means grow some plants in that room.

• Because it becomes depleted of nutrients, change the potting mixture in the pots of houseplants every year and replace it with a mix containing high organic matter content to aid moisture retention.

• Keep plants away from drafts and heating vents.

• If most houseplants, especially those that like high humidity, simply don't thrive in your home, grow cacti instead.

Coping with Problems Caused by High Humidity

Many diseases of garden plants need liquid water, from rain or irrigation, to complete their life cycles, and in so doing cause grief and trouble to gardeners. That's why you should try to keep the leaves of plants dry. However, some diseases thrive in humidity rather than free water. And these diseases can be just as difficult to manage as any others.

Botrytis

Description: The really accomplished fungal diseases can prey on a large number of species, and botrytis, also called gray mold, is one of the most accomplished. Botrytis can infect nearly all garden and landscape plants, and just about everyone has noticed it growing on strawberries or geraniums. There is always a little botrytis growing here and there, and some spores float about in the air throughout the growing season. When the relative humidity rises to about 85 percent and the temperature is between 60 and 75°F (18–21°C), the conditions exist for the spores to germinate and become established.

These optimum conditions need to exist only where the spore is germinating, which could be on a dead leaf atop a moist layer of mulch beneath a host plant. Conditions on the sunny lawn a few feet away may be substantially different. As long as the conditions remain favorable, the spores germinate, grow, and produce more spores. When the humidity changes, as it does often throughout different parts of the day, the fungus sheds the spores. The new generation of spores is often produced very near injured, decaying, or otherwise susceptible material, which provides an ideal site for the infection to explode now into an epidemic.

Symptoms: Along with brown spots on the flowers, stems, fruit, or leaves, you may observe fuzzy masses of gray mycelia on flowers, such as petunia, and fruit, such as strawberry.

Remedies: Apply a product containing clarified hydrophobic extract of neem as the active ingredient either before symptoms appear or when first noticed. Botrytis likes stagnant air, so improving air circulation helps. Also, proper sanitation, removing infected plants and plant parts, and cleaning away dead leaves from beneath the plants is helpful. Botrytis also doesn't like sunlight; some added light reduces infection.

Strategies: There are two steps to managing botrytis successfully. The first is sanitation. Gardeners are always advised to rake up dead leaves and remove spent flowers, but without proper explanation. Fallen leaves, spent blossoms, senescing foliage, and soft fruit are the most suitable environments for fungal growth. Removing them makes it much more difficult for a fungus to obtain a foothold in the garden.

The second step is reducing humidity. As a practical matter, you can reduce humidity only to the level of the air in the garden. However, most of the time the humidity in the garden is much higher than that of the ambient air. Space garden plants farther apart, so that foliage of separate plants does not touch. Prune plants to be as open as possible, given their form and growth habit. These tactics improve air circulation, which helps move moist air from around the plants in the garden, replacing it with drier air from elsewhere.

Botrytis is worst in cool weather, not because the fungus likes cool temperatures, but because of the humidity. As the temperature warms during the day, the relative humidity drops. As it cools in the evening, the relative humidity rises, often entering the moist zone preferred by botrytis. Increased air circulation can inhibit botrytis even during these optimal times.

Downy Mildew of Lettuce

Description: Downy mildew of lettuce is most common in greenhouse-grown crops and in warm regions where crops are grown through the winter. The disease is most serious when foliage is wet, humidity is high (above 60 percent), and temperatures range from 50 to 65°F (10–18°C).

Symptoms: Pale spots appear on the upper leaf surfaces, with downy spots underneath. Browning of the leaves follows, then death.

The Difference Between Azadirachtin and Neem Oil

To many people, azadirachtin is just another name for neem oil. While both are derived from the seeds of the neem tree, that is where the similarity ends. When the oil is removed from the neem seeds and treated with alcohol, neem oil separates from the seeds' other components, including azadirachtin. Azadirachtin is then used as the active ingredient in bioinsecticides that are registered to control many insect pests. The refined neem oil, called clarified hydrophobic extract of neem, is the active ingredient in EPA-registered bio-fungicides that control mildews, botrytis, alternaria, rusts, and other fungal diseases. The difference between azadirachtin and neem oil is pretty simple, therefore: Azadirachtin controls insect pests; neem oil is a fungicide.

Remedies: Apply a product containing clarified hydrophobic extract of neem as the active ingredient either before symptoms appear or when first noticed. Avoid excessive irrigation and keep the soil slightly drier than normal. Increase air circulation if possible.

Strategies: Keep plants well spaced. Keep leaves dry by watering with soaker hoses or drip irrigation. Remove old leaves promptly. Although many varieties are listed as resistant, it is common that a variety that's resistant in one location is not in another, due to the presence of different strains of the disease organism. Check with your local garden center or Cooperative Extension Service for varieties resistant in your area. Practice good sanitation by removing plant residue and weeds from the garden.

Alternaria Blights

Description: Alternaria blights include cucumber blight, carrot blight, early blight of tomato and potato, and blight of zinnia. These diseases are not vigorous and need high humidity to grow on their preferred hosts. They thrive on dead plant material and also prey on weak, diseased, or injured plants.

Symptoms: *Alternaria* fungi produce circular brown spots on leaves. These lead to browning of foliage and often the death of a plant.

Remedies: Apply a product containing clarified hydrophobic extract of neem as the active ingredient either before symptoms appear or when first noticed. (See The Difference Between Azadirachtin and Neem Oil on the facing page.) Improve air circulation and remove any susceptible plant material.

Strategies: Rotate plantings on a 3-year schedule. Use certified seed or plants. Practice proper sanitation.

Rust

Description: Rust comprises more than 4,000 species of specialized, complicated fungi responsible for thousands of different diseases on flowering plants and ferns. Often parasitic to two different species during different stages in their life cycle, rusts need high humidity to thrive.

Mildew-Resistant Plants

Trees

Crab apple (*Malus* spp. 'Adams', 'Arctic Dawn', 'Bob White', 'Callaway', 'Donald Wyman', and 'Ellwangerina')

Japanese flowering crab *(Malus floribunda)*

Flowering dogwood (*Cornus florida* 'Barton', 'Cherokee Brave', 'Cherokee Sunset', 'Rupka', and 'Sweetwater Red')

Kousa dogwood (*Cornus kousa* 'Angustata', 'Autumn Rose', 'China Girl', 'Milky Way Select', and 'Snowflake')

Rutgers hybrid dogwood (*Cornus florida* x *kousa* 'Aurora', 'Celestial', and 'Stellar Pink')

Phlox

Garden phlox (*Phlox paniculata* 'Blue Boy', 'David', 'Delta Snow', 'Natasha', 'Orange Perfection', 'Prime Minister', 'Robert Poore', 'Starfire')

Carolina phlox *(P. carolina)*

Meadow phlox (*P. maculata* 'Alpha')

Lilacs

Himalayan lilac *(Syringa emodi)*

Meyer lilac *(S. meyeri)*

Littleleaf lilac (*S. microphylla, S. microphylla* 'Superba')

Manchurian lilac (*S. patula, S. patula* 'Miss Kim')

Persian lilac *(S. persica)*

Japanese tree lilac (*S. reticulata, S. reticulata* 'Summer Snow')

Roses

Species Roses:

Lady Banks rose *(Rosa banksiae lutea)*

Swamp rose *(R. palustris scandens)*

Wingthorn rose *(R. sericea pteracantha)*

Virginia rose *(R. virginiana)*

Memorial rose *(R. wichuraina)*

Symptoms: Rust appears on plants as a yellowish discoloration on a leaf or stem, and orange-colored powdery spores.

Remedies: Apply a product containing clarified hydrophobic extract of neem as the active ingredient either before symptoms appear or when first noticed. This product, derived from the neem tree, is very effective. (See The Difference Between Azadirachtin and Neem Oil, page 260.)

Strategies: Follow the guidelines for air circulation and sanitation under Botrytis on pages 259–260. In humid weather, keep lawns mown short to allow faster drying. Grow rust-resistant varieties if available.

Rugosa Roses:
Rosa rugosa 'Frau Dagmar Hartopp'
R. rugosa 'Hansa'
R. rugosa 'Henry Hudson'
R. rugosa 'Jens Munk'
R. rugosa 'Linda Campbell'
R. rugosa 'Max Graf'
R. rugosa 'Rotes Meer'
R. rugosa 'Snow Owl'
R. rugosa 'Therese Bugnet'

Shrub Roses:
Rosa 'Assiniboine'
R. 'Bonica'
R. 'Carefree Delight'
R. 'Carefree Wonder'
R. 'Champlain'
R. 'John Cabot'

Floribundas:
Rosa 'Escapade'

R. 'French Lace'
R. 'Iceberg'
R. 'Sunflare'

Hybrid Teas:
Rosa 'Folklore'
R. 'Olympiad'
R. 'Pascali'

Miniatures:
Rosa 'Cinderella'
R. 'Green Ice'
R. 'Jean Kenneally'
R. 'Minnie Pearl'

Zinnias
Garden zinnia (*Zinnia elegans* 'Old Mexico', 'Orange Star', 'Pinwheel', and 'Star White')

Anthracnose

Description: Warm, wet weather with high humidity is tailor-made for anthracnose fungi. Affecting several plants, including beans, foxgloves, snapdragons, tomatoes, grains, geraniums, and strawberries, anthracnose loves crowded plantings with dead plant material and high humidity.

Symptoms: Dark spots appear on leaves and other plant parts. The spots enlarge, and the leaves turn brown and often die.

Remedies: Space plantings to improve air circulation. Keep plants dry — don't let leaves or other plant parts get wet during watering.

Strategies: In the vegetable garden, use a 3-year rotation and sow certified seed where available. Practice good sanitation by removing dead leaves and flowers. Use mulches, like bark chips, and renew every year.

Powdery Mildew

Description: Perhaps no other disease is so linked with humidity as powdery mildew. Unlike those of other fungal diseases, powdery mildew spores do not need water on a leaf surface to germinate, and it affects gardens in both low- and high-humidity areas.

If you grow phlox and lilac, you know powdery mildew will show up every year and you can pinpoint almost to the day when it will arrive because the conditions that cause it are so specific: when summer wanes and daytime temperatures begin to cool, rising only from 65 to 85°F (18–29°C), with humidity between 45 and 75 percent. If daytime temperatures rise above 85°F (29°C), the disease stops. Nights also need to be cool, with minimum temperatures around 60°F (16°C) and a relative humidity of near 90 percent.

Symptoms: White, powdery substance covers leaves.

Remedies: Apply a product containing clarified hydrophobic extract of neem as the active ingredient either before symptoms appear or when first noticed. Try altering the humidity, as spores germinate when the level of humidity at the leaf surface is just right. Wet the leaves to wash off the spores and change the conditions there so that spores won't be able to germinate.

Strategies: Some plants, such as garden phlox and French lilac, are very susceptible to powdery mildew. Some varieties are so sensitive that they are killed when infected for just a portion of a single growing season. Excellent resilient varieties exist, but for them to demonstrate that resilience year after year, it is best to remove any plants from your yard that many harbor the disease and replace them with one of the varieties listed on page 263.

Lightning

WARM, HUMID AIR HANGS OVER THE GARDEN LIKE A HAZY BLANKET. As the strong summer sun stirs the heavy air, it begins to move in immense invisible currents. Miles away, a cold front (a wall of cool air miles high) rolls quickly over the land. Like an enormous bulldozer, the front pushes into the hot air, sending updrafts surging into the sky. In just a few minutes, the invisible thermals become scores of white, billowing cumulous clouds. For a little while, the cottony clouds amid the blue sky make everything seem wonderfully peaceful, the perfect summer day.

The puffy clouds don't stay friendly and gentle for long. As the front pushes closer, clouds grow, rising higher and higher in great mushroom-shape clouds. Engorged with moisture, their once linen white surfaces harden into shades of steel gray. The moisture is swept up by winds into the tops of the clouds, getting bigger as they collide with other droplets. As the clouds grow taller, the droplets are driven higher until they pass into a region of the atmosphere where the temperature is just below freezing. In the freezing air, some droplets crystallize into ice, others remain liquid, and still more become a half-frozen mix. As the different forms of moisture continue to be tossed and blown about within the cloud, they begin to build up an electrical charge. The different rate at which the precipitation rises and falls causes either positive or negative electrical charges to accumulate in different places within the cloud.

A large area of positive energy develops in the cloud's cold upper region. Near its base, two more charged regions form, a large accumulation of negative energy and a smaller, positive one. Below the storm, the ground surface accumulates a negative charge. Like a bit of iron following a magnet, this reservoir of electricity moves through the ground, shadowing the clouds. As it slides silently through rocks and soil, positive energy momentarily concentrates within trees and buildings seeking a pathway into the clouds. It's the air between soil and sky that keeps the current in the ground. A good insulator, air blocks the current's discharge of current, until energy builds to such enormous levels that it overcomes air's insulating effect. At that point, lightning streaks across the sky.

The storm now passes over an area of fenced pastures and woodlots. Clusters of tidy homes are surrounded by tended lawns, shade trees, and

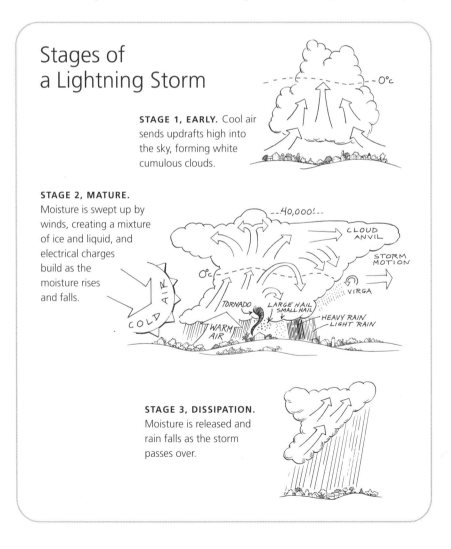

Stages of a Lightning Storm

STAGE 1, EARLY. Cool air sends updrafts high into the sky, forming white cumulous clouds.

STAGE 2, MATURE. Moisture is swept up by winds, creating a mixture of ice and liquid, and electrical charges build as the moisture rises and falls.

STAGE 3, DISSIPATION. Moisture is released and rain falls as the storm passes over.

colorful gardens. A dark, pregnant sky has driven people from their yards, except Norman and Sarah, who notice the danger but hurry to deadhead the last few plants in a border of peonies. As they work, the formless mass of electrical energy seeps through the ground beneath them as the first large raindrops splatter on the ground. At that moment, the insulating power of the air breaks down and an invisible channel of negatively charged particles begins a rapid, jagged descent from the cloud toward the ground. At the same time, streamers of positive energy momentarily coalesce within objects on the ground: a tall white pine, a rock ledge, and Norman and Sarah, who become very uneasy as an itchy tingle crawls over their bodies. These objects become launching pads for lightning. Instantly, invisible plumes of current shoot skyward from the tree, the ledge, and Norman and Sarah toward the channel descending from the cloud.

High over the garden, the descending channel meets one of the three plumes rising from below. Simultaneously a blinding flash and a deafening boom crash down on the countryside below. The bolt is only an inch in diameter and lasts just one 1000th of a second, but it delivers a shock measured in the millions of volts and cooks the air to nearly 50,000°F (27,760°C). The destruction is instantaneous. In stunned silence, Norman and Sarah stare at the shattered remains of the old field pine tree at the edge of the clearing a couple of hundred feet away. Waves of rain fall as another bolt strikes nearby, and a shaken Norman and Sarah hurry to the house. By the time the storm is over, three trees in the area have been hit by lightning bolts: the white pine in Norman and Sarah's garden, a large white oak in the arboretum down the street, and an American beech in a neighbor's yard.

An Awesome Power and Its Targets

When I was growing up, we had a large porch on the back of our house. When a thunderstorm gathered in the summer sky, the family filtered onto that porch in anticipation. The leaves on the red oaks near the house would stir and rustle in the swirling breeze. But when the leaves hung still and all the outdoors seemed to hold its breath, you knew the storm was just moments away. When the storm broke, the porch afforded everyone a front-row seat to watch some of the most powerful things on earth — lightning bolts.

On the porch all of us were brave, but I often wondered how sustained my calm would be if I were out in the garden or under the trees while lightning prowled about. Once in a while, a bolt would flash so brightly that the lightning seemed to etch a luminous trace on my eyes. The flash was followed instantly by an explosion of thunder so strong that the sound shoved past me like a schoolyard bully. But lightning that hit close took the fun out of the storm. It broke the rules and turned lightning from something that provides entertainment to what it really is — an immensely powerful force guided by an unforeseen occurrence that strikes whatever happens to be in the way — gardens, homes, or people.

There is little debate that the most common targets of lightning in the garden are trees. Exactly which trees are struck most often and why have been matters of argument for centuries. Many observers, including scientists and gardeners, have compiled lists of tree species struck by lightning, then sorted through the data in search of patterns and answers. What has emerged is a mass of circumstantial information that nearly obscures some valuable and useful facts. Assessing the risk of a single factor, such as tree species, is an oversimplification because it misses other important factors, such as a tree's height and location.

Location, Location, Location

As the electrical energy that precedes a lightning strike moves through the ground, it often gathers at a high place like a hill. If a tree is growing on the hill, then the distance between cloud and ground is that much shorter, making the lightning risk that much greater. If the hill is forested, the taller trees often carry the greatest risk. But there's an exception.

Water is a better conductor of electricity than is dry soil and can substantially change the risk for lightning strike, so a tree growing at the edge of a pond, even if it is below the level of nearby trees growing on well-drained soils, is often at a higher risk of being hit. This is because the roots interface with the water and create an easier path for the lightning to reach the ground.

Speaking of Species

Although height and location of the tree is important in assessing lightning risk, there is considerable evidence that the tree's species is also important. When all the data are taken into account, two types of trees stand out: one for qualities that increase the risk of lightning and the other for attributes that decrease the risk. Oaks are examples of the first; beeches are examples of the second.

Oaks. About 600 species of oaks *(Quercus)* exist around the world. The majestic shade trees in this genus are also the trees most often struck by lightning. This propensity may be due in part to the longevity of oaks — many survive for centuries, increasing their odds of getting struck. In addition, oaks are often the only trees in pastures and cornfields. More important, however, is the structure and content of oak wood.

Lightning's Good Side: Free Fertilizer

The good side of lightning is that each thundering bolt produces a measure of nitrogen fertilizer, which is delivered to your yard and garden by the raindrops that fall from the storm clouds. Nitrogen in the atmosphere exists as two nitrogen atoms bound together. As lightning rips through the atmosphere, it superheats the air, severing the molecular bonds and producing free nitrogen. Nitrogen atoms don't like being lonely, and they quickly recombine with oxygen in the form of nitrates. The nitrates dissolve in the raindrops and fall to earth, where they soak into the ground and enrich the soil.

Oak is heavy, and its wood contains a lot of moisture. The combined density and wetness creates a good pathway for current to run from a cloud to the ground. Another factor is the roughness and thick nature of oak bark. As it rains, the bark of an oak tree is moistened unevenly. Some believe that this trait influences the likelihood of a strike, but it more probably influences the degree of damage to the tree. Finally, oak has a deep taproot that creates a direct and easy-to-access channel from the top of the tree deep underground.

Beeches. In shape and form, a grand beech *(Fagus)* is similar to a classic oak. Both types of tree have a brawny trunk and multiple branches that form a spreading scaffold of strong limbs. But compared with oaks, beech trees rarely are victims of lightning. The secret to the beech's relative immunity may reside in the beech wood itself, the bark, and the roots.

Beech wood is a soft pink color with much less moisture than oak, making it less conductive to electricity. The roots of beech are shallow and spread out through the ground, dispersing the electrical energy rather than concentrating it. Plus, beech bark is very smooth and thin, while that of oak is thick and rough. As it rains, the bark of beech trees becomes more uniformly wet, which creates a pathway along the bark and on the

What Is Heat Lightning?

Heat lightning is flashes of light in the sky most often noticed around dusk or after dark during the summer months. It is a common belief in some parts of the country that heat lightning is different from other lightning — that it arises from the heat of the day and is silent. The truth is far less mysterious. Heat lightning is merely lightning generated in a thunderstorm that is too far away for the thunder to be heard.

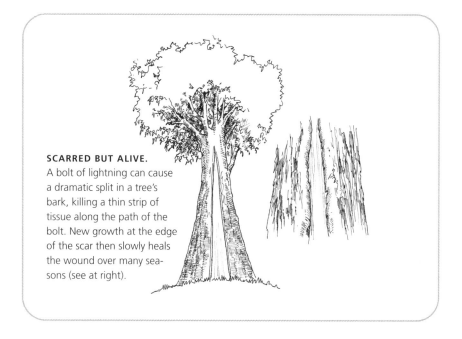

SCARRED BUT ALIVE.
A bolt of lightning can cause a dramatic split in a tree's bark, killing a thin strip of tissue along the path of the bolt. New growth at the edge of the scar then slowly heals the wound over many seasons (see at right).

outside of the tree. If lightning does strike, it often flashes over the tree, following the rainwater into the ground and doing little or no damage.

Bark: The Best Predictor?

The one consistent difference between trees that seem to be popular targets of lightning and those that seem to escape its notice is the bark. Cork forms most of the visible part of the bark that wraps around the outside of a tree. It is formed from a layer of cells called the *cork cambium.* In some trees, the cork cambium expands for a few years, then dies. A new cambium begins to grow beneath the old one. As a trunk continues to grow and expand, the old cork layer is stretched and breaks into cracks and plates. As repeated generations of cork cambium die, layers and layers of bark build up on the outside of the tree, creating the characteristic patterns by which individual species can be identified. These are the trees lightning seems to like.

In another, smaller group of trees, the cork cambium doesn't die — it continues to grow as the tree expands. This uninterrupted growth

Guidelines for Selecting Trees

Characteristics of Trees Least Likely to Be Struck by Lightning

Some trees have a knack for not getting hit by lightning as often as others. Though the list is short, all these trees are good additions to the landscape.

Oil in wood	Birch (*Betula* spp.)
Smooth bark	Beech (*Fagus* spp.)
	Smooth-bark cherries (*Prunus* spp.)
Short	California buckeye (*Aesculus californica*)
	Red buckeye (*Aesculus pavia*)
	Serviceberry (*Amelanchier* spp.)
	Stewartia (*Stewartia* spp.)

Characteristics of Trees Most Likely to Be Struck by Lightning

These trees are more prone than others to be struck by lightning, but this doesn't prohibit them from service in the landscape. Use the guidelines to distinguish those trees more likely to get zapped, and place them where they are least likely to be struck, such as in low areas.

Conifers	Fir (*Abies* spp.)
	Hemlock (*Tsuga* spp., especially eastern hemlock, *T. canadensis*)
	Pine (*Pinus* spp.)
	Spruce (*Picea* spp.)
Tall	Tulip tree (*Liriodendron tulipifera*)
Dense wood	Elm (*Ulmus* spp.)
	Maple (*Acer* spp.)
	Oak (*Quercus* spp.)
	Sycamore (*Platanus* spp.)
High moisture content	Aspen/cottonwood (*Populus* spp.)
	Willow (*Salix* spp.)
Starchy wood or starchy content	(*Fraxinus* spp.)
	Palms

produces a continuous but thin supply of smooth bark throughout the life of the tree. These smooth-barked trees are least likely to be struck by lightning. They include beech, some species of cherry, and birches.

Now the fine print. Some smooth-barked trees, such as quaking and bigtooth aspen, are commonly hit by lightning. This is because other lightning-attractive qualities outweigh the protective aspect of their bark. Aspen wood is heavy with water and the trees tend to rot in the heartwood. This makes them prone to lightning strikes that cause explosive damage.

The Forest for the Trees

At first, a woodland garden surrounded by forest can seem like a horde of easy targets. But woods can often protect from lightning rather than invite it. If the ground is relatively level and the tops of the trees are all about the same height, the risk of being struck by lightning is fairly low. If one or two trees poke up through the canopy, they are at greatest risk. Risk increases if the tree is older than its neighbors, is a high-risk species, and has any sign of rot in the heartwood.

Open gardens with few trees often seem like easy places to assess for lightning threats, but just as often they are not. If the garden has a nice big tree, such as a grand live oak, as a focal point and nothing else like it elsewhere, then yes, the tree is probably the greatest point of risk in the garden. However, large trees dominate only a relatively small area, and open areas nearby can have attractive locations that don't seem very obvious. These include smaller trees and structures, and other objects, such as watering systems.

Of special note are trees growing near (within 25 feet [7.5 m]) of electrical transmission lines, phone lines, buildings, and water pipes. If lightning strikes a tree growing in this proximity, the electricity often jumps to the lines or pipes. Once in the lines and pipes, the current goes wherever the path leads it — into electronic devices, such as computers, televisions, VCRs, telephones, and appliances. When tens of thousands of amps hit an appliance, it's "toast."

Take a Hard Look at Your Hardscape

Trees are obviously not the only targets of lightning strikes. Many hardscape elements, such as arbors, gazebos, and trellises, are often the tallest parts of the garden. Some naturally look best placed on a grassy rise that makes them more attractive to the gardener — but also to lightning. When hardscape elements are noticeably taller than other objects in the surrounding area, it helps if they are constructed of materials that are poor conductors, such as wood. If a taller structure, such as a trellis or an arbor, is located on a path, be sure that the path is well drained and not prone to pooling of water, which can create a conductive route to the element. Buildings, including homes; isolated structures, like gazebos; and large trees should be fitted with lightning protection systems. If the buildings and trees are within about 25 feet (7.5 m) of each other, make sure the systems are interconnected. (For more information on protective systems, see page 278.)

Give Me Room, Lots of Room

Lightning also seems to have bizarre and wholly unpredictable actions that occasionally affect the garden. The safety literature about lightning always suggests that people stay out of fields in a storm, but it doesn't say how much open space makes up a field. It turns out that lightning isn't very picky about topographical definitions and considers just about any break in the tree cover a "field." This could be a small pond or garden as small as 100 feet (30 m) across. The object of attraction can be almost anything a little taller than the surrounding terrain, especially when it is in proximity to water or electricity.

Conversely, gardens in climates not favorable for lush forest growth are often in a huge "field" hundreds of miles across. Whether prairie, high plains, or mountain plateau, the relief created by a garden's plants and landscape elements is sometimes the highest point, and thus the most attractive to lightning, for a considerable distance. All this means that lightning can and does strike places that don't at first seem to be likely targets for bolts to hit. Some garden spots that get struck by lightning are metal trellises, lawns, flower beds, water gardens, and even a driveway leading to the garden.

Though the locations of lightning strikes are unpredictable, the damage they cause is even more puzzling. When lightning strikes a lawn, for

A Gardener's Guide to Lightning Safety

Most people's gardens are a short walk from their homes, so when thunder threatens, they abandon their chores and quickly move indoors. There are three exceptions. The first are those who garden for others. The second are those whose property is large enough to draw them away from nearby shelter. The third exception are gardeners who enjoy the garden so intently that the sound of approaching thunder is drowned out by the hum of a honeybee dabbling atop a peony blossom, or who want to finish just one more task before the rain hits. Just about all gardeners are at risk from lightning sometime. Here are some rules.

The best safety tool you have is your brain — think ahead. Keep an NOAA (National Oceanic and Atmospheric Administration) weather radio with you when a chance of severe weather is present. The broadcasts often give precise tracking, timelines, and locations of dangerous storms in your area.

"Lightning safety" is almost an oxymoron, as lightning can find its way into many seemingly safe places. There are safer, as well as very dangerous, places to be in a thunderstorm.

Safer Places to Be in a Thunderstorm

• A solid, permanent structure, preferably fitted with lightning protection devices
• A fully enclosed metal vehicle, such as a car, truck, bus, van, or farm machinery, with the windows closed

Most Dangerous Places to Be in a Thunderstorm

• Small garden structures, such as a gazebo and an arbor
• Near picnic tables
• Near water, such as an irrigation line, pool, sprinkler, fountain, newly watered garden, and lawn
• Near bodies of water, such as a water garden, brook, lake, and river
• Open areas or elevated places
• Within 20 feet (6 m) of other people

example, it sometimes blows a hole through the turf into the ground. Other times, the only evidence is a brown, often circular patch of scorched grass. Flower beds have been wiped out by a single bolt of lightning that killed every plant.

The Path of Water

Some calamities occur when the electrical energy in a lightning bolt spills over from the initial target to other objects as it seeks a grounding path. Water is a better conductor of electricity than many other materials around the garden, including air and soil. Lightning can also streak through water faucets, showerheads, and washing machines, as well as garden hoses, soaker hoses, and sprinkler systems. People have died from shocks received while showering or putting clothes in the washer during a thunderstorm. Though some devices can minimize the risk of lightning damage in the home, it is still important to stay away from possible sources of shock, especially if trees are near your power lines. Lightning can also follow water you may not know is there, such as that in the fissures in the bedrock beneath the soil. Use the following measures to help minimize the chance of lightning strikes in the garden:

• Drain and roll up garden hoses.

• Disconnect and remove temporary irrigation systems, such as water towers, as soon as they are no longer needed.

• Disconnect (not just turn off) garden-related electrical devices, such as irrigation timers, water pumps, and decorative lighting.

Protecting a Tree from Lightning

A National Champion American elm tree grows in the Great Plains along the historic Oregon Trail in Louisville, Kansas. It stands stately at 100 feet tall (30 m) with a spreading canopy that spans 90 feet (27 m) and a rough trunk 8 feet (2.5 m) in diameter. A thunderstorm rolls over the prairie, and a sudden bolt of lightning flashes across the leaden sky. It strikes the upper scaffold of branches, severely damaging the tree.

The highest branches of a champion bigtooth aspen are over 90 feet (27 m) above the ground. It has been growing in the town of Hamlin in upstate New York for decades and has remained unscathed through a host of severe weather events, including hurricanes, droughts, and blizzards. This day, a billowing thunderstorm is cresting high above the tree. The massive aspen becomes the target of a single lightning bolt that strikes the tree high up the trunk. The instantaneous surge of millions of volts of electricity blows the tree to pieces.

In areas in which lightning is common, lightning protection installed on houses and buildings is an ordinary sight. Most of us never think that the same lightning protection is available for trees. But viable lightning protection systems have been installed on trees since the 19th century. Such protection could have saved the historic natural treasures that lightning destroyed in the above examples.

When St. Elmo Comes to the Garden

If you've ever seen light from a fluorescent bulb or neon sign, then you've seen a contained, if not very exciting, version of St. Elmo's fire. When you see the same phenomenon outdoors, hovering eerily over the yard as a thunderstorm departs, St. Elmo's fire and neon signs seem to have nothing in common at all.

During a thunderstorm, the ground beneath the clouds becomes charged with electricity. Sometimes the air between the clouds and the ground also contains a lot of electricity. If enough electrical energy enters, it begins to act on the very essence of the air (the protons and electrons that make up the air molecules). The result is a vapory, gossamer glow that can have many colors, including violet, red, and green. The misty light typically clings to such objects as the tops of flagpoles and the masts of ships, but it can also float above the ground.

Because St. Elmo's fire is the product of high electrical energy, it is often considered kin to powerful lightning strikes, but it is not lightning. Even though St. Elmo's fire is associated with thousands of volts of electricity saturating the air, this mysterious-looking phenomenon doesn't seem to damage garden plants or trees.

Which Trees Should Be Protected?

Protecting trees from lightning is not a cheap endeavor; each installation can cost thousands of dollars. If a large old picturesque tree calls your yard home, it may be worth protecting for both sentimental and economic reasons. Attractive large trees in the yard not only provide shade but also lend the landscape a sense of permanence that no other feature can match. Not to mention that such grand old trees are irreplaceable.

On a practical level, every tree within about 25 feet (7.5 m) of the home or other building should be protected. This is because the house, with its water and electrical system that often has connections deep underground, is a good launching pad for lightning. The lightning can easily jump to a nearby tree that carries a higher profile than your home.

Lightning protection for trees is the domain of arborists, urban foresters, and trained systems installers. Each protected tree needs a system designed just for it. These professionals will tailor one to fill the needs of a tree and its environment. Before you choose and have a lightning protection system installed, however, you can be a more educated consumer if you are familiar with the parts and purposes of the elements of a lightning protection system.

What Is a Lightning Protection System?

The function of a lightning protection system is not to deter lightning from striking a tree, but rather to disarm a lightning bolt's destructive power before damage occurs. The ruinous power of lightning is a product of its intensity — electrical power and high temperatures compressed into fractions of a second. The protection system disperses the lightning's force so that the bolt does not harm the tree.

To get an idea of what the system for your tree will look like, make a sketch of the tree. Draw both the main stem as well as the major branches. Now draw a line from the base of the tree to the top, connecting the tallest part of the tree to the top of the main stem with the shortest possible line. Use lines to interconnect the side branches with the main trunk. When you're done, you have a rough plan for the protection system.

The main element of the system is a network of woven copper conducting cables. When hit by lightning, the cables carry electrical energy harmlessly down the tree and into the ground, where it dissipates. The main cable runs from the base of the tree to the topmost accessible point, following the most direct line possible. Primary branches that could serve as alternate conduction points should also be fitted with woven copper cables, about half the diameter of the main cable. There should be fewer than 10 secondary cables, and they should be connected to the main cable.

All cables should retain enough slack that they are not damaged by the tree's movements in winds. If the tree has a large diameter, up to two main cables can be used; however, the separate lines must be interconnected. A poorly installed cable system may protect the tree but does nothing for the attractiveness of the yard. However, a well-trained professional can install cables so that they are inconspicuous.

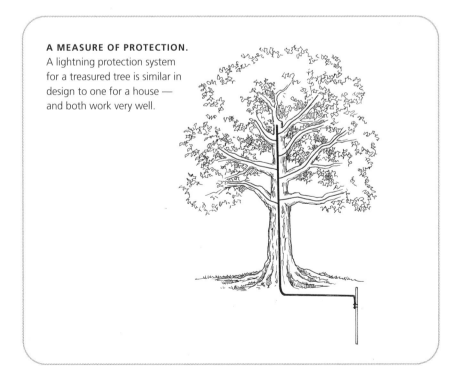

A MEASURE OF PROTECTION. A lightning protection system for a treasured tree is similar in design to one for a house — and both work very well.

Being Well Grounded

The installers will dig a 2-foot-deep (0.6 m) trench out from the base of the tree, beyond the drip line of the tree's canopy. (Thus, if the canopy extends 25 feet [7.5 m] from the trunk, the trench will be about 40 to 50 feet [12–15 m].) This ensures that the transferred lightning will not enter the ground amid the tree's roots. The main cable is then set into the trench. At the end of the trench, a 10-foot-long (3 m) copper grounding rod is attached to the cable. The copper grounding rod is then set firmly into the soil.

How the grounding rod is set, and how many rods are used, depends on the soil type and depth and whether other features, such as a rock ledge, are present. Deep, fine-textured soils often offer the simplest ground and usually need only a single rod set into the soil. A coarse-textured soil sometimes needs two connected grounding rods spaced at least 10 feet (3 m) apart. In shallow soils over ledge, the grounding rods are often longer and buried in trenches.

Each lightning protection system should be inspected every few years to be sure that it does not need repair. The installer should use copper or copper alloy for all cables, connections, and grounding rods, as copper provides the best and most reliable conductor for lightning protection systems. Do not use components made from other metals, such as aluminum.

When Lightning Strikes

When lightning damages a tree, the injury can be obvious, such as a split trunk, or concealed, such as damage to roots far underground. Hidden injury may not be revealed until months later. Damage — especially to large specimens — can vary considerably. And sometimes there is no damage at all. In cases of severe damage, or anytime you feel your knowledge isn't extensive enough, a professional can assess whether and how a tree can be saved.

In addition to obvious damage, such as split bark, an electrical surge also damages the tree right down to individual cells. Repairing this injury requires nutrients that can be quickly and efficiently delivered by applying appropriate fertilizers. When treating a tree struck by lightning, it is important to apply the fertilizer at the proper rate and in such a way that the nutrients uniformly reach all of the root system. The electrical charge may have injured many parts of the tree, such as the soft tissues at the ends of the roots and the generative cells under the bark. Improperly applied fertilizer can make things worse rather than better. Fertilizers should be applied in solution (as opposed to topdressing with dry preparations) so that the nutrients reach the roots quickly.

For those accustomed to fertilizing plants of modest size, like vegetables and perennials, taking care of trees can be surprising. Trees are big. A tree may have one or more trunks, plus a scaffold of branches. The first growing season after a lightning strike should be a restorative period for the tree. Provide enough nutrients to help the tree heal, but not so much that they encourage lush growth. Most trees should receive about

Lightning Rods, Then and Now

All the different types of lightning protection systems, whether installed on buildings or on trees, evolved from an invention by Ben Franklin. Franklin was a curious, innovative man who was not always appreciated by his peers. His interest in lightning led him to try kite flying in bad weather, and it was only good fortune that prevented his career from ending with a bang right then. After his adventure in the rain, Franklin tinkered with designs to protect buildings from the destructive power of lightning. In 1752, he invented the lighting rod, a metal rod with a sharpened tip that is still in use today. However, recent experiments have found that Franklin's design works even better if the tip of the rod is not pointed.

1 pound (0.5 kg) of available nitrogen per 1,000 square feet (93 sq m). (To calculate how much fertilizer your trees will need, see Fertilizer Amounts for Damaged Trees.)

Not all popular methods of fertilizing trees produce the even application desired in those with lightning damage. Fertilizer stakes or fertilizing via holes punched in the soil is not as desirable, because such methods can concentrate fertilizer salts in some areas and leave others without enough nutrients. Foliar feeding (spraying a dilute solution onto the leaves) can be effective if a tree isn't badly damaged.

Flashover

Description: Sometimes a tree may be struck during the storm but suffer little or no visible damage at all, due to a phenomenon called *flashover*. Lightning strikes that run down the outside of the bark often do very little damage to the tree. The bolt seems to spread out and slip down the tree cylinder in a bright burst of light. Flashover events most often occur to those species least likely to attract lightning, such as birch and beech, but can happen to any species.

Symptoms: Although some trees suffer no damage from flashover, others may display subtle injuries that appear days or up to a year later. This type of strike leaves no visible clues to the injury. The tree looks fine. The first hint of damage is often a yellowing (chlorosis) of the leaves. Sometimes the yellowing appears on a single branch; in other cases it is more

Different Strokes

There are three general paths lightning can follow once it hits a tree:

- Down the outside of the bark
- Between the inside of the bark and the outside of the sapwood
- Through the heartwood

Fertilizer Amounts for Damaged Trees

Size of area to be treated. The circumference of the canopy, the very edge of the branches, is called the *drip line*. The roots of a tree extend well beyond the drip line. To know how large a circle to fertilize, measure the distance from the trunk to the drip line and double it. That provides the radius of the circle.

To obtain the square footage of the circle, multiply 3.14 by the radius and by the radius again. For a tree with a root-zone radius of 30 feet (9.15 m), your calculations would be 3.14 x 30 x 30 = 2,826 square feet (or 3.14 x 9.15 x 9.15 = 83.7 sq m). If you apply a 10-10-10 fertilizer at 10 pounds (4.5 kg) per 1,000 square feet (93 sq m), you will need a large amount: 28.26 pounds (12.8 kg).

Amount of fertilizer. To determine how much available nitrogen a fertilizer contains, look at the analysis on the bag. A balanced 10-10-10 fertilizer contains 10 percent nitrogen, 10 percent phosphorus, and 10 percent potassium. One pound (0.5 kg) of available nitrogen is needed over 1,000 square feet (93 sq m), but the fertilizer contains only 10 percent nitrogen. To get the application amount needed, divide 100 into the percentage of nitrogen (10 into 100 = 10). The result, 10 pounds (5 kg), is the amount needed to be applied to the tree. A 20-10-10 fertilizer would be 20 into 100 = 5 pounds (2.25 kg) per 1,000 square feet (93 sq m).

uniformly spread over the canopy. The chlorosis can sometimes progress to leaf drop and death of selected branches.

Remedies: There are no remedies as such. However, applying a water-soluble fertilizer as noted above can reduce the symptoms.

Strategies: Periodically inspect the tree for damage over the next year or two. Check for yellowing leaves; pest infestations, such as caterpillar invasion; and diseases, especially root-related ones, such as *phytophthora*. If lightning related, these pest and disease problems can occur suddenly and seem to be centered on the tree that was struck. Fertilize the tree with a complete fertilizer if the bolt struck in spring to early summer. Otherwise, hold off until the following spring to fertilize. Keep the soil around the root zone properly watered throughout the growing season.

Scarred but Still Standing

Description: When lightning strikes a tree, it follows the wettest path to the ground, simply because water conducts electricity better than wood does. In many trees, this path is the moist cambium layer between the bark and the sapwood. The cambium layer is absolutely essential for a plant's survival, and it is a lot to ask that this fragile layer of cells survive being jolted by a few million volts of electricity. Amazingly, many times it does. Some trees, especially such oaks as live, bur, white, and overcup, can take repeated abuse from lightning and still manage to survive.

Symptoms: As the current of a lightning bolt reaches the tree, it shoots down a narrow path along the trunk's cambium to the roots, eventually dissipating in the ground. The current instantly boils the sap under the

Lightning Facts and Figures

• **Constant.** Every day of the year, every hour of the day, every minute of every hour, and every second of every minute, lightning bolts strike the earth. The barrage never ends, and it adds up to 8.6 million hits every day — 3 billion over the year.

• **Hot.** Lightning is much more than a huge surge of electrical energy; it is also incredibly hot. The surface of the sun is about 11,000°F (6,093°C). That means the sun is almost four times hotter than molten iron and over five times hotter than molten copper, gold, or silver. Now consider that a lightning bolt produces temperatures so hot that it doesn't just melt metals like copper and silver — it vaporizes them. Temperatures in a light-ning bolt can approach 50,000°F (27,760°C), making each jagged bolt one of the hottest objects in the solar system.

• **Fast.** The flash that signals a lightning bolt's race across the sky lasts for but a fraction of a second. When asked how fast lightning actually moves, some people say it travels at the speed of light, or about 186,000 miles per second. They're wrong. While light indeed moves at that incredible speed, lightning is not light; it is electricity. Electrical energy moves more slowly than light but still zips along at an amazing 20,000 to 100,000 miles (32,190–160,900 km) per second. That means a lightning bolt could travel all the way around the earth in roughly 1.2 seconds!

bark and blasts it from the tree, leaving a narrow, vertical scar. A light-ning bolt is about an inch wide, and the damage the stroke inflicts is fre-quently 1 to 2 inches (2.5–5 cm) wide as well, though it can be much wider. Sometimes thin strips of sapwood are also ripped from the tree. When the lighting strike travels deep into the roots, the current can superheat the sap there and instantly cook the tissues that conduct food and water. Symptoms of this damage are wilting leaves, yellowing leaves, dieback of branches, and pest and disease problems.

Remedies: Inspect the tree all along the scar, probing under the bark to see how wide the wound is. Lightning scars are continuous along the tree, and if a section of bark along the pathway appears to have escaped dam-age, carefully check beneath the bark to see whether it is loose. Also look to see if the scar forks along the route. Follow all the procedures for trees hit by flashovers (see page 283). Cleanly trim the bark along the scar and remove loose, damaged pieces. Tack loosened but otherwise undamaged sections in place. These measures help the wound heal. In trees suscepti-ble to bark beetles and similar pests, the open scar left by lightning can be an invitation, so watch carefully for these if warranted.

Blown Away

Description: Sometimes lightning pierces a tree to the heartwood, pro-ducing an explosion that blows the tree to pieces. While the result is sim-ilar, different trees are shattered in different ways. Most often, the bolt strikes a trunk about two thirds to three quarters of the way up the tree. This section of the trunk is annihilated, and the remainder of the tree above the strike point topples to the ground.

Symptoms: Where the bolt contacts the tree, a large portion of the trunk shatters like glass. The concussion fills the air with hundreds of wooden fragments, from slivers to logs. Sometimes every piece of wood, large and small, is permeated with thousands of volts — so much energy that the fragments glow with St. Elmo's fire. Like sparks of gleaming neon, they hurtle through the sky, creating tracers of ethereal light that last a second or two, then disappear.

Remedies: These trees are almost always a complete loss. The damage to the crown of a tree, which holds the foliage, is usually substantial. The trunk below is often split, and large cracks reach into the main roots. The power of the electrical charge and the temperature it generates are often enough to kill the tree outright. Sometimes enough branches and leaf area remain, such as on large white pines, that the tree can be topped and saved. The resulting tree won't win any beauty contest, but it will still be a living tree and that is enough in some cases. If the tree cannot be saved, it should be removed. Remember that damaged trees can be unstable and very dangerous to work around, so this is a job for a professional.

A Bolt out of the Blue

A lightning bolt that strikes in seemingly nice weather under a blue sky is wholly unexpected. Experts on thunderstorms and lightning repeatedly warn that if you can hear thunder, you're in danger from lightning. Perhaps this advice is overly cautious, as thunder can be heard long before the storm arrives and long after it departs. But the distant rolling tremors can often be heard in nice weather and under a blue sky.

Most lightning in a thunderstorm forms in the negatively charged lower portions of the cloud mass. Miles overhead, in the icy, anvil-shaped peak of the storm, another type of lightning can form that poses a special risk for people outdoors. The top of a thunderhead, sometimes 10 miles (16 km) above the ground, carries a positive charge. When a bolt traces from those cloud tops to the ground, it often strikes far from the storm, up to 10 miles (16 km) ahead or behind, in areas where the sun is shining and the sky is blue. Not only are these strikes unexpected, but they are also much more dangerous than most other lightning.

Because they carry a positive charge, these lightning bolts last longer, and transfer more electrical energy to the ground and nearby objects. This longer pulse of energy more often sparks fires in buildings and trees. It is also more likely to injure people, such as the gardener who wants to pull just one more weed before heading inside. To avoid bolts from the blue, head inside a building whenever you hear thunder.

Wind

THE WEATHER SYSTEM THAT DRIFTS OFFSHORE IS INVISIBLE, a mountain of dry air that manifests itself as a clear blue tropical sky. For days, the high-pressure system has moved west across the parched North African desert, a transparent monolith of air nearly 30,000 feet high. As it now edges out over the Atlantic and moves silently toward the Azores, something happens near the surface of the sea far below that begins a storm. The equatorial winds that blow over the warm ocean are heavy with water vapor, and conditions are right today for these winds to intersect. As they converge, the moist air is lifted into the sky, where it condenses into blossoms of towering white clouds.

As the moisture condenses, it releases heat, which warms the atmosphere thousands of feet above the sea. As the air is heated, the air pressure decreases, causing it to rise even higher into the sky. Moist air from below is drawn up to replace the rising air, establishing a system of thermals that drive winds from the ocean thousands of feet into the sky. As the clouds continue to grow, the winds begin to spiral in a counterclockwise direction. The white clouds have grown dark as water vapor collects into droplets and lightning courses through the veil of clouds, the bolts reflecting electric blue off the turbulent sea.

The latest satellite imagery at the National Hurricane Center shows a thunderstorm cluster south of the Azores. Tropical thunderstorms pop up and melt away all the time. But sometimes they form amid weather conditions that transform them into something far more than, and far different from, a cluster of thunderstorms. The winds thousands of feet aloft are strong and steady, reinforcing and strengthening the storm winds. As the growth of clouds continues, this random assembly of storms becomes organized. The blob of clouds on the last satellite image is now a storm with clouds rotating counterclockwise around a center — and the winds within are rising.

The storm is now a tropical depression, but the metamorphosis of the weather system continues. Bands of clouds heavy with rain begin to form and wrap around the storm center. The winds race in near-circular patterns, reaching speeds of 65 miles per hour. As the storm spins westward toward the Caribbean, it is upgraded to a tropical storm. This is the ninth named storm of the season, and the National Hurricane Center calls it Ishmael.

The lowest air pressures ever recorded on earth are in the eyes of hurricanes. As this storm intensifies, the air pressure in its center continues to drop. Meanwhile, the winds circulating around the center continue to increase in speed. In the final stage of metamorphosis, the circulation around the storm center becomes so strong that warm moist air is blocked from reaching the core, the clouds evaporate, the winds die down, and the eye of the hurricane opens amid a spiral of clouds. Hurricane warnings go up for Hispaniola, Puerto Rico, and other nearby islands in the Caribbean, but the winds have turned Ishmael west–northwest and offer the islands a passing shot of gales and rain.

In the past 2 days, the hurricane has grown from a category 1 storm, the weakest class of hurricane, with sustained winds of 75 miles per hour, to a category 3 storm. Hurricanes are rated according to the Saffir-Simpson Hurricane Scale and are assigned numeric values of 1 to 5 depending on their sustained wind speeds. Spawned from a thunderstorm off the west coast of Africa, Ishmael is now a massive hurricane 250 miles in diameter, producing 12 inches of rain per day and with sustained winds of 120 miles per hour. The National Hurricane Center posts hurricane warnings for parts of the Atlantic Coast. Forecasters predict that Ishmael will make landfall in hours.

About 20 miles from the coast are the similar homes of the Joneses and the Johnsons. Each house is situated on top of a low hill that is the highest point on the property. Gardens and shrub borders decorate both yards, and trees are scattered about the lawns. The Joneses have planted windbreaks of shrubs and trees on the windward edge of the property. Nearer the house is a berm windbreak planted in a deep hedge of roses, with a few old large oaks set behind it. The most fragile gardens are close to the house and protected by a hurricane fence covered with star jasmine. The Johnsons, however, have no windbreaks in their yard. The largest tree is close to the house. It has a hollow trunk and a large low branch where hangs a child's swing. A vegetable garden is nearby, and foundation plantings wrap around the house.

Ishmael picks up billions of tons of moisture from the ocean every day, and every day drops all of it as rain. As the storm plows its way onshore, it pushes a mound of water 10 feet high in front of it. Monstrous storm waves pound the shore and break over piers, knocking down pilings and curtain walls. The storm surge floods inland, washing over roads up to 3 miles away from the beach. Almost unbelievably, salt spray clipped from the whitecaps by the wind is whipped 50 miles inland. The gusts also sandblast shorefront homes and plants. As the storm crosses land, the peak winds drop down to 100 miles per hour, which is little comfort to those — like the Joneses and the Johnsons — with homes that lie in the hurricane's path.

As the storm reaches the Joneses' yard, the strongest winds first hit the windbreak of shrubs and low trees, which dampens the gusts and redirects them over the windbreak. Downwind, the berm and rose hedge steer the remaining winds up into the canopies of the oaks, which deflect the wind away from the house. Meanwhile, at the Johnsons', the wind rips across the yard in a rough, ragged assault. Some large branches are torn from trees, and with a horrific roar, the hollow old tree twists and cracks in the wind, then crashes to the ground. The wind tears shingles from the roof, and small branches hurled by the wind pound the house. The vegetable garden is flattened, and the leaves of most of the perennials and shrubs are tattered and torn. By the storm's end, both yards are covered with twigs and leaves and debris, but the Jones property has suffered much less than that of the Johnsons.

Hurricane Force

Hurricanes are the most powerful storms on the planet, vast engines of wind and rain that can span hundreds of miles. The furious energy that drives a hurricane comes from the water vapor that rises from the warm ocean. Only a tiny percentage of that energy is converted to mechanical energy in the form of winds. But the extent of that energy is almost incomprehensibly enormous. If the energy of Hurricane Ishmael were converted to electrical energy, it would be enough to meet all the power needs of the entire United States for months.

To understand their force, consider that hurricanes sank Spanish treasure galleons centuries ago. Even in our times, the iron hulls of warships cannot withstand these storms. In 1944, the U.S. Task Force 38, an immense armada of warships (including destroyers and aircraft carriers), battled a typhoon near the Philippines. Three ships were lost, nine others were disabled, 146 aircraft were destroyed, and 790 lives were lost.

Terrible Twisters

In a typical year, about 800 funnel clouds touch down in the United States, but the week of May 4–10, 2003, set a record no one ever wishes to see broken. In those 7 days, 384 tornadoes — nearly half of the *annual* number — swept across 19 states, killing 42 people. More tornadoes form

The Fastest Wind in the World

Mount Washington, in New Hampshire, holds the record for the fastest wind gust ever recorded on the surface of the earth. During a storm in April 1934, the wind gusted over the summit observatory at the ferocious speed of 231 miles (372 km) per hour.

over the United States than anywhere else in the world. And in America, the area with the most storms is the region east of the Rockies, particularly the Great Plains.

The strongest tornadoes produce the highest-velocity winds on the planet — winds of such awesome strength that they have yet to be measured directly by weather instruments. Instead, their speed must be judged by the damage they produce, and even those figures are almost unimaginable. The maximum winds estimated to occur in an F-5 tornado is 318 miles (511 km) per hour. (See Scales of Strength, page 292.) The most violent winds in the strongest hurricane are moving more than 100 miles (161 km) per hour *slower* than those of the most powerful tornado.

As you can see in Scales of Strength, the effective threshold for near total destruction of landscape and garden trees, shrubs, and other plants is 155 miles (249 km) per hour. This equates roughly to a very strong F-2 tornado. But what happens when an F-2 tornado passes over yards and gardens? Surprisingly, the seemingy less sturdy herbaceous annuals and perennials are most likely to survive and the "strong," towering trees are least likely. This was illustrated very clearly after the 1995 Memorial Day tornado that tore through Great Barrington, Massachusetts. As I walked through the debris area along the path of this F-2 storm, I found virtually every tree destroyed, including immense Norway spruce, sycamore, oak, white pine, larch, and maple. Smaller trees, such as serviceberry, hawthorn, and ironwood, were for the most part spared, and most perennials were undisturbed (unless something had fallen on them). The tornado was also very sharply defined, with devastation confined to an area about 200 yards (183 m) wide. Outside this zone it seemed that not a flower petal was damaged. The funnel cloud struck one forested mountainside hardest of all, however, and in one section, the woods were annihilated. A forest of hardwoods and hemlock in seconds became a field of boulders and bedrock. The trees, shrubs, and ferns, even most of the soil, just vanished. All that was left was bare rock. If this is the result of an F-2 tornado, it is difficult to imagine what an F-5 storm — more than twice as powerful — would do.

Birth of a Tornado

Tornadoes are most often associated with severe thunderstorms and result in part from the combination of strong updrafts of warm air entering the storm and colder downdrafts descending from the upper reaches of the storm cloud. The storm cell of a thunderstorm is often shaped like a box or a circle. Tornadoes tend to form in a certain region of the thunderstorm, an area about 2 to 4 miles (3–6 km) wide that exhibits a strong rotation. If the storm is approaching you, this area is to your left and the storm's rear corner. On weather radar, areas of tornado development often appear as hook- or comma-shaped.

Tornadoes are a spiraling circulation of air and are often invisible when they form. The funnel becomes visible when material such as raindrops, hail, or debris from the ground begins to circulate through the column of air. The first visible sign of a tornado is what scientists call a *rotating cloud wall*, which looks like a mass of clouds all moving in the same direction. The next sign is a nub-shaped funnel that forms at the base of the cloud wall and begins to expand and descend toward the ground. The funnel cloud changes from a mass of clouds with a soft sur-

Fujita Scale of Strength

Tornadoes are classed according to the Fujita Scale into one of six categories based on the damage the storm produces, as follows:

F-0: 40–72 mph (64–115 km), with light damage

F-1: 73–112 mph (117–180 km), with moderate damage

F-2: 113–157 mph (181–252 km), with considerable damage

F-3: 158–206 mph (254–331 km), with severe damage

F-4: 207–260 mph (333–418 km), with devastating damage

F-5: 261–318 mph (419–511 km), with incredible damage

face to the more defined, almost polished appearance of a mature storm. Weak tornadoes will often be thin and wobbly in appearance, while strong twisters will be massive and look impenetrable.

Once they touch ground, some tornadoes can travel up to 50 miles (80 m) and leave a debris field a mile wide. About two thirds of tornadoes that form are weak storms, classed according to the Fujita Scale (page 292) from F-0 to F-1, with winds of less than 112 miles (180 km) per hour and with a life span of less than 10 minutes. Fewer than 30 percent of storms are classed as F-2 or F-3, with winds of up to about 200 miles (321 km) per hour and a life span of around 20 minutes. Only two of every 100 tornadoes reach a strength rated as F-4 or F-5, yet these storms are responsible for nearly three quarters of all deaths caused by tornadoes. These monster storms can linger for over an hour before dissipating.

Given a tornado's power, there are no tornado-proof plants for the garden. There are plants that can, through good fortune, survive a tornado. However, they are usually battered and broken in a way that, even after the most careful pruning, shows they have suffered violence. Some people elect to remove these plants and trees and start afresh. Others let them stand, not as reminders of what once happened, but rather as symbols of endurance.

Tornado Safety

Any severe weather can be life-threatening. Floods, lightning, heat, and cold all can kill people. Yet perhaps nothing in nature is as terrifying as the sight of a funnel cloud approaching. To remain as safe as possible, here are some tornado-safety rules.

Have an information source. Keep an NOAA weather radio in the house, potting shed, and wherever else you spend time. These slim, trim radios are attractively styled and don't take up much space, and they are tuned to your local National Weather Service and broadcast forecasts, warnings, and, most important, detailed information on hazardous weather in your area. Many NOAA radios have an alert button that will automatically alert you to warnings issued for your area.

A Seasonal Thing

Tornadoes most frequently form in May and June and occur most often between 3:00 P.M. and 9:00 P.M.

Find safe shelter indoors. When a warning is issued that a storm is approaching, go to a basement or other storm shelter. Lacking such a spot, retreat to a small interior ground-level room, such as a bathroom.

If outdoors, take the best steps possible. If you are caught outdoors away from safe shelter, find a low place in an open area away from power lines and water, such as drainage ditches. Lie flat on the ground.

In addition to these positive actions, remember to follow this important "don't" list:

• Don't seek shelter in a big building with a large roof, such as a mall, office complex, or theater.

• Avoid large rooms of buildings with extensive unreinforced walls, such as gymnasiums, cafeterias, and auditoriums.

• Don't stay in a mobile home, near windows, or in your car.

• Don't stay under a highway bridge or an overpass.

• Don't open the windows in a building as a tornado approaches. Opening windows allows the tornado winds to enter the structure, causing more damage.

Gentle Garden Breezes

The first step toward protecting your garden from damaging winds is to evaluate the normal wind patterns that affect your property and plants. What direction do the prevailing winds come from? How strong are they? In what seasons do they occur and how often do they blow? Are there other conditions present that can magnify the effect of the wind in an area, such as full sun, slopes, and buildings? Be sure to notice even gentle wind patterns, as they can damage plants too. And be aware of the types of plants that are most easily damaged by wind.

Working in the garden on a warm, humid day, when the air is quiet and still can be physically uncomfortable. The heat clings to every part of you, taking away the pleasantness of working the soil. Then, from some place unknown, a breeze moves the branches and sweeps past the garden in a long, delicious exhalation. In a moment, the heat is exchanged for refreshment and discomfort for joy. Enjoying the sensation of a summer breeze is one of the delights of gardening. Gentle breezes are also an important part of a healthy garden in many other ways. The easy movement of air through foliage helps prevent outbreaks of diseases such as powdery mildew, and breezes help control infestations of pests, such as aphids. However, when the wind becomes too strong, persists for too long, or passes through as part of a violent storm, a garden can suffer a wide range of damage. Heeding warning signs, from weather forecasts to inspecting the trees in the yard for weakness, can help us reduce the damage and even turn a potentially devastating wind event into a force that helps the garden grow.

When designing a garden with an appreciation for the winds that will blow through it, the first thing to do is to survey the lay of the land. Watching the wind is a lot like looking for surface-drainage patterns of water. The flow of water is often contained by topographic features that define the paths of least resistance, such as the valleys and ravines that channel brooks, creeks, and rivers. Whatever the feature is called, the important thing to recognize is that it channels downslope not only water but also air. Sometimes the difference between the water temperature and that of the air, combined with the flow of water, produces a cool breeze that fills a streambed and overflows over a floodplain as well. These areas will consistently be up to 5 to 10 degrees F cooler than an area 100 feet (30 m) away but slightly higher in elevation.

Some winds form at day's end, when hilltops cool off before the valleys. The cool air flows down the slopes of the hills, following the topography. These breezes begin near sunset and can continue most of the night.

Other winds form early in the morning. The sun warms open areas, such as fields, faster than forested places, causing thermals to rise up from the open spaces and breezes of cooler air to sweep in to fill the spaces the warm air left behind.

Sea breezes are similar, but on a grander scale. Here, the land warms faster than the sea in the morning, so the breeze blows from water (sea or lake) onto the land. At night, the land cools faster than the water, and the air flow is reversed. Calm periods occur in between.

Drying Winds

The symptoms of drought, such as wilting of leaves, are most often associated with dry soil. However, symptoms that resemble drought can appear when there is plenty of water in the soil, as in flooded, frozen, or saline soils. In these examples, the water is unavailable to the plants because conditions stop the roots from absorbing it.

Wind produces symptoms similar to drought in another way. In wind-induced drought, the soil has adequate moisture and the moisture is readily available to a plant. However, the wind increases the transpiration rate to the point where the plant cannot absorb water fast enough from the soil to compensate for the moisture loss from its foliage.

Transpiration is the name given to what seems at first glance to be a pretty simple process. Roots absorb water from the soil, the moisture moves up the stem to the leaves, then the water evaporates from the leaf surfaces into the air. Transpiration helps transport minerals throughout

Stupendous Stomata

An apple leaf can have 250,000 stomata over every square inch of leaf surface. An orange tree leaf may have nearly 300,000, while an oak leaf can have upward of 350,000.

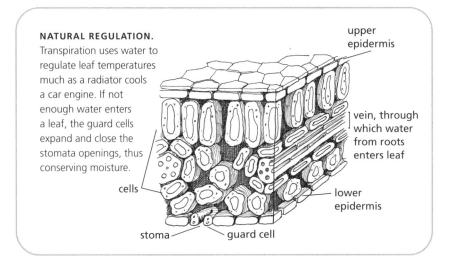

NATURAL REGULATION. Transpiration uses water to regulate leaf temperatures much as a radiator cools a car engine. If not enough water enters a leaf, the guard cells expand and close the stomata openings, thus conserving moisture.

upper epidermis

vein, through which water from roots enters leaf

cells

lower epidermis

stoma — guard cell

the plant and moves other substances, such as sugars. It provides necessary moisture for such processes as photosynthesis and helps keep leaves turgid and cool.

Once the moisture is in a leaf, it covers the interior cells with a wet film. Nearby are minute openings on the leaf surface called *stomata*. These are tiny holes into the interior of the leaf that are bounded completely by two boomerang-shaped cells called *guard cells*. The guard cells make the stomata bigger or smaller to increase or decrease the rate of moisture loss. (Even if the stomata are closed, moisture can still be drawn from a leaf.)

Wind increases a plant's moisture loss by increasing the rate of its leaves' moisture loss. The moisture moves from the roots to the leaves only so fast, and if the rate of evaporation outpaces the rate of replenishment, symptoms of wind drought such as the following begin to occur:
• Wilted leaves
• Scorched leaf margins
• Tip burn on leaves (especially monocots)
• Curling (either up or down) of leaves from margins
• Stunted or deformed growth from buds
• Dieback of emerging buds

A Combination That Changes the Odds

Although we've just seen that wind can increase the rate of transpiration in plants, the wind can also cool plants in the hot sun and actually reduce moisture loss in a plant. For instance, the transpiration rate of a plot of corn on a cloudy, calm day increases nearly 25 percent if the wind rises to a 5 mph (8 km) breeze. On a sunny day, however, the transpiration rate of that same patch of corn will decrease 25 percent when the conditions change from calm to a 5 mph (8 km) breeze. The difference between the wind's increasing or decreasing transpiration is the temperature of the corn. When plants are growing in full sun, the temperature dramatically rises within the leaves — and as the temperature goes up, so does the rate of evaporation. When the wind rises, it cools the leaves so much that it more than compensates for any increase in transpiration the breeze causes. The result is a net decrease in transpiration and improved conservation of water resources.

Plants Vulnerable to Wind Drought

Emerging seedlings. Seedlings have immature root systems and only a few — and fragile — true leaves. Wind desiccation can quickly wilt and kill unprotected seedlings. For vegetables and flowers sown in place, a light row cover effectively dampens breezes and speeds growth by increasing air temperatures. Protect grass seed from the wind by laying down a thin mulch at the time of sowing.

Newly planted transplants, divisions, and suckers. Transplants and newly planted divisions have had their root systems shocked, and the ability to provide moisture to the rest of the plant is compromised. For herbaceous perennials, such as irises and daylilies, cutting back the foliage by one half to two thirds (depending on the amount of root mass present at planting) will reestablish a balance between the amount of water the roots can provide and the surface area of the leaves, from which moisture will be lost.

Be forewarned that transplants, no matter how careful you are, suffer enough damage to their root hairs to temporarily reduce the volume of moisture absorption. Planting in a sheltered place is often enough to manage wind desiccation in these plants. For plants in an exposed area, install a row cover for 2 to 4 weeks until the plants become better established, or erect a temporary windbreak with snow fencing or some other barrier to break the wind. Avoid using a solid barrier, as this can produce wind currents where you don't want them.

Plants in the process of hardening. These plants have the disadvantage of having not just their leafy parts but also their root systems exposed to wind. In addition, the roots are still crowded into pots. One of the best ways to manage wind desiccation in hardening plants is to install a cold frame or similar structure that regulates temperature, manages wind, and allows appropriate light infiltration. Polycarbonate cold frames are excellent for this purpose.

It's a good idea to place a deep layer of mulch in the hardening area, then set the pots containing the plants into the mulch. This places the root zones at a more appropriate, cooler temperature and reduces moisture loss in the root-balls. If you must harden off plants in the open, at least select a shady spot that is sheltered from the wind.

Cuttings in the process of rooting. Although most propagation is done indoors, where breezes can be regulated, some gardeners root woody cuttings of easy, undemanding shrubs, such as red-osier dogwood and forsythia, in a special propagation bed outdoors. The hardwood cuttings are "struck" in spring, when the plants are in still the late stages of winter dormancy. The cuttings will root quickly, but they often leaf out before their root systems have matured, making them vulnerable to drying breezes. Drape the propagation bed with a light shade cloth or lightweight row cover to regulate light intensity and air movement.

Trees and shrubs within 2 years of transplanting. These plants are at risk of wind-drought damage solely because of their recent transplanting, yet they often can weather average breezy conditions without trouble. Keep the plants well watered throughout the period and fertilize each spring. Be sure to keep equipment and excessive foot traffic away from the root zones to avoid compacting the soil. In windy areas, stake young trees by using a three- or four-guy wire system to reduce wind rock (when a tree is rocked back and forth in the wind), which can damage their developing root systems.

Plants that have suffered root damage. Trees and other plants suffer root damage from several sources, from vehicles; chemical pollution, such as salt infiltration; destructive pests, such as ants; and various debilitating diseases, including root rot. Anything from an 80-foot-tall (24 m) aspen tree with girdled roots to a roughly transplanted marigold may have to cope with root damage. Often, the first symptom is wilting that is worse on windy days. But wind desiccation in this case can be an ally rather than a foe, because it flags the problem plant. Treat each plant individually and trace the source of the wilting problem. Trees with root damage severe enough to initiate wind wilt are also probably damaged enough to be a hazard and should be removed. Wind-wilted plants elsewhere in the garden may signal the presence of a pest or disease that needs your attention.

Plants with emerging leaves. Even healthy plants producing healthy leaves are vulnerable to wind desiccation for a few days or weeks each spring. Newly emerging leaves or flower buds need to harden, just like the vegetables and flowers you grow every spring. As the buds break, the new leaf tissue is very soft and easily desiccated. Over the course of a couple of weeks, the tissues harden and physiological changes toughen up the tender foliage so that it can endure breezy days. Damage usually is substantial if it is windy for several consecutive days, especially if the wind is accompanied by heat. To help plants along, keep the ground watered. Small shrubs can be covered with bird netting to break the wind flow until calmer weather returns.

Any part of a plant with new leaf and shoot growth. The guidelines for these plants are the same as those for plants newly leafing out. The difference is that new leaf and shoot growth can occur at many times of the year, not just in the spring, and is often spurred by pruning. Weather conditions can be harsher, such as heat and drought, and damage can occur very quickly.

Orchards and Wind

Wind is a special concern for those who grow fruit trees, as too much wind during almost any part of the fruiting cycle can injure an entire crop. In spring, good fruit set depends mainly on the work of honeybees. As bees go, honeybees are not an adventurous or courageous bunch. When it gets cold, misty, or windy, they simply stay home. Thus, too much wind during pollination time often results in poor fruit set. Wind at other times can disfigure fruit — you may observe scars left by twigs spearing the fruit as it is tossed about in the wind. Finally, wind that occurs near harvesttime can drop fruit prematurely from the trees.

The most effective defense against wind damage to orchards is good orchard layout. Choose a site that is to the lee of the prevailing winds and midway on a slope and you'll avoid most of the worst winds. If the topography doesn't cooperate, then a solution is to set windbreaks upwind from the orchard (and in some cases even within the orchard) to dampen the breeze.

Identifying Wind Hazards

Wind hazards are diverse and include:

Trees too close to structures. Often this means that if a tree comes down in a heavy wind, it will strike the house or another structure. Following this definition would leave everyone without any shade, so as a practical definition, "too close" means trees within about 25 feet (7.5 m) of structures. This definition refers to healthy trees.

Weak leaders. Multiple-leader trees are prone to failure but can be strengthened by a network of cables. Well-placed and well-installed cables can transform a large problem into a valuable asset.

Poor planting. Not everyone plants trees properly, and one of the most common errors is planting them too deeply. A tree that is set too deeply in the soil will develop a weak root system that either girdles the trunk or rots from intertwining. The effects of poor planting often take years to manifest, but eventually the tree will fall down in the wind or the trunk will snap.

Improper mulching. A cousin to deep planting is the recent fad of burying the area around trees in mulch. This damages the trees in a fashion similar to deep planting.

Trees with shallow root systems. Many trees, such as sugar maples, naturally have a wide, shallow network of roots without a taproot. Other trees grow in shallow soil, such as on ledge or above a high water table. Shallow roots don't offer the support that a more extensive root system provides. Pruning to reduce wind resistance can sometimes help.

Trees with girdling root systems. Such trees include quaking and bigtooth aspen. In this kind of tree, some of the roots grow around it, eventually weakening the tree so that it falls in a heavy wind. Avoid trouble by not planting such trees near the house.

A Proactive Approach to Wind Protection

If, as we have seen earlier, wind is stronger than the most powerful warship, how can our gardens hope to fare against such a tempest? Take heart from the knowledge that you *can* make your garden wind resilient by implementing various techniques, from pliancy to mass plantings, so the garden can not only weather a storm but help protect your home as well.

Windbreaks: Bending the Breeze

The old saying "to whistle down the wind" means to do something without purpose. Constructing a windbreak is the opposite, as this single tool can change the environment of a large part of your yard. A windbreak is a structure, such as a fence or a hedge, designed to break or lessen the impact of the wind. For gardeners, this broad definition has to be refined a little. In the garden and yard, a windbreak needs to do three distinct things to be most useful: modify the speed of the wind, redirect the course of the wind, and create places that are predictably free from the wind. Not every windbreak can supply all these things, and some windbreaks can make what you thought to be a solution to a problem just another part of the problem.

What's Wrong with a Wall?

The easiest way to construct a windbreak is to build a wall or fence the height you desire and set it in front of the area you want to protect. Unfortunately, the easy way is not always the right way, for the following reason. Wind is a mass of moving air that acts somewhat like a fluid flowing over a surface. Consider this parallel example with water: If you block a flow of water with a solid barrier, watch the powerful turbulence that erupts in front of and behind the blockage. White-water paddlers often see these currents on rivers. Known as *hydraulics,* they can be very dangerous if you become trapped in them. A solid windbreak does the same thing. As the wind contacts the barrier, the crush of air raises the air pressure in front of the wall. Some of the air sweeps up and over the windbreak, but other currents swirl up and back in damaging eddies. Behind the windbreak, in the supposedly protected zone, more currents form that roll the air in horizontal whirlpools. Just as water behaves in a river, windy hydraulics in a garden can really buffet your plants.

Windbreaks That Work

Some hard windbreaks, such as baffle fences, work well because their design allows the wind to filter through the fence rather than just slam up against it and create back currents. Any fence design that breaks the wind accomplishes what a baffle fence does, including chain-link hurricane fences with baffle strips woven among the links.

Traditional hurricane fences — metal chain-link fencing stretched between metal posts — aren't the most attractive additions to the garden, though they do their job well. Fortunately, they are excellent stages for some very attractive plants. In fact, a hurricane fence smothered in star jasmine is a more effective windbreak than the metal fence alone.

When constructing a fence in an exposed, windy area, set the fence posts securely in concrete to ensure a solid footing. And use corrosion-resistant fasteners where possible, especially near the shore. Finally, well before a forecast storm arrives, go out and inspect the fencing for structural integrity and repair as needed.

Windbreak Design Considerations

To design a windbreak that fits your property's needs and is also attractive, consider the following points:

Length. The length of the windbreak is generally equivalent to the distance of wind buffering downwind from it. So a windbreak that is 50 feet (15 m) long will have an area about 50 feet (15 m) downwind of it that experiences calmer winds.

Vines for Windbreak Fences

Not all attractive garden vines are good choices for growing on a hurricane fence or similarly designed structure. Because a vine growing on a hurricane fence is intentionally planted in harm's way, it must be wind resilient in order to endure the inevitable punishment and still look good enough to belong in or near a garden. For gardens along the coast or other areas in which the wind may pick up and carry salt, the windbreak plant should also be wind- and salt-spray resilient. The following plants are both:

Carolina yellow jasmine *(Gelsemium sempervirens)*

Lady Banks rose *(Rosa banksiae)*

Star jasmine *(Trachelospermum jasminoides)*

Trumpet creeper *(Campsis radicans)*

Wintercreeper *(Euonymus fortunei)*

If a strong storm with damaging winds is expected during a time when a covering vine is especially lush, you should thin the plant to reduce the leaf load by about a third. This allows more air through the windbreak, and helps reduce the chances of structural damage to the fence in event of very strong winds.

Width. A wider windbreak dampens the wind more gradually than a narrow break and produces far less turbulence. When you are planting your windbreak, widen it out wherever possible to take advantage of this quality.

Height. The height of a windbreak is very important in making a functional wind damper for the garden. The calm area (in feet) behind a windbreak is approximately five times the height of the windbreak. Thus, a windbreak 20 feet (6 m) tall will produce a protected area 100 feet (30 m) downwind.

Number of layers. The more layers in a windbreak, the more efficiently it will dampen the wind without generating eddies and other damaging currents.

Plant selection. This is where a good design can get better — or fail. Proper plant choice not only makes the windbreak perform more efficiently, but it allows it to modify even stronger winds as well, thereby protecting the garden even better.

Multiple windbreaks. If space permits, planting two or three windbreaks in sequence is a very effective way to manage the wind, especially the high winds.

The Three-Planting-Wide Windbreak

This windbreak requires a lot of room, as it is formed of three layers of plants: two rows of shrubs and one of trees. In cross section, the windbreak is tapered with low points at the leading and trailing edges and the high spot in the center. This design reduces turbulence as wind passes over the break. The planting is arranged to allow wind to gently pass through the windbreak as well as over it, again reducing trailing currents.

For this plan, choose shrubs and trees with mature heights that have a ratio of about 2:1 — that is, trees that will grow about twice the height of the shrubs. This produces a windbreak that will guide the wind up from ground level and direct it over the tops of the trees. The resulting flow pattern most effectively steers the wind away from the downwind structures on your property.

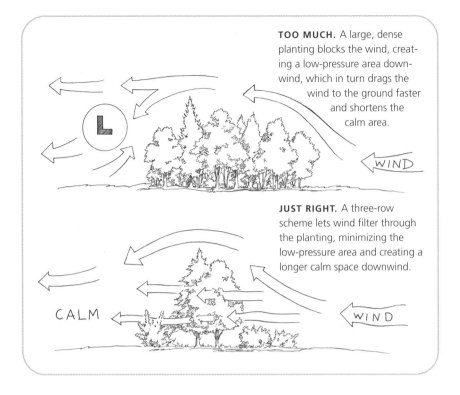

TOO MUCH. A large, dense planting blocks the wind, creating a low-pressure area downwind, which in turn drags the wind to the ground faster and shortens the calm area.

JUST RIGHT. A three-row scheme lets wind filter through the planting, minimizing the low-pressure area and creating a longer calm space downwind.

Set the windward edge of shrubs along the length of the windbreak and plant the shrubs every 4 to 5 feet (1 to 1.5 m) on center. About 10 feet (3 m) downwind of the shrubs, plant the trees in a staggered pattern in relation to the shrubs, 10 feet apart. Plant the last row of shrubs 10 feet downwind of the trees, in line with the first row of shrubs and the same distance apart. Follow this plan, and your property will have an excellent chance of withstanding even a hurricane with the power of Ishmael (see page 288).

Hedges as Windbreaks

When space is tight, a windbreak comprising a single or double row of sturdy, dense shrubs or small trees works very well. Unlike a solid wall, a hedge buffers the wind as it hits the windbreak, slowing it down and allowing the air to filter through to lessen turbulence. The hedge can be planted with plants set in a straight row or staggered.

Berms as Windbreaks

Earthen berms are effective tools to direct not only excess water, but also wind, away from homes and gardens. Residents of Cornwall, England, have a tradition of building windbreaks of stone that look like walls with hollow center troughs. The center is filled with soil and bushy plants are set atop the wall. The typical earthen berm begins with the same idea, but refines it a bit to better *direct* the wind flow (rather than *block* it, as the Cornish windbreaks do).

Earth berms are usually about 5 feet (1.5 m) tall and 10 feet (3 m) wide, with a uniform and graded slope from the peak to the base. This shape steers wind away from gardens and buildings. As the wind reaches the berm, air flows up the windward bank at the same angle of inclination as that of the berm. When it reaches the berm's peak, the lower portion of the airflow is intercepted by the shrubs and the wind is slowed as it filters through the plants. Meanwhile, the upper wind flow continues over the windbreak at the same upward angle as the berm, and for some distance downwind, the main wind flow stays well above ground level. At this

Good Plants for Windbreaks

Trees

Austrian pine *(Pinus nigra)*

Colorado blue spruce *(Picea pungens)*

Eastern hemlock *(Tsuga canadensis)*

Eastern red cedar *(Juniperus virginiana)*

Eastern white pine *(Pinus strobus)*

European larch *(Larix decidua)*

Monterey cypress *(Cupressus macrocarpa)*

Red maple (*Acer rubrum* 'Columnare')

Rocky Mountain juniper *(Juniperus scopulorum)*

Russian olive *(Elaeagnus angustifolia)*

Serviceberry (*Amelanchier* spp.)

Siberian pea *(Caragana arborescens)*

Shrubs

Apothecary's rose (*Rosa gallica* var. *officinalis*)

Pittosporum (*Pittosporum* spp.)

Podocarpus (*Podocarpus* spp.)

Rugosa rose *(Rosa rugosa)*

Simons cotoneaster *(Cotoneaster simonsii)*

Swiss mountain pine *(Pinus mugo)*

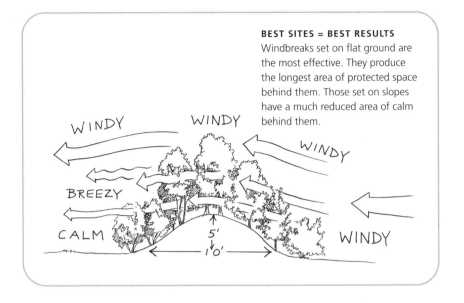

BEST SITES = BEST RESULTS
Windbreaks set on flat ground are the most effective. They produce the longest area of protected space behind them. Those set on slopes have a much reduced area of calm behind them.

point, anywhere within about 75 to 100 (22–30 m) feet downwind of the berm, large wind-deflector trees further protect homes and other structures. Very strong wind-resilient trees, such as live oak, southern magnolia, and white oak, can be used here to deaden the wind. (Trees need to be mature specimens to act as reliable wind deflectors.)

Depending on the availability of materials, a berm can have a core of stone covered by a mantle of soil or be constructed of solid soil. To stabilize the berm, it's wise to plant a ground cover or to sow a thick, deeply rooted grass. The plants also produce drag as wind flows over the berm, which slows the wind. If you wish, you may plant the very top of the berm with tough, wind-resilient shrubs, such as rugosa roses, which further dampen wind flow.

Taking Advantage of Structures

The gardens around the house, from foundation plantings to beds and borders, grow in an environment very different from that of the plants in garden beds a few yards away from the house. A structure can funnel more water to the garden from roof runoff, as well as warm the air and soil by acting as a solar collector. Structures also influence the wind that blows around, with the result that a planting on one side of the house may exist in a refuge of calm while one on the other side bears the brunt of every gale. Knowing how the wind changes the environment directly outside your door can help you in plant selection and care.

Some part of the house faces the prevailing winds, which means that the opposite side is going to be largely sheltered. The shelter wall will experience turbulence near both edges but a calm area will extend from the side of the house out about 10 to 15 feet (3–4.5 m) in a rough semicircle shape. The calm area in the lee of the house can be shaped by simply extending a barrier — for example — a fence, from its edges, angled slightly downwind.

The side of the house facing the wind can benefit from constructing windbreaks ahead of the house. The windbreaks should be staggered in increasing height so the wind rides up and over the structure. They can be wider near the house and narrower farther out. Patios bounded by fences, especially those with vines or buffered by shrubs on the windward side, are also beneficial.

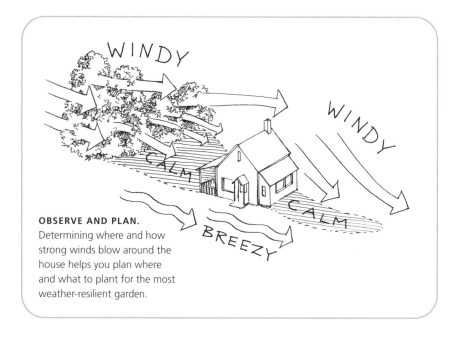

OBSERVE AND PLAN. Determining where and how strong winds blow around the house helps you plan where and what to plant for the most weather-resilient garden.

A structural wall that runs parallel to prevailing winds can create a windless, calm environment if you place barriers, either fences or hedges, at an angle slightly downwind to the wall.

A protected house, viewed as a rectangle with the prevailing wind hitting one of the narrow ends of the figure and all the windbreaks in place, takes on the appearance of an arrow. An arrow shape is perfectly streamlined to cut the air, and a home with windbreaks designed in this manner will slice the wind, allowing you to plant your gardens in a much more temperate environment. Even if the house itself isn't arrow-shaped, this technique produces calm areas that are more temperate than nearby unsheltered places.

The Wind in the Willows versus Resilience

The sound of the breeze passing through the boughs of trees has a soothing, peaceful tone. The sound of the wind in willow trees, especially, produces tranquillity, as long as the wind is light. When a storm comes along, however, choosing a cozy place beneath the willow boughs is a dangerous idea, given the vulnerability of willow trees. On the other hand, listening to the wind while sitting beneath the oaks would be less poetic but far safer.

Trees are the most permanent parts of the living landscape and are often costly or, in the case of large trees, impossible to replace. A tree is also the most obvious and spectacular victim of wind damage, with injuries ranging from broken branches at the very least to the entire tree being uprooted. Predicting which trees are going to be damaged by which storms is, of course, impossible. But you can substantially reduce the chances of wind damage to the trees in your yard by taking the following steps:

• Survey the trees in your yard for resilient traits.
• Inspect the trees for safety hazards and weaknesses.
• Remedy weaknesses in existing trees.
• Select species and varieties that are wind-resilient.

Wind-Resilient Trees and Shrubs

Trees

Bald cypress *(Taxodium distichum)*

Beech *(Fagus grandifolia)*

Cabbage palmetto *(Sabal palmetto)*

Coconut palm *(Cocos nucifera)*

Crape myrtle *(Lagerstromia indica)*

Live oak *(Quercus virginiana)*

Queen palm *(Syagrus romanzoffiana)*

Royal palm *(Roystonea elata)*

Southern magnolia *(Magnolia grandiflora)*

Sweetbay *(Magnolia virginiana)*

Tamarisk *(Tamarix* spp.)

Thread palm *(Washingtonia robusta)*

Tulip tree *(Liriodendron tulipifera)*

Weeping fig *(Ficus benghalensis)*

Shrubs

English holly *(Ilex aquifolium)*

Hebe *(Hebe* spp.)

Juniper *(Juniperus* spp.)

Red-osier dogwood *(Cornus stolonifera)*

Rugosa rose *(Rosa rugosa)*

Serviceberry *(Amelanchier* spp.)

Yaupon holly *(Ilex vomitoria)*

Going Out on a Limb

During windy conditions, branches often break at the point where the limbs join the trunk. This region, called the *branch union*, is a good indicator of whether the tree in general, or that branch specifically, is likely to suffer storm damage in the future. There are strong, wind-resilient branch unions and weak, damage-prone ones. You can easily tell the difference between the two by looking at the bark at the point of union and studying the angle at which a limb meets the trunk.

Strong branch unions. Limbs with strong wind resilience have a branch union called *bark out*. This merger is characterized by a very narrow line or ridge of bark beginning at the top of the branch union and running from that fork at a downward angle away from the branch. In some trees, a second line originates from the bottom of the union and runs up to the first ridge forming a V. The bark ridge is usually prominent and easy to find, especially in young trees and smooth-barked trees, such as beech. The ridge indicates a strong bond between branch and tree.

In addition to the ridgeline, strong, wind-resilient branches meet the trunk at close to right angles. These branches are held almost horizontal and join the tree fairly perpendicular to the trunk. As the angle of the branch to the trunk decreases, so does the strength of the branch union. Good wind resiliency is maintained until the branch-to-trunk angle becomes less than 45 degrees or so, or about halfway between horizontal and the line of the trunk.

Weak branch unions. The bark ridge on a tree is like a pressure ridge on a polar ocean. As two large ice floes move together, the leading edges of the ice crush against each other and the ice is pushed up into a ridge. The raised bark ridge of a tree is similar, if less dramatic. As the bark of the trunk and branch grow together, they push the bark out and away from the union, forming a bark ridge.

Weak unions grow together in an opposite fashion. Instead of the bark being pushed up and away in a ridge, it is drawn into the merger zone. This type of bond between limb and trunk has a recessed seam along the union (like two rollers or cylinders placed against each other). In these "bark-in" unions, a layer of bark grows between the branch and the trunk, effectively making a weak layer that compromises the union between

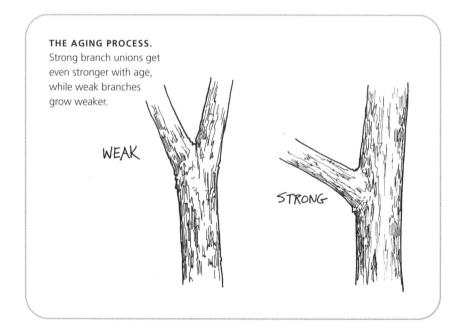

THE AGING PROCESS.
Strong branch unions get even stronger with age, while weak branches grow weaker.

WEAK

STRONG

limb and tree. A bark-in union acts like the abscission layer that appears in fall between a twig and a leaf. The adhesion becomes progressively weaker until a breeze knocks the leaf loose. Branches weakened by bark-in unions also progressively become weaker until a storm wind breaks the bond and the limb falls.

Weak branches are also often joined to the tree at a shallow angle. The closer to vertical the joint is, the weaker the union.

Double-Leader Trees, Double Trouble

Some trees, such as pines, are strongly inclined to have one main trunk. Other trees, such as cherry, have a growth habit in which some larger branches compete with the primary trunk for dominance. Either way, the result is a tree with double leaders, also called *codominant leaders.*

In trees like white pine, double leaders may be the result of a pest or disease that killed the original leader early in the tree's life. Two or three latent buds beneath the old leader then produced shoots that became the new leaders. If all new leaders continue to grow, the tree becomes very large, but the point of union where the multiple leaders joins the primary trunk is unstable. They combine the problems of a shallow angle, a bark-in union, and enormous stresses caused by the weight of the tree above.

Deciduous trees, such as cherry, may end up in similar circumstances, most often because of the growth habit of the tree rather than any pest or disease problem. This weak condition can then be made more fragile by pests, such as fall webworm, or diseases, such as black knot, that invade and weaken the union between the leaders and the trunk.

Strong winds will eventually take down a double-leader tree, usually in stages. Double-leader trees can grow rather large and thus can ride out the wind for a while. But as the trees grow, their equilibrium becomes more tenuous, until the right storm with the right wind flow knocks them down. A double-leader tree is most susceptible to gusty, swirling winds that twist a trunk. This breaks the union, toppling one of the main leaders and leaving the other leader intact. The remaining leader is very weak and dangerous and should be removed.

A Little Bit of Both

It would be easy if all trees had either strong branch unions or weak ones. But nature is rarely that tidy. Some trees, such as red maple, can have strong branch unions on one part of the tree and weak ones just a few feet away. We take for granted that pruning is a tool to maintain smaller plants, such as perennials and roses; similarly, pruning these trees, with some good branches and some bad, can turn a problem tree into a good one. A young tree is easiest to train. But don't neglect older trees. Careful pruning can make a great difference in these as well.

All That Rot

Rot is a decay of wood or other portion of a plant. It can compromise the strength of trees and eventually kill them outright. Strong trees can be weakened from pest and disease damage, which makes them vulnerable to the wind. Sometimes it's a gardener who begins the process, however, by improperly pruning branches, mowing around trees, or trimming with a line trimmer. Poor pruning can result in cuts that are excessively flush

Assessing Trees' Branch Unions

Trees with Strong Branch Unions

Beech (*Fagus* spp.)

Black tupelo *(Nyssa sylvatica)*

Hop hornbeam *(Ostrya virginiana)*

Hornbeam (*Carpinus* spp.)

Live oak *(Quercus virginiana)*

Southern magnolia *(Magnolia grandiflora)*

White oak *(Quercus alba)*

Trees with Weak Branch Unions

Box elder *(Acer negundo)*

Hackberry (*Celtis* spp.)

Mountain ash (*Sorbus* spp.)

Silver maple *(Acer saccharinum)*

Willow (*Salix* spp.)

Strong and Weak Branch Unions

Black locust *(Robinia pseudoacacia)*

Red maple *(Acer rubrum)*

Sugar maple *(Acer saccharum)*

The Effective Threshold

The plants most structurally able to endure high winds are trees. But even trees cannot survive the worst winds of the strongest storms. That effective threshold (approximately 155 miles [249 km] per hour) roughly equates to a category 5 hurricane on the Saffir-Simpson Scale. During such storms, one can expect all shrubs and trees to be blown down.

to the trunk, which may lead to weak branch growth and permit decay to enter the main stem. Cuts that result in stripping off the bark invite insects and disease to the open wound. Long stubs left behind often allow decay or new and weak branches to arise from the stub. Line trimmers and mowers can girdle small trees and shrubs, weakening the stems and root systems.

Rot of the roots and trunk is a common problem in many trees — and potentially more dangerous because it is harder to recognize. Rot in the heartwood of a large tree is often well camouflaged, with normal-looking bark all around the main stem. Examination of the base of the tree, the joint of branches, or the union of multiple leaders can offer clues to rot. Many decay diseases leave residues or discoloration at branch unions or near old wounds. Fine sawdust at the base of the tree or drizzled on the bark is a sign that the interior of the tree is a maze of ant tunnels. Woodpeckers in search of a meal open a hole large enough for other insects to enter. These insects are then eaten by the kinds of woodpeckers that make large holes. Small mammals or cavity-nesting birds enlarge the holes further, until eventually decay and rot assault the heart of the tree.

When to Take Preemptive Action

A rule of thumb is that if more than 50 percent of the wood is rotted or missing from a branch or trunk, its strength is therefore dangerously compromised. A professional arborist is the best person to assess the status and design a course of action for a tree. A weakened massive tree that gets caught in just the right gust of wind can produce drastic and tragic consequences. For example, backyard trees are not just decorative; they are also home to swings and tree houses and shade playgrounds and sandboxes where children and adults gather. The windfall of such a tree is chilling to consider.

Although some signs of wood rot can be sneaky and hide inside the branch and trunk, other signals may be in the open, waiting for you to notice them. Here are the most obvious symptoms of interior rot, and good reasons to call your arborist.

Bracket fungus growing on the bark of the tree. Bracket fungus is a hard, woody fungus that grows horizontally out from the tree. It comes in many types, with differing sizes, shapes, and colors. Technically, the bracket is the fruiting body of the fungus; much more fungus is growing beneath the bark. Bracket fungus likes to grow on rotted or weakened wood. Its presence almost always indicates a problem needing inquiry.

Moss growing on bark. Moss likes wet places, and once moss gets growing, it keeps places moist too. The moss in itself isn't the problem; it's the wet conditions that the presence of the moss indicates. Rot needs moisture to flourish, and while moss is not necessarily a sign of rot, it certainly is a signal to look further.

Seedlings or small ferns growing in the joints of branches and trunk. Some trees have branch unions that collect debris and moisture and inadvertently become little nurseries for a wide range of plants, from ferns to tree seedlings. The plants indicate that the branch joint is wet all the time, a condition that rot requires. As the plants grow, the roots often creep under the bark, opening the way for other organisms.

Large rectangular excavations in the wood. Large holes (up to 6 inches [15 cm] long and 3 inches [7.5 cm] wide) in a tree may indicate the presence of a pileated woodpecker. This bird is about the size of a crow, and black with a scarlet crest on its head. The species is found across all of eastern North America, as well as from the Pacific Northwest to northern

Selecting Plants for Hurricane Resilience

Very few plants are designed to survive steady winds of greater than about 155 mph (250 km) without suffering catastrophic damage. Many plants can endure wind speeds of about 120 mph (194 km) with little injury, however. Still others will fall when subjected to much less powerful gusts. Being able to tell which plants will survive and which ones won't is immeasurably helpful when selecting shrubs and trees for landscapes that commonly find themselves squarely in harm's way.

Trees that consistently endure hurricanes are fittingly called *survivor trees*. They can be of many different species, but they share traits that are critical to resisting strong winds:

Low center of gravity. A tree with a low center of gravity has an almost symmetrically tapered trunk and large branches low on the trunk. The limbs droop to near, or even touching, the ground. Some have multiple trunks arranged so that each trunk holds an almost equal share of the total of the branch load overhead. A low center of gravity stops the wind from using the mass of the tree to, in essence, topple the plant.

Roots. Survivor trees most often have a combination of a deep-rooted taproot and a wide mat of roots in shallow soils. These provide two different kinds of anchor for a tree.

Strong but thin canopy. Upper branches are fewer but strong, and they hold a moderate leaf cover rather than a heavy foliage load. This allows the wind to pass through the branches with less resistance.

Defoliation. Shrubs and trees that lose their leaves at fairly low wind speeds tend to survive storms better than those that cling to their foliage. As a tree loses foliage, wind resistance drops, which lessens the destructive force acting on the tree.

Native species. While some ornamental plants from other locations can weather hurricanes well, native plants seem to have an edge as to the ability to endure. Some of these native species are bald cypress *(Taxodium distichum)*, sweetbay magnolia *(Magnolia virginiana)*, live oak *(Quercus virginiana)*, and river birch *(Betula nigra)*.

California. Once thought to need vast acres of unbroken forest to thrive, pileated woodpeckers are now seen in town parks, backyards, and other areas of formerly untenable habitat. They love to eat carpenter ants, so if you spot them chipping away at a tree in your yard, chances are that tree has already been weakened by these destructive insects.

Repairing Wind-Damaged Trees

The damage left behind by wind and storm can range from cleaning up a yard littered with twigs and leaves to removing the remains of a prized tree. The interaction of branch and breeze can produce several different kinds of injuries to trees. The most common are described below.

Broken Branches

Description: The branch has broken but not separated from the tree and is left dangling.

Remedy: Remove a broken branch by sawing the limb free of the trunk near the branch collar. To ensure the tree's long-term health, use a three-cut procedure. (1) Make the first cut about one third of the way through the branch on the underside of the branch about 1 foot (30 cm) away from the branch union with the trunk. (2) Make the second cut on the top of the branch about 2 inches (5 cm) farther away from the branch union. Continue this cut until the branch falls. (3) Make the third cut about 1 inch (2.5 cm) away from the branch collar. Then saw away the stub.

You can rope larger branches before cutting, if you wish. Loop the rope over a higher, strong branch, then tie it to the branch you are removing. The helper on the ground should then keep light tension on the rope as the damaged branch is sawn free. Once the branch is sawn free of the tree, the helper can lower it to the ground in a controlled fashion.

Split Branches

Description: Sometimes limbs are cracked through, with the open split ranging from a few inches to many feet in length. If the crack isn't wide and the supporting branch is strong, a cracked limb can often be sound for years.

Strategy: Monitor split branches regularly for pests and diseases. If there is any question about the integrity of a limb, have it evaluated by an arborist and remove it if necessary.

Lost Leader of a Double-Leader Tree

Description: See page 313 for a description of double-leader trees.

Remedy: The structural integrity of a double-leader tree that loses one of its partners is so compromised that it may be dangerous. Once one leader is gone, most of the second will fail within a season or two. Under most circumstances, the tree should be removed. But it's always helpful to have the tree assessed by an arborist to be sure.

Broken Trunk

Description: A tree with a broken trunk is a total loss.

Remedy: Remove the entire tree.

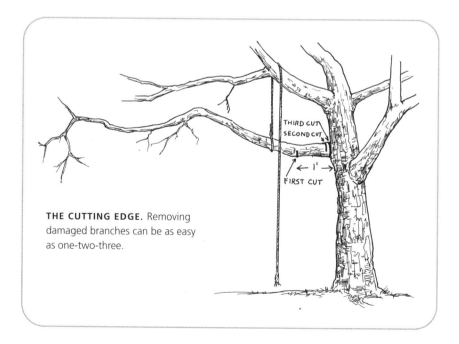

THE CUTTING EDGE. Removing damaged branches can be as easy as one-two-three.

Uprooted Tree

Description: Some uprooted trees can be straightened and staked, and they will grow beautifully for many years to come. It depends on the tree and the circumstances. Mario Cuomo, former governor of New York, often tells the story of his father and the spruce tree. The spruce tree toppled in the midst of a windy rainstorm, but rather than let events dictate actions, the elder Cuomo directed his sons to rope the tree and stand it up again. The tree, at last report, is still growing many decades later. None of the participants in this story was a horticulturist, but the family did everything right to save a windfallen tree.

Remedy: The first step is to set the tree back up as soon as possible. Quick action reduces damage to the main roots, root hairs, and supporting roots. Second, stake the tree with four guy wires, with the stakes set outside the area of root damage. Third, cover the root zone with an organic mulch to slow evaporation from the soil. Finally, water and fertilize the tree for at least five seasons.

Strategy: Watch an uprooted-but-rescued tree for symptoms of extensive root damage over the ensuing months. Yellowing of leaves, slow growth, and premature leaf drop are all signs that it might not be pulling through.

Leaning Tree

Description: Sometimes the wind presses so hard against a tree that the tree actually leans, though it doesn't go all the way down. Leaning trees should be straightened where possible, but they aren't hazards simply because they're leaning. I know of an old red maple in Connecticut that was tipped in the 1938 hurricane. It is still leaning — and still growing well.

Remedy: Rope the leaning tree and gently pull it straight. Once straight, stake the tree as for windfalls (above).

Strategy: Keep an eye on the tree over the next few months for symptoms of extensive root damage. In particular, be on the lookout for yellowing of leaves, slow growth, and premature leaf drop.

Travel Wind Damage

Description: Transporting plants from one place to another using an open truck is a great way to observe the effects of wind desiccation. Healthy plants that are subjected to 40- to 50 mph winds as a truck rolls down the highway suffer leaf damage and, sometimes, death of twigs and branches. Even bringing home a new foliage plant in your car can expose it to damage. If your car windows are open and the breeze buffets the plant all the way home, the foliage could experience substantial damage by the time you arrive.

Remedy: Keep plants out of direct sun, and water well, especially if they shows signs of wilting. Plant as soon as possible after transporting.

Strategy: If you are transporting your own plants, take care that larger plants are covered so that the leaves and root-ball are not exposed to wind or sun. Place smaller plants, such as houseplants, in protective paper or plastic sleeves that are then stapled shut for the ride home. And, if possible, keep the car windows up and the air-conditioning off for the journey. At journey's end, inspect the plants, checking especially for wilted leaves. Professional nurseries try to ward off wind damage by watering the plants before loading for delivery. They may also cover the plant material with tarps to deflect the breeze during the trip. All parts of the plants should be covered.

New-Home-Construction Damage That Weakens Trees

Description: If your home is new, the plants that were left in place during construction may have suffered damage as the result of the surrounding soil being rolled and crushed by bulldozers, trucks, and other heavy equipment. Trees weakened by such damage are more vulnerable to windstorms. Many contractors rope off areas around trees in an attempt to limit damage to the trees' root systems as they work. Still, it is very difficult to avoid all damage to the roots from compaction of the soil.

In addition to compaction, the depth of soil over the established roots of trees if often increased during grading, a practice that can smother the roots. This in turn can produce root damage that may take months or years to manifest. Symptoms include yellowing of leaves; dieback of twigs and branches, which can then drop in storms; and windfall, which can occur suddenly when a large storm blows through.

Strategy: If trees on your building lot seem sickly, it is smart to have an arborist come and assess the situation.

Windfall

Description: When building lots are carved from forest, the dynamics of the woodland are disrupted. The forest has grown together for years, and part of that growing together is an interdependence that lends wind protection. If you walk through the woods on a windy day, you'll notice that the tall, lanky trees move around a lot, swaying back and forth. All the trees together —the body of the forest — buffer each other from the wind. When a building lot is cut from the woods, the trees on the outside of the clearing suddenly lack the same protection. It is very common to see several trees windfall into the clearing over the next 2 to 5 years as the forest readjusts.

Strategy: If you build a house and plant a garden in such a setting, take the time before construction to survey and remove any weak or damaged trees along the forest perimeter. If possible, rather than clear-cutting a building lot, select a few strong trees to be left behind. These will soften the wind and provide some protection to exposed trees at the forest edge. Be prepared for storm damage to be above average in your yard for the first few years after you move in.

One Sign That Isn't Trouble

Lichens frequently grow on the bark of trees in areas with clean air and little pollution. These conglomerates of algae and fungi don't harm a tree and indicate only that the area you live in has clean air.

Part Three

Top 100

Weather-Resilient Plants

"We learn geology the morning after the earthquake."

— Emerson

Universities, government agencies, and other organizations regularly research and publish information about plants that are resilient to various weather conditions in their areas. By combining results from hundreds of sources, I have created a "Top 100" list, which describes those plants that are widely identified as the most resilient to multiple weather conditions in much of North America. The resilience categories are cold, deer, drought, fire, flood, hail, heat, humidity, ice and snow, lightning, salt, and wind and storm. The highest possible rating (that is, resilient in all categories) is 12. Plants are presented in order from most resilience to least; within each resilience level, they are listed in alphabetical order by common name.

Perennials

Blazing Star   *Liatris* spp.

Zones 4–9
Weather Resilience: 9
Resilient to: COLD, DEER, DROUGHT, FIRE, FLOOD, HAIL, HEAT, SALT, WIND AND STORM

Culture: Blazing star, also called gay-feather and liatris, has the tough weather resilience of many prairie wildflowers. It is most resilient when grown in average, well-drained soil and full sun.

Recommendations: The most popular garden species, *L. spicata*, prefers moist soil and is not as drought tolerant as other species. There are some very resilient

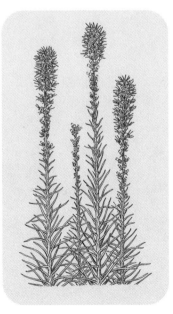

L. spicata cultivars, the best perhaps being 'Kobold'. Varieties grown in moist, rich soils can become weak-stemmed and lose their wind resiliency. The most flood- and salt-tolerant species is grass-leaved liatris *(L. graminifolia)*, although this is difficult to find in nurseries and garden centers.

Yarrow   *Achillea* spp.

Zones 4–8
Weather Resilience: 9
Resilient to: COLD, DEER, DROUGHT, HAIL, HEAT, FIRE, FLOOD, SALT, WIND AND STORM

Culture: Yarrow is adaptable to many soil types and pH values. A lean soil encourages more resilient growth, whereas rich soils produce weak, more succulent growth. Most species need full sun, the exceptions being *A. ptarmica* and *A. ageratum,* which like partial shade.

Recommendations: The most weather-resilient species are *A. millefolium* and *A. filipendulina.* Weather-resilient cultivars include 'Cerise Queen', 'Coronation Gold', 'Fire King', 'Moonshine', and 'Summer Pastels'. *A. ptarmica* (sneezewort) is vigorous and weather resilient, but it is not as drought tolerant as the first-mentioned species, and it is susceptible to humidity-related problems, such as powdery mildew and rust.

Yucca   *Yucca* spp.

Zones 5–10
Weather Resilience: 9
Resilient to: COLD, DEER, DROUGHT, FIRE, HAIL, HEAT, SALT, ICE AND SNOW, SALT, WIND AND STORM

Culture: Yucca plants have a taproot that grows deep into the ground, making them drought resilient but also hard to transplant. Container-grown plants are best for transplanting. Yucca is most resilient when grown in a light, deep soil in full sun, although it adapts to light shade and a range of soil types. Avoid overfertilizing it.

Recommendations: There are many weather-resilient species, but the one with the greatest strength and range of resiliency is *Y. filamentosa*. 'Bright Edge' is a cultivar with a yellow border on the leaf blade. Spanish dagger *(Y. gloriosa)* and *Y. recurvifolia* can also take the heat and humidity of southern summers. Species that thrive in arid areas of the Southwest and West are *Y. brevifolia* (Joshua tree), *Y. elata*, and *Y. whipplei* .

Daylily   *Hemerocallis* spp.

Zones 3–9

Weather Resilience: 8

Resilient to: COLD, DROUGHT, FIRE, FLOOD, HEAT, HUMIDITY, SALT, WIND AND STORM

Culture: Daylilies are exceptionally low-maintenance plants that thrive in a wide range of growing conditions. For strongest weather resilience, grow in mostly sun to full-sun locations, and divide clumps every 3 to 5 years.

Recommendations: Excellent weather-resilient varieties are 'Happy Returns', 'Hyperion', and the dwarf 'Stella d'Oro'. The tawny daylily *(H. fulva)* is the epitome of the weather-resilient perennial, yet its superb strength is marred by the fact that it often becomes invasive. Some *H. fulva* varieties that are more easily managed are 'Flore Pleno' and 'Kwanzo Variegata'. These need to be divided every 3 to 5 years for clumps to flower well.

Peach-Leafed Bellflower
Campanula persicifolia

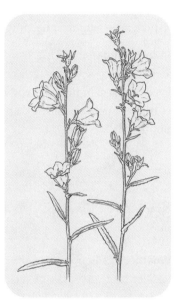

Zones 3–8
Weather Resilience: 8
Resilient to: COLD, DEER, DROUGHT, FLOOD, HAIL, HEAT, HUMIDITY, WIND AND STORM

Culture: Grow in partial to full sun in well-drained average soil. Overly rich soils produce weaker flower stems. This plant is very low maintenance. Deadhead to prevent the plants from self-sowing. The main floral display is in spring, with a few blossoms often appearing in early fall.

Recommendations: Peach-leafed bellflower is the most weather resilient of the bellflowers, a large group of plants with wide-ranging weather tolerances. It is strongly weather resilient in all listed categories except drought and flood, to which it is moderately resilient. *Campanula persicifolia* is very vigorous, to the point of being invasive in some areas. Good varieties are 'Alba Plena' and 'Telham Beauty'.

Red-Hot Poker
Kniphofia spp.

Zones 5–9
Weather Resilience: 8
Resilient to: DEER, DROUGHT, FIRE, HAIL, HEAT, HUMIDITY, SALT, WIND AND STORM

Culture: Red-hot poker is not a fussy plant and thrives in most soils except excessively dry or wet ones. The plants are native to southern Africa and are most resilient when they grow in full sun to mostly sunny sites. Drought resilience is moderate until a plant is well established, after which it becomes excellent.

Recommendations: This sturdy plant is vigorous and very weather resilient, but is underused in many gardens. Notable cultivars are 'Bees Sunset' and 'Royal Standard'.

Sedum   *Sedum* spp.

Zones 3–10
Weather Resilience: 8
Resilient to: COLD, DEER, DROUGHT, FIRE, HEAT, ICE AND SNOW, SALT, WIND AND STORM

Culture: Sedums are a large group of plants but are uniform in their needs. Plant in average soil amended with some (but not large amounts of) organic matter. The strongest weather resilience is attained in full sun. However, low-growing forms adapt well to partial shade. Once planted, sedums are fairly self-sufficient.

Recommendations: One of the most weather-resilient plants available is *Sedum* 'Autumn Joy'. Other tall sedums are close behind, like 'Ruby Glow' and varieties of *S. spectabile,* such as 'Atropurpureum' and 'Brilliant'. Some of the most weather-resilient, low-growing types are golden carpet sedum *(S. acre)*, October daphne *(S. sieboldii),* and two-row stonecrop *(S. spurium).*

Shasta Daisy
Leucanthemum × superbum

Zones 4–9
Weather Resilience: 8
Resilient to: COLD, DEER, DROUGHT, FIRE, FLOOD, HEAT, HUMIDITY, SALT

Culture: Conditions that produce the most flowers don't necessarily produce the best weather resilience. Shasta daisies grow most successfully in full sun and well-drained soil with plenty of organic matter, but not overly moist or fertilized ground. The plants naturally have a moderate drought tolerance that increases when grown in soil rich in compost.

Recommendations: The most weather-resilient varieties are those bearing small (less than 2 inches wide) blossoms on stems no taller than 24 inches. The variety 'Alaska' is a very cold-tolerant Shasta, being hardy to Zone 3.

Thyme   *Thymus* spp.

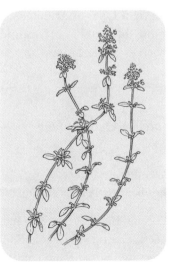

Zones 4–9
Weather Resilience: 8
Resilient to: COLD, DEER, DROUGHT, FIRE, HAIL, HEAT, HUMIDITY, WIND AND STORM

Culture: The many types of garden thyme are most resilient when grown in conditions resembling their Mediterranean origins: dry, well-drained soil in full sun. A breezy site is also beneficial. Overwatering, rich soil, and shady conditions will produce weak, disease-susceptible plants.

Recommendations: Garden thyme, including lemon thyme *(T. × citri-odorus)* and English thyme *(T. vulgaris)*, and species used for ground covers, such as creeping thyme *(T. praecox)* and wild thyme *(T. pule-goides)*, are fragile-looking plants that are nonetheless very resilient. Many varieties of each species are available.

Artemisia   *Artemisia* spp.

Zones 5–8
Weather Resilience: 7
Resilient to: COLD, DEER, DROUGHT, FIRE, HEAT, SALT, WIND AND STORM

Culture: Artemisias prefer full sun and average soil. Given these requirements, the plants become very drought- and heat tolerant. Many species are also very vigorous and require little fertilizing. Vigorous species need to be divided every 3 years.

Recommendations: Beach wormwood *(A. stelleriana)* is one of the most salt resilient of the artemisias; 'Boughton Silver' is especially attractive. 'Powis Castle' and 'Silver King' are both vigorous, sturdy varieties. Upright types of Artemisia, such as 'Silver King' and 'Silver Queen', are more tolerant of heat, humidity, and storms than are rounded varieties, such as 'Silver Mound'.

Blanket Flower   *Gaillardia* × *grandiflora*

Zones 3–10
Weather Resilience: 7
Resilient to: COLD, DEER, DROUGHT, FIRE, HEAT, SALT, WIND AND STORM

Culture: Blanket flower is native to open, sunny environments of the West, central states, and South. It thrives in average soil that has been amended with organic matter. You will see the strongest growth if you can provide soil that is moist but not excessively fertilized. The plants will suffer and decline if conditions are wet and humid, which encourages a number of problems, including powdery mildew and slugs.

Recommendations: The weather-resilient qualities of blanket flower are made stronger by growing it in company with other plants native to the prairies, such as *Achillea*, *Rudbeckia*, and *Echinacea*. Although weather resistant, blanket flower is naturally short-lived, surviving just 3 to 5 years. Extend their life by dividing the plants every other year. Cultivars include 'Goblin' and 'Burgundy'.

Crocus   *Crocus* spp.

Zones 4–8
Weather Resilience: 7
Resilient to: COLD, DEER, DROUGHT, HUMIDITY, ICE AND SNOW, LIGHTNING, WIND AND STORM

Culture: Plant the corms in early fall about 3 inches deep in well-drained soil. Most people like to plant crocus in lawns, which is an excellent environment for it. Deer don't like the corms, but other animals, such as chipmunks, sometimes bother newly planted ones.

Recommendations: The most weather-resilient crocuses are cloth-of-gold *(C. angustifolius)*, snow crocus *(C. chrysanthus)*, and sieberi crocus *(C. sieberi)*. Sieberi crocus grows best south of Zone 5. Dutch crocus *(C. vernus)* is slightly less resilient.

Daffodil *Narcissus* spp.

Zones 3–9
Weather Resilience: 7
Resilient to: COLD, DEER, DROUGHT, HEAT, HUMIDITY, ICE
AND SNOW, WIND AND STORM

Culture: Daffodil plants are drought tolerant but often fail to blossom when the flowering season is dry. Weather resilience seems to be strengthened when planted with cotoneaster, red buckeye, and vinca.

Recommendations: Hardy varieties include 'Avalanche,' 'Ice Follies', 'King Alfred', 'Minnow', 'Mount Hood', 'Scarlet Gem', and 'Tête-à-Tête'.

Echinacea
Echinacea spp.

Zones 4–9
Weather Resilience: 7
Resilient to: COLD, DEER, DROUGHT, FIRE, HEAT, SALT, WIND
AND STORM

Culture: Echinacea adapts to a range of conditions but grows best in fertile, deep soil in full sun. Plants grown in partial shade are not as strong as those that are grown in full sun. Echinacea is sensitive to wet soil and long periods of humid weather.

Recommendations: The deep taproots of echinacea allow the plants to grow and thrive even during extended droughts. The strong stems hold up to storms well. Some noteworthy varieties are 'Magnus', 'Robert Bloom', 'The King', and 'White Swan'.

Geranium   *Geranium* spp.

Zones 3–8

Weather Resilience: 7

Resilient to: COLD, DEER, DROUGHT, FIRE, HEAT, SALT, WIND AND STORM

Culture: Plant in fertile, moist soil well amended with organic matter and topped with a layer of organic mulch. Grow in full sun, except in Zones 6 through 8, where plants should be sited to receive afternoon shade. Vigorous varieties should be divided at least every 3 years.

Recommendations: All geraniums are lovely plants, but not all species are especially weather resilient. The most resilient plants are varieties of bigroot geranium *(G. macrorrhizum)*, bloody cranesbill *(G. sanguineum)*, and *G. endresii*.

Lavender Cotton   *Santolina* spp.

Zones 6–10

Weather Resilience: 7

Resilient to: DEER, DROUGHT, HAIL, HEAT, HUMIDITY, FIRE, WIND AND STORM

Culture: This undemanding plant prefers full sun to develop strong, resilient stems and leaves. Lavender cotton will grow well in poor or average soils that are well drained. Too much organic matter results in weak growth.

Recommendations: Compact varieties, such as 'Lemon Queen', 'Pretty Carol', and 'Weston', are more wind resistant than larger cultivars. A sturdy variety that is very popular is 'Lambrook Silver'.

Prickly Pear   *Opuntia* spp.

Zones 5–10

Weather Resilience: 7

Resilient to: COLD, DEER, DROUGHT, HEAT, ICE AND SNOW, SALT, WIND AND STORM

Culture: Prickly pear cacti thrive in sandy soils of average fertility and average amounts of organic matter. They are easily overwatered and prefer soil somewhat on the dry side.

Recommendations: The principal quality of *Opuntia* species is their uniform ability to withstand drought, heat, wind and storm, and saline conditions. Species that are weather resilient in the Southwest include bunny ears (*O. microdasys*), prickly pear (*O. ficus-indica*), and purple cactus (*O. violacea* var. *santa rita*). The prickly pear most resilient to cold and snow as well as the heat and humidity of the South is *O. compressa*.

Siberian Iris   *Iris sibirica*

Zones 4–9

Weather Resilience: 7

Resilient to: COLD, DEER, DROUGHT, HAIL, HEAT, FIRE, WIND AND STORM

Culture: Siberian iris is weather resilient in a wide range of soils. It is moderately drought tolerant in soils well amended with organic matter, but it loses this quality when grown in sandy soils. Grow in full sun or mostly sunny locations.

Recommendations: The varieties of Siberian iris are remarkably uniform in their weather resilience. This means that personal choice can have free rein. The plant is at home on the edge of a water garden as much as in the perennial border. Pretty 'Butter and Sugar' is unusual in that it offers yellow flowers.

Black-eyed Susan
Rudbeckia spp.

Zones 3–9
Weather Resilience: 6
Resilient to: Cold, deer, drought, heat, humidity, wind and storm

Culture: Black-eyed Susan needs deep, well-drained, average soil amended with some organic matter to maximize its weather-resilient potential. Grow in full sun except in the Southeast, where some afternoon shade is needed.

Recommendations: Gloriosa daisy *(R. hirta)* is a short-lived perennial that is as beautiful and showy as it is resilient. Good varieties include 'Becky Mixed', 'Marmalade', and 'Sonora'. The most weather-resilient and perhaps the best black-eyed Susan is a popular, widely available cultivar of *R. fulgida* var. *sullivantii* called 'Goldsturm'.

Boltonia   *Boltonia asteroides*

Zones 4–8
Weather Resilience: 6
Resilient to: COLD, DEER, DROUGHT, HEAT, FLOOD, SALT

Culture: Boltonia needs full sun to be weather resilient. After this criterion is satisfied, the plant is remarkably adaptable, thriving in many soil types and under conditions from wet to dry. Amend its soil with organic matter to encourage vigor and to strengthen stems. Extended periods of drought produce smaller-than-normal plants. In humid weather, powdery mildew and rust can occur.

Recommendations: Cultivars are more weather resistant than the species. 'Pink Beauty' bears flowers in late summer. 'Snowbank' is one of the best selections. Because its growth habit is more compact, it is more resistant than other boltonia varieties to storms and wind.

Butterflyweed
Asclepias tuberosa

Zones 4–9
Weather Resilience: 6
Resilient to: COLD, DEER, DROUGHT, HEAT, FIRE, WIND AND STORM

Culture: Plant in full sun. A member of the milkweed family, butterflyweed needs a well-drained sandy soil, lightly to moderately amended with organic matter. Avoid overwatering. Once established, the plant doesn't like to be fussed over.

Recommendations: One of the most popular, best-performing cultivars is 'Gay Butterflies'.

Candytuft   *Iberis sempervirens*

Zones 5–9

Weather Resilience: 6

Resilient to: DEER, DROUGHT, FIRE, HAIL, SALT, WIND AND STORM

Culture: Plant in poor to average, well-drained soil with some organic matter. For greater drought tolerance, mulch lightly. In northern regions, cut back winter-damaged stems in spring to encourage rampant spring bloom.

Recommendations: Low-growing 'Autumn Snow' blooms for weeks and withstands extremes without complaint. Small 'Little Gem' is fine for rock gardens. 'Purity' is named for the clear color of its white blossoms.

Coralbells   *Heuchera* spp.

Zones 4–8

Weather Resilience: 6

Resilient to: COLD, DEER, DROUGHT, FIRE, HEAT, SALT

Culture: Coralbells are most weather resilient when grown in partial sun to light shade, in soil with good amounts of organic matter. Most species are not drought tolerant and need shade in hot climates. Divide every 3 years.

Recommendations: *Heuchera sanguinea* is moderately drought- and heat resistant, but it does benefit from mulch. 'Pluie de Fue' and 'Splendens' are good. Varieties of *H.* × *brizoides* (e.g., 'Huntsman' and 'June Bride') are highly resilient to drought, heat, and wind. 'Palace Purple' is moderately salt resilient.

Coreopsis   *Coreopsis* spp.

Zones 4–9

Weather Resilience: 6

Resilient to: COLD, DEER, DROUGHT, FIRE, HEAT, WIND AND STORM

Culture: Coreopsis thrives in full sun and exhibits much weaker growth in shady spots. Plant in average soil amended with some organic matter (rich soils promote weak, succulent growth). Overwatering encourages disease.

Recommendations: One of the best varieties is 'Zagreb', a cultivar of threadleaf coreopsis *(C. verticillata)*, as it is more drought resistant and wind resilient than other types. Other varieties with similar qualities include *C. auriculata* 'Nana', *C. lanceolata* 'Goldfink', and *C. verticillata* 'Moonbeam'.

Note: Pink coreopsis *(C. rosea)* is not as weather resilient as other coreopsis species. It has a more fragile character and notably less drought tolerance.

Goldenrod   *Solidago* spp.

Zones 3–9

Weather Resilience: 6

Resilient to: DEER, DROUGHT, FLOOD, HEAT, SALT, WIND AND STORM

Culture: Goldenrod grows best in loose, sandy soils with poor to average fertility and light amounts of organic matter. Many species are vigorous and spread quickly.

Recommendations: There are over 100 species of goldenrod, with a vast array of characteristics. Cultivated varieties, such as 'Golden Baby',

'Goldenmosa', and 'Golden Wings', are best suited to the garden. However, the most weather-resilient species is probably seaside goldenrod *(S. sempervirens)*. This tall species is flood- and salt tolerant, qualities most other goldenrods lack.

Lavender   *Lavandula* spp.

Zones 5–10
Weather Resilience: 6
Resilient to: Deer, drought, fire, heat, salt, wind and storm

Culture: The strength of lavender's weather resiliency requires that the plant be grown in full sun and in light, sandy soil that isn't heavy with organic matter. In areas with poor drainage, grow in raised beds. For strongest stems, keep soil pH between 6.5 and 7.5. Wet soil and humid weather can result in root rot and botrytis.

Recommendations: The most weather-resilient species is probably English lavender *(L. angustifolia)*. 'Hidcote' is a fine variety. 'Munstead Dwarf' is prone to botrytis mold. Lavandin *(L. × intermedia* 'Grosso') is more resistant to moisture and humidity problems. Other species that are strongest in warm, dry climates are French lavender *(L. stoechas)* and spike lavender *(L. latifolia)*.

Penstemon   *Penstemon* spp.

Zones 4–9
Weather Resilience: 6
Resilient to: COLD, DROUGHT, FIRE, HAIL, HEAT, WIND AND STORM

Culture: The weather resiliency of nearly all penstemon species depends on their growing in sandy, deep, well-drained soil with just enough organic matter to make the soil look like a sandy loam. Grow in full or mostly sunny locations. Penstemon is not long-lived, and plantings should be renewed every 3 to 5 years.

Recommendations: There are about 250 species of penstemon and they are native to many very different climates and regions. Species most resilient in the Southwest are *P. barbatus, P. linariodes, P. palmeri, P. pinifolius*, and *P. pseudospectabilis*. In the Pacific Northwest, try *P. fruticosa, P. menziesii*, and *P. serrulatus*. In the Rocky Mountains and the plains, grow *P. barbatus, P. grandiflorus, P. strictus*, and *P. whippleanus*. Gardeners along the California coast can try *P. heterophyllus, P. rupicola*, and *P. spectabilis*. Weather-resilient penstemons for the Northeast include *P. digitalis* and *P. hirsutus*; in the hot and humid South, there are *P. smallii*, and *P. tenuis*.

Sea Holly   *Eryngium* spp.

Zones 3–10
Weather Resilience: 6
Resilient to: COLD, DEER, DROUGHT, HEAT, SALT, WIND AND STORM

Culture: Sea hollies are attractive, self-reliant plants that like full sun to produce strong growth. Soil needs vary depending on the species, but most garden types prefer loose, sandy soil with moderate amounts of organic matter. Rattlesnake master *(E. yuccifolium)* is native to the eastern United States and thrives best in more fertile, evenly moist soil.

Recommendations: A good all-around selection that is quite nicely adaptable is amethyst sea holly *(E. amethystinum)*. Rattlesnake master

(E. yuccifolium) thrives east of the Mississippi. 'Blue Cap' is a variety of flat sea holly *(E. planum)* that is resilient to conditions in the South. For semiarid western regions, try Mediterranean sea holly *(E. bourgatii* 'Oxford Blue') for good results.

Verbascum   *Verbascum* spp.

Zones 4–9

Weather Resilience: 6

Resilient to: COLD, DROUGHT, HAIL, HEAT, ICE AND SNOW, WIND AND STORM

Culture: Most verbascum species are native to dry, poor soils and waste places, and these lean, well-drained soils are what keep the plants so weather resilient. Grow plants in full sun in deep, sandy soil amended with small amounts of organic matter. Wet and rich soils reduce vigor and health.

Recommendations: Tall, stately verbascum adds a sturdy aspect to the garden, and its weather resiliency is a nice bonus. Olympic verbascum *(V. olympicum)* reaches 6 feet tall and grows best in warm, drier climates. Nettle-leaved verbascum *(V. chaixii)* reaches 3 feet tall and is adaptable to a wide range of environments. The most resilient is probably great mullein *(V. thapsus)*, which is so vigorous in some areas as to be invasive.

Rosemary   *Rosmarinus officinalis*

Zones 8–10

Weather Resilience: 5

Resilient to: DEER, DROUGHT, HEAT, SALT, WIND AND STORM

Culture: Rosemary needs a sharply drained, poor to average soil with modest amounts of organic matter to become strongly weather resilient. Soil that is too fertile or moist encourages disease and pests. Grow in full sun.

Recommendations: The variety 'Arp' is more cold hardy than other types, reliably wintering over in Zone 7. Creeping rosemary (*R. officinalis* 'Prostratus'), a ground cover, is resistant to hail and fire as well as being weather resilient. 'Tuscan Blue' is vigorous and fast growing.

Shrubs

Chokeberry *Aronia* spp.

Zones 5–9
Weather Resilience: 9
Resilient to: COLD, DEER, DROUGHT, FLOOD, FIRE, HEAT, ICE AND SNOW, SALT, WIND AND STORM

Culture: Chokeberries are resilient plants that thrive in a range of soils and under conditions that would stifle most plants. They prefer a well-drained, average soil amended with organic matter. Avoid alkaline soils and shallow saline soils. Plant in full sun to partial shade.

Recommendations: Chokeberries can tolerate both dry soils and wet soils, making them useful in challenging places. Excellent varieties include 'Brilliant' and 'Brilliantissima'; these not only are resilient but also offer radiant fall foliage and berries.

Forsythia   *Forsythia* spp.

Zones 4–9
Weather Resilience: 9
Resilient to: COLD, DEER, DROUGHT, FIRE, HEAT, HUMIDITY, ICE AND SNOW, SALT, WIND AND STORM

Culture: Grow in well-drained, average to fertile soil that has been amended with organic matter. Forsythia can grow in shady locations but flowers less and is notably weaker in weather resiliency; for best resiliency, grow in full sun. The plants establish quickly and are vigorous growers.

Recommendations: In northern climates, the chief drawback of forsythia has been the lack of hardiness of the flower buds. Fortunately, the newer varieties 'Northern Sun' and *Forsythia* × 'Meadowlark' (introduced by the North Dakota State University) produce flower buds that are hardy to –30°F and –35°F, respectively.

Note: Forsythia is only moderately resilient to salt and deer.

Rugosa Rose   *Rosa rugosa*

Zones 2–9
Weather Resilience: 9
Resilient to: COLD, DEER, DROUGHT, FIRE, HAIL, HEAT, ICE AND SNOW, SALT, WIND AND STORM

Culture: Rugosa roses accept a wide range of soils, including poor, sandy, and salty ones. 'Hansa' is a variety that seems to excel under these difficult conditions. Rugosas grow best in full sun, though some, such as 'Frimbriata', are resilient even when grown in part shade.

Recommendations: There is no such thing as the perfect weather-resilient plant, but rugosa rose comes very close. Exceptionally cold-hardy varieties are 'Therese Bugnet', 'Max Graf', 'Jens Munk', 'Henry Hudson', 'Hansa', 'Frau Dagmar Hartopp', and 'Frimbriata'.

Rugosa roses aren't as weather resilient in the South and Southwest (a class of rose that is weather resilient in both regions is the China rose). Some recommended varieties are 'Louis Philippe', 'Mutabilis', and 'Old Blush'.

Potentilla *Potentilla* spp.

Zones 3–8
Weather Resilience: 8
Resilient to: COLD, DEER, DROUGHT, HAIL, HEAT, FIRE, SALT, WIND AND STORM

Culture: Potentilla thrives in poor to average soil that is well drained and amended with some organic matter. An overly rich soil promotes weak growth.

Recommendations: Shrubby cinquefoil (*P. fruticosa*) is an adaptable, wonderfully cold-hardy plant that can be used for everything from windbreaks to a fire-resilient perennial border. Varieties include 'Everest', 'Gibson's Scarlet', and 'Katherine Dykes'. Potentilla species that make excellent ground covers are 'William Rollison' and wineleaf cinquefoil (*P. tridentata*).

Red-Osier Dogwood *Cornus stolonifera*

Zones 2–8
Weather Resilience: 8
Resilient to: COLD, DEER, FLOOD, HEAT, FIRE, ICE AND SNOW, SALT, WIND AND STORM

Culture: The shrubby dogwoods are resilient in a wide range of soils, but are most vigorous in fertile soils well amended with organic matter. They tolerate full sun to shade, but are most ornamental in full sun, where the stems take on rich color.

Recommendations: Redtwig dogwood *(Cornus alba)* has similar qualities to red-osier dogwood but is larger. *Cornus* 'Elegantissima' has attractive variegated foliage. Both make excellent plants for riparian areas, such as riverbanks and lakeshores. Other species with flood-resilient abilities are silky dogwood *(C. amomum)* and gray dogwood *(C. racemosa)*.

Sumac   *Rhus* spp.

Zones 3–9
Weather Resilience: 7
Resilient to: COLD, DROUGHT, FIRE, HEAT, ICE AND SNOW, SALT, WIND AND STORM

Culture: Sumac is very adaptable and thrives in just about any soil other than wet. It especially likes well-drained, dry, coarse soils with some organic matter. To ensure best wind resiliency, plant in full sun in groups of five or more. It is tolerant of saline soil, salt spray, and road salt.

Recommendations: Use sumac in fire-defensive landscapes to slow advancing fires. The most cold-hardy sumac is staghorn *(R. typhina)*, hardy to Zone 3. Cutleaf sumac *(R. typhina* 'Dissecta') has attractive, deeply cut leaves. Shining sumac *(R. copallina)* has glossy, winged leaves and is notably resilient to road salt and salt spray. Sugarbush *(R. ovata)* is suitable for deer-resistant landscapes in the Southwest.

Sweet fern *Comptonia peregrina*

Zones 4–7
Weather Resilience: 7
Resilient to: COLD, DEER, DROUGHT, HEAT, ICE AND SNOW, SALT, WIND AND STORM

Culture: Sweetfern, a cousin to bayberry, thrives in everything from nearly pure sand to peaty soils by the shores of ponds, but it prefers a sandy, lean soil amended with some organic matter. It is most resilient in full sun but tolerates light shade to mostly sunny conditions as well. Once established, it does not like to be moved.

Recommendations: Sweetfern is used in native gardens but is underused elsewhere. It creates a carefree, fragrant windbreak when planted en masse. It grows very well with many of the Mediterranean herbs, such as lavender and rosemary.

Bottlebrush Buckeye
Aesculus parviflora

Zones 5–9
Weather Resilience: 6
Resilient to: COLD, DEER, DROUGHT, FLOOD, ICE AND SNOW, WIND AND STORM

Culture: This very adaptive shrub will be resilient in dry to temporarily wet soils (it is not tolerant of extended flooding). Amending the soil with organic matter at planting time can hasten establishment of the plant.

Recommendations: Bottlebrush buckeye is vigorous and will spread into a large mass if not pruned back. This quality makes it an excellent windbreak or screen. It is native to the southern United States and flowers later in the season, often midsummer, than most shrubs. The variety

'Rogers' flowers a week or so later than the species.

Note: The foliage of other buckeyes and that of horse chestnuts uniformly get leaf scorch in late summer and enter fall looking burned and shabby. Bottlebrush buckeye doesn't have this problem; the foliage remains attractive throughout the growing season.

Burning Bush
Euonymus alatus

Zones 4–9

Weather Resilience: 6

Resilient to: COLD, FIRE, HEAT, ICE AND SNOW, SALT, WIND AND STORM

Culture: Burning bush is one of the easiest shrubs to care for, as it grows well in a range of soils and conditions — it is happy in dry as well as in fairly wet soils, and in full sun to shade. However, the best weather resiliency is attained in full sun and average soil lightly amended with organic matter. It is very tolerant of roadside salt.

Recommendations: Burning bush can be invasive and has become naturalized in portions of the East and Midwest. In the landscape, it is an excellent all-around shrub and is used extensively, even in areas where it has naturalized. The variety 'Compactus' has denser branching and a somewhat lower growth habit than the species.

Serviceberry   *Amelanchier* spp.

Zones 3–9

Weather Resilience: 6

Resilient to: COLD, DEER, ICE AND SNOW, LIGHTNING, SALT, WIND AND STORM

Culture: Serviceberries can be shrubs or small trees, depending on the species or variety. They all have similar weather-resilient qualities. The plants are adaptive to many soils, ranging from rocky and shallow to fertile and moist. Serviceberries grow well and seem equally strong in locations ranging from full sun to shade. Serviceberry is resilient to saline soils, road salt, and salt spray.

Recommendations: 'Ballerina', a variety of apple serviceberry (*A.* × *grandiflora*), is resistant to fire blight, which other service-berries are susceptible to. Developed in Canada, the Allegheny service-berry *(A. laevis)* 'R. J. Hilton' has abundant flowers and sweet berries.

   Note: Serviceberry is also called shadbush, shadblow, and juneberry. The names *shadbush* and *shadblow* refer to the coincidence of the appearance of the snowy white flowers with the shad swimming upstream to spawn in spring. The names *serviceberry* and *juneberry* refer to the dark, sweet berries that ripen in June and were once used in pies and jams.

Siberian Pea
Caragana arborescens

Zones 2–8
Weather Resilience: 6
Resilient to: COLD, DEER, DROUGHT, ICE AND SNOW, SALT, WIND AND STORM

Culture: Siberian pea shrub can thrive in slightly acidic soils as well as alkaline ones. It should have deep, well-drained soil with moderate amounts of organic matter. It needs little care or attention once established.

Recommendations: Siberian pea shrub can be planted in exposed loca-tions, in poor soil, and in very cold climates and be resilient in all. Its informal appearance makes it excellent for use as a windbreak with rugosa rose.

Pittosporum *Pittosporum* spp.

Zones 8–10

Weather Resilience: 5

Resilient to: DROUGHT, FIRE, HEAT, SALT, WIND AND STORM

Culture: Pittosporum species are native mostly to Australia and New Zealand and grow best in deep, fertile soil that is well drained. The most resilience is obtained by planting in full sun to mostly sun, although these shrubs will grow well in shade.

Recommendations: Plant lemonwood *(P. eugenioides)* in mild coastal areas, such as southern California; it makes an excellent windbreak or sheared hedge. Diamondleaf pittosporum *(P. rhombifolium)* needs warm climates, where it makes a tall, beautiful addition to landscapes and roadways. This species is widely grown in the Southwest and southern California. Japanese mock orange *(P. tobira)* is the hardiest pittosporum and is perhaps the most drought-resilient pittosporum species as well. It is popular as a hedge and landscape plant in the South and along the Pacific coast.

Star Jasmine *Trachelospermum jasminoides*

Zones 8–10

Weather Resilience: 5

Resilient to: DROUGHT, HEAT, FIRE, SALT, WIND AND STORM

Culture: This plant loves the heat and humidity of the South, where its fragrance hangs in the air as thick as fog. Grow in a well-drained, preferably deep soil amended with organic matter. It does best in fertile sites but thrives in average soils as well. It is moderately drought tolerant but doesn't like the cold.

Recommendations: Star jasmine is an excellent vine for hurricane fences. It can be grown farther north if set out in a warm, sheltered microclimate, such as the south wall of a house. It is also a dense, attractive ground cover that reaches about 2 feet tall and it is a good base plant for windbreaks.

Trees

Bald Cypress
Taxodium distichum

Zones 4–10
Weather Resilience: 10
Resilient to: COLD, DEER, HAIL, HUMIDITY, FIRE, FLOOD, ICE AND SNOW, LIGHTNING, SALT, WIND AND STORM

Culture: The signature tree of southern swamps, bald cypress is perfectly at home on dry land. It thrives in fertile, acidic soil amended with organic matter. Grow in full sun or partial shade. Small trees should be watered well until established.

Recommendations: The species is a strong, gorgeous tree with a graceful pyramidal form. The variety 'Prairie Sentinel' has a soft texture; 'Nutans' is narrowly conical and strongly upright. Both are selections of pond cypress, a botanical variety of bald cypress that may be slightly more cold hardy than the species.

Note: Bald cypress is a deciduous conifer that is so weather resilient and durable that an individual tree can live for roughly a thousand years! The tree produces woody knees that protrude up through the soil (or in swamps, through the surface water) to a height of 5 to 10 feet. When the tree is grown in well-drained locations, the knees on the tree may fail to form.

Eastern Red Cedar
Juniperus virginiana

Zones 3–10

Weather Resilience: 9

Resilient to: COLD, DEER, DROUGHT, HAIL, HEAT, ICE AND SNOW, LIGHTNING, SALT, WIND AND STORM

Culture: Eastern red cedar is a very self-reliant tree that thrives in all soils except waterlogged and very alkaline ones. The best weather resiliency seems to occur in coarse, well-drained soil with small to moderate amounts of organic matter. Avoid overwatering.

Recommendations: Some varieties are 'Burkii', 'Emerald Sentinel', and 'Skyrocket', a hybrid with Rocky Mountain juniper. Throughout its extensive range, slightly different forms of eastern red cedar have adapted to local weather conditions. The most weather-hardy ones can be found in pastures and other open places. Eastern red cedar is most vigorous east of the Rocky Mountains. To the West, Rocky Mountain juniper *(J. scopulorum)* is similarly weather resilient.

Note: Eastern red cedar is sensitive to fire. The plants become most drought resilient when the needles change from the prickly juvenile form of young trees to the scale type of mature trees. Long-lived species frequently reach 300 years old.

Kentucky Coffee Tree
Gymnocladus dioica

Zones 4–9

Weather Resilience: 9

Resilient to: COLD, DEER, DROUGHT, FIRE, HEAT, HUMIDITY, ICE AND SNOW, SALT, WIND AND STORM

Culture: Kentucky coffee tree grows best in slightly acidic to slightly alkaline soils in full sun. Plant in deep, well-drained fertile soil generously amended with organic matter. It tolerates drought but prefers moist soil conditions.

Recommendations: In addition to the weather-resilient traits noted above, Kentucky coffee tree is moderately flood resistant and tolerant of urban conditions. 'Expresso' and 'J. C. McDaniels' are robust male varieties that will eliminate the problem of pods falling onto the lawn, sidewalk, and driveway.

Bur Oak   *Quercus macrocarpa*

Zones 3–9

Weather Resilience: 8

Resilient to: COLD, DROUGHT, FIRE, FLOOD, HEAT, ICE AND SNOW, SALT, WIND AND STORM

Culture: As with most oaks, bur oak is easy to transplant when small and becomes increasingly difficult to move as it ages. The plants are adaptable to many soil types, from dry and gravelly to clay. Bur oak thrives in slightly acid soil but is also at home in an alkaline environment. Grow in full sun or in mostly sunny locations.

Recommendations: Bur oak is very long lived, with specimens that are many centuries old dotting the prairies. It is slow growing, but faster-growing, more vigorous varieties do exist, including 'Boomer' and 'Lippert'. As with other oaks, bur oak does not tolerate compacted soils.

Ginkgo   *Ginkgo biloba*

Zones 5–9
Weather Resilience: 8
Resilient to: COLD, DEER, DROUGHT, HEAT, FLOOD, ICE AND SNOW, SALT, WIND AND STORM

Culture: This very undemanding tree thrives in a range of soils. It develops the best resiliency when grown in full sun in well-drained soil that has been amended with organic matter. The tree grows slowly.

Recommendations: When young, ginkgo trees may look a little awkward, with sparse limbs and foliage that seems to hug the branches. But they fill out nicely as they age. The variety 'Autumn Gold' was selected for its fall color but also has a more symmetrical shape than the species.

Birch   *Betula* spp.

Zones 2–9
Weather Resilience: 7
Resilient to: COLD, DEER, HEAT, FIRE, FLOOD, LIGHTNING, SALT

Culture: Birches grow best in fertile, well-drained soil with abundant organic matter. Water in dry times to avoid leaf scorch and an increase in insect problems. Grow in full sun to light shade.

Recommendations: Birches are a large group of trees that have a wide range of weather tolerances. One of the most weather-resilient varieties is 'Heritage', a hybrid of river birch with heat resilience and tolerance to bronze birch borer. 'Grayswood Hill', a cultivar of Erman white birch *(B. ermanii)*, and 'Whitespire', a variety of Asian white birch *(B. platyphylla)*, are also good choices.

Buckeye   *Aesculus* spp.

Zones 5–8

Weather Resilience: 7

Resilient to: COLD, DEER, FIRE, FLOOD, ICE AND SNOW, SALT, WIND AND STORM

Culture: Grow in deep, fertile soil that has been amended with organic matter. Use an organic mulch to keep the soil moist. Plants are weather resilient in full sun but need less supplemental water in shade.

Recommendations: California buckeye *(A. californica)* is very heat resilient but needs moist soil, as do other *Aesculus* species. Red buckeye is a small tree that is perfect for small properties. Large buckeyes with similar weather resilience but cold-hardiness only to Zone 3 include Ohio buckeye *(A. glabra)* and yellow buckeye *(A. flava)*.

Cabbage Palm   *Sabal palmetto*

Zones 7–10

Weather Resilience: 7

Resilient to: COLD, DEER, DROUGHT, HEAT, FIRE, SALT, WIND AND STORM

Culture: Cabbage palm thrives in poor, sandy soil but grows well in slightly richer soils amended with some organic matter, as long as the soil remains well drained. Transplant during warm weather to hasten establishment of the plant. Plant in full sun or in a sunny location with afternoon shade.

Recommendations: Native to the Southeast United States, this large palm grows to a height of 100 feet with a 15-foot-wide spray of fan-shaped leaves. This is one of the most cold-hardy palms — it can tolerate hard freezes in addition to weathering hurricanes, salt spray, and wild-fires. Although cabbage palms are very resilient to salt spray, the plants are not as resistant to salt water. The palm named texas palmetto (*S. mexicana*) grows quite well in areas around southern Texas.

Colorado Blue Spruce
Picea pungens

Zone 3–8
Weather Resilience: 7
Resilient to: COLD, DEER, DROUGHT, HAIL, ICE AND SNOW, SALT, WIND AND STORM

Culture: Plant in any moist, well-drained soil that is amended with lots of organic matter. Plants are most weather resilient in full sun.

Recommendations: Colorado blue spruce should be used in large settings; trees con-fined to small yards can become less wind tolerant when they attain great height. White spruce (*P. glauca*) is notably more resilient to drought and wind than are other spruce species.

Note: In areas in which gall insects are a problem, plant white fir (*Abies concolor*) instead. It has similar, if not quite as strong, weather resilience as blue spruce and is just as attractive.

Honey Locust, Thornless
Gleditsia triacanthos

Zones 3–7
Weather Resilience: 7
Resilient to: COLD, DEER, DROUGHT, FIRE, FLOOD, HEAT, SALT

Culture: Honey locust grows and thrives in a variety of inhospitable sites, from compact alkaline soil to salty roadside and from coastal locations to hot, drought-prone parking lots. It prefers a deep, well-drained soil with lots of organic matter but will obviously settle for less.

Recommendations: On challenging sites, honey locust grows very slowly, sometimes no higher than a small tree. Certain varieties are more vigorous and resilient than others. The cultivar 'Shademaster' has been around for years and is still one of the top performers. 'Halka' produces strong, very resilient trees. 'Maxwell' is one of the most cold-tolerant forms of this tree.

Persimmon
Diospyros virginiana

Zones 5–9
Weather Resilience: 7
Resilient to: DEER, DROUGHT, FLOOD, FIRE, HEAT, HUMIDITY, SALT

Culture: The deep taproot of persimmon makes it important to transplant this tree when small. Water the first year after planting until the tree is established, after which it becomes drought tolerant. Trees are most weather-resilient when grown in full sun. Grow in deep, fertile soil that has been amended with organic matter. Trees should be planted in areas protected from wind and unseasonable cold.

Recommendations: Fire-damaged trees freely resprout. Named varieties provide better fruit quality and fall foliage color rather than improved resiliency.

Note: Persimmon is related to ebony, as evidenced by its dark black heartwood.

Eastern Hemlock
Tsuga canadensis

Zones 4–8
Weather Resilience: 6
Resilient to: COLD, DEER, FLOOD, HAIL, HUMIDITY, ICE AND SNOW

Culture: Grow in rich, moist, well-drained soil with lots of organic matter; it prefers acidic conditions but is adaptable to slightly alkaline soils. In hot climates, grow in shade; in cool climates, select locations from full sun to shade. The ultimate height of hemlocks is determined by geography as much as site. The tallest trees are in the Applachian states, where trees can reach over 160 feet. In the Northeast, the largest specimens are about 130 feet.

Recommendations: Eastern hemlock is excellent for waterside plantings. The species is extremely tolerant without having to be improved. Most of the cultivars are of dwarf or weeping forms that do not improve or even compromise its resiliency. Carolina hemlock *(T. caroliniana)* is more compact and not quite as cold hardy as the species but is slightly more heat tolerant. Hemlock is frequently used for windbreak hedges in areas in which winds are intermittent and not too strong. Avoid using where winds are persistent and don't plant on exposed sites.

Note: Hemlocks are very long-lived trees and can survive for many centuries. Starting in the 1920s, a serious insect pest, the woolly adelgid, began infesting hemlock; it can be controlled with horticultural oil. Biological controls are being researched.

Japanese Umbrella Pine
Sciadopitys verticillata

Zones 5–9
Weather Resilience: 6
Resilient to: COLD, DROUGHT, HEAT, HUMIDITY, ICE AND SNOW, WIND AND STORM

Culture: Umbrella pines prefer to grow in deep, acidic to near neutral fertile soil that is well drained and balanced between sandy texture and organic content. It thrives in moist soils but will grow well in drier soils once established. Umbrella pines are most weather resilient when grown where it is mostly sunny to partly shady.

Recommendations: Umbrella pines grow slowly and their sharply conical shape sheds ice and snow easily. The only possible weakness is the tree's tendency to have two leaders rather than one. Single-leader trees are more resilient to snow and wind, although many double-leader trees never suffer a problem. The needles on some trees can turn a dull brownish green in winter. The variety 'Wintergreen' keeps its green color all year long.

Live Oak   *Quercus virginiana*

Zones 8–10
Weather Resilience: 6
Resilient to: DROUGHT, HEAT, HUMIDITY, LIGHT-NING, SALT, WIND AND STORM

Culture: When young, live oak prefers a deep, friable soil that has been amended with organic matter. As a live oak ages, it becomes increasingly weather resilient and can thrive in conditions as diverse as coastal plains and city streets. Grow in mostly sunny to partly shady locations.

Recommendations: Live oaks are some of the oldest living plants in eastern North America; many trees are hundreds of years old. Live oak grows best within a few hundred miles of the ocean and thrives in humidity. The best resiliency is obtained by planting locally grown trees. Live oak should not be planted where oak wilt, a destructive disease, is common.

Russian Olive
Elaeagnus angustifolia

Zones 3–8
Weather Resilience: 6
Resilient to: COLD, DEER, DROUGHT, FIRE, SALT, WIND AND STORM

Culture: Russian olive grows well in any of a wide range of soils, from the wet soils of streams to dry sand. It prefers acidic to slightly alkaline conditions and becomes less weather resilient in alkaline soils. The tree grows best in full to mostly sunny locations.

Recommendations: People seem to either love or hate Russian olive. It is so vigorous as to be invasive in some parts of the United States, particularly in the West. In other areas, it is esteemed for use in riverbank reclamation, windbreaks, and wildlife habitat creation. The variety 'Quicksilver' has pewter-colored foliage.

Southern Wax Myrtle   *Myrica cerifera*

Zones 6–9
Weather Resilience: 6
Resilient to: DEER, DROUGHT, FLOOD, HEAT, SALT, WIND AND STORM

Culture: Southern wax myrtle is a small tree or large shrub that grows best in fertile, organic soils with even moisture. It is best in full sun.

Recommendations: Southern wax myrtle is excellent for windbreaks and screens, especially along the Atlantic and Gulf coasts. North of Zone 6, similar weather-resilient qualities can be obtained by growing bayberry *(M. pensylvanica)*, a very close relative of wax myrtle that is hardy in Zones 3 to 6 and is exceptionally resilient to salt and drought. It is also tolerant of very low pH soils, growing well in soils with values below 4.5. Another relative, sweet gale *(M. gale)*, grows in boggy locations in Zones 1 to 6 and is extremely resilient to flood and cold.

Swamp White Oak
Quercus bicolor

Zones 4–8
Weather Resilience: 6
Resilient to: COLD, DROUGHT, FIRE, FLOOD, ICE AND SNOW, WIND AND STORM

Culture: Grow swamp white oak in deep, fertile soil that has been amended with lots of organic matter. It grows best in moist soils; growth slows in drier ground. Trees are much easier to transplant when they are small and young. Young trees will thrive in sun to partial shade. Older trees are strongest in full sun.

Recommendations: Swamp white oak can endure weeks in standing water, but they thrive in drier locations. For areas prone to drought more than floods, grow white oak *(Q. alba)*, which is more drought resilient than swamp white oak. For very wet areas in the Deep South, grow overcup oak *(Q. lyrata)*, a warm-climate white oak species that is even more flood resilient than swamp white oak.

Washington Palm
Washingtonia spp.

Zone 10
Weather Resilience: 6
Resilient to: DEER, HEAT, HUMIDITY, FIRE, SALT, WIND AND STORM

Culture: Washington palms are sensitive to temperatures below about 45°F. Grow in full sun in fertile, well-drained soil amended with generous amounts of organic matter. Water as needed. Transplant in warm weather when plants are actively growing.

Recommendations: Thread palm *(W. robusta)* is resilient to storms and salt, making it an excellent plant for coastal areas. California fan palm *(W. filifer)* is good for dry, hot areas, such as southern California.

Beech   *Fagus* spp.

Zones 3–9
Weather Resilience: 5
Resilient to: COLD, DEER, ICE AND SNOW, LIGHTNING, WIND AND STORM

Culture: Beech trees thrive in rich, forest-type soil that contains abundant organic matter and is well drained. Give plenty of water during dry periods, and lightly mulch the soil beneath the canopy to conserve moisture. Grow in full sun to dappled shade. Beeches are very sensitive to fire damage.

Recommendations: American beech *(F. grandifolia)* is a benefit to any large yard, but you must acquire one by good fortune, as no commercial varieties are available. It is one of the few trees that seem resilient to damage from lightning. In contrast, for European beech *(F. sylvatica),* a truckload of superior varieties is readily available. The cultivar 'Riversii' has dark purple foliage and is especially attractive.

Coconut Palm *Cocos nucifera*

Zone 10
Weather Resilience: 5
Resilient to: DEER, FLOOD, HUMIDITY, SALT, WIND AND STORM

Culture: Coconut palms are for only the warmest areas and become most weather resilient when grown in a fertile, sandy soil that has been amended with plenty of organic matter. Grow in full sun.

Recommendations: This graceful palm is hurricane resilient and nearly immune to salt spray, sandy soil, and storm surge. A dwarf variety, 'Nana', grows just 10 feet tall.

   Note: A coconut can float across an ocean for thousands of miles, wash up on a beach, and sprout in the salty sand.

Golden-Rain Tree
Koelreuteria paniculata

Zones 5–9
Weather Resilience: 5
Resilient to: DROUGHT, FIRE, HEAT, HUMIDITY, SALT

Culture: This beautiful tree is easy to grow, thriving in soils from average to fertile, well drained, and amended with organic matter. Golden-rain tree is moderately resilient to drought and needs full sun to thrive.

Recommendations: Because golden-rain tree has weak wood, trees should be pruned to produce a strong branching form that can inhibit storm damage. Where possible, site trees in sheltered locations. The trees are also tolerant of urban conditions and moderately resilient to salty soils and spray. The variety 'September' flowers later in the summer than does the species.

Magnolia *Magnolia* spp.

Zones 6–9
Weather Resilience: 5
Resilient to: DEER, FLOOD, HEAT, SALT, WIND AND STORM

Culture: Southern magnolia prefers deep, moist organic soil with a sandy texture. Avoid wet soils, as the tree needs good drainage; it thrives on even moisture. Southern magnolia develops the strongest weather resilience when grown in full sun in areas where the winters are mild. In locations in which the ground freezes for longer than 1 month, grow in partial shade.

Recommendations: Although southern magnolia cannot be considered drought tolerant, it is more drought resilient than other magnolias. The variety 'Edith Bogue' is more cold hardy than most commercially available varieties. Sweetbay magnolia *(M. virginiana)* is generally similar to but smaller than southern magnolia. It is flood tolerant and a full zone more cold hardy; the variety 'Henry Hicks' is resilient to nearly –20°F.

Soapberry *Sapindus drummondii*

Zones 6–10
Weather Resilience: 5
Resilient to: COLD, DEER, DROUGHT, HEAT, WIND AND STORM

Culture: Soapberry is not readily available in nurseries. If you can't find any plants for sale, you can grow your own. Collect soapberry seed from the soapy fruits in early to late winter and sow it in seed flats. Germination is typically about 50 percent. (A caution: Soapberry fruit can produce skin irritation in some people.) Cuttings taken in mid- to late spring and treated with rooting powder containing 1  to 2 percent IBA root well. Root the cuttings in a well-drained mix of peat moss and perlite. Grow plants in full sun in soil near 7.0 pH.

Recommendations: This attractive tree can reach about 50 feet tall, with very large specimens topping 60 feet. Soapberry is able to thrive under some very rugged and demanding conditions. It grows well in soils of higher pH than many other forest trees and grows best in soils overlaying limestone bedrock. The trees can withstand drought and heat, as well as the unpredictable environment of stream banks. Once established, the trees are also resilient to wind, storms, and pollution.

Sweetgum
Liquidambar styraciflua

Zones 6–9
Weather Resilience: 5
Resilient to: DEER, FLOOD, ICE AND SNOW, SALT, WIND AND STORM

Culture: Sweetgum grows best on deep fertile soils, such as those found on floodplains and in Midwest farm fields. It is quite adaptable — it also thrives on dry, average soils as long as they are acidic. Plant in full sun.

Recommendations: Sweetgum is sensitive to fire and late-spring cold snaps. When grown at the northern edge of its hardiness range, it is subject to winter damage. 'Moraine' is more cold hardy and suffers less winter injury.

Vines and Ground Covers

Bearberry
Arctostaphylos uva-ursi

Zones 2–6
Weather Resilience: 10
Resilient to: COLD, DEER, DROUGHT, FIRE, FLOOD,
HAIL, HEAT, ICE AND SNOW, SALT, WIND AND STORM

Culture: Known also by its Native American name *kinnikinnick*, bearberry is the most resilient species in a genus full of weather-resilient plants. The plants grow best in well-drained, sandy to rocky acidic soils with some organic matter. Grow in full sun to mostly sunny locations.

Recommendations: In addition to the above resilient qualities, the cultivar 'Massachusetts' is disease resistant. Emerald carpet manzanita (*A.* × 'Emerald Carpet') has qualities similar to those of bearberry but is slightly taller, reaching 15 inches.

A bearberry for warm regions is 'Snow Camp', which looks remarkably like *A. uva-ursi* but is hardy in Zones 7 to 9.

Carpet Bugle   *Ajuga* spp.

Zones 3–9
Weather Resilience: 8
Resilient to: COLD, DEER, DROUGHT, FIRE, FLOOD, HAIL, HEAT, WIND AND STORM

Culture: Easy to grow in almost any soil, these versatile plants need very little care once established. Although they show the best leaf color and flowering when planted in full sun, they also grow quite well in shade.

Variegated forms should be grown in locations with mostly sun to shade.

Recommendations: For vigor and weather resiliency in a ground cover, carpet bugle *(A. reptans)* is at the top of the list. It spreads quickly and forms a dense, low mat of attractive foliage. It can be locally invasive. Varieties include 'Burgundy', with dark red leaves; 'Rainbow', with multicolored leaves; and 'Variegata', which spreads slowly. *Ajuga pyramidalis* doesn't spread but forms attractive pyramid-shaped clumps of foliage.

Juniper, Creeping
Juniperus spp.

Zones 3–9
Weather Resilience: 8
Resilient to: COLD, DEER, DROUGHT, HAIL, HEAT, ICE AND SNOW, SALT, WIND AND STORM

Culture: Creeping juniper thrives in soils ranging from slightly acidic to slightly alkaline. It grows well in dry, coarse soils and in moist, fertile ones, as long as the ground is well drained. The best weather resiliency is attained by most species when grown in sunny to mostly sunny spots, in a sandy soil amended with some organic matter.

Recommendations: Creeping juniper *(J. horizontalis)* combines vigor and excellent resiliency to a wide range of conditions. Outstanding varieties are the very salt-tolerant 'Bar Harbor' and 'Wiltonii' (also called blue rug juniper). Common juniper *(J. communis)* is a bristly evergreen that is also very resilient and durable. Creeping forms include 'Prostrata' and 'Repanda'. 'Emerald Sea' and 'Silver Mist' are forms of shore juniper *(J. conferta)* that are especially salt resilient.

Ice Plant *Delosperma* spp.

Zones 6–10
Weather Resilience: 7
Resilient to: DEER, DROUGHT, FIRE, HAIL, HEAT, SALT, WIND AND STORM

Culture: Ice plants prefer coarse, sandy, well-drained soil that has been amended with some organic matter. They are just about unmatched for holding loose sandy soils in place and resisting erosion. Most do not tolerate wet conditions. Grow in full sun.

Recommendations: *Ice plant* is the common name for many warm-climate, but otherwise very different, plants. *D. cooperii* and *D.* 'Alba' are strongly resilient to fire, salt, erosion, and drought as well as being deer resistant.

One very weather-resilient species, however, should not be grown. Highway ice plant *(C. edulis)* got its common name after being introduced to California a century ago for erosion control along highways. It is tolerant of fire, drought, salt, and wind; controls erosion; and tolerates wet sites. Unfortunately, it is also so invasive that it is considered a noxious weed.

Ivy *Hedera* spp.

Zones 5–10
Weather Resilience: 7
Resilient to: DEER, DROUGHT, FIRE, HAIL, ICE AND SNOW, SALT, WIND AND STORM

Culture: Ivy prefers a well-drained, fertile soil amended with organic matter and kept evenly moist. The plants grow more slowly and are more weather resilient under less fertile, drier conditions. Plants are less resilient in Zone 5, where they tend to need protection from winter conditions.

Recommendations: When beds of ivy are used as a fire buffer, grow the plants in soil that has been generously amended with organic matter and keep the area lightly moist when possible. Under dry soil conditions, the leaves hold less moisture and are less effective as a buffer. Algerian ivy *(H. canariensis)* and English ivy *(H. helix)* are moderately deer resistant. Baltic ivy *(H. helix baltica)* is strongly deer resistant.

Lilyturf *Liriope* spp.

Zones 5–10

Weather Resilience: 7

Resilient to: DEER, DROUGHT, FIRE, HAIL, HEAT, SALT, WIND AND STORM

Culture: Lilyturf prefers a moist, well-drained soil with a nice balance of sand and organic matter. It will tolerate more severe conditions, such as drought, once established. Grow in a sunny to partly shady location for best resilience. Lilyturf is not resistant to cold or to wind combined with cold.

Recommendations: Lilyturf is tolerant of shade, even the shade beneath trees. The difference in weather resilience among species is mostly a question of cold hardiness. *Liriope spicata*, for example, is hardy to Zone 5, spreads faster, and is more vigorous than *L. muscari*.

Vinca
Vinca minor

Zones 4–9

Weather Resilience: 7

Resilient to: COLD, DEER, FIRE, FLOOD, HAIL, ICE AND SNOW, WIND AND STORM

Culture: Vinca grows well in a range of soils unless persistently wet or dry, but it tolerates both for weeks if forced to. Dry conditions are best endured in shady locations. In colder areas, it can be grown in full sun to shade; in hot regions, it prefers partial to full shade.

Recommendations: Delicate-looking yet durable, vinca is a vigorous but easily managed ground cover. Includes white- and blue-flowered varieties. Greater periwinkle *(V. major)* is grown as an annual in cool regions and as a ground cover south of Zone 7. 'Variegata' has pale green, white-bordered leaves.

Cotoneaster   *Cotoneaster* spp.

Zones 3–9
Weather Resilience: 6
Resilient to: COLD, DEER, FIRE, HAIL, SALT, WIND AND STORM

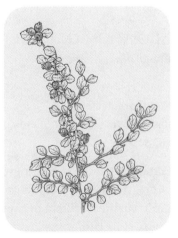

Culture: Cotoneasters are self-reliant shrubs with attractive glossy foliage and colorful fall fruits. For best fruits, low-growing forms need full sun to mostly sunny locations. Plant in well-drained, sandy soil that has been amended with organic matter for fastest growth; drier, less fertile soils lead to slower growth.

Recommendations: A slew of excellent species and varieties are available, with three ground cover forms standing out. The first is *C. salicifolius* 'Gnom', which produces a dense, foot-tall mat of shiny green leaves. *C. cashmiriensis* also grows just a foot tall and bears a carpet of glossy leaves. *C. adpressus* is similar to the above varieties but has a more open habit and fewer leaves; it is also much more cold hardy.

Mondo Grass

Ophiopogon japonicus

Zones 7–10
Weather Resilience: 6
Resilient to: DEER, DROUGHT, FIRE, HEAT, SALT, WIND AND STORM

Culture: In appearance, mondo grass is very similar to lilyturf (*Lirope* spp.) and is equally undemanding. Grow mondo grass in locations ranging from full sun to shade. It thrives in well-drained soil with average fertility and some organic matter.

Recommendations: Mondo grass makes an excellent ground cover and is valued for its dense habit and low growth. A dwarf form that reaches only about 6 inches tall is 'Nana'. Although mondo grass is not as cold tolerant as lilyturf, the thick mat it produces is even better at stabilizing the soil.

Snow-in-Summer

Cerastium tomentosum

Zones 3–7
Weather Resilience: 5
Resilient to: COLD, DEER, DROUGHT, FIRE, WIND AND STORM

Culture: Snow-in-summer grows well in all soil types except wet, heavy ones. It is most weather resilient on well-drained, coarse soils with some organic matter but can be quite vigorous on unstable banks and sandy soils.

Recommendations: Snow-in-summer is a very resilient plant for exposed places with poor soil. At the warmer edge of its range, snow-in-summer can suffer from humidity and heat, conditions that may lead to disease and pest problems.

Bougainvillea
Bougainvillea spp.

Zones 9–10
Weather Resilience: 4
Resilient to: DROUGHT, FIRE, HEAT, SALT

Culture: Pretty and tough, bougainvillea grows best in fertile, well-drained soil that has been amended generously with organic matter. The plants are strongest in locations receiving full sun. In winter, keep the soil barely moist, and always avoid overwatering.

Recommendations: Because the many species are fairly uniform in weather resiliency, you can base your selection largely on color, form, and other measures of personal preference. *Bougainvillea* × *buttiana*, *B. glabra*, and *B. spectabilis* are the most cold hardy. All bougainvilleas make excellent container plants in colder regions.

Ornamental Grasses

Blue Fescue *Festuca glauca*

Zones 4–8
Weather Resilience: 9
Resilient to: COLD, DEER, DROUGHT, FIRE, HAIL, HEAT, ICE AND SNOW, SALT, WIND AND STORM

Culture: Blue fescue is a very accommodating plant that is as beautiful as it is resilient. Grow in well-drained, average soil amended with organic matter. Soils with generous amounts of organic content or too much moisture, however, can result in weaker growth. It will thrive in poor, coarse soils or rocky spots. The best color and resiliency are obtained in full sun; blue fescue will tolerate a little shade.

Recommendations: Perhaps the best variety for combined weather resilience is 'Elijah Blue'. Other cultivars of excellent quality and resilience are 'Blue Finch', 'Blue Fox', and 'Sea Urchin'.

Maiden Grass
Miscanthus sinensis

Zones 4–9
Weather Resilience: 9
Resilient to: COLD, DEER, DROUGHT, FLOOD, HAIL, HEAT, HUMIDITY, ICE AND SNOW, WIND AND STORM

Culture: Maiden grass grown in a proper site requires little care. Plant it in full sun; when grown with less sunlight, the plants weaken and the clump thins out. It thrives in a deep, fertile soil that is well drained and amended with organic matter. This grass can tolerate short dry periods but is not truly drought resilient. Cut back old stalks before new growth shows in spring.

Recommendations: 'Silver Feather' is a vigorous variety. Zebra grass (*M. sinensis* 'Zebrinus') is a strong plant with broad leaf blades marked with yellow blazes. The foliage of 'Cabaret' and 'Gracillimus' has a silvery cast. *Miscanthus* 'Purpurescens' is all-around excellent.

Feather Reed Grass
Calamagrostis × acutiflora

Zones 5–9
Weather Resilience: 8
Resilient to: COLD, DEER, DROUGHT, FLOOD, HEAT, ICE AND
SNOW, SALT, WIND AND STORM

Culture: Feather reed grass grows well in a wide
range of soils, from wet to poor and sandy to
heavy clay. The plant grows best when some
organic matter is added. Grow in full sun to partial shade. Site in a breezy location to avoid
humidity-related diseases, such as powdery
mildew, that may occur (though infrequently).

Recommendations: The most widely grown and perhaps most resilient
variety is 'Karl Foerster', which has a compact habit and pliant but
strong stems. In warm regions, it is looser in habit. 'Stricta' has a form
similar to that of 'Karl Foerster'.

Prairie Cordgrass *Spartina pectinata*

Zones 4–7
Weather Resilience: 8
Resilient to: COLD, DEER, DROUGHT, FLOOD, HEAT, ICE AND
SNOW, SALT, WIND AND STORM

Culture: A North American native, prairie cordgrass grows best in fertile, well-drained soil
amended with organic matter; up to 5 feet tall.
This grass is resilient to saline soils as well as
extremes of wet and dry. It is a vigorous grower;
control it's spread by pulling out rhizomes in
spring. Site in full sun.

Recommendations: The variety 'Aureomarginata'
is particularly attractive, with golden-edged leaf blades.

Switch Grass
Panicum virgatum

Zones 5–9

Weather Resilience: 8

Resilient to: COLD, DEER, DROUGHT, FIRE, FLOOD, HEAT, SALT, WIND AND STORM

Culture: Switch grass prefers moderately fertile soils that are acid to slightly alkaline (pH range of 4.5 to 7.5). Amend the area with organic matter before planting, and keep the soil evenly moist for best growth. Overfertilizing makes stems floppy. Grow in full sun.

Recommendations: Switch grass can reach 6 feet tall and some varieties do sustain stem breakage in gusty winds. The variety 'Haense Herms', however, has very pliant stems, making it more wind resilient than most other cultivars. The most cold-hardy selection is probably 'Prairie Sky', which can be a full zone hardier than most varieties. Other excellent cultivars are 'Cloud Nine' and 'Heavy Metal'.

Blue Lyme Grass   *Leymus racemosus*

Zones 4–10

Weather Resilience: 7

Resilient to: COLD, DEER, DROUGHT, HEAT, ICE AND SNOW, SALT, WIND AND STORM

Culture: Blue lyme grass is excellent for hot locations, such as places in which heat radiates from pavement or buildings. It is drought resilient and salt tolerant as well. It grows about 4 feet tall and spreads vigorously once established, and it thrives in average to fertile soil that is well drained and evenly moist. Plant in full sun to achieve maximum resiliency.

Recommendations: The species is so vigorous as to be invasive; however, the cultivar 'Glaucus' is not as aggressive.

Blue Oat Grass
Helictotrichon sempervirens

Zones 4–9
Weather Resilience: 7
Resilient to: COLD, DEER, DROUGHT, HAIL, HEAT, ICE AND SNOW, WIND AND STORM

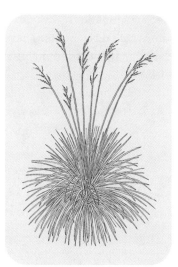

Culture: This handsome clumping grass has oatlike blossoms that age to gold. Blue oat grass grows well in dry soils but prefers a deep, average soil that is well drained and amended with organic matter. The plant grows best in soils that are alkaline, but does well in slightly acidic soils, too. Site in full sun in cool regions, light shade in warmer climates.

Recommendations: Cultivated varieties are not available, perhaps because the species is already attractive and resilient.

Northern Sea Oats
Chasmanthium latifolium

Zones 5–9
Weather Resilience: 6
Resilient to: COLD, DEER, DROUGHT, ICE AND SNOW, SALT, WIND AND STORM

Culture: Northern sea oats, native to eastern North America, grows atop sand dunes as well as in open woodlands and along stream banks. It is tolerant of heat as long as its soil is moist and fertile, although it also tolerates poor to average soils. One of the best ornamental grasses for wet or dry shade, it also thrives in full sun. Plants grown in shade are darker green than those grown in sun, but more likely to need staking.

Recommendations: Away from coastal areas, northern sea oats is sometimes called river oats. There are no cultivated varieties, but locally raised plants tend to do best in local conditions.

Annuals

Moss Rose
Portulaca oleracea

Zones 3–10 (seasonal)
Weather Resilience: 7
Resilient to: DROUGHT, FIRE, FLOOD, HAIL, HEAT, SALT, WIND AND STORM

Culture: Moss rose is tough as nails. It prefers a well-drained, light sandy soil with some organic matter and requires full sun to achieve best resiliency, but it is remarkably tolerant of environmental extremes. From deluge to drought, moss rose makes summer plantings carefree; it is particularly good in hanging baskets.

Recommendations: Moss rose is purslane, the weedy outlaw now re-formed into a pillar of the garden community. The often double rosy flowers are extraordinary. Excellent cultivated varieties include the Yubi series.

California Poppy
Eschscholtzia californica

Zones 4–10 (seasonal)
Weather Resilience: 6
Resilient to: DEER, DROUGHT, FIRE, HEAT, SALT, WIND AND STORM

Culture: California poppy is a hardy annual that grows vigorously in poor to average, well-drained soils that have been lightly amended with organic matter. Grow in full sun. The seeds germinate readily, and the seedlings grow quickly to flowering size. This is a very attractive, resilient plant that is also quite easy to grow.

Recommendations: Because the available varieties are uniformly weather resilient, you can choose largely based on flower color and height. Compact varieties include 'Dali', 'Mission Bells', and the Thai Silk Series. A cultivar that is slightly taller than the species is 'Orange King'.

Dusty Miller *Senecio cineraria*

Zones 8–10
Weather Resilience: 6
Resilient to: DEER, DROUGHT, FIRE, HEAT, SALT, WIND AND STORM

Culture: Dusty miller is hardy in warm climates but grown as an annual north of Zone 8. It is most resilient in a hot, dry climate, an environment that encourages a stout, full growth habit.

Recommendations: The woolly leaves protect the plant during drought and serve as a fire retardant in the landscape. Its excellent salt resiliency makes it a mainstay of coastal gardens. The varieties 'Cirrus' and 'Silver Dust' are particularly attractive. A surprise amid these drought-loving plants is *S. smithii*, which loves wet, soggy ground.

Rock Rose   *Portulaca grandiflora*

Zones 3–10 (seasonal)
Weather Resilience: 6
Resilient to: DROUGHT, FIRE, HAIL, HEAT, SALT, WIND AND STORM

Culture: Rock rose requires a well-drained, light soil with a little organic matter. It is most resilient in full sun with soil kept on the dry side. It often benefits from a light layer of organic mulch to reduce competition from weeds. Rock rose doesn't like pampering and grows quite nicely in rocky soil as well as sandy coastal gardens. It is hardy to about 35 to 40°F and is also an excellent choice for hot, dry climates.

Recommendations: The Sundial Series is especially resilient to climates, such as those in the Northwest and Northeast, that have more clouds, rain, and humidity.

Ageratum   *Ageratum houstonianum*

Zones 4–10 (seasonal)
Weather Resilience: 5
Resilient to: DEER, DROUGHT, HEAT, SALT, WIND AND STORM

Culture: Grow plants in a well-drained soil that has been amended with organic matter. The plants are strongest when provided with even moisture. They cannot tolerate frost but will endure drought (though flowering is often reduced). Overfertilizing encourages diseases and pests. Ageratum thrives in full sun but will also grow well in mostly sunny locations and those in partial shade.

Recommendations: The flowers of some varieties, such as 'Blue Danube' and 'Blue Horizon', hold up to weather better than others.

Begonia
Begonia × semperflorens-cultorum

Zones 4–10 (seasonal; this tender perennial is grown as an annual in cooler regions)

Weather Resilience: 5

Resilient to: DEER, DROUGHT, HAIL, HEAT, WIND AND STORM

Culture: These small plants are the mainstay of plantings near shopping mall entrances and in parking lots because they border on being indestructible. Plant in fertile, well-drained soil generously amended with organic matter. For best flowering and growth, keep soil evenly moist. Under dry conditions, growth stalls and flowering is reduced. Plant in full sun to partial shade.

Recommendations: Semperflorens begonias are excellent for planting in marginal places where the conditions can vary from wet to dry. The darker-leaved varieties thrive in full sun, whereas the green-leaved types prefer partial shade.

Morning Glory   *Ipomoea* spp.

Weather Resilience: 5

Resilient to: DEER, DROUGHT, HEAT, SALT, WIND AND STORM

Culture: Both annual and tender perennial species may be grown as annuals in cooler regions (moonflower, Zone 10, but Zones 5–9 as annual; sweet potato vine, Zones 9–10, but Zones 4–8 as annual; morning glory, Zone 10, but Zones 4–9 as annual). These climbing vines prefer full sun and average to moderately fertile, well-drained soil. Provide support for vines to climb. Amend poor soils with organic matter. In drought conditions, a sheltered location improves resilience. If well watered, the vines can take summer winds; however, they are not tolerant of cold weather.

Recommendations: Many species make excellent garden plants, including cardinal climber *(I. × multifida)*, moonflower *(I. alba)*, morning glory *(I. tricolor)*, red morning glory *(I. coccinea)*, and sweet potato vine *(I. batatas)*.

Sweet Alyssum
Lobularia maritima

Zones 4–10 (seasonal)
Weather Resilience: 5
Resilient to: COLD, DEER, DROUGHT, HAIL, SALT

Culture: Sweet alyssum is a hardy annual that can endure temperatures near freezing, once it has been properly acclimated. Grow in full sun and fertile, well-drained soil with good amounts of organic matter. Even moisture will help the plants grow their best.

Recommendations: Sweet alyssum is especially resilient in coastal gardens; it grows well in sandy, salty soil and tolerates salt spray. The variety 'Wonderland' is very vigorous, as are the cultivars of the Basket Series and the variety 'Rosario'.

Madagascar Periwinkle   *Catharanthus roseus*

Zones 4–10 (seasonal; grown as a tender perennial in Zone 10)
Weather Resilience: 4
Resilient to: DEER, DROUGHT, HEAT, WIND AND STORM

Culture: Madagascar periwinkle prefers soil that is well drained and fertile but not excessively rich; amending a sandy soil generously with organic matter produces a good growing medium. The plants thrive in hot weather and like full sun to partial shade.

Recommendations: The variety 'Parasol' is vigorous, generally more resilient than most other varieties, and very heat resist-ant. Its blossoms are symmetrical and nearly picture-perfect. Madagascar periwinkle should not be exposed to temperatures below about 45°F.

Marigold *Tagetes* spp.

Zones 4–10 (seasonal)
Weather Resilience: 4
Resilient to: DEER, DROUGHT, HEAT, WIND AND STORM

Culture: Grow marigolds in any well-drained, average to fertile soil that has been generously amended with organic matter; they do poorly in wet soils. The plants are most resilient when grown in full sun.

Recommendations: Blossoms of double-flowered varieties do poorly in wet, humid weather; single-flowered forms are much more resilient to stormy weather. Mexican tarragon *(T. lucida)* is more resistant to deer browsing than are other marigolds. In gardens, marigolds aid in reduc-ing nematode populations in the soil. The Antigua Series of African marigold *(T. erecta)* is more drought tolerant than many other types. The smaller French marigolds *(T. patula)* are more wind resilient, but dislike wet conditions.

Lawn Grasses

For lawn grasses, the USDA hardiness zone category is replaced by the categories "warm-season" and "cool-season." Cool-season grasses grow best in climates where the soil temperature remains below about 80°F. They thrive in the cooler temperatures of spring and fall, and do not go dormant until temperatures drop well below freezing. Warm-season grasses grow best in warm weather, and they do well even when soil temperatures rise into the 80s. They go dormant when the temperature approaches freezing. In areas where freezing temperatures are encountered, these grasses turn brown until they begin growth again in spring. Generally, cool-season grasses dominate from Zones 6 north, and warm-season types from Zone 6 south.

Bermuda Grass
Cynodon dactylon

Warm-season grass
Weather Resilience: 6
Resilient to: COLD, DROUGHT, FLOOD, HEAT, HUMIDITY, SALT

Culture: Bermuda grass needs full sun to become most weather resilient. It grows best in soil with a pH value of 6.0 to 7.0 but will tolerate more acidic and alkaline conditions. Bermuda grass is sown; hybrid Bermuda grass is established using plugs.

Recommendations: Bermuda grass is flood resilient but does not tolerate consistently wet locations. Although drought resilient, it is unattractive in dry periods unless irrigated. It is less expensive to establish than are hybrid types. Good varieties are 'Mohawk', 'Savanna', 'Sydney', and 'Yukon'. Hybrid types include 'Tifway' and 'Tifway II'.

Tall Fescue   *Festuca elatior*

Cool-season grass
Weather Resilience: 6
Resilient to: COLD, DROUGHT, FLOOD, HEAT, HUMIDITY, SALT

Culture: Tall fescue is a vigorous, coarse-textured lawn grass that establishes turf quickly. Fertilize lightly (1 pound of nitrogen per 1,000 square feet) once per season; excessive fertilizing reduces drought resiliency and increases cold-weather injury. Tall fescue adapts to many soil types. It grows best in slightly acid soils, but adapts to alkaline soils up to a pH of about 8.5. This tough lawn grass achieves its drought resistance by using its extensive root system to mine the soil for water. When the moisture is depleted, the grass weakens and dies quickly. Recharge moisture in the soil by giving the plant about ½ inch of water each week when possible. Tall fescue is flood resilient, tolerant both of salt and saline soils, and moderately cold tolerant.

Recommendations: Endophytic varieties, such as 'Shenandoah' and 'Titan', are resilient to many pests and diseases. Other excellent cultivars are 'Apache', 'Mustang', and 'Olympia'.

Buffalo Grass   *Buchloe dactyloides*

Warm-season grass
Weather Resilience: 4
Resilient to: COLD, DROUGHT, FIRE, HEAT

Culture: Buffalo grass grows best on clay soils and loams that have been amended with some organic matter; amend sandy soils generously with organic material. Sow or plant in spring. Keep sown seeds moist until germination. Grow in full sun. Avoid overwatering and fertilizing.

Recommendations: Buffalo grass grows more slowly than many cool-season types and is not appropriate for heavy traffic areas, as regrowth is slow. Buffalo grass will grow outside its native area but is most resilient in and around the prairies and similar low-rainfall climates. It is sensitive to saline soils. Varieties include 'Sharp's Improved' and 'Sharp's Improved II'. 'Prairie' and 'NE 609' are all-female varieties and produce more attractive lawns than do the mixed male/female varieties.

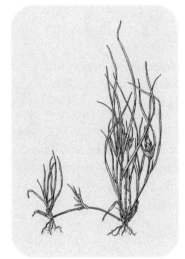

Zoysia grass *Zoysia* spp.

Warm-season grass
Weather Resilience: 4
Resilient to: COLD, DROUGHT, HEAT, SALT

Culture: Zoysia grass is a vigorous grass, forming thick stands of turf. It prefers to grow in full sun, though is tolerant of light shade. Zoysia grows strong in well-drained, light soils with some organic content but does poorly on heavy clay soils and wet sites.

Recommendations: In warm climates (Zones 8–10), Korean velvet grass *(Z. tenuifolia)* and manila grass *(Z. matrella)* produce fine-textured lawns. The most cold-resilient species is Japanese zoysia grass *(Z. japonica)*, which is hardy into Zone 5. Excellent cultivars are 'Diamond', 'Empire', 'Meyer', and 'Royal'. The variety 'Emerald' looks similar to Bermuda grass but has all the strengths of zoysia.

Appendix

Supplies and Resources

Plants and Planting Supplies

American Forests Historic Tree Nursery

8701 Old Kings Road, Jacksonville, FL 32218; Phone: 800-320-8733; Fax: 904-768-4630; www.historictrees.org. *Trees of historic significance from around the country are identified and cataloged and their seeds are collected to grow direct offspring trees.*

Bluestone Perennials

7211 Middle Ridge Road, Madison, OH 44057; Phone: 800-852-5243; Fax: 440-428-7198; www.bluestoneperennials.com. *Wide selection of perennials, herbs, ornamental shrubs, and bulbs.*

Carino Nurseries

P.O. Box 538, Indiana, PA 15701; Phone: 800-223-7075; Fax: 724-463-3050; www.carinonurseries.com. *Tree-shrub seedlings, evergreen and deciduous varieties, direct from the grower. Plants for landscaping, windbreaks, ornamentals, noise barriers, timber, wildlife food, and cover.*

Farmer Seed and Nursery

818 NW 4th Street, Faribault, MN 55021; Phone: 507-334-1623; www.farmerseed.com. *A wide range of perennials, shrubs, and trees especially suited for northern climates.*

Gardener's Supply Company

128 Intervale Road, Burlington, VT 05401; Phone: 888-833-1412; Fax: 800-551-6712; www.gardeners.com. *Gardening supplies, including watering systems and weather stations.*

GardenGuides

Phone: 800-274-0824; Fax: 770-216-1756; www.gardenguides.com. *Online growing resource for gardeners across all zones. Weekly newsletters; flower, vegetable, and herb guides; product reviews; tips and techniques; garden links directory; live chat and active discussion boards.*

Henry Field Seed & Nursery

P.O. Box 397, Aurora, IN 47001-0397; Phone: 513-354-1494; Fax: 513-354-1496; www.henryfields.com. *Flower and vegetable seeds, plants, fruit and shade trees, shrubs, perennials, and berries, plus growing aids and supplies.*

High Altitude Gardens/Seeds Trust

4150 B Black Oak Drive, Hailey, ID 83333-8447; Phone: 208-788-4363; Fax: 208-788-3452; www.seedstrust.com. *Encouragement, expertise, seeds, supplies for the gardener living through harsh winters (cold, wind) and dry summers.*

High Country Gardens

2902 Rufina Street, Santa Fe, NM 87505-2929; Phone: 800-925-9387; Fax: 800-925-0097; www.highcountrygardens.com. *Plants for the western garden; winter-hardy perennials, water-thrifty wildflowers, roses, native shrubs, water-wise lawns, and cold-hardy cacti and succulents.*

LandscapeUSA

13126 NE Airport Way, Portland, OR 97230; Phone: 800-966-1033; Fax: 503-255-9201; www.landscapeUSA.com. *A broad selection of products for lawn and garden.*

Mellinger's Inc.

2310 W. South Range Road, P.O. Box 157, North Lima, OH 44452-0157; Phone: 800-321-7444; Fax: 330-549-3761; www.mellingers.com. *Seeds (vegetables, herbs, trees), plants, and trees, plus "everything it takes to make them grow."*

Musser Forests, Inc.

1880 Route 119 North, Indiana, PA 15701; Phone: 800-643-8319; Fax: 724-465-9893; www.musserforests.com. *Northern-grown evergreen and hardwood tree seedlings, ornamental shrubs, nut trees, ground covers, and perennials.*

Park Seed Company

1 Parkton Avenue, Greenwood, SC 29647; Phone: 800-213-0076; Fax: 800-275-9941; www.parkseed.com. *Flower seeds, vegetable seeds, bulbs, and plants, along with a unique line of growing supplies and equipment.*

Stokes Tropicals

4806 E. Old Spanish Trail, Jeanerette, LA 70544; Phone: 337-365-6998 (info.); 800-624-9706 (orders); Fax: 337-365-6991; www.stokestropicals.com. *Exotic plants that thrive in the South.*

Thomas Jefferson Center for Historic Plants

P.O. Box 316, Monticello, Charlottesville, VA 22902-0316; Phone: 800-243-0743; Fax: 804-977-6140; www.monticello.org/chp/. *Collects, preserves, and distributes plants documented in American gardens before 1900, with a special emphasis on plants grown and documented by Thomas Jefferson at Monticello.*

Vesey's Seeds Ltd.

P.O. Box 9000, Charlottetown, Prince Edward Island, Canada, C1A 8K6; Phone: 902-368-7333; Fax: 800-686-0329; www.veseys.com. *Specializes in vegetable and flower seeds for shorter growing seasons as well as roses, shrubs, fruiting plants, and bulbs (bulbs are shipped only in Canada).*

Products to Control Hail and Wind

U.S. Global Resources USGR

10242 59th Avenue South, Seattle, WA 98178; Phone: 425-391-5646; Fax: 425-392-6713; www.usgr.com. *Agricultural fabrics for use as screens, covers, netting, shields, and fences including wind and hail control.*

Weather Information and Instruments

National Weather Service

National Oceanic and Atmospheric Administration, www.weather.gov. *Displays current Watches, Warning Advisories, and Statements on color-coded map of the United States. Special links to pages for dangers of fire, hurricanes, climate, rivers.*

Texas Weather Instruments, Inc.

5942 Abrams Road #113, Dallas, TX 75231; Phone: 800-284-0245; 214-368-7116; Fax: 214-340-6264; www.txwx.com. *Complete line of weather stations, which include anemometer, humidity, temperature, solar radiation, rain, barometric pressure, lightning, leaf wetness sensors, and wireless weather stations.*

Weather Sense: Canada's Weather Store

P.O. Box 2, 13 Nelson Street, Victoria Prince Edward Island, Canada C0A 2G0 Phone: 800-461-5525; 902-658-2993; Fax: 902-658-2366; www.weathersense.com. *Weather instruments, including tide clocks, lightning supplies, and weather stations.*

Wind and Weather

1200 N. Main Street, Fort Bragg, CA 95437; Phone: 800-922-9463; Fax: 707-964-1278; www.windandweather.com. *Weather instruments and garden ornamentals.*

Further Reading

A–Z Encyclopedia of Garden Plants, The American Horticultural Society (New York: DK Publishing, 1997)
Comprehensive plant encyclopedia, including trees, shrubs, and herbaceous plants.

Deerproofing Your Yard & Garden, by Rhonda Massingham Hart (North Adams, MA: Storey Publishing, 1997)
Suggestions for keeping deer off your land, based on understanding their habits, likes and dislikes, and behavior.

The Gardener's A-Z Guide to Growing Flowers from Seed to Bloom, by Eileen Powell (North Adams, MA: Storey Publishing, 2004)
A reference for sowing, raising, and propagating more than 500 annuals, perennials, and bulbs, including planning charts.

The Gardener's A-Z Guide to Growing Organic Food, by Tanya L.K. Denckla (North Adams, MA: Storey Publishing, 2004)
A guide to growing more than 750 varieties of vegetables, herbs, fruits, and nuts, including organic remedies for pest and disease problems.

The Landscaping Revolution: Garden with Mother Nature, Not Against Her, by Andy Wasowski with Sally Wasowski (Chicago, IL: Contemporary Books, 2002).
A manifesto on practical, responsible landscaping that is both empowering and entertaining.

Landscaping with Native Trees: THe Northeast, Midwest, Midsouth, & Southeast Edition, by Guy Sternberg and Jim Wilson (Boston, MA: Houghton Mifflin, 1996)
Includes where native American trees grow, where they shouldn't be grown, and their special strengths and weaknesses.

The Lawn and Garden Owner's Manual, by Lewis and Nancy Hill (North Adams, MA: Storey Publishing, 2000)
A comprehensive program for maintaining your home landscape.

Pruning Made Easy, by Lewis Hill (North Adams, MA: Storey Publishing, 1997)
Step-by-step illustrations demonstrate the time, equipment, and techniques for safely pruning trees, shrubs, hedges, vines, and flowers.

The Undaunted Garden: Planting for Weather-Resilient Beauty, by Lauren Springer (Golden, CO: Fulcrum Publishing, 2003)
An excellent and pioneering book, published in 1994, that gives not only hope, but also bountiful ideas and plant suggestions to gardeners coping with the challenging conditions of the mountainous West.

USDA Hardiness Zone Map

The United States Department of Agriculture (USDA) created this map to give gardeners a helpful tool for selecting and cultivating plants. The map divides North America into 11 zones based on each area's average minimum winter temperature. Zone 1 is the coldest and Zone 11 the warmest. Once you determine your zone, you may use that information to select plants that are most likely to thrive in your climate.

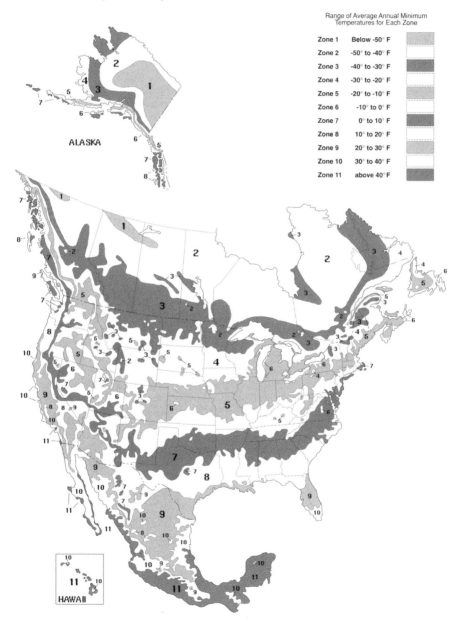

Range of Average Annual Minimum Temperatures for Each Zone

Zone 1	Below -50° F
Zone 2	-50° to -40° F
Zone 3	-40° to -30° F
Zone 4	-30° to -20° F
Zone 5	-20° to -10° F
Zone 6	-10° to 0° F
Zone 7	0° to 10° F
Zone 8	10° to 20° F
Zone 9	20° to 30° F
Zone 10	30° to 40° F
Zone 11	above 40° F

ALASKA

HAWAII

Botanic to Common Name Index

BOTANIC NAME	COMMON NAME	BOTANIC NAME	COMMON NAME
Abies	Fir	*Amelanchier*	Serviceberry
Abies fraseri	Fraser fir	*Amelanchier*	Shadblow
Abies koreana	Korean fir	*Amelanchier*	Shadbush
Acer	Maple	*Amorpha canescens*	Lead plant
Acer × freemanii	Freeman maple	*Anacyclus depressus*	Anacyclus
Acer buergeranum	Trident maple	*Angelonia angustifolia*	Angelonia
Acer campestre	Hedge maple	*Antennaria*	Pussytoes
Acer circinatum	Vine maple	*Aquilegia chrysantha*	Yellow
Acer ginnala	Amur maple		columbine
Acer globrum	Rocky Mountain	*Arbutus menziesii*	Pacific madrone
	maple	*Arctostaphylos uva-ursi*	Bearberry
Acer negundo	Box elder	*Arctotheca populifolia*	African daisy
Acer palmatum	Japanese maple	*Arecastrum*	Queen palm
Acer platanoides	Norway maple	*romanzoffianum*	
Acer rubrum	Red maple	*Armeria*	Thrift
Acer saccharinum	Silver maple	*Armeria maritima*	Sea thrift
Acer saccharum	Sugar maple	*Armeria maritima*	Thrift
Acer tataricum ginnala	Amur maple	*Aronia*	Chokeberry
Achillea	Achillea	*Artemesia*	Wormwood
Achillea	Yarrow	*Artemisia*	Artemisia
Achillea filipendulina	Yarrow	*Artemisia schmidtiana*	Silvermound
Achillea millefolium	Yarrow		artemisia
Adiantum pedatum	Maidenhair fern	*Asarum*	Wild ginger
Aesculus	Buckeye	*Asclepias tuberosa*	Butterflyweed
Aesculus × carnea	Red horse	*Asimina triloba*	Paw-paw
	chestnut	*Asparagus densiflorus*	Asparagus fern
Aesculus californica	California buck-	*Aurinia saxatilis*	Basket-of-gold
	eye	*Baptisia australis*	False indigo
Aesculus glabra	Ohio buckeye	*Begonia × semperflorens-*	
Aesculus hippocastanum	Horse chestnut	*cultorum*	Begonia
Aesculus parviflora	Bottlebrush	*Berberis*	Barberry
	buckeye	*Berberis thunbergii*	Japanese
Aesculus pavia	Red buckeye		barberry
Aethionema	Stonecress	*Bergenia*	Bergenia
Agapanthus africanus	Lily-of-the-Nile	*Betula*	Birch
Agave americana	Century plant	*Betula alleghaniensis*	Yellow birch
Agave victoriae-reginae	Victoria Regina	*Betula lenta*	Sweet birch
Agave vilmoriniana	Octopus agave	*Betula nigra*	River birch
Ageratum houstonianum	Ageratum	*Betula nigra* 'Heritage'	Heritage birch
Agropyron	Wheatgrass	*Betula papyriferya*	Paper birch
Ajuga	Carpet bugle	*Betula platyphylla*	White birch
Ajuga reptans	Carpet bugle	*Boltonia asteroides*	Boltonia
Albizia julibrissin	Silk tree	*Bougainvillea*	Bougainvillea
Albizia julibrissin	Mimosa silk tree	*Brachychiton populneus*	Bottle tree
Alcea rosea	Hollyhock	*Bracteantha*	Bracteantha
Allium moly	Lily leek	*Buchloe dactyloides*	Buffalo grass
Aloe	Aloe	*Buxus sempervirens*	Boxwood
Amelanchier	Juneberry	*Caladium*	Angel wings

Botanic Name	Common Name	Botanic Name	Common Name
Caladium	Caladium	*Clematis* hybrids	Clematis
Caladium × *hortulanum*	Angel wings	*Clematis paniculata*	Sweet autumn
Calamagrostis ×	Feather reed		clematis
acutiflora	grass	*Cocos nucifera*	Coconut palm
Calendula officinalis	Pot marigold	*Coleus*	Coleus
Callicarpa americana	Beauty berry	*Comptonia peregrina*	Sweet fern
Callistemon	Bottlebrush	*Cordyline australis*	Giant dracaena
Calluna	Heather	*Coreopsis*	Coreopsis
Caltha palustris	Marsh marigold	*Coreopsis verticillata*	Coreopsis
Campanula persicifolia	Peach-leafed	*Coreopsis verticillata*	Threadleaf
	bellflower		coreopsis
Campsis radicans	Trumpet creeper	*Cornus*	Dogwood
Capsicum annuum	Ornamental	*Cornus florida*	Japanese
	pepper		flowering crab
Caragana arborescens	Siberian pea	*Cornus florida*	Flowering
Carpinus	Hornbeam		dogwood
Carya	Pecans	*Cornus florida* × *kousa*	Rutgers hybrid
Carya	Hickory		dogwood
Carya aquatica	Water hickory	*Cornus kousa*	Kousa dogwood
Carya glabra	Pignut hickory	*Cornus nuttallii*	Pacific dogwood
Caryopteris	Caryopteris	*Cornus racemosa*	Gray dogwood
Cassia artemisioides	Wormwood	*Cornus stolonifera*	Red-osier
	senna		dogwood
Catalpa	Catalpa	*Corylus cornuta*	California hazel
Catharanthus roseus	Madagascar	*californica*	
	periwinkle	*Cosmos bipinnatus*	Cosmos
Cedrus atlantica	Blue atlas cedar	*Cotoneaster*	Cotoneaster
Celosia cristata	Celosia	*Cotoneaster simonsii*	Simons
Celtis	Hackberry		cotoneaster
Celtis occidentalis	Hackberry	*Crataegus crus-galli*	Cockspur
Cerastium tomentosum	Snow-in-summer		hawthorn
Ceratonia siliqua	Carob	*Crataegus phaenopyrum*	Washington
Cercis canadensis	Redbud		hawthorn
Cercocarpus ledifolius	Mountain	*Crocus*	Crocus
	mahogany	*Cryptomeria japonica*	Japanese cedar
Chaenomeles	Flowering quince	× *Cupressocyparis*	Leyland cypress
Chamaecyparis	False cypress	*leylandii*	
Chamaecyparis	Lawson false	*Cupressus*	Cypress
lawsoniana	cypress	*Cupressus macrocarpa*	Monterey
Chamaecyparis thyoides	Atlantic white		cypress
	cedar	*Cycas revoluta*	Sago palm
Chasmanthium	Northern sea oats	*Cynodon dactylon*	Bermuda grass
latifolium		*Dasylirion wheeleri*	Desert spoon
Chelone lyonii	Turtlehead	*Delosperma*	Ice plant
Chionanthus virginicus	Fringe tree	*Delphinium*	Delphinium
Chitalpa × hybrids	Chitalpa	*Dianthus*	Dianthus
Cinnamomum	Camphor tree	*Dianthus*	Pink
camphora		*Dianthus* × *allwoodii*	Allwood pink
Cistus	Rock rose	*Diospyros virginiana*	Persimmon
Cistus ladanifer	Crimson spot	*Dodonaea viscosa*	Purple hop bush
Cladrastis lutea	Yellowwood tree	'Purpurea'	

Botanic Name	Common Name	Botanic Name	Common Name
Dorotheanthus	Ice plant	*Helianthemum*	Sun rose
Dorotheanthus bellidiformis	Ice plant	*nummularium*	
Duchesnea indica	Mock strawberry	*Helichrysum braceteatum*	Strawflower
Echinacea	Echinacea	*Helictotrichon sempervirens*	Blue oat grass
Echinops ritra	Small globe thistle	*Hemerocallis*	Daylily
Elaeagnus angustifolia	Russian olive	*Hesperaloe parviflora*	Red yucca
Erianthis ravenae	Plume grass	*Heuchera*	Coralbells
Eriobottya japonica	Loquat	*Heuchera sanguinea*	Coralbells
Eriogonum umbellatum	Sulfur flower	*Hibiscus moscheutos*	Rose mallow
Eryngium	Sea holly	*Hibiscus syriacus*	Rose-of-Sharon
Eryngium amethystinum	Amethyst sea holly	*Hosta*	Hosta
		Iberis sempervirens	Candytuft
Eschscholtzia californica	California poppy	*Ilex aquifolium*	English holly
Eucalyptus sideroxylon	Red ironbark	*Ilex opaca*	American holly
Eucommia ulmoides	Hardy rubber tree	*Ilex vomitoria*	Yaupon holly
		Ipomoea	Morning glory
Euonymus alatus	Burning bush	*Iris*	Iris
Euonymus fortunei	Wintercreeper	*Iris ensata*	Japanese iris
Euphorbia	Spurge	*Iris pseudacorus*	Yellow flag
Fagus	Beech	*Iris sibirica*	Siberian iris
Fagus grandifolia	Beech	*Jacaranda mimosifolia*	Jacaranda
Festuca	Fine fescue	*Juglans nigra*	Black walnut
Festuca elatior	Tall fescue	*Juniperus*	Juniper
Festuca glauca	Blue fescue	*Juniperus communis*	Common juniper
Ficus benghalensis	Weeping fig	*Juniperus horizontalis*	Creeping juniper
Ficus pumila	Creeping fig	*Juniperus scopulorum*	Rocky Mountain juniper
Forestiera neomexicana	Desert olive		
Forsythia	Forsythia	*Juniperus silicifolia*	Southern red cedar
Fraxinus americana	White ash		
Fraxinus pensylvanica	Green ash	*Juniperus virginiana*	Eastern red cedar
Fremontodendron × 'California Glory'	Flannel bush		
		Justicia californica	Chuparosa
Gaillardia	Blanket flower	*Kalmia latifolia*	Mountain laurel
Gaillardia × grandiflora	Blanket flower	*Kniphofia*	Red-hot poker
Gaillardia pulchella	Blanket flower	*Kniphofia uvaria*	Red-hot poker
Gaultheria procumbens	Wintergreen	*Koelreuteria paniculata*	Golden-rain tree
Gelsemium sempervirens	Carolina yellow jasmine	*Lagerstromia indica*	Crape myrtle
		Lantana	Lantana
Geranium	Geranium	*Larix decidua*	European larch
Ginkgo biloba	Ginkgo	*Larix laricina*	Eastern larch
Gleditsia triacanthos	Honey locust	*Larix occidentalis*	Western larch
Gomphrena globosa	Globe amaranth	*Larix siberica*	Siberian larch
Gymnocladus dioica	Kentucky coffee tree	*Laurus nobilis*	Laurel
		Lavandula	Lavender
Hamamelis virginiana	Witch hazel	*Lavandula angustifolia*	English lavender
Hebe	Hebe	*Lavandula stoechas*	Spanish lavender
Hedera	Ivy	*Leucanthemum × superbum*	Shasta daisy
Hedera canariensis	Algerian ivy		
Hedera helix	English ivy	*Leucophyllum frutescens*	Texas ranger
		Leucothoe	Leucothoe

Botanic Name	Common Name	Botanic Name	Common Name
Leymus racemosus	Blue lyme grass	*Oenothera missouriensis*	Missouri
Leymus racemosus	Giant beach		primrose
'Glaucus'	grass	*Olea europaea*	Olive
Liatris	Gayfeather	*Olneya tesota*	Desert ironwood
Liatris	Blazing star	*Ophiopogon japonicus*	Mondo grass
Liatris	Gayfeather	*Opuntia*	Prickly pear
Ligularia	Ligularia	*Opuntia fiscusindica*	Prickly pear
Ligustrum	Privet	*Opuntia microdasys*	Bunny ears
Limonium latifolium	Sea lavender	*Originum*	Oregano
Liquidambar styraciflua	Sweetgum	*Osmunda regalis*	Royal fern
Liriodendron tulipifera	Tulip tree	*Ostrya virginiana*	Hop hornbeam
Liriope	Lilyturf	*Panicum virgatum*	Switch grass
Liriope muscari	Lilyturf	*Parkinsonia aculeata*	Jerusalem thorn
Liriope spicata	Lilyturf	*Parthenocissus*	Virginia creeper
Lobelia	Lobelia	*quinquefolia*	
Lobelia cardinalis	Cardinal	*Paspalum notatum*	Bahia grass
	flower	*Paspalum vaginatum*	Seashore
Lobularia maritima	Sweet alyssum		paspalum
Magnolia	Magnolia	*Pelargonium* hybrids	Geranium
Magnolia grandiflora	Southern	*Pennisetum*	Fountain grass
	magnolia	*Penstemon*	Penstemon
Magnolia virginiana	Sweetbay	*Penstemon eatonii*	Eaton's
Mahonia aguifolium	Mahonia		penstemon
Malus	Crab apple	*Perovskia atriplicifolia*	Russian sage
Malva moschata	Musk mallow	*Petunia* × hybridus	Petunia
Matteuccia struthiopteris	Ostrich fern	*Phlox paniculata*	Garden phlox
Melaleuca linariifolia	Flaxleaf paper-	*Physocarpus*	Nine-bark
	bark	*Picea*	Spruce
Melampodium	Blackfoot daisy	*Picea abries*	Norway spruce
leucanthum		*Picea engelmannii*	Engelmann
Melampodium	Melampodium		spruce
poludosum		*Picea glauca*	White spruce
Metasequoia	Dawn redwood	*Picea mariana*	Black spruce
glyptostroboides		*Picea omorika*	Serbian spruce
Mimulus	Monkey flower	*Picea pungens*	Colorado blue
Miscanthus sinensis	Eulalia grass		spruce
Miscanthus sinensis	Maiden grass	*Picea rubens*	Red spruce
Mitchella repans	Partridgeberry	*Pieris japonica*	Pieris
Morus rubra	Red mulberry	*Pinus*	Pine
Myrica	Bayberry	*Pinus banksiana*	Jack pine
Myrica cerifera	Wax myrtle	*Pinus contorta*	Lodgepole pine
Myrica cerifera	Southern wax	*Pinus echinata*	Shortleaf pine
	myrtle	*Pinus edulis*	Pinyon pine
Myrica pensylvanica	Bayberry	*Pinus eldarica*	Afghanistan pine
Myrtus communis	Myrtle	*Pinus elliottii*	Sand pine
Narcissus	Daffodil	*Pinus halepensis*	Aleppo pine
Nerium oleander	Oleander	*Pinus lambertiana*	Sugar pine
Nierembergia caerulea	Nierembergia	*Pinus mugo*	Swiss mountain
Nyssa aquatica	Water tupelo		pine
Nyssa sylvatica	Black tupelo	*Pinus nigra*	Austrian pine
Nyssa sylvatica	Black gum	*Pinus ponderosa*	Ponderosa pine

Botanic Name	Common Name	Botanic Name	Common Name
Pinus radiata	Monterey pine	Quercus luarifolia	Laurel oak
Pinus resinosa	Red pine	Quercus macrocarpa	Bur oak
Pinus strobus	Eastern white pine	Quercus palustris	Pin oak
		Quercus rubra	Northern red oak
Pinus sylvestris	Scotch pine	Quercus rubra	Red oak
Pinus taeda	Loblolly pine	Quercus shumardii	Shumard oak
Pinus thunbergiana	Japanese black pine	Quercus velutina	Black oak
		Quercus virginiana	Live oak
Pistacia chinensis	Chinese pistachio	Ratibida columnifera	Prairie coneflower
		Rhaphiolepis umbellata	Yeddo
Pittosporum	Pittosporum	Rhododendron	Azalea
Pittosporum tobira	Japanese pittosporum	Rhododendron	Rhododendron
		Rhus	Sumac
Platanus	Sycamore	Rhus lancea	African sumac
Platanus occidentalis	Sycamore	Rhus typhina	Staghorn sumac
Platycodon grandiflorus	Balloon flower	Robinia	Black locust
Poa pratensis	Kentucky bluegrass	Robinia × ambigua	Hybrid locust
		Robinia pseudoacacia	Black locust
Podocarpus	Podocarpus	Rosa banksiae lutea	Lady banks rose
Populus	Cottonwood	Rosa gallica var. officinalis	Apothecary's rose
Populus	Aspen		
Populus deltoides	Eastern cottonwood	Rosa palustris scandens	Swamp rose
		Rosa rugosa	Rugosa rose
Portulaca grandiflora	Moss rose	Rosa sericea pteracantha	Wingthorn rose
Portulaca grandiflora	Rock rose	Rosa setigera	Prairie rose
Portulaca oleracea	Portulaca	Rosa spinosissima	Scotch rose
Portulaca oleracea	Purslane	Rosa virginiana	Virginia rose
Portulaca oleracea	Moss rose	Rosa wichuraina	Memorial rose
Potentilla	Potentilla	Rosa woodsii var. fendleri	Sierra Nevada rose
Potentilla fruticosa	Potentilla		
Potentilla neumanniana	Spring cinquefoil	Rosmarinus officinalis	Rosemary
Prosopis glandulosa	Mesquite	Rosmarinus officinalis 'Prostratus'	Creeping rosemary
Prunus	Smooth-bark cherries	Rosmarinus officinalis 'Prostratus'	Prostrate rosemary
Prunus americana	Wild plum		
Prunus caroliniana	Cherry laurel	Roystonea elata	Royal palm
Prunus lyonii	Catalina cherry	Rudbeckia	Rudbeckia
Prunus serotina	Black cherry	Rudbeckia	Black-eyed Susan
Pseudotsuga menziesii	Douglas fir	Sabal mexicana	Texas palmetto
Pyrus calleryana 'Bradford'	Bradford pear	Sabal palmetto	Palmetto
		Sabal palmetto	Sabal palmetto
Quercus	Live oak	Sabal palmetto	Cabbage palm
Quercus	Oak	Sabal palmetto	Cabbage palmetto
Quercus alba	White oak	Salix	Willow
Quercus bicolor	Swamp white oak	Salvia	Sage
		Salvia greggii	Autumn sage
Quercus coccinea	Scarlet oak	Sansevieria	Snakeplant
Quercus garryana	Oregon white oak	Santolina	Santolina
		Santolina	Lavender cotton
Quercus ilex	Holly oak	Sanvitalia procumbens	Creeping zinnia
Quercus laevis	Turkey oak	Sapindus drummondii	Soapberry

Botanic Name	Common Name	Botanic Name	Common Name
Sassafras albidum	Sassafras	*Tristania conferta*	Brisbane box
Scaevola aemula	Scaevola	*Tsuga*	Hemlock
Schinus molle	California pepper	*Tsuga canadensis*	Hemlock
Schinus terebinthifolius	Brazilian pepper	*Tsuga canadensis*	Eastern hemlock
Sciadopitys verticillata	Japanese umbrella pine	*Ulmus*	Elm
		Ulmus parvifolia	Chinese elm
Sedum	Sedum	*Ulmus pumila*	Siberian elm
Sedum	Sundrop	*Ungnadia speciosa*	Mexican buckeye
Sedum	Stonecrop	*Uniola paniculata*	Sea oats
Sedum × 'Autumn Joy'	Autumn joy sedum	*Vaccinium angustifolium*	Lowbush blueberry
Sempervivum	Hen-and-chicks	*Vaccinium pallidum*	Dry-land blueberry
Senecio cineraria	Dusty miller	*Venedio*	Venedio
Serenoa repens	Saw palmetto	*Verbascum*	Verbascum
Solidago	Goldenrod	*Verbascum thapsus*	Mullein
Sophora secundiflora	Texas mountain laurel	*Verbascum thapsus*	Verbascum
		Verbena	Verbena
Sorbus	Mountain ash	*Verbena bonariensis*	Verbena
Spartina pectinata	Prairie cordgrass	*Veronica*	Speedwell
Stachys	Lamb's ears	*Viburnum dentatum*	Arrowwood
Stachys byzantina	Lamb's ears	*Viburnum lentago*	Nannyberry
Stenotaphrum secundatum	St. Augustine grass	*Viburnum prunifolium*	Blackhaw viburnum
Stewartia	Stewartia	*Viburnum suspensum*	Sandankwa viburnum
Syragrus romanzoffiana	Queen palm		
Syringa	Lilac	*Vinca minor*	Vinca
Syringa emodi	Himalayan lilac	*Waldsteinia ternata*	Barren strawberry
Syringa meyeri	Meyer lilac		
Syringa microphylla	Littleleaf lilac	*Washington filifera*	California fan palm
Syringa patula	Manchurian lilac		
Syringa persica	Persian lilac	*Washingtonia*	Washington palm
Syringa reticulata	Japanese tree lilac	*Washingtonia robusta*	Washington palm
Tagetes	Marigold	*Washingtonia robusta*	Thread palm
Tamarix	Tamarisk	*Yucca*	Yucca
Taxodium distichum	Bald cypress	*Yucca brevifolia*	Joshua tree
Thuja	Arborvitae	*Yucca schidigera*	Mojave yucca
Thuja occidentalis	Arborvitae	*Zauschneria californica*	California fuchsia
Thymus	Thyme		
Tilia americana	American linden	*Zelkova serrata*	Zelkova
Tilia cordata	Littleleaf linden	*Zinnia*	Zinnia
Tithonia rotundifolia	Mexican sunflower	*Zoysia*	Zoysia grass
Trachelospermum jasminoides	Star jasmine		
Trillium	Trillium		

General Index

Page numbers in **bold** indicate charts; page numbers in *italic* indicate drawings.

A

Acclimating (hardening) plants, 43–44, 51, 55–58, *56*, 299
Achillea (*Achillea* × 'Coronation Gold'), **167**
Acidity (pH) of soil, 15, 91, 105, 106, 107, 122, 141
Aerobic bacteria, 121
Afghanistan pine (*Pinus eldarica*), **166, 240, 241**
African daisy (*Arctotheca populifolia*), **189**
African sumac (*Rhus lancea*), **166, 240, 241**
Ageratum (*Ageratum houstonianum*), **99,** 231, **233,** 378, *378*
Air (oxygen) for fire, 176–77
Aleppo pine (*Pinus halepensis*), **166, 240, 241**
Algerian ivy (*Hedera canariensis*), **98**
Alkali grasses, 99, **99**
Alliums, 123, **123**
Allwood pink (*Dianthus* × *allwoodii*), **99**
Aloe (*Aloe* spp.), **168**
Alternaria blights, 261
Amending soil, 10–16, **12,** *13,* **14,** *16,* 229
American holly (*Ilex opaca*), **80**
American Horticultural Society, 24
American Horticultural Society's A-Z Encyclopedia of Garden Plants, 57
American linden (*Tilia americana*), **81**
Amethyst sea holly (*Eryngium amethystinum*), **238**
Amur maple (*Acer ginnala*), **165**
Amur maple (*Acer tataricum ginnala*), **80**
Anacyclus (*Anacyclus depressus*), **165**
Anaerobic bacteria, 121
Angelonia (*Angelonia angustifolia* 'Blue Summer Orchid'), **233**

Angel wings (caladium) (*Caladium* 'Pink Gem,' 'Red Frill'), **233**
Angel wings (*Caladium* × *hortulanum*), **214**
Annuals
 drought resilient, **165–66**
 hail damage, 217–18
 heat resilient, 232–33, **233**
 salt resilience, 99, **99**
 "Top 100" list, 376–81
Anther, 252, *252*
Anthracnose, 263–64
Apothecary's rose (*Rosa gallica* var. *officinalis*), **307**
Arborvitae (*Thuja occidentalis*), **81,** 85, *85*
Arborvitae (*Thuja* spp.), **156**
Arnold Arboretum, 23
Arrowwood (*Viburnum dentatum*), **238**
Artemisia (*Artemisia* spp.), **99, 165, 168,** 330, *330*
Asparagus fern (*Asparagus densiflorus* 'Sprengeri'), **167**
Aspen (*Populus* spp.), **81,** 272, *272,* **272,** 273
Astilbe, 155
Atlantic white cedar (*Chamaecyparis thyoides*), **81**
Austrian pine (*Pinus nigra*), **307**
Autumn joy sedum (*Sedum* × 'Autumn Joy'), **167, 238**
Autumn sage (*Salvia greggii*), **68**
Azadirachtin, 260
Azalea (*Rhododendron* spp.), **81**

B

Back-burner system for compost, *13,* 13–14
Background climate, microclimates, 25, 26
Bacteria damage, 51, 114, 120–21

Bahia grass *(Paspalum notatum)*, 123, **123, 162**

Bald cypress *(Taxodium distichum)*
drought resilience, **167**
flood resilience, **134**
hail resilience, **213**
ice and snow resilience, **80**
"Top 100" list, *350*, 350–51
wind resilience, **311**, 317

Balloon flower *(Platycodon grandiflorus)*, **212**

Barberry *(Berberis* spp.), **68**

Bark-in branch unions, *312*, 312–13

Bark of trees as lightning predictor, 271, *271*, 273

Bark-out branch unions, 311–12, *312*

Bark splits from cold, *61*, 61–62

Barren strawberry *(Waldsteinia ternata)*, **165**

Barriers, 109, 111

Basket-of-gold *(Aurinia saxatilis)*, **126**

Bayberry *(Myrica pensylvanica)*, **98**

Bayberry *(Myrica* spp.), **165**

Bearberry *(Arctostaphylos uva-ursi)*, **68, 165, 212**, 365, *365*

Beauty berry *(Callicarpa americana)*, **167**

Beeches *(Fagus)* and lightning, 270–71

Beech *(Fagus grandifolia)*, **311**

Beech *(Fagus* spp.), **80**, 272, **272, 314**, *361*, 361–62

Begonia *(Begonia* × *semperflorens-cultorum)*, **233**, 379, *379*

Bending of plants under pressure, 83–85, *85*

Bergenia *(Bergenia* spp.), **213**

Berms, 128, **128**, 307–8, *308*

Bermuda grass *(Cynodon dactylon)*, **99**, 123, **123, 162**, 181, 382, *382*

Bermuda high, *221*, 221–22

Bermuda 'Princess,' 242, *242*

Birch *(Betula* spp.), **81**, 85, **172**, 272, **272**, *353*, 353–54

Birds, protecting, 210–11

Black cherry *(Prunus serotina)*, **81**, 123, **123**

Black end, 172

Black-eyed Susan *(Rudbeckia* spp.), **165**, 335, *335*

Blackfoot daisy *(Melampodium leucanthum)*, **167**

Black gum *(Nyssa sylvatica)*, **80**, 123, **123**

Blackhaw viburnum *(Viburnum prunifolium)*, **238**

Black locust *(Robinia pseudoacacia)*, **314**

Black locust *(Robinia* spp.), **81**

Black oak *(Quercus velutina)*, 123, **123**

Black spruce *(Picea mariana)*, 73

Black tupelo *(Nyssa sylvatica)*, **188, 314**

Black walnut *(Juglans nigra)*, **80**, 123, **123**

Bladder cells, 97

Blade-leafed evergreens and fire, 186

Blanket flower *(Gaillardia pulchella)*, **233**

Blanket flower *(Gaillardia* spp.), **99, 126, 165**

Blanket flower *(Gaillardia* × *grandiflora)*, **238**, 330–31, *331*

Blazing star (gayfeather) *(Liatris* spp.), **165, 213, 239**, *324*, 324–25

Blindness, drought, 172–73

Blooming vs. non-blooming plants, 34

Blossom-end rot, 173

Blown away trees, 285–86

Blue atlas cedar *(Cedrus atlantica* 'Glauca'), **166, 168**

Blue fescue *(Festuca glauca)*, **213**, *371*, 371–72

Blue fescue *(Festuca glauca* 'Elijah Blue'), **99**

Blue gramma grass, **162**

Blue lyme grass *(Leymus racemosus)*, **165**, *374*, 374–75

Blue oat grass *(Helictotrichon sempervirens)*, **165, 213**, *375*, *375*

Bog (ground) fires, 178

Bolting, 235

Boltonia *(Boltonia asteroides)*, 335–36, *336*

Botrytis (gray mold), 258–60

Bottlebrush buckeye *(Aesculus parviflora)*, **68**, *346*, 346–47

Bottlebrush *(Callistemon* spp.), **168**

Bottle tree *(Brachychiton populneus)*, **166**

Bougainvillea *(Bougainvillea* spp.), **98, 168**, 371, *371*

Box elder *(Acer negundo)*, **81, 314**

Boxwood *(Buxus sempervirens)*, **68**

Brace grafting, 75, *75*

Braces, 76

Bracket fungus, 316

Bracteantha (*Bracteantha* spp.), **233**
Bradford pear (*Pyrus calleryana* 'Bradford'), **81**
Brain (human), water contents of, 18
Branches, broken, 82–83, *83*, 86, 138–39, 318–19, *319*
Branch unions, 311–13, *312*, 314, **314**
Brazilian pepper (*Schinus terebinthifolius*), **166**
Breezes, 294–95
Bridge grafting, 78–82, *79*, 197, 198
Brisbane box (*Tristania conferta*), **166**
Broadleaf evergreens, snow-removal, 78
Broken branches, 82–83, *83*, 86, 138–39, 318–19, *319*
Broken treetops, 86
Broken trunks, 87, 319
Brush (surface) fires, 178
Buckeye (*Aesculus* spp.), 354, *354*
Buffalo grass (*Buchloe dactyloides*), **162**, 181, **189**, 383–84, *384*
Buffer areas, 181–82
Buffers
  microclimates as, 22–32, 48–49, *49*
  soil resilience, 7–16
  water for weather resilience, 16–22
Bunny ears (*Opuntia microdasys*), **167**
Burning bush (*Euonymus alatus*), **238**, 347, *347*
Bur oak (*Quercus macrocarpa*), **165**, **168**, *352*, 352–53
Butterflyweed (*Asclepias tuberosa*), **165**, 336, *336*

C
Cabbage palmetto (*Sabal palmetto*), **98**, **311**
Cabbage palm (*Sabal palmetto*), **168**, 354–55, *355*
CA (calcium), 15
Caladium (angel wings) (*Caladium* 'Pink Gem,' 'Red Frill'), **233**
Calcium (CA), 15
Calcium chloride, 102, *102*, **104**
California buckeye (*Aesculus californica*), 272, **272**
California fan palm (*Washington filifera*), **168**, **188**
California fuchsia (*Zauschneria californica*), **167**

California hazel (*Corylus cornuta californica*), **188**
California pepper (*Schinus molle*), **166**, **240**, **241**
California poppy (*Eschscholtzia californica*), **165**, 377, *377*
Camphor tree (*Cinnamomum camphora*), **241**
Candytuft (*Iberis sempervirens*), **167**, **189**, 337, *337*
Canopy of survivor trees, 317
Capillary flow, 93, *93*, 94
Capillary water, 132, *148*, 148–49
Cardinal flower (*Lobelia cardinalis*), 134, **134**, 155
Carob (*Ceratonia siliqua*), **166**
Carolina yellow jasmine (*Gelsemium sempervirens*), **168**, 304, **304**
Carpet bugle (*Ajuga reptans*), **165**, **189**, **238**
Carpet bugle (*Ajuga* spp.), **212**, 365–66, *366*
Carrots, 216, 234
Carthage, 101
Caryopteris (*Caryopteris* spp.), **68**
Catalina cherry (*Prunus lyonii*), **166**
Catalogs for buying plants, 33
Catalpa (*Catalpa* spp.), **80**
Cation exchange capacity (CEC), 10
Celosia (*Celosia cristata*), **233**
Center of gravity of tree, 317
Century plant (*Agave americana*), **99**, **168**
Cherry laurel (*Prunus caroliniana*), **168**
Chill damage, 43–46, 53–54, 216
Chill requirements, 223–24
Chinese elm (*Ulmus parvifolia*), **81**
Chinese pistachio (*Pistacia chinensis*), **166**
Chitalpa (*Chitalpa* × hybrids), **166**
Chloroplasts and chill damage, 44–45
Chlorosis, 135–36
Chokeberry (*Aronia* spp.), 342, *342*
Chuparosa (*Justicia californica*), **166**
City microclimates, 26–27
Clay pots, 95–96
Clay soils, 8–9, *8–9*, 32, 94
Clean landscape for fire protection, 185, 187
Clematis (*Clematis* hybrids), **126**
CMI (Crop Moisture Index), 151

Coarse loam, 7–11, *8–9,* 12
Cockspur hawthorn *(Crataegus crusgalli),* **239**
Coconut palm *(Cocos nucifera),* **98, 311,** 362, *362*
Codominant leaders, 313
Cold, 38–62. *See also* Ice and snow
Cold air, flow of, 40–41, *41*
Cold composting, 14
Cold-damaged roots, 59
Cold frames, 51, 54–55, 56, *56,* 207–8
Cold spots, identifying, 40–41, *41*
Cold-weather and water, 17–19, *19*
Coleus *(Coleus* spp.), 214
Coleus *(Coleus* × *hybridus* 'Burgundy Sun'), **233**
Colloids, 121–22
Colorado blue spruce *(Picea pungens),* 163, **171, 307,** 355, *355*
Colorado blue spruce *(Picea pungens glauca),* **68,** 73
Color of snow, 66
Comatose garden, 144
Common juniper *(Juniperus communis),* 163
Compact myrtle *(Myrtus communis* 'Compacta'), **166**
Companion planting, 20, 209
Compatible solutes, 96
Compost
    back-burner system for, *13,* 13–14
    cold composting, 14
    drought resilience and, 157
    salt resilience and, 101
    soil amending, 10, 11, 12, *13,* 13–14, *14*
Conifers, 272, **272**
Conservation laws, 127
Container plants, 54–55, 243–45, *244*
"Controlled" fires, 199
Cool-season grasses, 382
Coralbells *(Heuchera sanguinea),* 154, **167, 238**
Coralbells *(Heuchera* spp.), **126,** 337, *337*
Coreopsis *(Coreopsis* spp.), 123, **123, 126, 165,** 338, *338*
Coreopsis *(Coreopsis verticillata),* **238**
Cork cambium, 271, *271,* 273
Cosmos *(Cosmos bipinnatus),* 165
Cotoneaster *(Cotoneaster* spp.)
    drought resilience, 164, **165, 168**
    fire resilience, **189**

hail resilience, **212**
ice and snow resilience, **68**
"Top 100" list, 369, *369*
Cottonwood *(Populus* spp.), 272, **272**
Crab apple *(Malus* spp.), **81, 262**
Crape myrtle *(Lagerstromia indica),* **168, 311**
Creeping fig *(Ficus pumila),* **168**
Creeping juniper *(Juniperus horizontalis),* **238**
Creeping red fescue, **189**
Creeping rosemary *(Rosmarinus officinalis* 'Prostratus'), **189**
Creeping zinnia *(Sanvitalia procumbens),* **233**
Crimson spot *(Cistus ladanifer),* **166**
Crocus *(Crocus* spp.), 331, *331*
Crop Moisture Index (CMI), 151
Crown fires, 178
Crown (top) kill, 198–99
Cuomo, Mario, 320
Cuttings, vulnerability to wind, 299
Cypress *(Cupressus* spp.), **168**

D
Daffodil *(Narcissus* spp.), 332, *332*
Dawn redwood *(Metasequoia glyptostroboides),* **80**
Daylily *(Hemerocallis* cultivars), 134, **134,** 218
Daylily *(Hemerocallis* spp.)
    drought resilience, 155, **167**
    fire resilience, **189**
    flood resilience, 123, **123,** 134, **134**
    heat resilience, **233**
    salt resilience, **99**
    "Top 100" list, 33, *326,* 326–27
Deaths from hail, 210
Deciduous trees
    fire damage, 195
    ice and snow resilience, 80–81, **80–81**
    salt resilience, 108–9
    snow- and ice-sensitivity, *81*
Decks for fire protection, 183
Deep (too) planting of trees, 301
Deer, 67–68, **68**
Defensible space landscaping, 175, 180, *180*
Defensive landscaping, 4–5. *See also* Designing gardens and lawns
Defoliation, 317

Deicing products, 91, 92–93, *102*, 102–4, **104**

Delphinium (*Delphinium* spp.), 123, **123**, **126**

Depth and temperature of water, 124, 125

Desert ironwood (*Olneya tesota*), **241**

Desert olive (*Forestiera neomexicana*), **167**

Desert spoon (*Dasylirion wheeleri*), **167**

Desiccation, 48

Designing gardens and lawns. *See also* Plant selection

  cold resilience, 48–49, *49*

  drought resilience, 154–56, *155*

  fire resilience, 179–85, *180*, *185*, 192–94

  flood resilience, 113–16

  hail resilience, 208–10, *209*, 215, 216, 217

  heat resilience, 229–31

  humidity resilience, 248–54, 255–56, *256*

  ice and snow resilience, 72–78, *75*, *77*

  lightning resilience, 274, 276–80, *279*

  salt resilience, 100–107

  wind resilience, 294–302, *297*

Dew point, 42

Dianthus (*Dianthus* 'Melody Pink'), **233**

Dieback, 62

Direct salt damage, reversing, 107–11

Dittmer, H. J., 115

Divisions, vulnerability to wind, 298

Dogwood (*Cornus* spp.), **80**

Dominant trees, 134, **134**

Double-leader trees, 313, 319

Douglas fir (*Pseudotsuga menziesii*), **188**

Downy mildew of lettuce, 260–61

Drainage and salt, 92, *93*, 93–94, 104–6

Drip irrigation, 160, *160*

Drip line, 231

Driveways and access, 192–93

Drought, 145–73

Drought tolerance, 164–69, **165–68**

Dry climate plants, 154

Drying winds, *297*, 297–97

Dry-land blueberry (*Vaccinium pallidum*), **165**

Dry streambeds, 129–30, **130**

Dry wells, 131–32, **132**

Dust Bowl, 151–52

Dusty miller (*Senecio cineraria*), **99**, 164, **167**, 377, *377*

E

Eastern cottonwood (*Populus deltoides*), **134**

Eastern hemlock (*Tsuga canadensis*), 272, **272**, **307**, 357, *357*

Eastern larch (*Larix laricina*), 171

Eastern red cedar (*Juniperus virginiana*), **98**, 163, **165**, **238**, **307**, 351, *351*

Eastern white pine (*Pinus strobus*), **307**

Eaton's penstemon (*Penstemon eatonii*), **167**

Echinacea (*Echinacea* spp.), **165**, **233**, 332, *332*

Eggplant, 54, 57, **235**

Elevation dependent storms, 27

Elm (*Ulmus* spp.), 123, **123**, 272, **272**

Emergency-response-unit, 191

Endophytic tall fescue, 242, *242*

Engelmann spruce (*Picea engelmannii*), 73

English daisy, 231

English holly (*Ilex aquifolium*), **311**

English ivy (*Hedera helix*), **98**

English lavender (*Lavandula angustifolia*), **167**, **168**

Enzymes of plants, 228

Epinasty, 135

Equilibrium, 96–97

Erosion, 137–38

Escape routes, 191

Eulalia grass (*Miscanthus sinensis*), **238**

European larch (*Larix decidua*), **307**

Evaluation of weather-resiliency, 4–5

Evergreens

  blade-leafed evergreens, 186

  broadleaf evergreens, 78

  fire damage, 196

  hail resilience, **213**

  ice and snow resilience, 80–81, **80–81**

  needled evergreens, 77, *77*, 186

  snow-removal strategies, 77, *77*

Excavations in wood, 316, 318

Extracellular spaces, 46, 48

F

Fair-weather systems, 221

False cypress (*Chamaecyparis* spp.), **68**, 72, **80**

False indigo (*Baptisia australis*), **165**

Fats and oils in plants and fire, 186–87

Feather reed grass (*Calamagrostis* × *acutiflora*), 372–73, *373*
Feather reed grass (*Calamagrostis* × *acutiflora* 'Karl Foerster'), **99**
Fe (iron), 15
Fence microclimates, 31–32
Fences, 303–5, 304, **304**
Fertilizer
  cold weather and, 49, 53
  heat and, 231
  lightning, fertilizer from, 269
  lightning damage and, 281–82, 283
  salty soil and, 92, 96
  weather-resilient garden and, 15
Field capacity, 149
Filipendula, 155
Fine fescue (*Festuca* spp.), **99,** 100
Fir (*Abies* spp.), **80, 156,** 272, **272**
Fire, 71, 174–99
Fire scars, 197
Flammable materials, storage of, 194
Flannel bush (*Fremontodendron* × 'California Glory'), **167**
Flash floods, 119, **128–33**
Flashover, 282–83, 285
Flaxleaf paperbark (*Melaleuca linariifolia*), **166, 241**
Floods, 112–44
Flowering dogwood (*Cornus florida*), 47, 123, **123, 156**
Flowering quince (*Chaenomeles* spp.), **165, 168**
Foehn, 174
Forsythia (*Forsythia* spp.), 343, *343*
Foundation plantings, 194
Fountain grass (*Pennisetum* spp.), **99**
Fractional analysis, 8–9, *8–9*
Franklin, Ben, 281
Fraser fir (*Abies fraseri*), **213**
Fraxinus spp., 272, **272**
Free capillary water, *148,* 148–49
Freeman maple (*Acer* × *freemanii*), **239**
Freeze damage, 42–43
French drains, *130,* 130–31, 132
Fringe tree (*Chionanthus virginicus*), 47
Frost, Robert, 84
Frost blankets, 50–51
Frost damage, 42–43
Frost heaving, 58–59
Frost protection devices, 49–51, *50*
Fuel for fire, 176

Fujita Scale of Strength, 291, 292
Fungi, 116, 250–51
Funnel cloud, 292–93

G

Gardener's A-Z Guide to Growing Flowers from Seed to Bloom, The, 57
Gardening in the heat, 220, 227
Garden phlox (*Phlox paniculata*), **262**
Gayfeather (blazing star) (*Liatris* spp.), **165, 213, 239,** *324,* 324–25
Genus and drought, 171
Geography
  of hail, 205
  of heat, 222–23, 224, 226
  of ice storms, 74
Geologic material, weathering and salt, 92
Geranium, hardy (*Geranium* spp.), **126**
Geranium (*Geranium* spp.), 333, *333*
Geranium (*Pelargonium* hybrids), 123, **123**
Giant beach grass (*Leymus racemosus* 'Glaucus'), **99**
Giant dracaena (*Cordyline australis*), **166**
Ginkgo (*Ginkgo biloba*), **68, 80, 98, 166,** 353, *353*
Girdling, 198, 302
Global warming, 222, 254–55
Globe amaranth (*Gomphrena globosa*), **165**
Golden-rain tree (*Koelreuteria paniculata*), **166, 240,** *362,* 362–63
Goldenrod (*Solidago* spp.), *338,* 338–39
Grasses. *See* Lawn grasses; Ornamental grasses
Gravitational water, 132, 148, *148*
Gray dogwood (*Cornus racemosa*), **188**
Gray foliage plants for drought, 164
Gray mold (botrytis), 258–60
Gray snow mold, 89
Green ash (*Fraxinus pensylvanica*), **134**
Green floods, 113, 116–17, **128–33,** 137
Greenhouses (holding houses), 17–18
Greensand for soil, 11, 12
Ground (bog) fires, 178
Ground covers. *See* Vines and ground covers
Growth after flood, lack of, 143–44
Guard cells, 297, *297*
Guttation, 250
Gypsum (white alkali), 106–7

H

Hackberry (*Celtis occidentalis*), **188, 239, 240**
Hackberry (*Celtis* spp.), **81, 314**
Hail, 200–218, 387
Hail netting, 207, 217, 218
Hail shaft, 202
Hardening plants, 43–44, 51, 55–58, *56*, 299
Hardiness changes through seasons, 41–42
Hardiness mysteries, 47
Hardiness zone map, 22–24, 40, 389
Hardscapes, 183–84, 209–10, 274
Hard surface microclimates, 31
Hardy rubber tree (*Eucommia ulmoides*), **239, 240**
Healing methods and fresh starts, 35–37
  cold, 38–62
  drought, 145–73
  fire, 71, 174–99
  flood, 112–44
  hail, 200–218
  heat, 219–46
  humidity, 53, 247–64
  ice and snow, 63–89
  lightning, 265–86
  salt, 90–111
  wind, 287–322
Heat, 219–46
Heat canker, 246
Heat exhaustion, 220, 227
Heat for fire, 176
Heather (*Calluna* spp.), **212**
Heat index, 219–20
Heat lightning, 270
Heat-shock proteins of plants, 228
Heat wave, 222, 224, 226
Hebe (*Hebe* spp.), **311**
Hedge maple (*Acer campestre*), **239, 240**
Hedges, 181–82, 306
Height of target and lightning, 268–69
Hemlock (*Tsuga canadensis*), **80, 156**
Hemlock (*Tsuga* spp.), 272, **272**
Hen-and-chicks (*Sempervivum* spp.), **165**
Heritage birch (*Betula nigra* 'Heritage'), **68, 172**
Hexagon shape of snow, 65
Hickory (*Carya* spp.), 123, **123, 188**

High-sodium (sodic) soils, 91, 94–95, 106–7
Hilltop microclimates, 27
Himalayan lilac (*Syringa emodi*), **262**
Holding houses (greenhouses), 17–18
Hollyhock (*Alcea rosea*), **165, 212**
Holly oak (*Quercus ilex*), **168**
Home protection from fire, 191–94
Honey locust, thornless (*Gleditsia triacanthos*), 356, *356*
Honey locust (*Gleditsia triacanthos*), **81, 134, 165, 168**
Hop hornbeam (*Ostrya virginiana*), **188, 314**
Hornbeam (*Carpinus* spp.), **314**
Horse chestnut (*Aesculus hippocastanum*), **98**
Hosta (*Hosta* spp.), 214
Hot caps, 51
House microclimates, 30–31
Houseplants and humidity, 256–58, *257*
Humidity, 20, 53, 247–64
Humidity microclimates, 32
Hurricanes, 287–90
Hybrid locust (*Robinia* × *ambigua* 'Idahoensis'), **166**
Hydraulics, 303
Hyphae, 251

I

Ice and snow, 63–89. *See also* Cold
Ice buffer, 20
Ice damage, 69–70, 72
Ice-jam floods, 118
Ice plant (*Delosperma* spp.), 367, *367*
Ice plant (*Dorotheanthus bellidiformis*), 97, **189**
Ice plant (*Dorotheanthus* spp.), **99, 212**
Ice storms, 73, 74
Impatiens, 155
Inspecting landscape for fire protection, 185
Instruments for weather station, 28–29, *29*, 387
Intermediate climate plants, 155
Internal temperatures of plants, 40
Interspecies planting, *158*, 159
Iris (*Iris* spp.), 123, **123**
Iron (Fe), 15
Ivy (*Hedera* spp.), **189**, *367*, 367–68

J

Jacaranda *(Jacaranda mimosifolia)*, **166,** 168

Jack pine *(Pinus banksiana)*, **80, 165**

Japanese barberry *(Berberis thunbergii)*, 165

Japanese black pine *(Pinus thunbergiana)*, **168**

Japanese cedar *(Cryptomeria japonica)*, **68, 81, 240**

Japanese flowering crab *(Cornus florida)*, **262**

Japanese iris *(Iris ensata)*, 134, **134**

Japanese maple *(Acer palmatum)*, **156**

Japanese pittosporum (*Pittosporum tobira* 'Variegata'), **167**

Japanese tree lilac *(Syringa reticulata)*, **262**

Japanese umbrella pine *(Sciadopitys verticillata)*, **80,** 358, *358*

Jerusalem thorn *(Parkinsonia aculeata)*, **166**

Jet stream, 38, 39

Joshua tree *(Yucca brevifolia)*, **188**

Jug-tree-watering system, *155,* 155–56

Juneberry. *See* Serviceberry *(Amelanchier* spp.)

Juniper, creeping *(Juniperus* spp.), 366, *366*

Juniper *(Juniperus* spp.), **81, 98,** 164, **165, 213**

K

Kentucky bluegrass *(Poa pratensis)*, 123, **123,** 162

Kentucky coffee tree *(Gymnocladus dioica)*, **80, 165,** 352, *352*

Korean fir *(Abies koreana)*, **213**

Kousa dogwood *(Cornus kousa)*, **262**

K (potassium), 15

L

Lady banks rose *(Rosa banksiae lutea)*, **262,** 304, **304**

Lamb's ears *(Stachys byzantina)*, **167**

Lamb's ears *(Stachys* spp.), **165**

Lantana *(Lantana* spp.), **98, 167, 168, 233**

Late blight (phytophthora), 122, 248–49, 283

Laurel *(Laurus nobilis)*, **166, 168**

Laurel oak *(Quercus luarifolia)*, **168**

Lavender cotton *(Santolina* spp.), **126, 165, 189, 240, 241,** 333, *333*

Lavender *(Lavandula* spp.), 123, **123, 126,** 154, **165,** 339, *339*

Lawn grasses
   burned lawns, 199
   drought resilience, 161–62, **162**
   fire resilience, 181, **189**
   flood damage, 141
   heat resilience, 242, *242*
   mulch vs., 52
   salt resilience, 99, **99,** 100
   "Top 100" list, 382–84

Lawson false cypress *(Chamaecyparis lawsoniana)*, **81**

Leaching the soil, 106

Leader trees, hazard, 301

Lead plant *(Amorpha canescens)*, **165, 168**

Leaf drop, 136–37

Leaf hairs, 164

Leaf scorch, 195–96

Leaning tree, 320

Leaves (emerging), vulnerability to wind, 300

Leaves of plants and drought, 164

Lenticels, 125

Lettuce, 235, **236,** 260–61

Leucothoe *(Leucothoe* spp.), **68**

Leyland cypress (× *Cupressocyparis leylandii)*, **240**

Lichens, 322

Light differences, microclimates, 25, *25,* 26

Lightning, 265–86

Ligularia *(Ligularia* spp.), 214

Lilac *(Syringa* spp.), **68, 262,** 264

Lily leek *(Allium moly)*, **126**

Lily-of-the-Nile *(Agapanthus africanus)*, **99**

Lilyturf *(Liriope muscari)*, **99**

Lilyturf *(Liriope spicata)*, **239**

Lilyturf *(Liriope* spp.), **189, 213,** 368, *368*

Limb damage, 82–83, *83,* 86, 138–39, 318–19, *319*

Linnaeus, Carolus, 47

Littleleaf lilac *(Syringa microphylla)*, **262**

Littleleaf linden *(Tilia cordata)*, **80**

Live oak *(Quercus* spp.), **98**

Live oak *(Quercus virginiana)*

Live oak (*Quercus virginiana*) (*continued*)
  drought resilience, **165, 168**
  fire resilience, **188**
  heat resilience, **240, 241**
  salt resilience, **98**
  "Top 100" list, *358, 358–59*
  wind resilience, **311, 314,** 317
Loam, 7–11, *8–9,* 12
Lobelia (*Lobelia* spp.), 123, **123**
Loblolly pine (*Pinus taeda*), 123, **123**
Location of lightning target, 268–69
Lodgepole pine (*Pinus contorta*), **80**
Loquat (*Eriobottya japonica*), **168**
Lost leader of double-leader tree, 319
Lowbush blueberry (*Vaccinium angusti-folium*), **238**
Lupine, 155

M

Madagascar periwinkle (*Catharanthus roseus*), 380–81, *381*
Madagascar periwinkle (*Catharanthus roseus* 'Parasol'), **233**
Magnesium (Mg), 15
Magnolia (*Magnolia* spp.), 363, *363*
Mahonia (*Mahonia aguifolium*), **189**
Maiden grass (*Miscanthus sinensis*), 372, *372*
Maidenhair fern (*Adiantum pedatum*), 214
Manchurian lilac (*Syringa patula*), 262
Manganese (Mn), 15
Manual of Cultivated Trees and Shrubs (Rehder), 23
Maple (*Acer* spp.), 272, **272**
Maps, hardiness zone, 22–24, 40, 389
Marigold (*Tagetes erecta,* Antigua series), **233**
Marigold (*Tagetes* spp.), 381, *381*
Marsh marigold (*Caltha palustris*), 134, **134**
Maximum annual temperature, 23
Mayonnaise jar test, 8–9, *8–9*
Melampodium (*Melampodium poludosum* 'Derby'), **233**
Melons, 54, 173, **235**
Memorial rose (*Rosa wichuraina*), **262**
Mesophytes, 166
Mesquite (*Prosopis glandulosa*), **166**
Mexican buckeye (*Ungnadia speciosa*), **167**

Mexican sunflower (*Tithonia rotundifo-lia*), **165, 233**
Meyer lilac (*Syringa meyeri*), **262**
Mg (magnesium), 15
Michigan State University, 47
Microclimates, 22–32, 48–49, *49*
Microorganisms in soil, 70, 114, 120–21
Mildew, **262**
Mimosa silk tree (*Albizia julibrissin*), **240**
Minimum annual temperature, 23
Missouri primrose (*Oenothera missouriensis*), **167**
Mn (manganese), 15
Mock strawberry (*Duchesnea indica*), **189**
Moist climate plants, 155
Moisture meters, 151, 161
Moisture of soil, recharged by snow, 71
Mojave yucca (*Yucca schidigera*), **188**
Mondo grass (*Ophiopogon japonicus*), **99,** *370, 370*
Monkey flower (*Mimulus* spp.), 134, **134**
Monterey cypress (*Cupressus macro-carpa*), **307**
Monterey pine (*Pinus radiata*), **188**
Morning glory (*Ipomoea* spp.), **165, 168,** *379, 379–80*
Moss growing on bark, 316
Moss rose (*Portulaca grandiflora*), **233**
Moss rose (*Portulaca oleracea*), **99,** 376, *376*
Mountain ash (*Sorbus* spp.), **314**
Mountain laurel (*Kalmia latifolia*), **68, 80**
Mountain mahogany (*Cercocarpus ledi-folius*), **167**
Mulch
  cold resilience and, 49, 52, 55
  drought resilience and, 159
  fire resilience and, 181
  heat resilience and, 230
  lawn grasses vs., 52
  salt resilience and, 101
  wind resilience and, 302
Mullein (*Verbascum thapsus*), **239**
Murphy's Oil Soap, 8
Musk mallow (*Malva moschata*), **165**
Mycelia, 251
Mycorrhiza, 116

N

Naming fires, 175–76
Nannyberry *(Viburnum lentago)*, **238**
National Oceanic and Atmospheric
     Administration (NOAA), 275, 293
Native plants and microclimates, 24
Native species for survivor trees, 317
Needled evergreens, 77, *77*, 186
Neem oil, 260, 261
New growth, vulnerability to wind, 300
New-home-construction and wind,
     321–22
Nierembergia *(Nierembergia caerulea)*,
     233
Nine-bark *(Physocarpus* spp.), **165**
Nitrogen, 15
NOAA (National Oceanic and
     Atmospheric Administration), 275, 293
Normay maple *(Acer platanoides)*, **80,**
     240
Northern red oak *(Quercus rubra)*, **80**
Northern sea oats *(Chasmanthium lati-*
     folium), **99,** *375,* 375–76
Norway maple *(Acer platanoides)*, **239**
Norway spruce *(Picea abries)*, 73
Nurseries and microclimates, 24
Nutrient imbalance after flood, 141–42
Nutrients conservation from snow, 70
Nutrition and chill damage, 53

O

Oak *(Quercus* spp.), 123, **123,** 269–70,
     272, **272**
Octopus agave *(Agave vilmoriniana)*, **167**
Oenothera, 155
Ohio buckeye *(Aesculus glabra)*, **98**
Okra, 235, **235**
Oleander *(Nerium oleander)*, **68, 98, 168**
Olive *(Olea europaea)*, **166**
Open space areas, 180
Open spaces, 274–76
Orchards and wind, 301
Oregano *(Originum* spp.), **165,** 235
Oregon white oak *(Quercus garryana)*,
     188
Origin of plants and drought, 163
Ornamental grasses
     salt resilience, 99, **99**
     "Top 100" list, 371–81
Ornamental pepper *(Capsicum annuum)*,
     233

Ostrich fern *(Matteuccia struthiopteris)*,
     214
Overwintering, 17–19, *19,* 54–55
Oxygen (air) for fire, 176–77

P

Pacific dogwood *(Cornus nuttallii)*, **188**
Pacific madrone *(Arbutus menziesii)*, **189**
Palmer, Walter, 150–51
Palmer Drought Severity Index (PDSI),
     150–51
Palmetto *(Sabal palmetto)*, **98**
Palms, 98, **98, 168,** 272, **272**
Paper birch *(Betula papyriferya)*, **189**
Paper birch *(Betula papyriferya* 'Varen'),
     172
Paracelsus, 56
Parking lots, 245
Partridgeberry *(Mitchella repans)*, **212**
Passive protection, 50
Paths of lightning strike, 282
Patios for fire protection, 183
Paved surface microclimates, 31
Paw-paw *(Asimina triloba)*, **68**
PDSI (Palmer Drought Severity Index),
     150–51
Peach-leafed bellflower *(Campanula per-*
     sicifolia), **212,** 327, *327*
Peas, 236
Pecans *(Carya* spp.), 123, **123**
Penstemon *(Penstemon* spp.), **126,** 155,
     165, 212, 239, 339–40, *340*
Peppers, 54, 173, 234, 237
Perennials
     drought resilience, **165–68**
     fire resilience, **189**
     flood resilience, 134, **134**
     hail damage, 218
     heat resilience, 238, **238–39, 241**
     salt resilience, 99, **99**
     "Top 100" list, 324–42
Perlite for soil, 10–11, 12
Permanent wilting point, 149
Persian lilac *(Syringa persica)*, **262**
Persimmon *(Diospyros virginiana)*, **134,**
     188, *356,* 356–57
Petunia, 231
Petunia *(Petunia* × *hybridus* Carpet
     series, 'Happy Dream'), **233**
Phases (states) of water, 16, 17–20, *19*
Phlox for humidity, **262,** 264

pH of soil, 15, 91, 105, 106, 107, 122, 141
Phosphorus (P), 15
Photosynthesis of plants, 227–28
Phytophthora (late blight), 122, 248–49, 283
Pieris *(Pieris japonica)*, **68**
Pignut hickory *(Carya glabra)*, **165, 168**
Pileated woodpecker, 316, 318
Pine *(Pinus* spp.), 272, **272**
Pink *(Dianthus* spp.), **126**
Pink snow mold, 89
Pin oak *(Quercus palustris)*, **81, 165, 168, 188**
Pinyon pine *(Pinus edulis)*, **166**
Pittosporum *(Pittosporum* spp.), **98, 189, 307,** 349, *349*
Plant Heat-Zone Map, 24
Plant selection. *See also* Designing gardens and lawns
    cold resilience, 47, **47,** 57–58
    drought resilience, 154–55, **156, 162,** 163–71, **165–68, 171**
    fire resilience, 181–83, 186–91, **188–89**
    flood resilience, 123, **123,** 126, **126,** 134, **134**
    hail resilience, 211–14, **212–13,** 215, 216, 217
    heat resilience, 230, 231–42, **233, 235–36, 238–42**
    humidity resilience, 258, 261, **262–63**
    ice and snow resilience, 68, **68,** 72, 73, 80–81, **80–81**
    lightning resilience, 272, **272**
    salt resilience, 98–99, **98–99,** 101, 111
    weather-resilient garden and, 5, 32–34
    wind resilience, 304, **304,** 305, **307, 311, 314,** 317
Plants' reaction to injury, 36–37
Plastic-covered hoops, 74
Plume grass *(Erianthis ravenae)*, **165**
Podocarpus *(Podocarpus* spp.), **307**
Pollen sac, 252
Pollination and humidity, 251–54, *252*
Ponderosa pine *(Pinus ponderosa)*, **188**
Ponding floods, 113, 117, **128–33**
Pores, 114
Portulaca *(Portulaca oleracea)*, **233**
Potassium (K), 15
Potatoes, **236,** 237
Potentilla *(Potentilla fruticosa)*, **171**
Potentilla *(Potentilla* spp.), **165,** 344, *344*

Pot-in-pot system, 244–45
Pot marigold *(Calendula officinalis)*, **99**
Powdery mildew, 264
P (phosphorus), 15
Prairie coneflower *(Ratibida colum-nifera)*, **165**
Prairie cordgrass *(Spartina pectinata),* 373, *373*
Prairie cordgrass *(Spartina pectinata* 'Aureomarginata'), 97, **99**
Prairie rose *(Rosa setigera),* 169
Praus, 2
Pressures endured by weather-resilient garden, 3, *3*
Prickly pear *(Opuntia fiscusindica),* **167**
Prickly pear *(Opuntia* spp.), **165, 168, 241,** 334, *334*
Privet *(Ligustrum* spp.), **165**
Prostrate rosemary *(Rosmarinus officinalis* 'Prostratus'), **213**
Pruning plants, 49, 185, *185*
Purple hop bush *(Dodonaea viscosa* 'Purpurea'), **167, 240, 241**
Purslane *(Portulaca oleracea),* 232
Pussytoes *(Antennaria* spp.), **166**

Q

Queen palm *(Arecastrum romanzoffi-anum),* **168,** 223
Queen palm *(Syragrus romanzoffiana),* **311**

R

Radiational cooling, 38–39
Rain gauges, 151, 161
Raised bed microclimates, 31
Raised beds, 105–6, 127–28, **128,** 157–58
Red buckeye *(Aesculus pavia),* 272, **272**
Redbud *(Cercis canadensis),* **80,** 123, **123, 188**
Red horse chestnut *(Aesculus × carnea),* **240**
Red-hot poker *(Kniphofia* spp.), **99, 189, 212, 239,** 327–28, *328*
Red-hot poker *(Kniphofia uvaria),* **167**
Red ironbark *(Eucalyptus sideroxylon),* **166**
Red maple *(Acer rubrum),* **156, 189, 239, 240, 314**
Red maple *(Acer rubrum* 'Columnare'), **307**

Red mulberry *(Morus rubra)*, 123, **123**
Red oak *(Quercus rubra)*, 123, **123, 189**
Red-osier dogwood *(Cornus stolonifera)*, **68, 311,** 344–45, *345*
Red pine *(Pinus resinosa)*, **81**
Red spruce *(Picea rubens)*, 73
Red yucca *(Hesperaloe parviflora)*, **167**
Refrigerator, chill damage from, 54
Rehder, Alfred, 23
Relative humidity, 257
Repairing soil, 104–7
Resources for weather-resilient garden, 386–387
Respiration of plants, 227–28
Retaining walls, 183–84
Reverse transpiration, 250
Rhododendron *(Rhododendron* spp.), **68, 80**
Ripeness and chill damage, 54
River birch *(Betula nigra)*, **172,** 317
Riverine floods, 113, 117–18, **128–33**
Road salt spray, 108–9
Rock and rock garden microclimates, 31
Rock rose *(Cistus* spp.), **189, 241**
Rock rose *(Portulaca grandiflora)*, **166,** 378, *378*
Rocks, weathering and salt, 92
Rocky Mountain juniper *(Juniperus scopulorum)*, **307**
Rocky Mountain maple *(Acer globrum)*, **188**
Rodent damage, 66, 78–82, *79*
Roof protection from fire, 194
Root damaged plants, vulnerability, 300
Roots and root hairs, 115–16, 119–20
Roots of survivor trees, 317
Rose mallow *(Hibiscus moscheutos)*, **99,** 134, **134**
Rosemary *(Rosmarinus officinalis)*
    drought resilience, 154, 164, **168**
    heat resilience, **235, 241**
    ice and snow resilience, **68**
    salt resilience, **99**
    "Top 100" list, 341–42, *342*
Rose-of-Sharon *(Hibiscus syriacus)*, **68**
Rot, 314–16, 318
Rotating cloud wall, 292
Row covers, *50,* 50–51, 52
Royal fern *(Osmunda regalis)*, 214
Royal palm *(Roystonea elata)*, **311**
Rudbeckia *(Rudbeckia* spp.), **239**

Rugosa rose *(Rosa rugosa)*
    drought resilience, **165, 168,** 169–70, **171**
    fire resilience, **189**
    heat resilience, **238**
    humidity resilience, **262, 262–63**
    salt resilience, **98**
    "Top 100" list, *343,* 343–44
    wind resilience, **307**
Russian olive *(Elaeagnus angustifolia)*
    drought resilience, **165, 166, 171**
    ice and snow resilience, **68**
    salt resilience, **98**
    "Top 100" list, 359, *359*
    wind resilience, **307**
Russian sage *(Perovskia atriplicifolia)*, **126**
Rust, 261–62
Rutgers hybrid dogwood *(Cornus florida × kousa)*, **262**

S

Sabal palmetto *(Sabal palmetto)*, **188**
Safety
    lightning, 275, **275**
    tornadoes, 293–94
Sage *(Salvia* spp.), **166**
Sago palm *(Cycas revoluta)*, **168**
Saline soils, *93,* 93–94, 104–6
Salt, 90–111
Salvia, 154
Sandankwa viburnum *(Viburnum suspensum)*, **167**
Sand percentage, determining, 8–9, *8–9*
Sand pine *(Pinus elliottii)*, **168**
Sandwich boards, 74
Sandy soil, 32
Santa Ana winds, 174–75
Santolina *(Santolina* spp.), 123, **123**
Saprophytes, 250
Sassafras *(Sassafras albidum)*, 123, **123, 188**
Saturated soil, *139–40,* 139–41
Saw palmetto *(Serenoa repens)*, **168**
Scaevola *(Scaevola aemula)*, 232, **233**
Scales of Strength, 291, 292
Scarlet oak *(Quercus coccinea)*, **189**
Scarred trees, 284–85
Scotch pine *(Pinus sylvestris)*, **68, 171**
Scotch rose *(Rosa spinosissima)*, 170
Screens for hail, 207

Sea holly (*Eryngium* spp.), **166**, *340*, 340–41

Sea lavender (*Limonium latifolium*), **99**

Sea oats (*Uniola paniculata*), **168**

Sea-salt damage, 111

Seashore paspalum (*Paspalum vaginatum*), **99**, 242, *242*

Sea thrift (*Armeria maritima*), **99**

Sedimentation, 118, 124, 125, 142–43

Sedum (*Sedum* 'Autumn Joy'), **99**

Sedum (*Sedum* spp.), *328*, 328–29

Seed damage from hail, 217

Seedlings, 298, 316

Serbian spruce (*Picea omorika*), 73

Serviceberry (shadbush, shadblow, juneberry) (*Amelanchier* spp.)

    ice and snow resilience, **68, 80**

    lightning resilience, 272, **272**

    "Top 100" list, 347–48, *347*

    wind resilience, **307, 311**

Shallow root systems, hazard, 302

Shape of snow, 65

Shasta daisy (*Leucanthemum* × *superbum*), 329, *329*

Shields, 72, 74, 82, 85, 86, 87, 88

Shortleaf pine (*Pinus echinata*), **81**

Shrub damage from hail, 215–16

Shrubs

    drought resilience, **165–67**

    fire resilience, 183, **189**

    heat resilience, 238, **238–41**

    salt resilience, 98, **98**

    "Top 100" list, 342–50

    wind resilience, **307, 311**

Shumard oak (*Quercus shumardii*), **165, 168**

Siberian elm (*Ulmus pumila*), **81**

Siberian iris (*Iris siberica*), 134, **134, 212,** *334*, 334–35

Siberian larch (*Larix sibirica*), 171

Siberian pea (*Caragana arborescens*), **165, 171, 307,** 348, *348*

Sidewalk salt, 109–10

Sierra Nevada rose (*Rosa woodsii* var. *fendleri*), 170

Silk tree (*Albizia julibrissin* 'Rosea'), **166**

Silt percentage, determining, 8–9, *8–9*

Silver maple (*Acer saccharinum*), **81, 134, 189, 314**

Silvermound artemisia (*Artemisia schmidtiana*), 123, **123, 126**

Simons cotoneaster (*Cotoneaster simonsii*), **307**

Site of garden, 229

Sleet vs. hail, 203

Slope microclimates, 28–30

Small globe thistle (*Echinops ritra*), **212**

Smooth-bark cherries (*Prunus* spp.), 272, **272**

Smudge pots, 19

Snakeplant (*Sansevieria* spp.), **241**

Snow. *See* Ice and snow

Snow, uniqueness of, 65–66

Snow-in-summer (*Cerastium tomentosum*), **166, 189,** 370, *370*

Snow-removal strategies, 76–78, *77*

Snow to ice transition, 68–69

Snow traps, 76, 255–56, *256*

Soaker hoses, 160

Soapberry (*Sapindus drummondii*), 363–64, *364*

Sodic (high-sodium) soils, 91, 94–95, 106–7

Sodium chloride, **104**

Soil

    drought and type of soil, 163

    fire changes to, 177

    floods, soil before floods, 113–16

    floods damage, 119–20, 121–22

    heat and, 226

    microclimates, soil differences in, 25, *25, 26*

    salt damage, 91

    snow benefits for, 70–71

Soil heaving, 70, 83–84

Soil microclimates, 32

Soil needles, 161

Soil resilience, 7–16

Soil tests, 14–16, *16*, 105, 106, 142

Soil triangle, 9, *9*

Southern magnolia (*Magnolia grandiflora*), **168, 188, 240, 241,** 311, **314**

Southern red cedar (*Juniperus silicifolia*), **168**

Southern wax myrtle (*Myrica cerifera*), **98,** 359–60, *360*

Spanish lavender (*Lavandula stoechas*), **167**

Species of plants and flood, 124, 125

Species of tree and lightning, 269–71

Specific heat, 16, *21*, 21–22

Speedwell (*Veronica* spp.), 134, **134**

Split branches, 318–19
Split stems, 87–88
Spot fires, 178
Spring, 88–89
Spring cinquefoil (Potentilla neumanniana), **189**
Sprinklers for hail protection, 208
Spruce (Picea spp.), 73, **80**, 272, **272**
Spurge (Euphorbia spp.), **166**
Squash, 173
St. Augustine grass (Stenotaphrum secundatum), **99**, 123, **123**
St. Elmo's fire, 277, 285
Stabilization, 4–5
Staggered rows for planting, 158, 158–59
Staghorn sumac (Rhus typhina), **165, 167**
Staking trees, 140, 140
Star jasmine (Trachelospermum jasminoides), **98, 168, 189**, 304, **304**, 349–50, 350
Stewartia (Stewartia spp.), 272, **272**
Stigma, 252, 252
Stomata (leaf pores), 122, 296, 297, 297
Stonecress (Aethionema spp.), **166**
Stonecrop (Sedum spp.), **166, 189**
Stone wall microclimates, 31–32
Stone walls, 184
Straight rows for planting, 158, 158
Strawflower (Helichrysum braceteatum), **166**
Structures for protection, 308–10, 309
Style, 252, 253
Suckers, vulnerability to wind, 298
Sugar maple (Acer saccharum), **156, 189, 314**
Sugar maple (Acer saccharum 'Green Mountain'), **239**
Sugar pine (Pinus lambertiana), **188**
Sulfur flower (Eriogonum umbellatum), **167**
Sumac (Rhus spp.), 345, 345
Sundrop (Sedum spp.), **166**
Sun rose (Helianthemum nummularium), **166**
Sunset National Garden Book, 23–24
Supercell, 202
Supercooling, 46
Surface (brush) fires, 178
Surface tension and water, 16, 20
Survivor trees, 317
Swales, 128–29, **129**

Swamp rose (Rosa palustris scandens), **262**
Swamp white oak (Quercus bicolor), 360, 360
Sweet alyssum (Lobularia maritima), **99**, 123, **123**, 380, 380
Sweet autumn clematis (Clematis paniculata), **239**
Sweetbay (Magnolia virginiana), **188, 311**, 317
Sweet birch (Betula lenta), **156**
Sweet fern (Comptonia peregrina), **98, 165, 168**, 346, 346
Sweetgum (Liquidambar styraciflua), **80, 134**, 364, 364
Sweet potatoes, **235**
Swimming pools for fire protection, 184
Swiss mountain pine (Pinus mugo), **213, 307**
Switch grass (Panicum virgatum), 374, 374
Sycamore (Platanus occidentalis), **134**
Sycamore (Platanus spp.), 272, **272**

T

Tall fescue (Festuca elatior), **99**, 100, 123, **123, 162**, 383, 383
Tamarisk (Tamarix spp.), **168, 311**
Taproot system, 141
Targets of lightning, 267–76, 271, **272**
Temperature differences in microclimates, 25, 26
Temperature of soil moderated from snow, 71
Tepee, water-filled plastic, 21, 21–22, 51
Testing plant for fire resilience, 190
Texas mountain laurel (Sophora secundiflora), **68**
Texas palmetto (Sabal mexicana), **98**
Texas ranger (Leucophyllum frutescens), **167, 241**
Threadleaf coreopsis (Coreopsis verticillata 'Moonbeam'), **167**
Thread palm (Washingtonia robusta), **98, 311**
Three-planting-wide windbreak, 305–6, 306
Thrift (Armeria maritima), 123, **123, 126**
Thrift (Armeria spp.), **166**
Thunder and lightning, 286

Thyme (*Thymus* spp.), **166, 189, 212, 235, 239,** *329,* 329–30
Tile drains, 133, **133**
Time and chill damage, 53
Time of year and floods, 124–25
Timers for watering, 161
Timetable for plant tolerance, 123, **123**
Tip burn, 235
Tomatoes, 21, 54, 173, 207, 216, 234, **236,** 237
Top (crown) kill, 198–99
Tornadoes, 200, 208, 290–94
Transpiration, 249–50, *297,* 297–97, 298
Transplants, vulnerability, 34, 230, 298–99, 299–300
Travel wind damage, 321
Tree microclimates, 31
Trees
   drought resilience, **156, 165–68,** 172, **172**
   fire resilience, 182, 188, **188–89**
   flood resilience, 134, **134**
   hail damage, 215–16
   heat resilience, 238, **238–41**
   humidity resilience, **262**
   lightning, protection from, 276–80, *279*
   lightning resilience, 272, *272*
   limb damage, 82–83, *83,* 86, 138–39, 318–19, *319*
   salt resilience, 98, **98**
   structures, trees too close to, 301
   "Top 100" list, 350–64
   uprooted trees, 87, 320
   water contents of, 18
   wind resilience, **307,** 310–18, **311,** *312,* **314,** 317
Triage approach to gardens, 4–5
Trident maple (*Acer buergeranum*), **239, 240, 241**
Trillium (*Trillium* spp.), 214
Trumpet creeper (*Campsis radicans*), **168,** 304, **304**
Trunks, broken, 87, 319
Tulip tree (*Liriodendron tulipifera*), **188,** 272, **272, 311**
Tull, Jethro, 158
Turkey oak (*Quercus laevis*), **168**
Turtlehead (*Chelone lyonii*), 123, **123**
Twain, Mark, 6
Tying branches, 85, *85*

U
Ultraviolet light, 225
Understory trees, 134, **134**
Uprooted trees, 87, 320
USDA, 225
USDA Hardiness Zone Map, 22, 23, 40, 389

V
Vacuole, 97
Valley microclimates, 27
Varieties of plants, caution, 33
Vegetables
   drought resilience, 156–61, *158, 160*
   hail damage, 214, 216–17
   heat resilience, 233–37, **235–36**
Venedio (*Venedio* spp.), **233**
Verbascum (*Verbascum* 'Southern Charm'), **212**
Verbascum (*Verbascum* spp.), 341, *341*
Verbascum (*Verbascum thapsus*), **166**
Verbena (*Verbena bonariensis*), **233**
Verbena (*Verbena* spp.), **99**
Victoria Regina (*Agave victoriae-reginae*), **167**
Vinca (*Vinca minor*), **189, 212,** 368–69, *369*
Vine maple (*Acer circinatum*), **188**
Vines and ground covers
   drought resilience, **165–66, 168**
   fire resilience, 181, **189**
   hail resilience, **212**
   salt resilience, 98, **98**
   "Top 100" list, 365–71
   wind resilience, 304, **304**
Virginia creeper (*Parthenocissus quinquefolia*), **98, 168**
Virginia rose (*Rosa virginiana*), **165, 262**

W
Walkways for fire protection, 184
Warm-season grasses, 382
Warm-weather water, 19–20
Washington hawthorn (*Crataegus phaenopyrum*), **165, 239, 240, 241**
Washington palm (*Washingtonia robusta*), **168**
Washington palm (*Washingtonia* spp.), **98,** 361, *361*
Wastebasket syndrome, 187
Water
   cold and, 51–53

conductivity of, 276
fire protection from, 184, 193
flood and water movement, 124, 125
heat resilience, 230–31
microclimates, water differences in, 25,
    26, *26*
soil, water movement in, *148*, 148–49
stress vs. drought, 150
weather resilience and, 16–22
Water-filled plastic tepee, *21*, 21–22, 51
Water hickory *(Carya aquatica)*, **134**
Watering tools, *155*, 155–56, 159–61, *160*
Watermelon and chill damage, 57
"Water thief," 147. *See also* Drought
Water tupelo *(Nyssa aquatica)*, **134**
Wax myrtle *(Myrica cerifera)*, **168**
Weather-resilient garden, 1–34. *See also*
    Annuals; Designing gardens; Lawn
    grasses; Ornamental grasses;
    Perennials; Plant selection; Shrubs;
    Trees; Vegetables; Vines and ground
    covers
  blooming vs. non-blooming plants, 34
  catalogs for buying plants, 33
  cold resilience, 38–62
  defensive landscaping, 4–5
  drought resilience, 145–73
  evaluation of garden, 4–5
  fire resilience, 71, 174–99
  fixing gardens, 4–5
  flood resilience, 112–44
  hail resilience, 200–218, 387
  healing methods and fresh starts,
    35–37
  heat resilience, 219–46
  humidity resilience, 53, 247–64
  ice and snow resilience, 63–89
  lightning resilience, 265–86
  microclimates, 22–32, 48–49, *49*
  plants' reaction to injury, 36–37
  praus, 2
  pressures endured by, 3, *3*
  resources for, 386–87
  salt resilience, 90–111
  soil resilience, 7–16
  stabilization, 4–5
  triage approach to gardens, 4–5
  varieties of plants, caution, 33
  water for weather resilience, 16–22
  wind resilience, 41, *41*, 287–322, 387
Weather station, 28–29, *29*, 387

Weeping fig *(Ficus benghalensis)*, **311**
Western larch *(Larix occidentalis)*, 171,
    188, 196
Western wheatgrass, **162**
Wet growth, 202
Wheatgrass *(Agropyron* spp.), **99**
White alkali (gypsum), 106–7
White ash *(Fraxinus americana)*, **98**, **189**
White birch *(Betula platyphylla)*, **239**,
    240, **241**
White oak *(Quercus alba)*, **80**, **165**, **188**,
    314
White spruce *(Picea glauca)*, 73
Wildfires after ice storms, 71
Wild ginger *(Asarum* spp.), **213**
Wildlife, 66–68, **68**
Wild plum *(Prunus americana)*, 123, **123**
Willow *(Salix* spp.), **81**, 272, **272**, **314**
Wilting, 136, 242–43
Wilting point, 149–50
Wind, 41, *41*, 287–322, 387
Windbreak microclimates, 31–32
Windbreaks
  drought resilience, **171**
  hail resilience, 208–9, *209*
  humidity resilience, 255–56, *256*
  ice and snow resilience, 76
  salt resilience, 111
  wind resilience, 302–10, **304**, *306*, **307**,
    308–9
Wind differences in microclimates, 25, *25*,
    26
Windfall, 322
Windows of home and fire, 194
Wingthorn rose *(Rosa sericea
    pteracantha)*, 170, **262**
Wintercreeper *(Euonymus fortunei)*, **168**,
    304, **304**
Wintergreen *(Gaultheria procumbens)*,
    68
Winter leaf sunscald, 60–61
Winter sunscald, 48
Winter trunk sunscald, 60
Witch hazel *(Hamamelis virginiana)*, **189**
Woods and lightning, 273
Worms, 115, 120
Wormwood *(Artemesia* spp.), **189**
Wormwood senna *(Cassia artemisioides)*,
    167
Wyman, Donald, 23
Wyman's Gardening Encyclopedia, 23

X

Xeriphytes, 163, 166

Y

Yarrow (*Achillea filipendulina*), **99**
Yarrow (*Achillea millefolium*), **189**
Yarrow (*Achillea* spp.), 134, **134, 166,**
   239, 325, *325*
Yaupon holly (*Ilex vomitoria*), **68, 98,**
   241, 311
Yeats, William Butler, 1, 36
Yeddo (*Rhaphiolepis umbellata*), **167**
Yellow birch (*Betula alleghaniensis*), **156,**
   188
Yellow columbine (*Aquilegia chrysantha*),
   239

Yellow flag (*Iris pseudacorus*), 134, **134**
Yellowwood tree (*Cladrastis lutea*), 47
Yucca (*Yucca* spp.)
   drought resilience, **166, 167, 168**
   hail resilience, **212**
   heat resilience, **239**
   ice and snow resilience, **68**
   salt resilience, **99**
   "Top 100" list, 325–26, *326*

Z

Zelkova (*Zelkova serrata*), **168**
Zinc (Zn), 15
Zinnia (*Zinnia* spp.), **166, 263**
Zonal flow, 38
Zoysia grass (*Zoysia* spp.), **162,** 384, *384*